Being Human

in safety-critical organisations

How people create safety, what stops them and what to do about it

Dik Gregory and **Paul Shanahan**

Published by TSO (The Stationery Office), part of Williams Lea Tag,
and available from:

Online
www.tsoshop.co.uk

Mail, Telephone, Fax & E-mail
TSO
PO Box 29, Norwich, NR3 1GN
Telephone orders/General enquiries: 0333 202 5070
Fax orders: 0333 202 5080
E-mail: customer.services@tso.co.uk
Textphone 0333 202 5077

TSO@Blackwell and other Accredited Agents

Commissioned by:

Printed in the United Kingdom for The Stationery Office

J003349311 C20 09/17

Contents

Being Human in safety-critical organisations

List of figures

List of tables

Preface

Gretchen Haskins

CEO, HeliOffshore

Formerly Group Director of Safety at the Civil Aviation Authority, 2010–2013 and Group Director of Safety at National Air Traffic Services (UK), 2000–2010

If you read one book on human factors, make it this one! I picked it up and couldn't put it down. During more than 30 years working to apply human-factors principles to real-world operational and business priorities, I have thought, every once in a while, that I should try to write a book to give back the most important lessons learned through experience – the things that actually work in practice. I am delighted to say that I no longer need to write that book, because Dik Gregory and Paul Shanahan have done it!

It's the apparently small but fundamental things that seem to make the difference, like considering that the human is an essential part of an effective safety system, not the part that makes the errors that we then try to fix. Although both views may be argued, working proactively to improve safety by focusing on system performance is much more inspiring – and much more effective. You can cover the same ground and measure progress more quickly.

Once you've read enough accident and incident reports, you know that it is very rare that the people in the system set out to cause an event. So, an understanding of their mindset, the pressures they face, and how they decide on what to do becomes central to creating a system that supports them in doing their jobs consistently well.

The authors' SUGAR model, described in this book, provides an excellent framework to systematically review the context in which people perform their work. It helps us consider how we can influence and shape those human factors that may have seemed beyond our reach. The book's real-world stories, when viewed in this context, really bring things to life.

The stories exemplify the significant costs – loss of productivity, income and, most importantly, lives – that occur when human factors are not addressed. The opportunity to enhance human performance in day-to-day operations is something for which we can create a business case that is both deliverable and measurable. All it takes is a greater understanding of the mindsets of the people doing their jobs, creating the right support structure around them, and measuring the difference in terms of effective actions every day. This can be done proactively – as part of design, test and operations – before an accident happens. In fact, all organisations would benefit from such an investment strategy, based on a clear understanding of those things that support effective human performance in their company.

I am grateful to Dik and Paul for writing such an interesting, practical and useful book. It is wonderful to see theory, practice and potential solutions all in one place.

Foreword

Sir Alan Massey

Chief Executive, Maritime & Coastguard Agency

Maritime & Coastguard Agency

"Where is safety – in people or in rules?"

Dik Gregory and Paul Shanahan's previous book, *The Human Element – a guide to human behaviour in the shipping industry*, posed this very question. It argued that whilst the traditional focus on rules and procedures seemed a reasonable way to improve safety, the role of people was increasingly apparent. Real safety, the authors contended, lies very much in the expertise, understanding, risk mitigation and decision-making of operators – or, in other words, normal human behaviour, at all organisational and regulatory levels.

Being Human examines what it means to be human in complex, safety-critical systems. It explains how we perceive; how we think, act and react; what can distract us, confuse us and throw us off course; what are our strengths and limitations; and what we can all do – both as individuals and as organisations – to deal with these realities. It steers us towards an understanding of people's behaviour and capabilities on a systemic level, and clearly illustrates why we need to take this matter very seriously.

The book has been written for the majority of us who are not ourselves human-factors experts but who want to benefit from the knowledge, expertise and experience of others to improve operational and safety performance in our own organisations. It is a well-blended mix of theory, compelling case studies and practical guidance designed to increase the resilience of both individuals and organisations.

The Maritime & Coastguard Agency is committed to improving safety at sea and around the coast through a wide range of initiatives. An effective understanding of human behaviour in normal and safety-critical contexts is a key component of this. We are confident that *Being Human* will support our own work, and we are delighted to have been closely associated with its development.

Foreword

Chris Bailey

**Vice President Operations,
BP Shipping**

The Human Element book and training film have both been used extensively within
BP Shipping – and with great success. They helped to introduce and explain human factors
to the maritime industry in a way that could be easily understood by all.

Human beings sometimes act in a most unexpected manner, which can lead – and has led
– to incidents or accidents. *The Human Element* gave us more insight into how and why this
'human error' occurs. I believe that it has helped us to improve our safety performance by
truly understanding why humans act as they do.

It is also worth recognising the importance of senior leadership in creating an environment
and working conditions that contribute to our people's performance. However, there is still
much more to be done to improve safety in our industry.

I was therefore very keen to support this follow-up book. It does not replace the first book,
but rather sits alongside it and takes our understanding of human behaviour in the maritime
sector to a new level. The safety of our seafarers is my first priority and I feel that this new
book will help us to continue to improve our safety performance and, thereby, deliver
success to the industry as a whole.

Foreword

John Adams

Managing Director
Teekay Shipping (Glasgow) Limited

The maritime sector has made good progress in improving operational safety and environmental impact in recent years. At Teekay, we recognise the need to go beyond review of policy and procedures in acknowledging the human element. That means getting the right people, making them fit for the job, understanding their approach, managing their behaviours and motivating them for success. Communicating our values and the *spirit* in which our employees should approach their work goes a long way in ensuring they return safely to their families at the end of each tour on board.

It's all about having a clear focus on hearts and minds, with supporting strategies. Human capital is the differentiator, offering our business a clear competitive advantage. Human resources are distinct, relevant, complex and, not least of all, resourceful. Yet the strategic value of this most important asset makes us continually strive for a better understanding of the influences, situational awareness, thought processes and decision-making that can impact safety. And that includes the safety of our ships, the safety of our environment and, ultimately, the safety of our people.

'Operational Leadership' is a strategy and a concept that we have been progressing at Teekay for some time. We believe that study of the human element can achieve positive outcomes for our business, our people and the wider community.

Being Human provides valuable, specific insights into the human element in the maritime industry – along with practical tools for the application of this knowledge.

We are proud sponsors of this book – this innovative approach and philosophy are completely aligned with the way we want to manage our business. I highly recommend this important piece of work to the industry!

Foreword

Capt. Yves Vandenborn, AFNI

Director of Loss Prevention, The Standard Club

"It is not the ship so much as the skilful sailing that assures the prosperous voyage."

George William Curtis, writing in the 19th century, could have been describing the shipping industry today. A reputable shipowner, operator or manager will understand this imperative, and will arrange extensive professional training and education for their crew to ensure a prosperous voyage. As a result, the overwhelming majority of ships, cargoes and crews arrive safely at their final destination.

However, when issues do occur, 'human error' is usually at the heart of the problem. Dik Gregory and Paul Shanahan's book delves more deeply into why humans make errors despite their training and how we can look beyond this.

Today, ships are more sophisticated, larger and faster. Operating procedures on board may appear comprehensive and robust enough to manage this challenge, but this can only be the case if officers and crews follow them. During ship visits, our surveyors have witnessed behaviours among officers and crews that were contrary to the safety management system on board and, frequently, the crew members were not aware of the risks that they were taking. In other words, they appeared blind to their own blindness. This book discusses why this occurs and what safeguards can be put in place to minimise the associated risks.

As the authors explain, we now have a much better understanding of how humans behave, how we perceive and make sense of the world, how we make decisions, what really motivates us at work, how we are affected by technology and, most importantly, how we communicate and work with each other as a team. With this knowledge, human error can be combated.

The Standard Club is delighted to support this publication to enhance understanding and management of *the human element* – a critical area of ship operations deserving greater appreciation.

Acknowledgements

The authors warmly acknowledge Marc Williams and David Turner of the Maritime & Coastguard Agency, John Adams of Teekay Shipping, Iain Bruce and Chris Bailey of BP Shipping, and Yves Vandenborn of the Standard P&I Club. Without their remarkable vision and support, the book might never have left its intellectual starting blocks.

We would also like to acknowledge the valuable feedback we received on earlier drafts of the book from our sponsors, as well as from Erik Hollnagel, Professor & Industrial Safety Chair at MINES ParisTech – Centre for Research on Risks and Safety, and Gretchen Haskins, CEO of HeliOffshore. Without their counsel, the book would not have been so sharply focused or practical to use.

Our sincere thanks go to commissioning editor Lucy de Best of TSO. Without her, our journey through the publication process would have been a lot more fraught.

We are hugely grateful to Jane Edmonds for her work on the initial drafts and to Dominic Fenn, our copy editor at TSO. Without their diligence and skilful attention to detail, the book would not have achieved the quality and consistency that we always intended for it.

Our sincere appreciation also goes to Adam Ray of TSO, who designed and typeset the pages and cover. Were it not for his efforts, you would be reading a collection of Word files, rather than the attractive volume you hold in your hands today.

We are heavily obliged to the many operational and management staff in a wide range of safety-critical enterprises who spent time with us over many years. Without them, we would not have seen the patterns that connect, nor learned from their astonishing stories.

Finally, we are enormously indebted to Hillary Gregory and Roswitha Shanahan over their lifetimes. Without their understanding and love, we would never have found time for the countless conversations over many years that were required to generate this book.

Dik Gregory and Paul Shanahan

Dedication

This book is dedicated to cybernetician Professor Gordon Pask (1928–1996), without whom many of the conversations that were required for this book could not have started.

1

About this book
how people create safety, what stops them and what to do about it

Being human

For most of us, most of the time, going to work is a safe and uneventful activity. Sometimes, though, despite doing our usual best to act responsibly, we may end up as unwitting participants or bystanders – or perhaps victims – in things that go wrong. This book provides a structured approach to understanding how and why this happens, and how to adjust our thinking at both individual and organisational levels to deal with the many, ever-present influences on our behaviour at work.

The maritime industry is one of the most dangerous business activities that humans undertake. This book is the result of the responsible action of a consortium of maritime companies to do what they can to understand, accommodate, harness and assure safe human behaviour at work. As such, it is highly relevant to anyone – at any level – who is involved in the operation of safety-critical activities, whether in maritime or in sectors such as aviation, chemical, defence, healthcare, highways, nuclear, rail or space. The many different examples used in the book reflect the behavioural common denominators relevant to all these areas of people at work.

The underlying drivers of our behaviour – evolved over millions of years – will not go away and cannot be ignored.

It is our contention that dealing with them effectively and responsibly will not only make work a genuinely and sustainably safer activity; it will also make it a more honestly human one. We also believe the reverse is true: making work more human will make it safer.

A new perspective

About 40 years ago, a new understanding of major industrial accidents emerged. It crystallised out of the incident at the Three Mile Island nuclear plant in 1979. Such disasters have occurred at regular intervals: the Deepwater Horizon oil-rig explosion and subsequent pollution in 2010 is one among many more recent examples. What was new about our understanding of these accidents was the realisation that they could not be explained in terms of simple cause and effect. The complexity of the operations defied full understanding, both by those working at the time and, later, by accident investigators.

In recent years, a number of engineers, system designers, safety specialists, psychologists and organisational theorists have grown increasingly curious about the character of such accidents. To solve the mystery, they have had to break out of older ways of thinking. The result is a new approach to understanding how and why complex systems go wrong, known as *resilience engineering*.

A key aspect of resilience engineering is how it looks at the role of humans. Traditionally in safety thinking, people have been viewed as the weak link in otherwise soundly engineered systems. This is reflected in the great majority of accident reports, which usually implicate 'human error'. Resilience engineering starts by recognising that today's complex systems are necessarily underspecified. It is simply impossible to predict all the states the system can be in and how all the numerous components will work in combination. This problem becomes even more intractable when the system is embedded in a highly variable environment that can – and frequently does – throw up novel demands.

This inherent unpredictability means that the people working in the system must develop and apply deep expertise so that they can continually adjust the working of the system to cope with unexpected technical glitches and environmental demands. Far from being the weak link, humans literally create safety. But of course, being human, they will sometimes make errors or be confronted with challenges beyond their capacities.

Human beings: it seems it's difficult to live with them and even harder to live without them.

At the same time as our understanding of the nature of complex systems has increased, there has been rapid growth in our knowledge of human behaviour. Psychologists, human-factors specialists, sociologists, neuroscientists, physiologists, evolutionary biologists and anthropologists have developed a vast and fascinating body of behavioural knowledge. We understand much better how humans perceive and make sense of the world; how we make decisions; what really motivates us at work; how we are affected by technological, environmental and organisational factors; how we communicate and work cooperatively with each other; and much more.

This book brings together the emerging knowledge of resilience engineering with recent insights into our behaviour. By understanding how resilience engineering and human nature fit with each other, operators, managers, regulators and others involved in safety-critical industries can adopt a more proactive approach to preventing industrial disasters and can have greater insight into what goes wrong when accidents do happen.

The book draws on many case studies and experiences from a range of safety-critical sectors. The lessons learned can be applied everywhere that humans are to be found creating safety in the midst of uncertainty.

A new framework

Being Human is constructed around a simple but powerful model of human behaviour – SUGAR – that helps people at all levels put these ideas into practice. The SUGAR model is introduced and developed in Chapter 3 (Being framed) and Chapter 4 (Being sufficient).

Together, Chapters 2, 3 and 4 describe the approach and framework for the book, exposing what we believe to be the true problems of safety in a complex, globalised world that is here to stay.

Chapters 13 and 14 give practical guidance and tools that will help individuals and organisations address their safety issues more effectively – and with proper regard to the humans at the centre of these issues.

In between, Chapters 5 to 12 provide evidence, examples and stories that amply illustrate the perspective that this book takes.

The authors are both organisational psychologists who have spent many years learning at first hand the realities of working in and with complex, safety-critical systems. We are grateful to the many seafarers, aviators, soldiers, railway signallers, healthcare workers, air traffic controllers and others who, over the years, have helped us understand their work and their lives.

We offer our deep respect to the vast majority who continuously sustain each other with their professionalism and mindfulness. And we pay tribute to those who suffer when things go wrong somewhere in the system of which they are a part. There will be more. This book aims to make their number less than it would have been.

2 Being at work
the curiousness of the problems we really face

What's the real issue with people?

What does normal work look like?

Why can't we eliminate human error?

Why can't we predict and eliminate accidents?

The puzzle of people

In the past few decades, the proportion of accidents due to equipment failure has steadily decreased. We have got a lot better at understanding how materials work and how they fail. But over the same period, the proportion of accidents that implicate human behaviour has stayed stubbornly the same. Around half of all work-related accidents involve people doing something – or failing to do something – that contributes to a bad outcome. This is despite all the training, safety campaigns, lessons learned, and new rules and procedures – not to mention the distress that is caused when yet another accident impacts another industry, another business, and another set of family lives for ever.

What are we to do? How are we ever going to improve this stubborn statistic? Or are we looking at this the wrong way – measuring the wrong thing?

The authors of this book think so. This book is all about looking at the human relationship with safety in a different way. A way that is much more constructive, much more effective, much more consistent with our everyday experience of safety – and, in the end, much more human.

What do humans actually *do*?

Sidney Dekker is an airline pilot, professor of human factors and psychology, and author of several books on safety. Let's start with his idea about the true place of humans in modern systems. Systems that involve humans are best characterised as both complex and adaptive. That is to say, they are composed of lots of smart, interacting components – including humans. Such components are 'smart' not only because they communicate with each other, but because each may have a different agenda, a different capability and a different range of applicability. Within their respective limitations, each component seeks to achieve its goals by coordinating and adjusting its activities with other components – all with the least effort, so as to conserve limited energy and resources.

So, for example, a surgeon with a particular range of knowledge, skills, experience and expectations – and in a particular emotional or physical state – prepares to operate on a patient. The patient has a certain set of capabilities to deal with the forthcoming surgical assault. The surgeon is supported by a number of medical staff, each with their own goals, knowledge and attentiveness. The surgical team members are all using sets of instruments with a particular functionality, readiness and reliability. And all this happens within an operating space that imposes its own demands and constraints, in a context in which the operating schedule is routinely paced or perhaps highly pressured by an external calamity that is producing more patients by the minute.

As the surgery proceeds, attention is focused and switched, information is requested and provided, assumptions are made and challenged, decisions are considered and enacted, suggestions are solicited and offered, techniques are tried and evaluated, and priorities are created and changed. The whole process is mutually coordinated in a fluid dance in which every element plays its part. This is true even of inanimate tools. A scalpel is either sharp, sterile and to hand when it is needed or it is not – in which case the drama takes a new turn as the team adapts to changed circumstances and reconfigures its actions and priorities.

Although this is a surgical example, the same underlying principles apply to every other human system. Recognition of these principles is especially important in safety-critical enterprises such as maritime, aviation, rail, construction, mining, space, nuclear and the highways.

A system may comprise many humans and pieces of equipment, or just a few. Whether it's a bridge team, a cockpit crew, a military fire team, a construction gang, a surgical team or a road full of cooperating car drivers, the characteristics are the same. The space in which the system plays out is prescribed by sets of rules, procedures, processes and techniques that specify part, but never all, of what, how and when things get done. The space of operations – be it a ship's bridge, a flight deck, a building site, an operating theatre or a highway – is always filled with uncertainty. Its users are always uncertain about who exactly will do what and when, and what this might mean in the moment in which it is done, given the many other things that may also arise in that moment. Our task within the uncertainty of the space in which we operate is always underspecified.

This is why Dekker says that the essential place of humans in systems is to *complete the design*.[1]

The story that unfolded on 17 January 2008 at London's Heathrow Airport is a wonderful example of humans completing the design. It is also an example of an accident that was due entirely to equipment failure. The fact that the situation was recovered by the humans involved is something that occurs frequently in the vast amount of everyday work in which there are no accidents. We hardly ever notice them – but the stories are there, if we only care to look.

Accident investigations often focus on the shortcomings of system components – and people are an easy target. So it is especially interesting to find an accident that involves an

---

1   Dekker (2005)

extended and disparate team of people doing almost everything right to successfully avert what would otherwise have been a monumental disaster.

This is the story of British Airways 'Speedbird' 38.[2, 3]

Speedbird 38 – plucked from the jaws of disaster by human agency

As British Airways (BA) flight 38 lifted off from Beijing, China on 17 January 2008, its pilots had no idea that less than 11 hours later they would be at the centre of one of the most remarkable dramas ever to unfold at London Heathrow.

In fact, no-one had any idea about the impending drama until just one minute before touchdown at 12.42 on runway 27L. It was a cloudy, dry London winter's day and, at 10°C, a mild day for the time of year. The aircraft – call sign Speedbird 38 on this flight – was a Boeing 777. It had been in uneventful service for seven years, clocking 28,675 hours over the course of nearly 4,000 take-off/landing cycles.

In the commander's seat was 43-year-old Captain Peter Burkill, a married father-of-three from Worcester – his youngest just ten weeks old. He had 8,450 hours of flying experience on Boeing 777s. Alongside him was co-pilot John Coward, aged 41, with 7,000 hours. When not working, Coward lived with his wife at their home in France.

They were both highly experienced and highly trained, having met the rigorous and regular simulation and certification requirements demanded of all BA pilots.

For all but the last minute of Speedbird 38's flight that day, the trip was apparently routine and uneventful. What the crew did not know was that a peculiar and previously unknown malfunction had been developing in the fuel system throughout the entire flight.

Abnormally high levels of soft ice had built up in the fuel. Ice in fuel is quite normal and comes from water that occurs naturally in the aviation mix. The difference here lay in the combination of very cold conditions at the start of the flight, a long period of cruising with low fuel flow, a fuel temperature that increased significantly in the latter part of the flight, and a fuel/oil heat exchanger whose design could not cope with the resulting large amounts of soft ice that detached from inside the fuel lines as the aircraft manoeuvred for its final approach. The effect of these circumstances had never been simulated or imagined by the aircraft's designers – or its pilots.

As Speedbird 38 descended towards London, Captain Burkill had the controls. Under the guidance of the UK *en route* air traffic controller (ATCO) at Swanwick, 60 miles (100 km) away on England's south coast, Burkill descended the aircraft from 4,000 feet. The Swanwick ATCO handed over the aircraft to the London Heathrow control tower, and Burkill responded to new ATCO instructions to enter a hold pattern at 1,100 feet. After five minutes, the tower instructed a further descent to 900 feet. As he did so, Burkill prepared the aircraft for an Instrument Landing System (ILS) approach to Runway 27L. This put the aircraft on an automated glide path and set things up for the aircraft's control to be handed to co-pilot Coward for a manual landing.

---

2 AAIB (2010)

3 Wikipedia

At 1,000 feet, and 83 seconds before touchdown, the aircraft was fully configured for the landing. The landing gear was down and flap 30 selected, as normal. This flap setting would increase lift in exchange for the lower speed required for a safe and smooth landing.

Around this time, as planned, Burkill handed over control to Coward, who now became the 'pilot flying', releasing the captain to maintain a trouble-shooting, supervisory role for the landing. It was just as well.

In the Heathrow control tower, the duty ATCO was in full charge of the normal, high-intensity operations at one of the world's busiest airports. Here, there is a major aircraft movement every 60 seconds or so, a tempo that is enabled by the support, research and training provided by NATS (National Air Traffic Services – the British ATC organisation).

Coincidentally, at that exact moment, the authors of this book were at NATS in Swanwick, having just finished a meeting with *en route* ATCO managers. In the spirit of continuous improvement that makes NATS world-class, we had been discussing ways in which human-element thinking could be even more deeply entrenched into NATS' already sophisticated operational practices.

At a height of 720 feet, 3 miles (5 km) and now less than a minute from touchdown at London Heathrow, the fuel flow to the right engine of the 777 suddenly stopped. Seven seconds later, at 620 feet, the same thing happened to the left engine. The pilots didn't know it, but ice in the fuel had starved the engines just as a final demand for thrust was needed.

At 590 feet, and 48 seconds before impact, Coward became acutely aware of a serious thrust failure. The problem distracted Coward from disengaging the autopilot at this point, as he had intended.

At 430 feet, with 34 seconds to go, as Coward struggled to comprehend the problem, the following calm and understated exchange took place:

Captain Burkill: *"[Is the aircraft] Stable?"*

First Officer Coward: *"Well, not exactly. I can't get any power from the engines ... Looks like we have a double engine failure."*

The aircraft was not going to make the runway. In fact, it was starting to stall as the autopilot lifted the nose to try to maintain the glide slope.

At 240 feet, Burkill retracted the flaps. The action was instinctive and not taught in the simulators. It had the desired effect. It reduced drag and (as it turned out) increased the distance to touchdown by a vital 50 metres. Although Burkill knew it would have little impact on the forthcoming stall, he had done what he could to clear the perimeter fence. Accident investigators later calculated that if the flap setting had been left alone, the impact would still have been within the airfield boundary – just – but the aircraft would have collided with the ground-based ILS antenna, causing substantial structural damage and potentially multiple passenger injuries.

At 200 feet, the stick shaker activated, telling the pilots that the aircraft was stalling. They were dropping like a stone. At 150 feet, Coward pushed hard on the controls. His action caused the autopilot to disconnect and the aircraft to keep flying with the wings level. As the aircraft glided very low over Hatton Cross tube station, to the left of a busy petrol station and to the right of a dense residential area and school, the pilots had an unusual and terrifying view.

They were diving towards the ground at 125 mph. Burkill transmitted "MAYDAY ... MAYDAY ... Speedbird ... Speedbird ... 95 ... 95." As the pilots continued their struggle with the stalling aircraft, there was no time to instruct the passengers to "brace, brace".

It was three seconds before impact.

In the tower, the final-approach ATCO had been managing several aircraft in various stages of transit. Included in these had been a series of transmissions to Speedbird 38, giving clearance to land and post-touchdown taxiing instructions. After hearing the MAYDAY transmission, the ATCO took a few beats to comprehend the situation.

He ignored the fact that, under extreme pressure, Burkill had used the wrong call sign (Speedbird 95 instead of Speedbird 38). Interestingly, 'Speedbird 95' is the call sign reserved for use in BA's 777 simulator. Under stress, people tend to revert to what they know best. It is a measure of the quality of BA pilot training that what Burkill knew best was his training, although even that had not anticipated the present circumstances.

The aircraft skimmed the perimeter fence, missed the ILS tower and finally stalled 10 feet from the ground, dropping to the soft, rain-soaked grass. Coward flared the nose of the plane to reduce the speed of impact. Initial touchdown was 1,000 feet short of Runway 27L. The main landing gear tore gouges 18 inches deep before the aircraft bounced and touched again, breaking up as it slid along the grassy apron and up onto the southern edge of the runway itself. The left main landing gear had seriously bent, puncturing the wing. The right main landing gear had torn off at first impact, causing the aircraft to veer to the right and puncturing the fuselage. The penetrating wheel assembly broke the leg of the unlucky passenger in seat 30K – the only serious injury sustained among the 152 people on board.

Now aware of the crisis, the tower ATCO instructed another aircraft preparing to depart, Speedbird 229, to hold position. He then transmitted clearly, but with arresting urgency, *"Aircraft accident ... Aircraft accident ... the position is the threshold runway two seven left ... aircraft type is a triple seven ... nature of the problem is 'crash' ... aircraft has crashed. Rendezvous point is south."*

This message contained all the essential information for the fastest possible fire, medical and police response.

As the plane came to a stop, there was an eerie silence in the cockpit. To the pilots' surprise, they appeared to be uninjured. They were not so sure about the passengers, many of whom they feared must be dead. But now the risk was fire and Burkill made the announcement *"This is the captain. This is an emergency: evacuate, evacuate."*

Hearing this, the ATCO immediately realised that, in the continued stress of the moment, the captain had made the announcement on the wrong circuit – on the VHF radio to the tower, rather than on the public-address (PA) system to the passengers. The ATCO responded calmly and effectively: *"Transmitted on ATC, sir. Fire service on the way."* Without missing a beat, he immediately switched his attention to another aircraft on approach: *"Qatari 011 go around ... I say again, go around, acknowledge."*

The approaching Qatari aircraft acknowledged immediately and the ATCO spent the next few minutes on VHF, intercom and telephone, coordinating the emergency services, managing the multiple approaching aircraft and liaising with his ATC colleagues in the tower and at Swanwick.

Meanwhile, at Swanwick, high-alert procedures were being implemented. All ATCOs were recalled from their breaks to the operations room and visitors (including ourselves) were asked to vacate the premises, pending a potential lockdown, until the source of the problem at Heathrow was understood. The possibility of a terrorist attack was clear – especially since one of the passengers in a waiting aircraft, just a few hundred metres from the crashed 777, was the British Prime Minister, Gordon Brown, on his way to China for an official five-day visit.

As soon as the crashed aircraft had come to rest, some of the passengers left their seats to seek an exit. Under the leadership of Cabin Service Director Sharon Eaton-Mercer, the cabin crew took immediate control, firmly instructing people to stay in their seats. Moments later, the captain gave the evacuate command and flashing red lights picked out the exits.

The cabin crew held back the passengers until the escape slides were fully inflated, blocking access to slides that had too much debris at the bottom. They then helped the passengers to jump. Passengers began leaving the aircraft just 58 seconds after first impact. The passenger with the broken leg in seat 30K was helped by a neighbouring passenger, who accompanied him down the slide. The cabin crew were the last out, following an operation carried out with textbook clarity and care.

Even though they had no prior warning of a developing emergency, the fire services arrived at the crash site within two minutes of first impact. This was just as well. Nearly 7,000 kg of fuel had leaked out of the aircraft and oxygen was escaping from ruptured passenger emergency cylinders. The attending fire officers neutralised the problem with 300,000 litres of water and 17,000 litres of foam.

As might be expected, London Heathrow was severely disrupted for days afterwards. But this impact was nothing compared with what might have been.

What was good here?

The crew were presented with a potentially catastrophic situation at a critical moment and with very little time to sort it out. Sudden double engine failure 2 miles (3 km) from landing was unprecedented, unimagined and unrehearsed.

What was needed were high levels of professionalism and knowledge. Deep technical knowledge – in this case about flight – was required so that effective action could be generated. A high degree of emotional training was also required, so that panic could be averted and minds could remain analytically focused on the problem.

 Read more about the nature of emotions and understanding in **Chapter 7**, and the nature of expertise in **Chapter 10**

But far more than this was delivered on the day that Speedbird 38 crashed. High levels of teamwork, coordination and shared understanding were displayed by the cabin crew, the London tower ATCOs, their *en route* colleagues miles away in Swanwick, the airport emergency services and ground staff, and the flight crews of other aircraft in the area. Fundamental to this coordination was the use of effective, unambiguous and crystal-clear communication made at the right time and in the right way, allowing priorities to be correctly set and actions to be synchronised.

Read more about the nature of teamwork and communications in **Chapter 11**

The coordination was not perfect, of course. The evacuation checklist was split between the captain and first officer. While one operated the engine cut-off switch, the other operated the engine fire switches. But they were done in the wrong order. In the stress of the moment, the fire switches were thrown first, and a large amount of fuel leaked out of the engines. Fortunately, there was no fire, even though the risk was heightened due to leaking oxygen.

All unintended results within complex systems occur when many components (including humans), each with their own variability, combine in an unimagined way to create a unique event. When the event is negative and people are hurt or property is damaged, we call it an accident. When the event is positive and a new material is discovered or a new insight is glimpsed, we call it an invention. When the event is neutral and (for example) aviation fuel leaks but there is no fire, we call it luck. If we are wise, we attempt to learn by removing the reliance on luck via better design.

Humans have deployed such learning throughout their evolution. What we need to understand, however, is that multiple interacting components – each with their own agendas and capabilities – will always generate unique combinations with unintended consequences. No amount of learning will result in a finite space of operations in which all combinations are knowable and all eventualities can be catered for. In fact, the opposite is the case: the more we learn, the more new components emerge, with new degrees of freedom and potential new combinations. That means unimagined, unprecedented possibilities.

It is only when an accident occurs, such as the one involving Speedbird 38, and forensic analysis follows, that we suddenly see humans doing what they do unnoticed the rest of the time. When people go about their work apparently uneventfully, or when 'luck' works in our favour, we usually fail to think of them as doing what the crew of Speedbird 38 did: 'completing the design' of underspecified processes.

Instead, our perception of what humans spend most of their time doing is often distorted. When, with hindsight, we see people making decisions that appear to be on the critical path to catastrophe, we can become seduced by the desire to blame, re-train or eliminate them. Such temptation often goes hand in hand with the desire to create a new procedure, which we then insist everyone else uses.

Read more about the problems of hindsight in **Chapter 9**

Get help with enhancing hindsight analysis in **Chapter 14**

Unintended consequences – what happens when you poke a system with a stick

If it seems clear to us with hindsight that a new procedure would have prevented the observed accident, it is easy to convince ourselves that adopting the new procedure will create a safer workplace. Unfortunately, this logic only works to the extent that the unique combination of degrees of freedom that created the bad results will occur again. The logic can be further undermined to the extent that the new procedure produces a new range of possibilities. If its use interferes with the ability of other system components to achieve their function or goals, then the behaviour of those other components will also change, leading to a new set of uncertainties.

This dynamic was established in chemistry by Le Chatelier in 1898, and it has since been generalised for use in biology and other realms. Le Chatelier's principle basically says that any change in the stability of a system provokes an opposing reaction, leading to a new status quo. If you fuss with the system by changing how one of its components operates, it will respond by trying to find a new stability. All sorts of unintended consequences may then follow as other components adjust their behaviour to compensate. In human circles, this is known as 'playing the system', but in many cases it is a natural and organic phenomenon in which the system is simply trying to re-optimise itself in the interests of efficiency.

In 2002, the UK government tried to reduce the time that casualty patients were waiting to be seen by a doctor. It decided that 98% of patients should be dealt with within four hours. In 2010, this was eased to 95%. Both targets were virtually impossible to achieve without radical system redesign and extra resources. Despite this, average waiting times appeared to get a lot better. How come?

What is interesting is what the highly pressured hospital system did to help itself. One response was to delay the four-hour clock from starting by holding patients in ambulances until the hospital staff could take them. Another was to transfer casualties out of the queue into 'assessment wards', so stopping the clock. A third was to discharge patients and then immediately re-admit them.

It would be easy to assume that staff were simply evading the means of measuring their performance. However, this view assumes a world of simple systems, governed by linear cause and effect. In the real, complex, adaptive world consisting of many constantly negotiating parts, these are effective strategies that introduce a new degree of freedom to replace the one that was taken away.

It is important to understand that such compensations do not return the world to the way it was. Instead, they move the system into a new space, leading to new negotiations and a new balance that may or may not be fundamentally more dangerous than the one it replaced.

Detailed scrutiny of an event with a bad outcome seems to reveal problems that then skew our perception of the role of people in their everyday work. When we see people make apparently avoidable mistakes, we want to blame them. Alternatively, we set about creating procedures that are designed to prevent others from making the same mistakes.

The curiousness of the problems we really face

The curiousness of the problems we really face at work is twofold.

The uncertainty of operations First, as we have just seen, we operate in an uncertain, underspecified world where we must function as designers in order to complete the specification in an operational setting. This means it is of limited value to keep adding more rules and procedures.

The capacity for surprise Second, it is often not obvious how the human behaviour at the centre of accidents is any different from that on days when no accident occurs. This means that we must look not so much at what people do, as at what influences them to do the things they do at the time they do them.

Underlying both of these problems is the curiousness of the kind of world in which we live and work. A fundamental distinction needs to be made between complex, adaptive systems on the one hand and systems that are simple – or merely complicated – on the other.[4]

Simple systems have few elements, variables and states. Here, checklists, stepwise procedures and simple look-up tables can be applied by almost anyone to diagnose and fix problems.

Complicated systems may have very large numbers of elements, variables and states, but, like simple systems, they have been designed and assembled. Problems will occur, but their solutions will be found in some giant virtual look-up table (although it will normally take an expert to analyse and find them).

Complex systems are radically different from those that are simple or merely complicated. Modern humans live and work as agents in complex, adaptive systems where everything is tightly connected and small changes in one part can have huge implications elsewhere, producing lock-up and confusion.

 Read more about complex systems in **Chapter 12**

A good example of lock-up is when a car driver in heavy traffic lightly touches their brake pedal, causing the driver behind to do the same. The knock-on effect results in total stoppage several kilometres behind – and the potential danger of rear-end shunts. As the bunched-up traffic gets going again, drivers are mystified to discover that there is no accident ahead – just free-moving traffic. Naturally, there is no trace of the briefly illuminated brake light.

The answer to such problems does not lie in more complicated layers of rules and procedures, but in some means of detecting when the system is becoming fragile and then damping the particular behaviour that is responsible. In the UK, Highways England[5] found a great way to do this. Sensors detect when the density of traffic has built up to a critical threshold, at which point compulsory variable speed limits come on. The traffic controls itself by means of a damping feedback loop. The result is that traffic slows, but moves much more continuously – and much more safely – with greatly reduced 'stop–start' effects.

There are many examples of the confusion that arises when overcomplication develops. Hundreds of alarms were triggered in the first few seconds of the near meltdown at Three Mile Island nuclear power plant in 1979.[6] In a more recent case, engineers were puzzled by negative-pressure test results on BP's Deepwater Horizon platform in the Gulf of Mexico in 2010.[7] What they didn't realise was that a giant bubble of hydrocarbons was heading

---

4   Dave Snowden (2016) distinguishes a further type of system – the chaotic – in which agents are unconstrained and behave independently of each other, with little or no mutual regard. Chaotic systems lend themselves to modelling by probability theory, which is good at describing the world of unconnected random events. Chaos, random events and probability inhabit a strange world that is extremely difficult for most humans to understand – as we shall see in Chapter 8 (Being in the know – part III). See http://cognitive-edge.com [accessed April 2017].

5   Highways England is the UK government authority that operates and maintains England's motorways and major roads.

6   Kemeny (1979)

7   National Commission on the BP Deepwater Horizon Oil Spill and Offshore Drilling (2011). Deepwater Horizon was the name of the platform from which drilling operations had been taking place at BP's Macondo Prospect oil well on the seabed 1 mile (1,600 metres) below.

towards them from the seabed with the force of a 500-ton train. The resulting explosion killed 11 people and produced huge environmental damage, five years of lawsuits, worldwide corporate opprobrium and a bill for $60 billion.

Is it possible to turn a complex system into a simple one? It might seem so, but this is just an illusion.

Prosecution lawyers, the media, accident enquiries and gossiping onlookers do it all the time. By applying hindsight, it is possible to manufacture a coherent and clear causal chain that tells just one story of a single trajectory through a simple space that inevitably ends in what was observed to happen. The problem, of course, is that the imagined simplicity of the space didn't exist at the time the participants were involved in it. Instead, there was highly selective attention, prioritising in the face of deep uncertainty, imperfect knowledge, calculated guesswork, intuition, the guidance (and possible misdirection) produced by previous experience, and the attempt to predict future interactions between components that are in principle unpredictable.

Explanations of things as simple causal chains of events are compelling, but not very useful. In the complex, adaptive systems exemplified by safety-critical industries such as aviation, chemicals, defence, healthcare, highways, maritime, nuclear, rail and space, we need a different approach, a different way of framing our understanding: a matter to which we turn in the next chapter.

3

Being framed
how context makes us blind

> How is it possible to hide in plain sight?
> Why do things surprise us?
> Why do different people see different things?
> Why do the same things have different meanings for different people?
> Where do context and meaning come from?

A question of perspective

Here's an easy question. Look at everything around you. What do you see? For everything that you silently pick out, ask yourself why you chose it. Now ask the person you are with to do the same thing. If there is no-one with you, imagine what they might say. What about a forensic scientist?

Why are the accounts different? Did the other person literally fail to see the things you saw? Or maybe they did see them, but they considered other things to be more meaningful?

Lee Ross is Professor of Humanities and Sciences at Stanford University. As a social psychologist, he is interested in the influence of context on cooperation. With his colleagues, he came up with a variation on the Prisoner's Dilemma game in which two people are better off if they both cooperate, but neither can communicate with the other. There are three possible outcomes. If both cooperate, they both get light sentences. If there is asymmetric trust and only one attempts cooperation while the other remains uncooperative, the cooperative one will receive a very heavy sentence while the other gets off completely. If neither cooperates, they both end up with medium sentences.

So what do people tend to do? Logic says that it is best for each isolated individual to fail to cooperate, because it potentially leads to the best result. However, if both do this, they end up with medium sentences. People aren't strong on logic, so what actually happens is a tendency to risk trusting the other: they both cooperate and they both end up with light sentences.

In Ross's variation, two groups of people played an identical game. However, one group were told they were playing the Wall Street Game, while the other group were told they were playing the Community Game. If players thought they were in the cut-throat world of big business, 70% never cooperated. Furthermore, in repeated games, the other 30% started out cooperating but gave up when there was no cooperative response from the other side. In the Community Game, it was the opposite: 70% cooperated from the start and kept on doing so.

People get a lot of clues about what to do and think from the context they believe they are in. Psychologists sometimes call these kinds of contextual clue the *demand characteristics* of the situation, and they have to be careful to take account of them in order to draw meaningful conclusions from their investigations. We will have more to say about the extraordinary and often unfelt power of others around us in Chapter 11 (Being together).

In everyday life, demand characteristics are everywhere. What people see around them and what they do depends on their perspective, values, goals, priorities, expectations and experience. It depends not just on who you are, but on who you are today. Actually, it depends on who you are *right now*: how you feel, what you know and what you are trying to achieve. These things fluctuate from moment to moment, in a constant dance between your psychology and your physical surroundings. So much so, in fact, that you won't notice exactly the same things if you repeat the 'look around you' exercise in a few minutes, let alone tomorrow.

Hiding in plain sight

It's worse than this, however. While you're busy noticing the things that seem to be important right now, there are huge amounts of information that you're simply ignoring.

In January 1995, Boston police officer Kenny Conley leapt out of his cruiser at the end of a *cul de sac* in his patrol area. He was in hot pursuit of a black man who, with three others, was suspected of shooting a fellow officer just minutes earlier. As he gave chase, he ran past a group of officers who were brutally beating another black man. After Conley had run past, the officers realised that they had made a terrible mistake and that the man they were attacking was in fact one of their own – Michael Cox, a plain-clothes policeman who had arrived on the scene moments before them. Rather than help him, though, they melted into the night. Later, no-one came forward to confess their participation.

Cox suffered extensive injuries that kept him off work for six months. The case achieved notoriety. The only person to admit being anywhere near Cox was Kenny Conley. However, like all the others, he claimed to have seen nothing – a fact that he said was a complete mystery to him.

He wasn't believed. It was obvious to the court that if he had been as close as he indicated, he simply must have seen what was happening. The court decided he was covering for his fellow officers. Conley was convicted of perjury and sentenced to 34 months in prison.[1]

Harvard psychologists Christopher Chabris and Daniel Simons became intrigued. They were convinced that Conley was a real-life victim of something they called *inattentional blindness*. Their most famous demonstration of this was inspired by the Conley case and has now been seen by millions. (If you haven't seen it, you can easily find it on YouTube.)

The video features a group of people playing basketball. Viewers are instructed to count the number of times the players pass the ball. Halfway through, a person in a full-size gorilla suit

---

1   Lehr (2010)

ambles on to centre screen, turns to the camera, beats his chest, turns again and ambles off. The gorilla's appearance is a huge and obvious event. However, the viewer's focus on the task of counting the number of ball passes is such that around 50% of first-timers fail to see the gorilla. Indeed, when the scene is replayed, many people are so shocked that they claim the video has been switched.

The reality of inattentional blindness is striking for two reasons. First, it is shocking that we can miss large events that are in plain sight simply because we are not attending to them. (Furthermore, the evidence shows that the more we are absorbed with a task, the more we will miss other things that are happening.) Second, the reason we are shocked is that it runs counter to our belief that we see everything there is to see. It seems an insult to our intelligence to accept otherwise.

If you are a car driver, you will have had the experience of suddenly realising that you can't remember anything about the last few miles. You realise with a start that you have been driving on some kind of inner autopilot. This often happens when we are bored or preoccupied with a pressing problem and our thoughts start to wander. We can convince ourselves that we must nevertheless have been paying sufficient attention to the task, but the fact is that we get away with it only to the extent that the demands on us remain low level and routine.

The thing is, we are all inattentionally blind most of the time. Most of what is around us simply passes us by, unnoticed. And so it must be. Attention is a precious and finite thing. It is a pie that is capable of division into only so many slices. Once the last slice has been served, the pie has gone and we will not see a gorilla, however obvious it may seem to others with an attentional slice left to give. Only when we free up our attention are we able to notice what was there (or in the process of arriving) all the time. As mathematician Ron Atkin put it: *"A surprise is the answer to a question that hasn't been asked yet."* [2]

 Read more about the limits of attention in **Chapter 7**

A nasty surprise

So, attention is highly limited. But there is a wider issue here that was hinted at in 1890 by William James, an early modern psychologist, in the language of his time:

"Only those items which I notice shape my mind: without selective interest, experience is utter chaos. The function of ignoring, of inattention, is as vital a factor in mental progress as the function of attention itself." [3]

If attention is used up as a result of 'selective interest', how do we decide what is interesting? And how do we prevent ourselves from becoming too focused and immersed in things for our own good – as cargo surveyor Jorge Santos did one day in 2001?

The day attention ran out on *Emilia Theresa*

On 17 January 2001, *Emilia Theresa*, a 3,335 GT chemical tanker, was berthed in Santa Clara, Brazil, loading benzene, a highly flammable hydrocarbon. By lunchtime, 10 of her 12 tanks had been loaded. Loading of the final two tanks was completed at 16.30. During their

---

2   Atkin (1981)

3   James (1890)

loading, a shore-based cargo surveyor, Jorge Santos, came on board. He began taking samples, starting with the after-most tanks and progressing forward to the tanks loaded last. At 16.50, as Santos introduced a metallic sample can into one of the final tanks, a static spark ignited vapours in the ullage space above the main load. The explosion blew the lid off the cargo tank, injuring Santos and causing some structural damage on the deck. The crew did well to control the resulting fire; their actions prevented the incident from developing into a much more serious one.

How did this accident happen? It is true that there were some breaches of the company safety management system. Santos should not have been left alone to do the sampling – especially since he did not share the ship's working language (English). Although the correct sampling equipment was stowed on board, Santos used equipment that was only permitted to be used 30 minutes after loading was complete. This period allowed the electrostatic charges caused by the contact of the benzene with the sides of the tank to disperse to safe levels.

Santos's problem, as he approached the 11th tank, was that he was on a roll, operating in a powerful context established by his successful sampling of the first ten tanks. This behavioural groove (combined with his lack of either English or supervision) meant that he failed to suspect that the final tanks had not been loaded long enough for the electrostatic charges to eliminate themselves.[4]

Attention can become too much of a good thing

Such behavioural grooves are commonplace. People get into an operational rhythm in the interests of efficiency. When such efficiency narrows into a micro-efficiency at the expense of the bigger picture, the results can be catastrophic. That was what happened to the crew of Eastern Airlines flight 401 in December 1972. They all became focused on the failure of a little green cockpit light and no-one noticed that they were spiralling into the Florida Everglades. They hit the ground at 227 mph – an impact that killed 103 people, including everyone in the cockpit. Incredibly, 75 people survived.[5]

It's not just individuals or close teams who create and inhabit these deep behavioural grooves. Whole organisations do it too, drawing upon the stories that they create for themselves to provide a comfortable context for their decision-making. So it was in January 1986 that NASA decided to launch the space shuttle *Challenger* even though they knew that the O-rings separating the fuel components were cracked. Much earlier, any cracking at all was considered to be unacceptable. However, when some cracking was observed without any ill effect, criteria were relaxed, a familiar context was established and the organisation embarked upon a drift towards failure. The eventual result was an explosion shortly after launch, the catastrophic breakup of the shuttle, the deaths of all the crew and the grounding of all NASA shuttles for much of the next three years.[6]

Isn't this just complacency?

Some refer to those who follow such behavioural grooves as complacent. Unfortunately, doing so doesn't explain anything about the source of such behaviour. Nor does it deal with

---

4   Marine Administration Oaseirys Lhuingys (2001)

5   National Transportation Safety Board (1973)

6   Rogers Commission (1986) and Vaughan (1986)

the fundamental human propensities to find shortcuts, create rules of thumb or respond to the pressure to become more efficient. We have more to say about complacency and its relationship with efficiency in Chapter 4 (Being sufficient) and Chapter 5 (Being in a state), and what you can do about it in Chapters 13 and 14 (Being practical).

Behavioural grooves are not fashioned only from an uncritical desire to become more efficient. Sometimes, the purpose being served is the maintenance of safety. A good example of this occurred in the US in December 2015.

A tale of two cities[7]

At 22.20 on the evening of Monday 14 December 2015, a senior Los Angeles (LA) school official received a chilling email. The anonymous writer said that they had been a victim of bullying at a district high school and had now become a 'jihadist'. The 360-word email went on to say that *"schools will be attacked with pressure cooker bombs, nerve gas agents, machine pistols and machine guns"*, that the attacks would be carried out by *"32 jihadist friends"* and that students *"at every school will be massacred, mercilessly. And there is nothing you can do to stop it."*

In a news conference at 07.00 on Tuesday morning, LA Schools Chancellor Ramon Cortines explained the joint decision by the LA Police Department (LAPD) and the Schools Authority, taken 30 minutes earlier, to close the city's 1,100 schools. The disruption was vast: the lives of millions of people were sent into disarray – both emotionally and logistically – as arrangements were made, amid considerable fear, to keep 640,000 students at home during final exams week. Cortines made clear his priority: *"I, as superintendent, am not going to take a chance with the life of a student,"* he said.

Unknown to Cortines, a virtually identical email had been received at the exact same time 3,000 miles (5,000 km) away by New York (NY) school officials – at 01.20 on Tuesday morning their time. The only differences in the emails were the naming of different cities and the statement that the NY attacks would be carried out by *"138 comrades"*. In view of the hour, the official receiving the email did not read it until 05.08. It was forwarded to the New York Police Department (NYPD) by 06.30. An hour later, students began arriving at NY schools without any knowledge of the threat. At 09.30, the threat was ruled a hoax in NY. Simultaneously, and with no knowledge of each other's problem, LA officials were announcing the closure of the LA school system.

It is rare in real life that there is an opportunity to observe the impact of context on the interpretation of an identical message by two equivalent organisations in the same culture. What drove the very different responses in NY and LA?

Timing was one thing. LA received the email at a time that made school closure more practicable than in NY. But there was a much more powerful contextual difference between the two cities. Less than two weeks earlier, there had been a real and deadly 'jihadist' attack at a San Bernardino community centre just 50 miles (80 km) from LA. It had left 14 people dead and 22 injured. The authorities were on edge about the possibility of another attack, so LA officials found their attention focused on the email's description of a radicalised Muslim. They saw significance in the fact that he appeared to be very familiar with the structure of

---

7   This account was compiled from contemporaneous news stories published by the BBC (2015), *The New York Times* (2015) and ABC News (2015).

the LA Unified School District. And they knew their investigators were already assessing the possibility that the husband and wife who carried out the earlier San Bernardino shootings had been planning an attack on schools.

In a very different NY context, officials focused on different elements of the message. They decided that the number of attackers was not credible, and nor was the claim to have access to nerve gas. They, too, noted the author's claim to be *"a devout Muslim"* but found it unlikely that such a person would spell 'Allah' with a lower-case 'a', as the email did. Same evidence, different interpretation, informed by a different context: LA's *"credible threat"* was NY's *"outlandish hoax"*. And different conclusions led to different rationales, too. While LA's Cortines was justifying the $29 million decision with *"I think it's important to take this precaution based on what has happened recently"*, NY's Mayor, Bill de Blasio, was justifying the decision to keep NY schools open: *"... it's important – very important – not to overreact in situations like this,"* he said.

Who was right? You will have your own view. Ours is that both were. The fact is that, like all decision-makers, they were in genuinely different situations. What was important was not the single 'objective' reality of the same email message, but the different possibilities raised by the different contexts in which the email landed. Hindsight shows that the NY interpretation was more consistent with the hoax status of the email, but hindsight is an illusory luxury that is only ever available to auditors and never to decision-makers. We will return to the illusion of hindsight later in this book, in Chapter 9 (Being in the know – part IV).

 Get help with making more of hindsight with Mindset Analysis in **Chapter 14**

The impossibility of a single, objective context

There is a crucial implication to the fact that we all have a particular field of view at any particular time. It is that we do not – nor ever can – live in an objective world in which we can know everything there is to know. The perspective we happen to have is only ever one of many. That perspective is both informed by, and contributes to, the context that gives us meaning.

There is an old conundrum about whether a glass is half full or half empty. It is claimed that optimists tend to see the former, while pessimists tend to take the latter view. Such personality attributes are, of course, long-term shapers of context. However, it is quite easy to exchange pessimist and optimist perspectives by manipulating local context. Take a full glass and publicly empty exactly half into an identical empty glass. Spectators will readily agree that the formerly full glass is now half empty, while the formerly empty glass is now half full.

Isolated facts mean very little and are often a source of ambiguity as we attempt to make sense of them. When they are made part of a narrative – a story – their 'true' meaning suddenly becomes clear. Except, of course, this clarity is not a property of the fact itself, but of our interpretation of it. We impose meaning.

We live in a world that we continually create and shape in accordance with our reasons and purposes for doing so. It is a world that is inter-subjective at best, ie one that we can make shared sense of. It is never objectively knowable.

The fact that humans – all of us – live inside stories of our own making, and can never – in principle – have the whole picture, turns out to be fundamental to the business of how organisations can create an effective and resilient safety culture. Understanding this is one of the central points of this book. Responding to it will throw off the shackles that are holding organisations back from achieving optimal levels of safety.

The power of shared context

In his epic history of humankind, *Sapiens*, Yuval Harari[8] identifies the 'moment' of the Cognitive Revolution, 70,000 years ago, when we transformed ourselves from *"an animal of no significance"* to a species that would come to dominate the planet (at least for now). Until that moment, *Homo sapiens* had subsisted the same way, doing the same things, for 130,000 years. For 130 millennia we were quite happy eating, sleeping, breeding and making very little progress at all.

Then something happened.

We developed the ability to express and communicate concepts, stories and meanings for things that exist only in our *imagination*. This imaginative power to create, share and cooperate in our ideas, purposes and enterprises wonderfully complemented our individually restricted fields of view. We suddenly sprang forward from lives fettered by the constraints of immediate, everyday context. We began to share the meanings we derived from such context to first imagine, and then cooperate in, the creation of our own collective future.

The generation of context

But where does the context come from in the first place? If we make things up and share them, what are the psychological ingredients we use for our stories? Where do they come from, how are they influenced – and what does this mean for operational safety in a complex world of our own making?

In this book, we use a simple descriptive model – the SUGAR model[9] – to organise the ingredients from which we create and maintain the context in which we find ourselves moment by moment.

---

8 Harari (2014)

9 The SUGAR model was introduced in the KVH Media/Pukka film (2012) *The Human Element*, based upon the eponymous book by Gregory & Shanahan (2010).

Figure 3.1 The three main ingredients in our creation of context

State (S), Understanding (U) and Goals (G), which provide context for Action (A), after which the cycle is repeated (R)

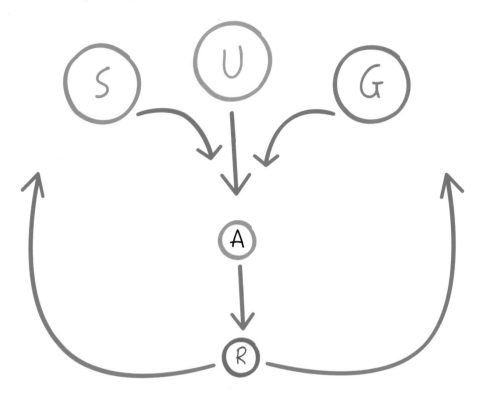

 Get help with using SUGAR to retrieve context in accident investigation in **Chapter 14**

State (S) refers to both our physical and mental state. Our state is determined at any particular moment by longer-term attributes such as our general level of health and fitness, size, strength, personality, and chronic stress. It is also affected by shorter-term factors such as hunger, thirst, drugs, exertion, fatigue, boredom and mood. We explore some of these behavioural influences in more detail in Chapter 5 (Being in a state).

Understanding (U) refers to what we know, or think we know, and how we have come to know it. It refers to how we sense the world around us, how we make sense of what our senses tell us, the role and impact of emotion and, crucially, the true nature of the relationship between all three (sensing, making sense and emotion). It includes not just what we have learned formally and informally, through experience, but the extensive world of unconscious biases on our behaviour and our dynamically changing perception of risk. We explore these behavioural influences in more detail in Chapters 6 to 9 (Being in the know).

Goals (G) refers to the complex and dynamic structure of the values, purposes and objectives we maintain to inform and drive our professional, social and personal behaviour in one direction rather than another. We explore these behavioural influences in more detail in Chapter 10 (Being on target).

Together, our momentary State, Understanding and Goals provide the psychological context for any particular **Action (A)** that we take at any particular moment. Action includes both physical and psychological action, including decisions not to act. Action can be focused on making a change to the world with which we are interacting, or it might be focused on changing one, some or many of the more controllable S, U, G ingredients. For example, action could involve making further progress in a task that is under way. Or it could involve changing an explicit goal or a goal priority. Or it might be urgently focused on fixing some aspect of our state, such as sleeping when we are tired. The mix of ingredients also includes less accessible aspects, such as our emotions, instincts, fears and values. All of these play a part in the complex mix that moves us towards one action or another.

Once an action has occurred, the whole cycle **Repeats (R)**. However, the new cycle operates in a changed world, with a new mix of ingredients. This is why, for LP Hartley, *"the past is a foreign country"*. And it's why, some 2,000 years before, Heraclitus saw that *"you can't step twice into the same river"*. Our knowledge of how the world has changed is determined by the collective values and meaning of the new mix. And we use this new mix to figure out – both consciously and unconsciously – what new action, if any, to take next.

How is the SUGAR model used in this book?

In Chapter 5 (Being in a state), Chapters 6 to 9 (Being in the know) and Chapter 10 (Being on target), we explore in more detail the three sets of ingredients – State, Understanding and Goals – and see how increasing our insights into them can improve our approach to safety.

In Chapter 11 (Being together), we discover the nature of the 'social glue' that allows us to coordinate our actions with others. We discover what teamwork and diversity are really all about and how they are crucial to the development of safe behaviour at work.

In Chapter 12 (Being human), we take a step back and examine the organisational implications of construing human behaviour at work through the framework of the SUGAR model. In doing so, we begin to see clearly in what way organisational culture needs to develop in order to make a real difference to the human element in safety.

In Chapters 13 and 14 (Being practical), we present some pragmatic guidelines for using the information in this book, leading to strategies for greater individual and organisational resilience that will help us in the important business of creating safety.

But first, in Chapter 4 (Being sufficient), we need to complete the SUGAR model by incorporating the tricky question of efficiency. Given that our working days are filled – and often overfilled – with many competing demands, how do we decide that what we have done is good enough before allowing ourselves to move on? What happens when we get this wrong – and how much of a safety problem is it?

4 Being sufficient
how much is enough?

How much safety is enough?

Why isn't safety always 'paramount' – despite what people say?

Where does safety come from?

What's the relationship between safety and productivity?

How can human factors be used more effectively to promote safety?

Absolute must or relative need?

There is an old joke with many variations. Here is one.

Two swimmers were resting against a small platform in the middle of a bay when a large shark appeared and started circling around them. One of the swimmers immediately began to put on his flippers. His companion expressed surprise: *"Surely you don't think you can outswim a shark?"* *"I don't have to,"* came the reply. *"I just have to outswim you."*

This nicely introduces a key distinction. The concept of 'enough' has both absolute and relative components. For the swimmer in the joke, the flipper strategy is useless if he can't actually swim, so swimming is an absolute or minimal requirement. Similarly, if the officer of the watch (OOW) on a ship's bridge has no idea about collision regulations (COLREGS) or no knowledge of the relationship between helm changes and the time lag before the ship responds, then no amount of his attention will make any difference to the ship's fate.

But let's assume the absolute requirements of the situation can be met. Our flippered friend knows how to swim. (How else did he get to the middle of the bay?) And the OOW knows perfectly well what the COLREGS say and understands system lag. After all, he is qualified and has the certificate to prove it(!). What does 'enough' depend on now? This is where we have to rely on the relative sense of the word.

The flippered swimmer makes decisions based on his perception of his swimming ability *relative* to his companion and the shark. For the OOW, he makes decisions about how much attention to pay and what to do about what he sees *relative* to his insight into his own experience and confidence levels, among other things (many of which are what this book is about).

A large part of 'enough' is always relative to the perceived resources and purpose of the people in the situation in which they perceive themselves to be.

Natural sufficiency

Sharks are generally white on their underbelly and blue or grey on top. The combined result is an exquisitely fine camouflage. Seen from above, they are hard to discern from the ocean. Seen from below, they blend with the diffused light coming from above. Their lower jaws are connected to their heads at two points in such a way that they can dislocate their lower jaw at will, allowing it to be opened very wide. They never run out of teeth, since they can just grow new ones, and they can smell blood at 100 metres in dilutions of one drop per Olympic-sized swimming pool. They can hear their next meal with internal ears from more than a kilometre away. They were swimming in every one of Earth's oceans 200 million years before dinosaurs appeared, and today's sharks are almost identical to those living 100 million years ago.

So, sharks are an exquisite blend, and they have earned respect as highly evolved killing machines. But they aren't perfect. They suffer from viruses and they get cancer.[1] If they ever stop swimming and lose the lift from their pectoral fins, they sink and drown. And despite their formidable predatory equipment and over 400 million years of evolution, in a fight with an Orca killer whale they have only a 50–50 chance.

Nature is not concerned with perfection, but with 'good enough'. For sharks, 'good enough' was reached 100 million years ago, and since then nothing has changed in their ecosphere to demand any further refinement. So how come they still suffer from cancer?

The answer lies in the realisation that nature has no purpose. It is not trying to achieve anything, and nor is natural selection or evolution. These are simply descriptive names for an automatic, self-regulating, blind process that works across many generations. Within its ecosphere, chance variations in an individual's repertoire either favour its survival long enough to breed, or count against it. The key phrase is 'long enough to breed'. If the development of cancer comes late enough in an individual's life so as not to interfere with creating or nurturing the next generation, then natural selection has nothing to say about the cancer. In fact, if a cancer has genetic roots, the opposite may occur: selection of those cancers that develop late.

Natural selection supports the development of a balance among all the inhabitants of any particular ecosphere. This balance is always subject to disruption, change and rebalancing.

For centuries, the light-coloured peppered moth[2] liked to rest by settling on the bark of trees, where it blended in nicely among the light-coloured bark and lichens. Enough survived via this camouflage year-on-year to generate sufficient numbers of progeny so as to take advantage of the available food supply and, for the moth, for life to go on in the UK. But then the Industrial Revolution happened. The trees turned dark with soot from factory pollution, and the light-coloured moths became increasingly easy for hungry birds to spot.

There was nothing purposive in what happened next. What happened was that the tiny proportion of peppered moths with darker wings produced by natural variation survived in

---

1 Until quite recently, it was thought that sharks did not get cancer at all. This is now known to be incorrect.

2 The case of the peppered moth is hugely significant and counts today as the first solid evidence for Darwinian evolution. This evidence was available to Darwin, but it was only scientifically accepted in 1896, 14 years after the great man's death.

Being Human in safety-critical organisations

disproportionate numbers relative to their lighter-coloured friends. Over a few generations, the entire species turned dark and a new natural balance was found. When the effects of the Industrial Revolution were reversed by cleaner manufacturing processes, the trees got lighter again, and so did the moths.

Everyday behaviour

What have peppered moths and natural selection got to do with human behaviour at work?

Well, it should be no surprise that our everyday behaviour tends to be governed by the same natural principles. As the swimmers in the joke demonstrate, it's often a question of just doing enough. And so it is that in our everyday work we naturally seek what is 'good enough' to satisfy what we take to be the requirements that we need to meet. So often, the work required of us is constrained by time and available resources, by the other things that we know we must get done, and by the many purposes we are trying to serve.

It is important to note, though, that 'good enough' is not the same as compromise. Real-world decisions are often compromises in suboptimal circumstances that we judge to be good enough to permit progress. However, the task in which we are engaged may or may not be vulnerable to compromise. If we are learning to play a violin to public acclaim, or hand-crafting a pair of made-to-measure shoes for a specific customer, or if we are a doctor conducting a heart bypass operation, there is little room for compromise. In these kinds of endeavour, 'good enough' needs to be close to perfection against some absolute criterion, or else there is little point in conducting the activity.

So, the amount of compromise in 'good enough' is always defined by the overall context in which we find ourselves. The more our context is defined by externally prescribed standards, rules and expectations (including those we impose upon ourselves), the less room there is for compromise. And the less room there is for compromise, the more tightly coupled everything is, and the more devastating the effects of any variation can be. The incidents we describe in this book show what can happen when the interdependencies between system elements are broken. But there are many everyday examples as well – sometimes with surprising results.

Route 1 is the main road through Alexandria, Virginia, just outside Washington DC. For a dozen blocks it follows a dead straight line through as many light-controlled intersections. There is a speed limit of 25 mph the whole way and the Highways Department found a clever way of encouraging adherence. If you move off from the first green signal and keep to 25 mph, every one of the remaining lights turns green just before you get to it. Any faster and you get brought to a stop.[3] Clever – except when the lights get out of sync or fail-safe to red, and gridlock quickly ensues.

What's interesting is what happens when the external controls are removed and the lights are turned off altogether. Driver progress is surprisingly efficient. Everyone moves slowly, making eye contact as they negotiate their way past each other. It turns out that giving people more control and responsibility, rather than micro-managing their behaviour, can produce positive results.

---

3   Similar, albeit much simpler, systems are being introduced on main roads that run through French villages. If drivers approach a traffic light faster than the speed limit, the light turns red, stopping them. Drivers quickly learn that it is far more efficient to reduce their speed and proceed through a light that cooperatively stays green.

In the UK, recent experiments have been done to simplify and remove roadway signage and street furniture. In their place, painted chicanes and other features have been introduced to create visual uncertainty. The aim is to transfer the focus of safety from signs on the road to inside people's heads – that is to say, transferring absolute 'good enough' to relative 'good enough'; and transferring degrees of freedom from the external to the internal.

Herb Simon was a social psychologist, Nobel prize-winning economist and one of the founding fathers of artificial intelligence. In 1956, he introduced the word 'satisfice' to capture the notion of 'good enough'. It is an amalgam of the two words 'satisfy' and 'suffice', and he coined it originally in the context of his work on decision-making. He wanted to understand the behaviour of human decision-makers where there was not enough information to come up with a perfect solution. For Simon, satisficing was achieved in everyday tasks either when people simplified things in order to come up with an optimum solution, or when they found an imperfect solution that would, nevertheless, do the job.

"Safety is paramount"

Senior company spokespeople are sometimes heard to say "*in our organisation, safety is paramount*". They often say this shortly after an accident that calls into question the very thing that the company is anxious to defend.

The meaning of 'paramount' is unambiguous. The Oxford English Dictionary defines it as "*more important than anything else; supreme*". The underlying message of such company spokespeople is that whatever has gone wrong has nothing to do with deficient safety procedures or inattention to safety, and therefore must be something else. Bad luck or bad people. Definitely not bad policy.

While such speakers may be sincerely motivated, such declarations fail to represent the reality of human safety perception and the real, satisficing world of human behaviour. The fact is that our perception of safety is a moving thing. On one day we are keen to don all the personal protection equipment that the rule book says we must, and on another we find it easy to decide not to. One day we scrupulously follow a written medical checklist, and the next we rely on our memory to administer part of the drug round. We will explore the factors that make our perception of safety change from one moment to the next in Chapter 8 (Being in the know – part III).

For now, we want to highlight how our decision-making at work is driven by satisficing, how this impacts our sense of safety, and how it is possible for organisations to sincerely believe that 'safety is paramount' immediately after the most appalling accident has occurred.

Erik Hollnagel's efficiency–thoroughness trade-off

An important piece of the story was provided by Erik Hollnagel in 2009, when he explored the implications of human decision-making for something he called the efficiency–thoroughness trade-off (ETTO) principle. Here is how he described the central idea:

"The ETTO principle refers to the fact that people and organisations frequently – or always – have to make a trade-off between the resources (time and effort) they spend on … an activity. The trade-off may favour thoroughness over efficiency if safety and quality are the dominant concerns, and efficiency over thoroughness if throughput and outputs are the dominant concerns. It follows from the ETTO principle that it is never possible to maximise

efficiency and thoroughness at the same time. Nor can an activity expect to succeed, if there is not a minimum of either."[4]

The ETTO principle is, of course, a more finely analysed dissection of 'good enough'. For example, a wading bird foraging in the mud for food (efficiency) needs to adopt a head-down position. However, it also needs to maintain a certain degree of vigilance against predators (thoroughness), which requires a head-up position. Its answer is to alternate positions in a proportion that fits its current sense of danger versus hunger. As it satiates, the risk ratio changes and it spends proportionately more time being vigilant. As it approaches migration time, the ratio changes the other way, in favour of efficiency, as the need to increase food intake becomes more pressing.

Hollnagel's insight is that something like this dynamic trade-off is a constant feature of human decision-making. In order to be productive, get things done, make progress and achieve our goals – both our own and those of our organisation – we need to focus on efficiency. But in order to do things properly, safely, by the rule book and to the standards required by our training, trades, professions, employers and the law, we need to focus on thoroughness. Depending on our frame of reference and the situation we perceive we are in, the trade-off point between the two will shift either towards efficiency (and greater risk) or towards thoroughness (and less productivity).

Hollnagel lists and exemplifies a number of ETTO rules of thumb that we often use to guide our trade-off decisions. Some of these are used by individuals, while others appear to operate across the whole organisation. Table 4.1 highlights a few of these 'good enough' rules.

Table 4.1 ETTO rules

Individual ETTO rules	Organisational ETTO rules
'It looks fine' – so there's no need to do anything	Negative reporting – so the absence of reports is taken to infer that nothing's wrong
'It's not really important' – so it can be left for now	Invisible managers – who tend to focus on administrative issues rather than operators
'It will be checked later by someone else' – so we can skip it and save time	Supplier under-reporting – economies of the truth by suppliers to avoid undue penalties
'It has been checked by someone else' – so there's no need to do it again	Cost-reduction – in which unwise choices are made about costs that are deemed unnecessary
'Doing it this way is much quicker' – even though it does not quite follow procedure	Double binds – in which people are conflicted by mixed messages about the importance of both safety and productivity

Reproduced from *The Etto Principle: Efficiency–Thoroughness Trade-Off: Why Things That Go Right Sometimes Go Wrong* (Hollnagel, 2009: Ashgate) with kind permission

It should be noted that all the rules of thumb in Table 4.1 favour increased efficiency at the expense of thoroughness. This is unsurprising in a commercial context that is driven by the need for competing organisations to maintain and increase profits through increased volume, leaner processes and minimised costs. However, as Hollnagel points out, *"it is only in hindsight, when the outcome is the wrong one, that the choice of efficiency over thoroughness conveniently is labelled 'human error'".*[5]

---

4   Hollnagel (2009), pp. 28–9

5   Hollnagel (2009), p. 133

We shall have more to say on the illusion of hindsight and the problem of human error in Chapter 7 (Being in the know – part II).

ETTO rules such as the ones in Table 4.1 are not causes or explanations of behaviour at work, but simply descriptions of it. A bosun may decide to skip a scheduled instrument reading on the assumption it won't have changed since he last checked it. He may instead use the time saved to fix a problem he considers (or has been told) is more pressing, or to take much-overdue rest after a long shift. What he actually decides to do will be impacted by a very large constellation of human factors.

In December 2014, the chemical tanker *Orakai* collided with the Dutch-crewed fishing trawler *Margriet* in the North Sea. The trawler was severely damaged. Her wheelhouse was partially destroyed and 8 tonnes of fuel oil leaked into the sea. It was a small miracle that *Margriet* did not sink and that no-one was hurt.

Although *Margriet*'s watchkeeper was on the ship's bridge, he was not keeping an effective lookout to the seas. Instead, the trawler crew were relying on Rule 18 of the Collision Regulations (COLREGS), which says that when a ship is trawling, other powered ships are required to take evasive action. The main problem was that, heavily influenced by fatigue, the chief officer of *Orakai* was focused on searching the ship for a cable tie to secure a light. Intending only to leave the bridge for a few minutes, his preoccupation with an inconsequential task kept him away for the 22 minutes it took for the collision to occur.[6]

The chief officer had left the bridge for short periods before, all without any issues developing. For him, there was no difference this time, and the short period of absence he had intended did not appear to warrant arranging a replacement officer[7] to accompany the unqualified and increasingly panicked lookout he left on the bridge. The chief officer was pursuing his task with great efficiency, as well as trying to be efficient with the time of others who were resting. The problem was that he was focused on efficiently pursuing one task at the expense of the thoroughness that was required for another.

In Chapter 3 (Being framed), we introduced an organisation of these factors in the descriptive SUGAR model. We can now complete that model as follows:

---

6   MAIB (2015)

7   Laughery (undated) notes that tag-out procedures are often ignored for the same reason, leading to incidents when other workers come along and turn the unprotected machine back on – all in a time period that was so short as to be thought impossible to compromise safety.

Being Human in safety-critical organisations

Figure 4.1 The SUGAR model

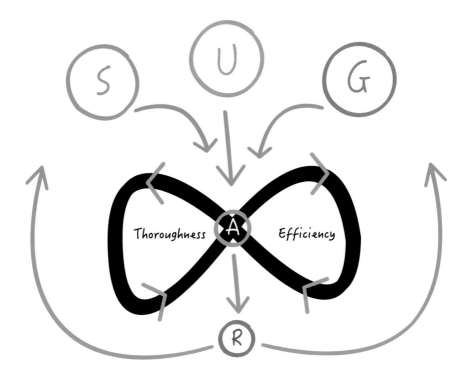

The bow-tie-shaped object in Figure 4.1 is instantly recognisable as the symbol for infinity. Using this symbol to represent Hollnagel's efficiency–thoroughness trade-off cycle is highly appropriate. It captures the idea of human cognition as a continuous decision loop whose every iteration both impacts, and is impacted by, the current complex mix of State, Understanding and Goals. Each iteration describes a point on an individual's decision path over time. Each decision timeline is a trace of an individual's moment-by-moment resolution of the need to trade efficiency with thoroughness, based on the situation in which they perceive themselves to be at the time. Each moment may involve a conscious decision, including a conscious decision not to act. However, all such moments are impacted by factors and biases operating at deeper or even unconscious levels. This may make a lot of the decision-making timelines we create seem relatively effortless, even though there is an awful lot going on.

All of our decision trajectories may include trade-offs that turn out to be unnecessarily thorough (and so wasteful of resources) or over-efficient (and so unnecessarily risky). Either way, they crystallise out of the constellation of SUGAR influences (ie human factors) relevant to us at the time. Within the frame created by that constellation, they are in most cases the individual's best attempt at 'good enough'.

But sometimes, despite best intentions, 'good enough' turns out not to be good enough. We may start to compromise where we shouldn't and thereby lose some of the coupling that keeps us working in a coordinated way. Once you've broken your diet with one biscuit (*"just one biscuit won't hurt"*), you are likely to go on to eat the whole packet. The initial crossing of the threshold is what matters.

There are a host of reasons why S, U and G factors can mislead, misinform and otherwise beguile us, and we will delve into these individually in Chapters 5 to 10. In the meantime, let's take a look at the catastrophic case of *Herald of Free Enterprise* to see all of them at work.

The *Herald of Free Enterprise* catastrophe

Herald of Free Enterprise was a roll-on/roll-off (ro-ro) cross-channel ferry operated by Townsend Thoresen between Dover and Calais in the 1980s. The Channel Tunnel would not open until 1994, and cross-channel freight traffic was increasing. To remain competitive with other ferry operators, Townsend Thoresen required ships designed to permit fast loading and unloading, and quick acceleration. With their adjustable ramps allowing vehicles to drive on and off their flat steel decks, ro-ro ships saved huge amounts of unproductive port time.

Commercial changes in the ferry industry had recently complicated the picture. They included:

- New high-capacity mixed freight and passenger 'jumbo' ferries
- Reductions in crew levels, despite strong union opposition
- New freight-only ro-ro ferries
- New dock-side facilities to accelerate ferry turnaround time
- New fare tariffs to attract day trippers and off-peak travellers.

On 6 March 1987, the 9,000 GT *Herald* left her berth in the inner harbour of the Belgian port of Zeebrugge at 18.05 GMT. She was overloaded. She carried 459 passengers, 80 crew, 81 cars, 47 trucks and 3 buses. Within 20 minutes she had passed completely out of the harbour, was rapidly picking up speed and was heading for the open sea at just over 18 knots. No-one had yet noticed that the vast bow loading doors were still open.

As the ship reached a critical forward speed, the bow dipped and scooped a huge mass of seawater through the open doors. With no watertight compartments, the water flooded through the entire deck. In seconds, the ship listed 30 degrees to port, righted herself, then listed port again past the point of no return. She capsized in shallow water 1 km from the shore, coming to rest on her side on a sand bar. Within moments of the capsize, the power failed and the ship lay creaking and groaning in darkness, in the freezing waters of the North Sea.

The entire event took just 90 seconds. One hundred and ninety-three people died.

It was the worst peacetime disaster involving a British ship in over 70 years. Many passengers were returning from a cheap day promotion offered by *The Sun*, a British national newspaper. Most were trapped inside the vessel, falling victim to hypothermia in the 3°C water.

Many more would have died but for the quick response of a nearby dredger that raised the alarm, a passing ferry that effected early rescue, the Belgian Navy who were on exercise nearby, and the Zeebrugge port rescue authorities who quickly provided helicopter services.

Naturally, a full investigation and public inquiry followed. This was chaired by British Lord Justice Sir Barry Sheen.[8] The following were among the particular points he noted, as summarised by the authors.

---

8 Sheen (1987)

The ship and crew that day

- There was poor workplace communication – identified as part of the 'root cause' of the accident.
- The assistant bosun (responsible for closing the bow doors) had worked long hours before the vessel left Zeebrugge.
- The ship was under pressure to leave the berth: a sense of urgency to sail at the earliest possible moment had been increased by an internal memorandum sent to assistant managers, stating that sailing 15 minutes early was the new expected norm.
- Careless counting meant that the freight weight exceeded the declared weight by approximately 13%, and the number of passengers was excessive.
- The ship's design made her naturally top-heavy, yet trimming of the ship with ballast water to lower her centre of gravity had been careless and inefficient.
- The design of the ship made it impossible for the master to see the bow doors from the bridge.

The company

- There was a *"stand-off"* relationship between ship operators and shore managers – identified as part of the 'root cause' of the accident.
- There was a *"disease of sloppiness"* and negligence at every level of the company hierarchy.
- The company directors did not have any proper comprehension of their duties.
- The board demonstrated an inability or unwillingness to give clear orders.
- No director was solely responsible for safety.
- Shore management took very little notice of what they were told by their masters.
- In October 1983, *Herald's* sister ship, *Pride of Free Enterprise*, had sailed from Dover to Zeebrugge with the bow doors open after her assistant bosun fell asleep.
- Issues relating to the breaking of waves high on the bow doors while under way were dismissed by company management because *"ships' masters would come and 'bang on the desk' if an issue was truly important"*.
- Requests to have an indicator installed on the bridge, showing the position of the doors, were dismissed by management because it was thought frivolous to spend money on equipment to indicate if employees had failed to do their job correctly.
- The risks posed by the lack of watertight compartments on the vehicle decks of ro-ro vessels had been known since two other ro-ro vessels had been lost prior to the *Herald* disaster.

What is it possible to see – over and above these highly pertinent observations – when the event is examined from the point of view of SUGAR (State, Understanding, Goals, Action, Repeat)? In Table 4.2, we set out some additional human issues that can be straightforwardly derived from the official investigation reports.

Table 4.2 *Herald of Free Enterprise*: investigation highlights and possible SUGAR influences

Role	Investigation highlights	SUGAR influences	
Assistant bosun	Had been busy with cleaning and maintenance on the car deck. Went to his cabin before the departure, fell asleep and did not wake when 'harbour stations' was called. As a result, was not available to close the bow doors, as expected by normal practice. Identified as the immediate cause of the accident.	**S**	• Fatigue – for which sleep is the only remedy
		U	• Could go to sleep without risk – since either someone would wake him or someone else would close the bow doors
		G	• To sleep
		A	• It seemed 'enough' to give in to sleep without ensuring a timely return to duty through a fail-safe means
Bosun	Had been loading vehicles. After the last was loaded, he knew the bow doors should be closed, but went to his harbour station. Said it was *"not his duty"* to close the doors. Identified as *"the most immediate"* cause of the accident.	**S**	• Under pressure to go to 'harbour stations' (which the chief officer had called), as everyone else was doing
		U	• Assumed the assistant bosun would close the doors, as normal and as expected • Own narrow definition of his job was sufficient for operational safety
		G	• To move efficiently to his next duty • To avoid involvement in operational delay
		A	• It seemed 'enough' to pay attention only to his own duties as he – somewhat narrowly – interpreted them

Role	Investigation highlights	SUGAR influences
Chief officer	Took over loading supervision from second officer. Believed it was his responsibility to ensure the assistant bosun was in position to close the doors, not to actually check himself the doors were shut. Believed he had seen the assistant bosun going towards the doors and assumed he would close them. Then went to his harbour station on the bridge.	(S) • Under pressure to finish loading, call 'harbour stations' and then get back to the bridge • Feeling some (unexplained) tension with the second officer, whom he unusually relieved from loading minutes before it was finished
		(U) • Assumed the assistant bosun would close the doors, as normal and as expected • Expectation bias (or memory flaw) meant he thought he saw the assistant bosun returning • Relied upon unquestioned, ambiguous instruction that meant he did not consider it his job to check the bow doors
	There was an implicit conflict here, in that he was required to be both loading cars and on the bridge 15 minutes before the departure time. Was very conscious of pressure from management to leave on time.	(G) • To complete vehicle loading as quickly as possible • To call 'harbour stations' as soon as possible • To get to the bridge to assume next duty, for which he was late • To get the ship on her way as soon as possible • To avoid censure from shore management
		(A) • It seemed 'enough' to rely on a few untested assumptions so as to achieve multiple, partly conflicting objectives in the conditions and time available

Role	Investigation highlights	SUGAR influences	
Master	Been at sea for over 30 years, ten of them in command. Was on the bridge. Had to configure ship loading to one deck at a time via ballast operations due to incompatibility of Zeebrugge dock. (The ship was designed for Dover–Calais ports.)	**S**	• Under pressure to hasten turnaround and depart on time in suboptimal loading conditions
		U	• Stress contributed to overlooking the need to trim the ship after filling ballast tanks to allow loading • Familiarity with uneventful operations contributed to underestimating bow-doors risk – made worse by no visual indicator for bow doors • Cued for departure by 'harbour stations' call and return of chief officer to the bridge • No attention paid to potential impact of company issues on crew
	Saw the chief officer come onto the bridge, but did not ask him for a report on the ship's status. Not asking for a report was common practice. Could not see the bow doors from the wheelhouse, and no indicator light was fitted.	**G**	• To get the ship on her way as soon as possible • To avoid censure from shore management
		A	• It seemed 'enough' to rely on familiar, untested cues both in spite of, and because of, company pressures and unhelpful culture
Company management	Ignorant of how to run a safe ferry company. Unaware and seemingly uninterested in numerous earlier failures, including a capsize and ferries sailing with the bow doors open.	**S**	• Culture of cavalier inattention, non-learning and blame
		U	• Preoccupation with profitability and commercial competition • Little knowledge of ship operations • Little knowledge of interacting network of shared responsibilities • Little interest in increasing operational knowledge • Ignorant about their ignorance and its potential impact
	Had little contact with masters and did not listen to them when they did have contact. Did not support masters in maintaining discipline.		
	Did not issue clear instructions. Tolerant of ships carrying excessive numbers of passengers.	**G**	• To do well relative to their competition • To make profits by cutting corners • To appear to be tough-minded
	These aspects of the company culture were identified as the root cause of the accident.	**A**	• It seemed 'enough' to insist on efficiency in a vacuum of knowledge about the shipping industry, and to rely on ships' crews for thoroughness with little regard for the impossibility of maximising both efficiency and thoroughness

The Sheen Inquiry determined that the capsizing of *Herald of Free Enterprise* was partly caused or contributed to by serious negligence in the discharge of their duties by the master, the chief officer and the assistant bosun, and partly caused or contributed to by the owners, Townsend Car Ferries Limited. The Townsend Thoresen name disappeared and the ships were quickly rebranded as P&O Ferries by their new owners, the European Ferries Group. The Sheen Inquiry suspended the master's certificate for one year and the chief officer's certificate for two years, and directed Townsend to pay £400,000 ($600,000) for legal and court costs.

In 1989, as a direct result of the disaster, the UK's Marine Accident Investigation Branch (MAIB) was formed.

In 1990, a case of corporate manslaughter collapsed in the British courts when the various acts of negligence could not be pinned on any specific individual who was a 'controlling mind' on behalf of the company that day. The failure of this case led – ten years later – to legal reform in the UK. Since 2007, *"A corporation, be it a company, government department or other Crown body, will be liable to face prosecution where a gross failing by its senior managers to take reasonable care for the safety of their workers or other individuals causes death."* [9]

Had the new law been available for the *Herald* case, there is little doubt that greater accountabilities would have been determined and these would have been met with greater redress. There is no doubt that everyone involved in the calamity suffered greatly – as did the thousands who made up the extended family and friends of the victims.

In all cases like this, there is a tendency to determine and apportion blame. While it is entirely reasonable to determine accountability, it needs to be done in a way that takes proper and reasonable account of the circumstances in which those involved were embedded at the time. What context did they judge themselves to be in? Why were they attending to the things they were and not to other aspects of their situation? How far was it reasonable for them to behave in the way they did, given the context they were in?

 Read more about blame and accountability in **Chapter 12**

Herald operated with three sets of crew and five sets of officers. Would a different crew have behaved differently in the same circumstances of increasing pressure from a senior management bent on ever greater efficiency?

Are we talking about 'bad apples'? Or are we talking about a series of interacting system components, each of whom is behaving in a way that is within normal operating limits, but whose drift over time and combination at a critical moment was disastrous? And if so, is there any way that those interacting system components – the crew, the officers, the managers, the organisation – can be provided with additional knowledge about the true nature of the enterprise in which they are participating? Knowledge that will help?

We think so.

We do not offer any of the SUGAR observations in Table 4.2 as primary causes or excuses for what took place on that cold winter's day off Zeebrugge. What is important about them is

---

9   UK Corporate Manslaughter and Corporate Homicide Act 2007

that they suggest clues as to why the individuals involved defined 'enough' as they did. What they offer are additional lines of enquiry – pathways – to where this book is headed. To a place that begins with the acknowledgement of the inevitability of individual – and highly constrained – points of view, how those points of view come about, and what it takes for us as individuals, team members, supervisors, senior managers and company directors to deal with them effectively.

A spoonful of SUGAR

It is traditional in the discipline of human factors, and in the enlightened commercial enterprises that already pay attention to it, to start with an interest in how to deal with human failure. The thinking goes like this: if we can work out how and why humans fail, then we can come up with strategies and interventions that stop this occurring, or at least reduce the risk of it happening.

And, of course, much has been achieved with this approach.

Figure 4.2 expresses this traditional view. In the top left, it captures a set of conditions that are often held to be causes of human failure; and in the top right, there is a systematic set of ways for dealing with them.

Over the past two or three decades, a lot of effort has been spent on developing best practice in areas such as design, selection, training, procedure writing and so forth. In addition, effort has gone into methodologies that integrate these areas into the acquisition of technology. Examples are the US Department of Defense's (DoD) Manprint programme in the 1980s and the UK Ministry of Defence's (MOD) Human Factors Integration (HFI) programme in the 1990s.

In fact, the authors of this book were heavily involved in these developments.[10] We were also involved in distilling, summarising and enhancing a lot of this best practice to the rail industry in the 2000s.[11] These remain useful developments and provide a comprehensive source of human-factors information and principles.

 Get help with design, selection and training in **Chapter 14**

---

10 Dik Gregory spent three years in the mid-1980s on exchange to the US Army Research Institute in Virginia, working alongside American psychologists involved in creating tools to support the emerging Manprint programme. In the early 1990s, both authors of this book were heavily involved in evaluating the contribution of US Manprint tools to UK MOD procurement and in developing specific UK guidance for MOD desk officers and HFI staff.

11 Gregory & Shanahan (2008)

Figure 4.2 The traditional view of the contribution of human factors

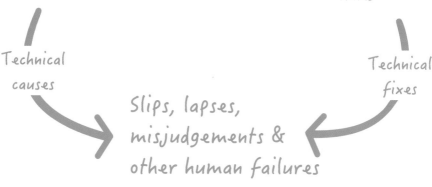

- Human fallibility
- Insufficient capability
- Insufficient training
- Insufficient time
- Bad design

- Design
- Selection
- Training
- Automation
- Policies
- Procedures
- Rules

Technical causes

Technical fixes

Slips, lapses, misjudgements & other human failures

While useful, the traditional view assumes a world that is merely complicated. The degree of assumed complication may be very large, but, as we explained in Chapter 2 (Being at work), 'complicated' is very different from 'complex'. When we re-construe the world of operational safety as a world of complex, adaptive systems, we find we must shift our attention from linear notions of cause and effect to systemic notions of circular causality, disproportionate effect and unintended consequences that may be very far-reaching. We must move our focus away from 'cause' and 'effect' and towards 'drivers' and 'improvers' of performance and safety. And we must re-construe the position of humans in this mix – not as weak links or as sources of failure that must be fixed – but as the source of system safety. This perspective has been missing to date.

 Read more about complexity and why it is crucial to safety in **Chapter 12**

Figure 4.3 introduces it – not as a replacement for the traditional view, but as a fundamental enhancement that changes the quality of the whole enterprise of understanding the contribution of human factors.

Figure 4.3 A more comprehensive view of the contribution of human factors

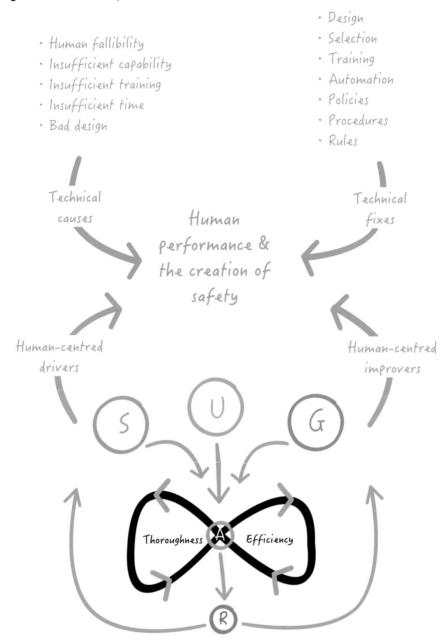

The addition of a spoonful of SUGAR is the 'best of both worlds', in which we incorporate traditional human-factors concerns with an explicit account of the influences on humans as they go about the business of creating safety.

In the next six chapters, we take a closer look at the human factors represented by the SUGAR model's State, Understanding and Goals components. These are always present and affect our decision-making in ways that are sometimes surprising.

5

Being in a state
what does our state do to our sense of safety?

How much of a problem is fatigue and stress?
How do negative states such as fatigue and stress contribute to accidents?
What causes stress and how can it be avoided?
What part do boredom and complacency play in safety at work?
Do positive moods and emotions matter at work?

Fitness for work

In Chapters 3 (Being framed) and 4 (Being sufficient), we introduced our SUGAR model to identify three major sources of influence on human behaviour as we continuously trade off between efficiency and thoroughness – State, Understanding and Goals.

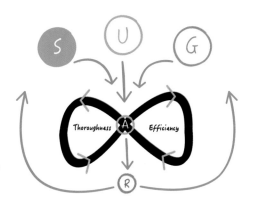

This chapter explores the first of these sources of influence, State, with a focus on fatigue and stress. Although we necessarily have to discuss State, Understanding and Goals separately, it is important to remember that they are not independent silos. All three work together, each one influencing the other two.

In the history of safety-critical systems, humans play two opposite roles. On the one hand, accidents are often blamed on human error and people are seen to make mistakes that are direct or indirect causes of things going wrong. On the other hand, human operators are seen as carrying the burden of system safety, covering those situations that are too difficult – or too hard to predict – to be managed by automation.

In other words, when the designers of complex systems no longer know how to build safety into the system, or there are hazards they do not know about, human operators have to try to fill the gap. As the Columbia Accident Investigation Board[1] noted, "*complex systems almost always fail in complex ways*", and what was always a hard task for a human suddenly becomes even harder.

The ability of human operators both to avoid errors causing incidents and to find ways of keeping the system within its safety boundaries when things are going wrong depends to a large extent on the state they happen to be in at the time. Both fatigue and stress can lead to poor judgements. If too much emphasis is placed on efficiency, then thoroughness (including safety) is put at risk. Conversely, too much emphasis on thoroughness may mean that the job does not get done on time, with the risk of commercial damage.

In this chapter, we focus on how some of our most common physical and mental states influence the trade-off decisions we make between efficiency and thoroughness. Accident investigations commonly identify problems of fatigue and stress. But other states often play an important part too, including complacency and boredom – and nor should we overlook positive states, such as happiness.

 Get help with fatigue, stress, boredom and complacency in **Chapter 13**

Fatigue
Tiredness and accidents

In June 2009, Air France Airbus AF447, *en route* from Rio de Janeiro to Paris with 228 passengers and crew, disappeared over the Atlantic Ocean. For two years the cause of its disappearance remained a mystery. Finally, the wreckage of the plane was located on the seabed and the two black-box recorders were recovered.

It emerged that in a tropical thunderstorm the plane had begun to roll dangerously. The problem was made worse because the airspeed sensors were not working, probably because they had frozen up. The two co-pilots who were flying the Airbus could not bring it back under control, so they called the pilot, who was asleep. He took over a minute to respond and, when he reached the cockpit, he behaved in ways that suggested he was not fully awake – a state known as 'sleep inertia'. When the plane stalled, the pilots raised the nose. The normal procedure is to lower the nose. AF447 went into a dive that lasted for three-and-a-half minutes before it hit the ocean.

It emerged that the pilot had only had one hour's sleep the night before the flight. Both co-pilots were also seriously short of sleep. One of them had been asleep shortly before the accident.

It appears that the fatigue problems of the flight crew of AF447 were largely due to their intense leisure-time activities during their three days in Rio.[2] This case highlights the importance of using rest periods wisely.

---

1 Columbia Accident Investigation Board (2003). The space shuttle *Columbia* broke up over Texas as it re-entered Earth's atmosphere at the end of its 28th mission on 1 February 2003, killing all seven crew. The disintegration resulted from damage to the thermal protection tiles on the shuttle's left wing, due to impact from a large piece of insulating foam that fell off an external fuel tank during the launch two weeks previously.

2 BEA (2012)

Often, of course, fatigue is due to the work itself and the associated working and manning practices. In March 2013, the general cargo vessel *MV Danio* ran aground in the Farne Islands. The subsequent UK Marine Accident Investigation Branch (MAIB) inquiry established that:

- The chief officer, who was on watch at the time, had been asleep for more than three hours before the vessel ran aground. No lookout was posted and the bridge watch alarm was turned off.

- The chief officer had worked for 17 hours in the previous port and was likely to have been suffering from the effects of cumulative fatigue, sometimes known as 'sleep debt'. The hours of work and rest on *Danio* had been falsified.

The MAIB report[3] further noted that the *"very high workload placed on the two deck officers was typical of that found on many near coastal vessels trading in European waters"* and that it was common to bypass safety procedures such as alarms and the use of lookouts.

Given that people *always* get tired and, if they get too tired, they *will* make potentially catastrophic mistakes, these remarks are deeply worrying. But the MAIB report is even more extraordinary than at first it seems.

Twenty-five years before, in 1989, the problem of fatigue in the shipping industry had been officially recognised after the most devastating man-made disaster in history at that time. *Exxon Valdez* ran aground in Alaska, spilling 11 million US gallons (36,000 tonnes) of crude oil, which then spread over 11,000 square miles (28,000 square km) of ocean. Hundreds of thousands of sea creatures died. By 1991, the local marine population and fishing industry had collapsed. Several of the affected residents committed suicide and the Alaska Native Corporation was bankrupted. Billions of dollars were paid in damages and fines. The shoreline is still not expected to recover until at least 2020.

At the time of the accident, there were two crew members on the bridge. After an exhausting day, neither had been given any time off before a new 12-hour duty began. The officer of the watch (OOW) in charge of delicate navigation around an icefield was the third mate. He had worked 20 hours in the previous 24, much of it physically demanding work supporting cargo-loading operations. His level of fatigue had the same effect on his performance as being twice over the drink-driving limit in many countries. The investigation concluded that this played a significant part in mistiming a critical turn, leading to the tanker grounding on a well-known outcrop of land known as Bligh Reef.[4]

According to accident reports right up to the present day, fatigue continues to play a significant part in the bad reasoning and decision-making that contributes to accidents in which people, business and the environment suffer. And it's not just a maritime problem. The US National Transportation Safety Board (NTSB) says that around 20% of all of its major investigations involve significant fatigue.[5] The UK Royal Society for the Prevention of Accidents (RoSPA) says that fatigue contributes to 25% of fatal and serious accidents on UK roads.[6] A report concerned with fatigue in aviation[7] concluded that *"shift work, night work, irregular work schedules, unpredictable work schedules ... pose known challenges to human physiology, and ... a risk to safety"*.

---

3 MAIB (2014)

4 Skinner & Reilly (1989)

5 NTSB (2016)

6 RoSPA (2011)

7 Akerstedt et al (2003)

All the research shows that these remarks apply more generally to all transport sectors and safety-critical industries. Offshore oil and gas operations, the chemical process industry, nuclear power and hospitals (especially those dealing with acute cases), to name just the most prominent, all impose demands on staff that have to be met on a more or less continuous basis.

In 2012, Project HORIZON[8] delivered a definitive report following a comprehensive set of highly realistic trials examining the relationship between maritime watches and fatigue. The report confirmed much of what is known about fatigue and provided rigorous, well-researched results. In particular, the study used a highly realistic simulation to conclusively demonstrate the links between specific watch patterns and performance degradation. A key finding was that the 'six hours on, six hours off' schedule commonly used by seafarers produces significantly increased risk when demands are high (eg in passages through difficult waters).

The fact that fatigue continues to figure in accidents means that widely available information such as this is being ignored by those at the working level, as well as by those at senior levels, who are in a position to act on it.

Why?

In fact, there is a more general problem here. Clues emerge from a distinction that Erik Hollnagel[9] makes between 'work as imagined' at senior organisational levels (and by regulators), and 'work as done' at operational levels. It is in the nature of organisational life that senior management tend to focus on performance (ie efficiency). In view of their ultimate responsibility for safety, they must insist on the workforce following copious rules and procedures, but the way in which senior management believe that work is carried out is often very different from the way in which those on the front line actually do the work. The rules and procedures imposed by senior managers are likely to conflict with what practical experience has shown to be efficient or safe ways of working.

Like all of the topics in this book, fatigue is an area that needs to be considered in a new light. If we want safety-critical systems that are actually safe, then they must at least be manned by people who are themselves behaving safely.

How does fatigue arise?

Demands arising from the relentless systems in which people work are often made worse as increasing commercial pressures cause management to reduce staff numbers to a minimum (and sometimes beyond). Fatigue arises in a number of ways:[10]

- **Lack of sleep** This is the most obvious cause of fatigue. Most people need around seven hours of sleep to function properly. To get seven hours of sleep means that, as well as time spent working, you need enough time to do all the other things you have to do: attending to family needs, preparing food and eating, cleaning yourself and the place

---

8   Warsash Maritime Academy (2012)

9   Hollnagel (2014)

10 There are numerous guidance documents on fatigue in safety-critical industries. For example, in the maritime sector there are Maritime & Coastguard Agency (2014) and International Maritime Organization (2001). Other examples can be found in the aviation sector (IATA/IFALPLA/ICAO, 2011), railways (Rail Safety & Standards Board, 2012), nuclear power (US Nuclear Regulatory Commission, 2009), petrochemical industry (American Petroleum Institute, 2010) and healthcare (Registered Nurses' Association of Ontario, 2011; Association of Anaesthetists of Great Britain and Ireland, 2014).

where you live, travelling to and from work. Ideally, you also have some time for social and leisure activities. Neglecting these is likely to contribute to your stress levels, as we discuss later in this chapter.

- **Fractured sleep** Ideally, you are able to take the seven hours of sleep you need consecutively. However, in many occupations where staff are on shift/watch patterns or on call, this is not possible. You may have to snatch two or three hours of sleep as the opportunity arises. But sleep goes through a number of stages. The most restorative stage only occurs when you have been asleep long enough to pass through other stages. If your periods of sleep are too broken up, you may never reach this stage of deeper sleep. Tiredness then accumulates. You may be slightly short of sleep for one day and still be able to cope. The same pattern may repeat the next day, and you may still be OK. Over several days, however, the accumulated lack of sleep (sometimes called 'sleep debt'[11]) is associated with an increasing risk of making a mistake or having an accident. Notably, we are not very good at assessing our own level of fatigue. Our performance steadily gets worse, but we believe we are still working fine.

- **Hours on shift/watch** Long periods of work without a proper break mean that the physical and mental demands of your work build up, contributing to your tiredness. Your risk of having an accident rises steadily with the number of hours you have been at work. By the time you have worked more than ten hours, you are roughly four times more likely to have an accident than you were after the first hour on shift/watch.

- **Time of day** Humans evolved to be active in the daytime and to sleep at night. Our physiology reflects this rhythm. Body temperature, blood pressure, hormone levels, reaction speed, state of alertness and many other body parameters all follow a 24-hour cycle, known as the circadian rhythm. Sleep in the daytime is never as beneficial as sleep at night. In many areas of safety-critical work, staff have to work at all times of day and night. While we can adjust to night work up to a point, the natural rhythms of our bodies mean that we generally perform better at certain times of day. This means that our risk of having an accident is lowest early in the morning. It then climbs steadily during the day, until the risk is greatest in the hours following midnight.

- **Crossing time zones** High-speed airliners have created another problem: jet lag. We can cross many time zones in a single flight. The problem is that our body's daily rhythm is no longer matched to the place we have travelled to. Our body may be telling us it is time to go to bed when the sun is coming up. Or we may feel it is time to get up as the sun is going down. This obviously affects airline pilots and crew, but it can also affect other workers who travel long distances; for example, seafarers who fly from Europe to Australia to join a ship. You may be expected to start work when your body is in the low-performance phase of its daily cycle. The sleep disturbances associated with jet lag can make this worse. It takes three weeks for the body to fully adjust to a new time zone.

 Get help with ways to deal with fatigue and jet lag in **Chapter 13**

- **Working environment** Hot, noisy, badly lit workspaces that are prone to vibration or motion are measurably more tiring to work in.

---

11 Sleep debt builds up over several days of interrupted sleep. While it can never be fully 'paid back', recovery from significant sleep debt requires seven to eight continuous hours of sleep in each 24-hour period over two or three days.

How does fatigue affect us at work?

Being tired affects all aspects of physical and mental functioning. We concentrate here on mental functioning because work has become less physical and more mental. Also, as a general rule, a bad decision has more potential than a physical error to cause a major disaster.

Studies of fighter pilots in World War II identified many of the problems caused by fatigue. Under the impact of fatigue, pilots' ability to attend suffered. They developed tunnel vision, so their field of attention became more and more narrow, thus making worse the normal problems arising from attention being a limited resource. They failed to notice important things they were not directly attending to. For example, tired fighter pilots might fixate on the altimeter and totally ignore the fuel gauge, risking running out of fuel. At the same time, they became more easily distracted by things that were not relevant. They forgot things. They could not take in and remember new information as easily as normal. They could not make plans or cope with complexity. Actions were mistimed, movements that were previously skilled and smooth broke down and became poorly coordinated.

 Read more about the limits of attention in **Chapter 7**

We have all experienced how tiredness affects our mood, making us irritable. If it isn't controlled, bad temper can damage relations with colleagues.

As we have already noted, missing one night's sleep has the same effect on performance as being well over most European countries' drink-driving limit. The effect of fatigue on humans is that they are much more likely to be involved in an incident through making an error that they would not normally make.

Fatigue has a particular significance here. When people are tired, their capacity for divergent thinking suffers. Divergent thinking is what you need when you have to come up with a creative solution to some problem you have not experienced before. Yvonne Harrison and James Horne[12] emphasise the importance of the loss of this ability in the kind of complex systems that typify safety-critical operations. They note that sleep deprivation is implicated in some major disasters and near-disasters involving nuclear reactors:

- At Davis-Besse (Ohio, 1977), the single reactor on the site shut down after a problem developed in its feedwater system, which caused a relief valve to stick open. There were no leaks or injuries, but the US Nuclear Regulatory Commission categorised it as the fourth-highest related nuclear safety incident after the three below.
- At Rancho Seco (California, 1978), a failure of the power supply to the plant's instrumentation system led to the steam generator drying out. Fortunately, no additional failures occurred and the potentially disastrous results of the accident were contained.
- At Three Mile Island (Pennsylvania, 1979), a coolant valve that had not been returned to its operational state following maintenance contributed to a misdiagnosis of the status of the overall system. The result was a partial nuclear meltdown and a loss of radioactive coolant. Fortunately, a full-blown hydrogen explosion did not occur and most of the lost radioactive material was confined to the reactor site.

---

12 Harrison & Horne (2000)

- At Chernobyl (Ukraine, 1986), a vessel ruptured in one of the plant's four reactors and steam explosions followed a series of unexpected power surges. The resulting fire sent a plume of radioactive fallout into the atmosphere, which then drifted over the Soviet Union and Europe. Four hundred times more radioactive material was released than in the Hiroshima atomic bomb. Thirty-one people died as a direct result of the accident and it has been calculated that a further 4,000 people living in the affected area will develop cancer because of the leak.

The US Nuclear Regulatory Commission rates the three American incidents outlined above among the top four most serious. In all four nuclear incidents, sleep deprivation was a factor in human operators failing to deal with unexpected and unusual control-room malfunctions.

Fatigue is an insidious danger. It creeps up on us unnoticed, all the time undermining our performance. The pilots in the World War II studies of fatigue stubbornly believed they were doing just fine, although objective measures showed their flying skills were severely degraded.

There is only one way to truly remedy fatigue, and that is to sleep, preferably for six hours or more at a stretch. But this is often not possible. Working in a complex system imposes its own demands, rhythms and timescales.

 Get help with ways to manage fatigue in **Chapter 13**

Stress
What is stress?

The UK's Health and Safety Executive (HSE) defines work-related stress as "*a harmful reaction people have to undue pressures and demands placed on them at work*".[13] Stress is widely reported as a major problem in workplaces of every kind. The HSE reported that in 2014/15 there were 440,000 cases of work-related stress in the UK. This translated to around 10 million days of lost time. Overall, 43% of all working days lost due to ill health were attributed to stress. The common factors related to stress were said to be workload pressures (including tight deadlines), too much responsibility and a lack of managerial support.

In some industries, there are particular factors that give rise to stress. For example, seafarers often suffer from long periods away from home, loneliness and social isolation.[14] Although the picture of work-related stress in the UK is dire, a 2013 survey[15] of the countries in the European Union (EU) found that the UK had a lower reported incidence of stress than the EU as a whole (44% versus 51%). Furthermore, 65% of UK respondents reported that stress was well managed in their workplace, compared with 54% of EU respondents overall.

It is worth noting that these figures indicate stress is a major problem in normal workplaces – that is, offices, factories, shops and the like. Many of these are not safety-critical or high-risk working environments. If we now consider workplaces where people are working

13 UK Health and Safety Executive (2016)

14 For a review of stress among seafarers, see Carotenuto et al (2012)

15 European Agency for Safety and Health at Work (2013)

with complex, safety-critical systems, then there are numerous sources of stress that are not found in normal workplaces, or certainly not at the same intensity. In these situations, stress is close to what the military calls 'combat stress'. This is defined as *"the perception of an imminent threat of serious personal injury or death, or the stress of being tasked with the responsibility to protect another party from imminent serious injury or death, under conditions where response time is minimal"*.[16]

Jan Cannon-Bowers and Ed Salas are two psychologists who worked on the Tactical Decision-Making Under Stress (TADMUS) programme that was set up in the wake of USS *Vincennes'* shooting down of an Iranian Airbus in 1989. (For an account of this incident, see Chapter 7: Being in the know – part II.) Cannon-Bowers and Salas[17] identified the following stressors that were present in *Vincennes'* control room at the time of the incident:

- Multiple information sources
- Incomplete, conflicting information
- Rapidly changing, evolving scenarios
- Requirement for team coordination
- Adverse physical conditions
- Performance pressure
- Time pressure
- High work/information load
- Auditory overload/interference
- High perceived threat.

Many, if not all, of these stressors are faced by workers dealing with an emergency in any safety-critical system. How people cope with these stressors will be a significant factor in how safe system operation proves to be.

What does stress do to people?

Research[18] has identified a wide range of effects attributable to stress:

- Physiological changes (eg quickened heartbeat, laboured breathing and trembling)
- Emotional reactions (eg fear, anxiety, frustration)
- Loss of motivation
- Narrowed attention
- Reduced search for information
- Longer reaction time
- Decreased vigilance
- Degraded problem-solving
- Performance rigidity (ie inability to change behaviour as circumstances change)
- Loss of team perspective
- Decrease in willingness to help others.

---

16 Grossman & Siddle (2000)

17 Cannon-Bowers & Salas (1998)

18 Driskell & Johnston (1998)

While this list presents a negative view of stress, it is important to keep in mind that stress has a positive side.[19] The UK's HSE further clarifies its definition of stress, concluding that "*Stress is not an illness – it is a state. However, if stress becomes too excessive and prolonged, mental and physical illness may develop.*"[20]

In fact, far from being an illness, stress is essential for our survival. When we detect a threat – and threats can come in many kinds – our brains respond by releasing several hormones.[21] These are chiefly adrenaline, cortisol and norepinephrine, which increase heart rate and blood pressure, and switch blood flow from digestion and the skin to the muscles. Overall, there is a release of energy. Evolution has prepared us to respond to threats by fight or flight (or sometimes by freezing). The physiological effects of stress are thus designed to help us survive.

In the short term, stress is valuable – or at least there is value in the physiological reactions produced by detection of a threat. In our evolutionary past, the situations calling for flight or fight would usually have been very short-lived. When out hunting, we find a prey. We run after it and either we quickly overcome it or it gets away (due not least to the release of its own stress hormones!). Similarly, if we encounter a predator that sees us as prey, we run away or – if escape is not an option – get ready to fight. Either way, there will soon be an outcome.

The trouble is that in today's world we often find ourselves in situations where stress endures over hours, days, or even months. If we can't remove the source of stress or remove ourselves from the stressful situation, then all those physiological reactions – so helpful in fight or flight – begin to do serious damage to our bodies, creating conditions for all kinds of illness, notably heart disease and the so-called 'silent killer', high blood pressure.

Of course, stress can arise outside of work, for many reasons. Marital problems, financial problems, the death of a loved one, moving house, disputes with neighbours or family, and so on can all be highly stressful. This 'domestic' stress is not left behind when you come to work; it continues to have an effect, possibly degrading your performance in your job.

As we have seen, stress arises to help us in situations demanding instant action. It helps us produce large physical actions that require little thought, such as throwing a spear or running away. It tends to make worse those actions that require fine motor movements, the coordination of a number of movements, or some measure of thought. Fine motor control suffers because one of the stress reactions is to constrict blood vessels in the more peripheral parts of the body, eg the hands. This is to reduce blood loss in the event of injury. Under stress, hands may shake. You don't want to be trying to thread a needle when under acute stress. At the same time, much of the blood directed to the muscles comes from the brain, reducing the capability for coordination of movements and for thinking. We look more at the impact on decision-making later in this chapter.

It is important to note that the stress reaction to a perceived threat is automatic. It cannot be prevented. The information that triggers a stress reaction goes directly from the senses (eg vision, hearing) to that part of the brain that initiates the release of hormones. The thinking part of the brain only gets involved after the stress reaction is well under way.

---

19 Some authorities, such as Tom Cox (1978), distinguish between stress and arousal, and argue that stress is always bad. For our purposes, we treat stress as a continuum in which either too little or too much will have a negative impact on human performance.

20 UK Health and Safety Executive (2016)

21 Hormones are signalling chemicals released into the bloodstream by glands in response to perceived demands. They travel very quickly around the body to stimulate distant organs and muscles into appropriate action.

How does stress work?

Let's consider a typical experience of stress at work.

Imagine you are working in the control room of a nuclear power station. To begin with, there may be indications that something is going wrong, but the signs may be unclear or contradictory. You take some actions but the indications of possible problems don't go away.

You are puzzled and also beginning to feel a bit stressed.

Now you get an indication that is the opposite of what you expected. This doesn't seem to make sense. So for the moment you ignore it and concentrate on those things that do seem to make sense.

As we saw earlier, one of the major effects of stress is tunnel vision: we focus on one thing and miss other things going on around us. You may focus on one or two indicators and not attend to others that collectively might tell a different story about the problem. If you are under time pressure, you may stop searching for new information before you know enough.

If there are aspects of the situation you find especially scary, you may 'look the other way', consciously or unconsciously avoiding information that might confirm your worst fears. Stress also exaggerates our usual tendency to see what we expect to see. This works together with the human confirmation bias: our tendency to look for evidence that supports what we already believe. Evidence that this is not the 'usual' problem may go unnoticed.

 Read more about the confirmation bias and other unconscious biases in **Chapter 7**

You have tried out some ideas to correct the problem, but things keep on getting worse. More and more alarms are coming on. Your stress levels are rising, and stress is beginning to become fear. You know that if you do not get the situation under control, it could go critical, but the information you are getting does not seem to 'add up'.

You try to make sense of the situation. Making sense means that you try to connect the different bits of information you have perceived into a meaningful whole. You try to find a 'story' that explains all the disconnected, possibly conflicting, possibly ambiguous information you have gathered. As well as the information from your current perceptions, you draw on information from your memory. Your past experiences play a key role in making sense of your present ones.

The mental function involved in this process is known as your *working memory*, a temporary store analogous to the volatile random access memory (RAM) in a computer. The effect of stress – and especially fear – is to reduce the capacity of your working memory. You can't think about so many bits of information at the same time. You can't manipulate them so well. Retrieval of information from your longer-term store takes longer and is more likely to be erroneous: you can't think of things that you know you know, you misremember things and your recall is inaccurate.

You realise now that you must *do something*, but the question is what? Stress tends to limit our capacity for coming up with options. One tendency when under stress is that we revert to doing the things we first learned as novices, possibly years before. Airline pilots flying four-engine jets under stress may regress to ways of handling the single-engine propeller-driven plane in which they first learned to fly. You can't think long term, so any plan you do come up with will be short term, lacking any consideration of what might happen later. As Jeff Wise has said, *"fear makes us stupid"*.[22]

The problem has not gone away, in spite of your best efforts, and you are now confronted by the need to make another decision. You realise that you may be approaching the point when you should close the system down completely and maybe order an evacuation. But if you raise a false alarm, then the consequences for you, your career and the company could be dire. You are horribly aware of the risks of both action and non-action.

Now a new wave of alarms has gone off. You feel totally paralysed, unable to make any decision or take any action. Just then, a member of the relief shift arrives. He has not had the several hours of increasing confusion and stress you have been exposed to. He can look at the situation through fresh eyes and almost immediately sees the wrong assumptions you have been making. He asks a key question about the status of one of the system elements. This makes you realise that you've been thinking about the problem all wrong. For the first time, you begin to feel you understand what is happening. You act accordingly and the alarms begin to diminish. Your stress levels slowly begin to reduce.

The reason you hadn't thought of this possibility is because neither your training nor the written procedures for the system had allowed for such an unlikely combination of problems occurring simultaneously. This exemplifies the difficulty of identifying in advance all possible scenarios for a highly complex system.

The relationship between stress and complex system operations

We loosely based the story above on the near-meltdown incident at Three Mile Island in 1979. A number of such near-disasters are examined by Charles Perrow.[23] Perrow's central argument is that complex systems such as nuclear power stations, however well designed and operated, will sooner or later have a major accident. The subsequent disasters at Chernobyl (1986)[24] and Fukushima Daiichi (2011),[25] among others, have done little to weaken his case.

Your inner chimp

Psychiatrist Steve Peters has developed a simplified model of brain functioning, which he describes in his book *The Chimp Paradox*.[26] Using this model, Peters has worked with a number of leading sportspeople, including top footballers and gold-medal-winning Olympic cyclists. The model is a rich source of insights into behaviour under pressure. Here we describe just some of its aspects.

Peters divides the brain into the Human and the Chimp. The Human is the conscious, rational, thinking part of the brain – the part that you think of as You. The Chimp is the emotional, largely unconscious part of the brain. The job of the Chimp is to ensure survival – both of you and the species. It is constantly on the lookout for threats, and tends to see the world in terms of life and death.

22 Wise (2009)

23 Perrow (1984)

24 Read (1993)

25 Lochbaum et al (2015)

26 Peters (2012)

When something happens, the Human and the Chimp each interpret the event in their own way. The Human will look for evidence and facts, and try to draw logical conclusions. The Chimp will form impressions, make untested assumptions, have feelings, and use instinct and gut reactions. While both the Human and the Chimp may form a plan based on their interpretation, the Chimp is much faster and will be ready to act long before the Human.

The Chimp's plan has the benefit of speed, but it may bear only a limited relationship to reality. The Chimp only cares about the present moment. It will not care about any possible longer-term adverse consequences of its plan, and nor will it care about morality: what is right or wrong. Thinking long term, worrying about truth and caring about morality are solely concerns of the Human.

If the plans of the Chimp and the Human are compatible, then there is no problem. Problems arise when the Human disagrees with the Chimp's plan. The Chimp is not only faster but is also much stronger than the Human. The Human cannot simply override the Chimp.

It is because the Chimp often gets its way that we often act out of emotion, in ways we subsequently regret. Peters makes an important point when he says we cannot change our Chimp but we do have a responsibility to *manage* the Chimp.

How do we manage something that is faster and stronger than us?

Peters stresses that the Chimp presents the Human with an emotion and a plan of action. This is not a command but an *offer*. The Human can accept or reject the offer. If they simply reject the offer without in any way managing the Chimp, then the Chimp and the associated emotions will become very disruptive. The Human needs to realise that the Chimp's concern is survival, and, consistent with this, it has many powerful drives: food, shelter, security, sex, approval from powerful authorities, and so on. The Human cannot change or stop these drives, but they can find ways of meeting them that are socially acceptable and not harmful.

The Human must also recognise that little can be done with the Chimp while it is in an emotional state. It may be necessary to let the Chimp express its feelings. The Human can help by finding a time and place where strong emotions can be expressed without damage. Once the Chimp has calmed down, the Human can try to persuade it of the benefits of their plan.

Peters gives the example of going to the dentist. The Chimp may have anxiety about this. Left to itself, the Chimp may choose the 'flight' option, ie avoid going. The Human, however, can use truth and logic to convince the Chimp of the benefits of going to the dentist: preventing future toothache, lost teeth, pain and the expense of dental treatment.

There is a third part of the brain in Peters' model, the Computer. Here, we just mention one aspect of the Computer that is relevant to managing your Chimp. The Computer is a store for behaviours and beliefs that the Human and the Chimp have put there in the past. The Computer is a source of reference that both Human and Chimp consult for guidance. When confronted by a challenging situation, the Human or the Chimp may find a habit or over-learned skill in the Computer that can take over and act without any further conscious intervention. Peters calls these habits and skills 'auto-pilots'.

If you have already read Chapter 7 (Being in the know – part II), you will spot the direct parallels between Peters' Chimp/Human and Daniel Kahneman's *System 1/System 2*.[27]

Boredom and complacency

In this part of the chapter, we look at two states that seem very different from stress, but are actually closely related to it: boredom and complacency.

Why is boredom boring?

Boredom seems to be a low-key problem, but its consequences can be catastrophic – as shown in the following incident involving a National Airlines DC-10 over Albuquerque, New Mexico in 1973.

"Out of boredom, the captain and flight engineer decided to experiment and see what would happen to the autothrottle system if the circuit breakers which supplied power to the instruments which measured the rotational speed of each engine's low pressure compressor were tripped. This led to engine overspeeding and destruction of the engine. Pieces struck the fuselage, breaking a window, causing rapid explosive decompression and a passenger was sucked out of the plane. The plane landed safely." [28]

We normally experience stress when we feel we have too much to do and too little time in which to do it. Boredom arises when we don't have enough to do. We need a certain level of stimulation to feel comfortable. Nearly every job will involve periods of boredom, which you may recognise as *"a pervasive lack of interest in the current activity"*.[29] To feel bored, you need to feel a certain level of energy, a desire to do something, combined with relative current inactivity. If you are lacking energy, then a period of low activity will be experienced as relaxing, not boring. Boredom also requires that there is something else you would rather be doing and your mind keeps wandering to this. Boredom tends to arise when you are not in control of the situation.

Figure 5.1 is a well-known graph that shows the relationship between performance and stress. It is named after the scientists who first drew it, in 1908: Robert Yerkes and John Dodson.

---

27 Kahneman (2011)

28 Strange and Unusual Accidents, http://www.planecrashinfo.com/unusual.htm [accessed April 2017].

29 Fisher (1991)

Figure 5.1 The Yerkes-Dodson inverted U curve

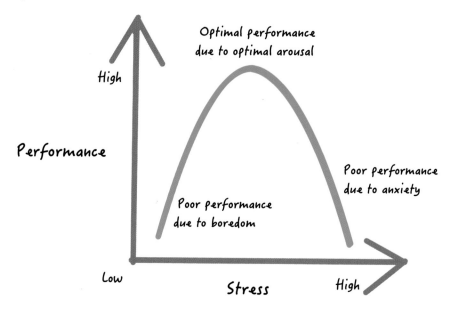

Like too much stress, boredom can narrow your attention and reduce your working-memory capacity. You are more likely to miss some event that you should take notice of. Boredom can also lead to depression, impulsiveness or inappropriate anger and aggression.

There can, however, be a positive side to boredom. Like all states we experience as unpleasant, boredom can motivate us to seek another state. This can make us creative. A bored child may start to learn something or begin some worthwhile activity to escape this state (parents beware!).

But this has dangers for people working with safety-critical systems. A bored operator may decide to try things out 'to see what would happen'. The result may be a serious incident. Not long ago, the authors interviewed a senior air traffic controller (ATCO). He told us that few incidents occurred when the ATCOs were busy. At these times, procedures are followed correctly. However, when little is happening, ATCOs are tempted to experiment – or they may seek other distractions unrelated to the job – and things can quickly go wrong.

On 8 August 2009, a small private plane – a Piper Cherokee Lance carrying the pilot and two passengers – collided over the River Hudson with a Eurocopter AS350 helicopter carrying a pilot and five sightseeing Italian tourists. All nine people died. The investigation found that the ATCO in the tower at Teterboro Airport, New Jersey, who had been controlling the plane, had been immersed in a personal phone conversation at the time. As a result, he had failed to notice a collision alert on his radar and had failed to correct the plane pilot's incorrect readback of the critical radio frequency.[30]

It has also been reported that in the accident involving two jumbo jets colliding on the runway at Tenerife in 1977, the ATCOs were listening to a football match on the radio.[31]

---

30 National Transportation Safety Board (2010)

31 Subsecretaría de Aviación Civil (1978). See Chapter 8 (Being in the know – part III) for an account of this accident in the context of human risk perception.

A recent study in the UK found that nearly a third of drivers are often bored and overtake or speed as a result. An insurance company's[32] analysis of 65,000 fatal car accidents in the US showed that 'daydreaming', a state closely related to boredom, is a factor in many accidents. To overcome boredom when driving, we are likely to turn to other activities, such as chatting with passengers, tuning the radio or – increasingly – looking at our smartphones. Our attention is not on our primary task and we miss the vital indication that leads us to crash. Similar things happen in work situations.

In terms of our SUGAR model, the state of boredom impacts both efficiency and thoroughness through withdrawal from the task at hand. Efficiency suffers because the operator is doing nothing of any productive value – and is certainly underachieving, given the skills that they could be deploying instead. However, thoroughness also suffers because attention is wandering away from the task, towards more interesting thoughts or activities. When boredom sets in, the operator is no longer on an efficiency–thoroughness loop of relevance or value to their job or the organisation. Instead, the operator has effectively abdicated and is no longer psychologically present.

What is complacency?

Complacency is similar, but not identical, to boredom. Boredom often seems to be a 'justifiable' state: "*Nothing was happening, so I got distracted.*" Complacency implies a higher level of culpability: "*Something was happening that I should have acted on, but I chose not to.*" In terms of stress: "*I should have been stressed, but wasn't.*"

Complacency is a common explanation for a wide variety of accidents, scandals and crises. Examples of organisations that have been accused of being complacent include NASA (for the loss of the space shuttle *Columbia*) and the Bank of England (for the 2008 banking crisis). In attributing the 2010 Deepwater Horizon disaster to complacency, the President's Commission commented: "*There are recurring themes of missed warning signals, failure to share information, and a general lack of appreciation for the risks involved.*"[33] Individuals and organisations have similarly been blamed for complacency in countless other accidents at sea, on the railways and in industrial operations.

But while it is emotionally satisfying to blame someone for being complacent, the trouble is it does not explain very much. Even worse, it provides few clues about how to avoid such things happening again. To describe someone's behaviour as complacent provides a feeling of explanation, but this doesn't bear any deeper analysis. Different people understand complacency very differently. For some, it means extreme self-satisfaction or smugness. For others, it refers to a natural human consequence resulting from familiarity with a task or operation. These are very different interpretations and suggest very different responses.

In this book, we take complacency to mean that someone has failed to take action to prevent something bad from happening *when they could have done so*. This assumes that indications were available to the person that there was an actual or emerging problem, and they had the possibility of doing something to prevent or minimise the problem.

---

32 Erie Insurance (2013)

33 National Commission on the BP Deepwater Horizon Oil Spill and Offshore Drilling (2011)

This view of complacency implies two possible reasons why the person failed to act. First, they may have failed to recognise the problem. Second, they may have recognised that there was a problem but made a decision not to act. We now look at each of these possibilities in more detail.

Failure to see the problem

There are two broad reasons why someone may fail to see a problem. First, they may not notice the signs that a problem is present, or developing. Second, they may see the signs but not recognise that they point to a problem. We often accuse someone of complacency when we see that the danger signs were glaringly obvious. However, this usually entails the use of hindsight, which by definition was not available to the people involved at the time.

 Read more about the illusion of hindsight in **Chapter 9**

Why do people overlook signs that seem obvious now but were not then?

One reason is that attention is a limited resource. If we are devoting our attention to one matter, we can easily miss something very large but unexpected, even when it is in our field of view. This is strikingly demonstrated in the famous 'gorilla' video made by psychologists Daniel Simons and Christopher Chabris,[34] which we described in Chapter 3 (Being framed).

Inattention has particular significance for a person who is working with a system that is normally very reliable, or who is carrying out a familiar task. The operator may not see the problem because they are not looking for any sign of it. If we expect something to go well, we tend to look for confirmation that all is well, rather than for evidence that might suggest things are going wrong. We see what we expect to see.

This may explain the alleged complacency of the Bank of England when the governor and his colleagues failed to see the impending financial collapse in 2008. The Bank's primary task at that time was to manage inflation. By focusing on possible indications of inflation, they failed to notice all the indications of other troubles brewing in the finance and banking sectors.

Another reason a person may fail to notice warning signals is that they may be trying to process a large volume of information from many sources. The signals get lost in the 'noise'. People also tend to fail to notice problems if they emerge very slowly. This is illustrated by the old story of the frog placed in a pan of cold water that fails to jump out if the water is slowly brought to the boil.[35]

Sometimes, people focus too closely on one part of the picture and get 'tunnel vision'. This happens especially as a response to the stress that comes from information overload. When this happens for air traffic controllers (ATCOs), they speak of 'losing the picture'. Observers can sometimes tell when this is happening, because the nose of the affected ATCO can get closer and closer to their screen as they focus on less and less, literally to the exclusion of the whole radar picture. Fatigue also increases the likelihood of tunnel vision.

As we noted above, the operator may see the signs but fail to recognise them as warnings of danger. Many problems, especially if they involve complex social or technological situations, do not immediately present themselves as problems. Correctly recognising the problem

---

34 Viscog (2003)

35 The story is apocryphal. If you place a real frog in cold water and heat it up, the frog jumps out.

often involves putting together a lot of clues. These clues may only emerge one by one, over time. They may be widely scattered across locations and sources. They will often require the person to make inferences, to join the dots, in ways that go beyond the presenting data. Until the problem manifests itself unmistakably, there is always uncertainty and ambiguity. This provides scope for our many unconscious biases to come into play. One that deserves special mention here is the *normalcy* bias, our tendency to believe that there is nothing unusual about the situation we think we are in.

 Read more about unconscious biases in **Chapter 7**

So, correctly diagnosing a problem may be mentally challenging. It may also be emotionally challenging. The problem itself may pose a threat that the person would rather deny than admit to. For example, many people with symptoms of serious illness prefer to rationalise away the signs, coming up with all sorts of reasons that explain them away, rather than face up to the feared reality.

Lastly, there is a particularly subtle bias known as the *centrality fallacy*. This is paradoxically a problem for the person with long experience, an extensive professional network and good information sources. The fallacy held by this person is that if there were a problem, someone with their experience would surely know about it. Since they don't know about it, there can be no problem.

Failure to act on the problem

Sometimes a person in a responsible position will recognise there is a problem but fail to take the appropriate action. Another of our many human biases is the tendency to overestimate our capabilities. We may think we can readily fix the problem on our own. We may not inform others who need to know or we may fail to ask for help that we really need. As a result, the problem is given time to grow until it is out of control.

The person may fear that, if they report the problem, they may be blamed for causing it or even for drawing attention to it. Many organisations still operate on the 'shoot the messenger' principle where bad news is concerned – the very opposite of what might be expected in a 'just' culture. Of course, in some relatively rare situations, the person has indeed caused the problem and may wish to cover up what they have done.

 Read more about the place of 'just' culture in **Chapter 12**

Another reason may be that other people around them are not acting as if there were a problem. As we have said, problems – especially in complex technological or social situations – often involve a high degree of uncertainty. The person who is beginning to suspect there is a problem may believe that the others know more than they do, and so they may take their cue from the lack of action around them. This is especially likely if the others are more senior or more experienced.

 Read more about the influence of groups and social pressure in **Chapter 11**

If there are others involved who seem unaware of the problem, this creates an extra level of difficulty for the person who believes or knows there is a problem. By voicing their concerns, they may appear to be criticising the others by drawing attention to their mistakes or lack of awareness. They may fear they will get into trouble or simply wish to spare the others embarrassment.

Co-pilots have been known to sit silently and let their captains crash the plane, rather than challenge their actions. In 1982, Air Florida flight 90 crashed in the Potomac River after taking off from Washington National Airport. The co-pilot failed to intervene strongly when the captain failed to switch on the engine ice protection system. In 2013, Asiana Airlines flight 214 crashed at San Francisco International Airport after the co-pilot did not warn the captain about the low-speed landing.[36]

 Get help with how to challenge others in **Chapter 13**

Positive states, performance and safety

So far in this chapter, we have concentrated on the negative states that are often associated with the problems that arise in safety-critical industries: fatigue, stress, boredom and so on. In this final part of the chapter, we go to the opposite end of the spectrum and consider the effects of positive states: happiness, enthusiasm, joy, excitement, etc. If negative states have a negative effect on workplace performance and safety, can we expect positive states to have a positive effect? Put simply, are happy[37] workers more productive and do they behave more safely than unhappy workers?

First, we must ask whether it's possible to be happy working in a safety-critical job. By definition, a safety-critical job entails the possibility of danger, and for most people danger precludes happiness.

Some years ago, one of the authors went on an exercise on a Royal Navy destroyer. He became friendly with the pilot and observer who made up the crew of the ship's Lynx helicopter. A lot of the time they were sitting around in the officers' mess (the wardroom), looking bored and fed up. We were far out in the North Atlantic in winter. It was the middle of the night. There was a force 9 or 10 wind blowing. Then there came a call from the operations room, ordering the helicopter to undertake some task. Immediately the mood of the pilot and observer was transformed. They became energised in a way that can only be described as happy. This was what they lived to do, although for the rest of us it seemed scary beyond words.

How is it possible to be happy in such circumstances? Part of the answer is provided by two recent books on the role of attention in happiness.[38] Happy people focus on the positive things in their situations and lives. The pilot and the observer were highly trained professionals, and they well knew the risks involved. But they gave most of their attention to

---

36 Wheeler (2016)

37 There are numerous moods or emotions that can be regarded as positive. We focus here mainly on happiness. What happiness is has been a topic of dispute among philosophers and scientists for centuries. We do not attempt a definition here, but rely on an everyday, common-sense understanding of the word.

38 Newport (2016) and Dolan (2014)

the challenge of their task, to the pleasure of being part of a cohesive, elite team, and to the sheer emotional buzz of what they were undertaking. The helicopter crew did not ignore the dangers but they paid them only as much attention as they deserved in the moment. They did not let the dangers dominate their thinking and their experience.

This still leaves the question whether being happy in your work makes you perform better and/or more safely. In fact, the conclusion from the research is that a happy workforce is more productive.[39] But which comes first – happiness or productivity? Again, the research seems conclusive: being happy makes workers more productive.

On a different note, there is plenty of evidence that a safe working environment promotes happiness. There is much less evidence in the other direction: how far operator happiness promotes safety.

The most striking finding comes from a global survey which revealed that highly engaged workers are much safer than those who are less engaged.[40] This is a highly significant piece of evidence to which we return in Chapter 10 (Being on target). It is worth noting that being engaged, though certainly a highly positive state, is not the same as being happy. Presumably volunteer doctors and nurses working in battle zones to treat injured children are highly engaged and feel their efforts are worthwhile – but it is less clear that they are happy.

To answer this question, we must extrapolate from research on the influence of emotion on risk and decision-making. Dr Jennifer Lerner is a co-founder of the Harvard Decision Science Laboratory and a steering-committee member of Harvard's Mind, Brain, and Behavior Initiative. She and her colleagues see human decision-making as a channel through which emotions guide our everyday attempts to avoid negative feelings (eg guilt, fear, regret) while increasing positive feelings (eg pride, happiness, love). And this happens even though we often lack awareness of this everyday process.[41]

 Read more about the relationship between emotion and decision-making in **Chapter 7**

Barbara Fredrickson is a professor of social psychology at the University of North Carolina. For nearly 20 years, she and her colleagues have been concerned to discover what positive emotions are actually for. While anger creates the urge to attack, and fear creates the urge to escape, what is the value to us of their positive counterparts? The result of her research is the well-received theory of positive emotions known as 'broaden and build'.[42] Fredrickson says that emotions such as happiness, joy and amusement act to increase the flexibility of our thought, increasing our options and broadening our repertoire of possible actions.

It is clear that a state which maximises the creation of new ideas is a valuable capability for an operator within a complex system who is confronting a novel, difficult, potentially dangerous situation.

---

39 See, among many examples, Oswald, Proto & Sgroi (2015), Seppala & Cameron (2015)

40 Rigoni & Nelson (2016)

41 Lerner et al (2015)

42 Fredrickson (2001)

Cynthia Fisher, Professor of Management at Bond Business School, Australia, concludes her large-scale review of happiness in the workplace with these words:

"There is reason to think that improving happiness at work is a worthy goal ... The happy–productive worker hypothesis may be more true than we thought ... Happiness-related constructs such as job satisfaction, engagement, and affective commitment have important consequences for both individuals and organizations. Happiness at the person and group level is related to core and contextual performance, customer satisfaction, safety, attendance, and retention." [43]

In the light of these findings, some companies have introduced programmes to promote happiness. We should sound a note of caution here, though, and report that efforts by companies to *make* workers happy can have the opposite effect. This is especially the case when there is pressure on workers to *"be happy"*.[44]

Attempts by organisations to make their employees happy are always likely to be perceived as manipulative. A better approach is to seek to work with the fundamental motivations that drive most people's moods and behaviour at work, as we discuss in Chapter 10 (Being on target).

43 Fisher (2010), p. 49

44 Spicer & Cederström (2015)

6

Being in the know – part I
how our senses deceive us

Why can't you write down everything you know?

Why is seeing not always believing?

How is it possible to sense things that aren't there?

What do our senses really tell us?

Why is understanding the way human sensing works important to safety?

What is it to know something?

How we understand the world is a large and complex topic. This is the first of four chapters looking at different aspects of understanding.

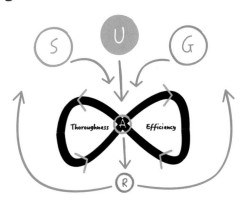

Let's start with the short answer to the first question above. The impossibility of writing down everything you know has nothing to do with how much you know or how fast you can write. It's because knowledge itself is infinite. And knowledge is infinite because it's not a set of facts that exist 'out there' independently of us, but rather the product of questions that we happen to be able to ask. Every question we ask yields answers that lead to more questions that we weren't able to ask before. In the end, knowledge is not an objective set of 'things' to be known, but a particular *way of understanding* that we develop, share and challenge with each other. And as we do so, our understanding can suddenly and quite radically change. Like the universe itself, the history of knowledge is one of exponential expansion.

So, what influences the questions that we ask?

Sensing is what we do to keep ourselves connected with the physical world in which we live. That is the topic of this chapter.

What our brains do with the information we gather through our senses is a separate matter, which, logically enough, is referred to as *sense-making* – the subject of Chapter 7 (Being in the know – part II).

In these two chapters, we look at the everyday ways in which both sensing and sense-making can be influenced. This influence is often significant and unsuspected. We will see that our knowledge of what goes on around us does not result from a simple process of absorbing external information and then integrating it into some ever closer map of reality. Instead, it is necessarily very *subjective* and highly *selective*. We will see that even things that are taken to be facts are not so straightforward. Neville Morley, a noted professor of ancient history, concludes emphatically that *"facts don't speak".*[1] Instead, they only acquire meaning after they have been incorporated into the observer's particular way of understanding them.

And so it is with all of us, whatever stories we wish to communicate to one another.

In what follows, we shed some light on what it is to know something – anything at all – and we will see more clearly why it is impossible to know everything there is to know. We will see how it is that the significance of the world in which we live is one that we create. We will see what the implications are for the safety of people and organisations, and how we, and the organisations we work for, have to change if we are all to become what we can be – *resilient* – as opposed to what we cannot be – *error-free*.

In Chapters 8 and 9, we look at two topics of particular importance in how we understand the world: how we perceive risks (obviously a central issue in safety) and how the understanding we gain by looking back at events after they have happened (hindsight) is necessary but can lead to erroneous conclusions about the way accidents happen.

Our senses

Five basic sense channels are available to most humans: vision, hearing, touch, taste and smell. There are others too, such as senses that help with our orientation in space. *Proprioception* depends on receptor cells in our muscles to let us know where our limbs are without having to look for them. Proprioception (sometimes called kinesthesia) works with our sense of *balance* – controlled by a delicate mechanism in the inner ear (the vestibular system) – to create a stable sense of which way is up.

In most working situations, we get the majority of our information through our eyes (especially) and ears, although on occasion our noses can play a vital role – for example, in detecting smoke or escaping gas. In this chapter, we focus largely on vision, say a little bit about sound and briefly touch on the other senses.

The sky is blue – isn't it?

Let's start with something simple that we all know: the sky is blue. Well, OK, not here, right now. As we write this, it's a cold, rainy November day in the UK and the sky appears to be various shades of grey. This afternoon, as the clouds roll away to the east and the sun sets in the west, the greys transform into the most glorious shades of yellow and orange, changing all the time until the last rays disappear and the sky turns more of a black colour.

---

1   Morley (1999), p. 15, original emphasis

Let's revise what we say we know. The sky is blue sometimes. Except that even when it's blue, without a cloud in the sky, it's not blue all over. The deepest blue is where the atmosphere is thinnest, directly overhead. Towards the horizon, as the atmosphere thickens relative to our line of sight, the blue gets paler, until it becomes white. Except in more populated areas, where the whiteness will be more of an off-white due to particulate matter suspended in the otherwise fresh air.

We won't distract ourselves here with the physics of why the sky is blue at all (when it's blue) and not green. The point is that statements about blue skies – or indeed anything at all – have different meanings for different observers in different places and with different purposes.

Statements about colour should make little sense at all to people born with certain sight defects, for whom the colour spectrum describes a set of distinctions that they cannot directly sense. However, this is not quite the case. In the 1990s, the neurologist Oliver Sacks visited Pingelap, a tiny Pacific atoll, where an abnormally large percentage of the population suffer from congenital achromatopsia – total colour blindness from birth.[2] He described how achromatopic people integrate with their peers by developing a detailed *theoretical* knowledge of colour, so that, for example, they can trade appropriately in bananas that, to the rest of us, are yellow or green.

In other words, although some Pingelapese can see only shades of grey, they know when the sky is blue and bananas are yellow. They can agree with unaffected Pingelapese that they are all looking at the same thing, even though they are most definitely not having the same experience.

This turns out to contain a crucial point – a particularly clear instance of what we, as humans, are doing all the time. Remember this as you turn the pages of this book: you and I may share an agreement on things; we may even agree to disagree; but no matter how extensive our agreement or disagreement appears to be, just like the Pingelapese, we are not experiencing the same thing. It is the constant presence of the differences between us (and where they come from) that generates danger for us in our operational lives – usually through misunderstandings and diverging priorities. Importantly, it is these same differences that are also the source of our mutual safety – but only if we, our colleagues and our managers are able to expect such differences and communicate with each other about them.

It is, of course, a function of training to increase the similarity of different trainees' approach and response to common operational issues, and to eliminate irrelevant, ineffective or dangerous variability. As a result, highly trained people become a lot more *entrained* with their task and with each other. However, it would be wrong to conclude that, faced with a specific situation, they have the same experience, or that understanding will consistently be the same from moment to moment, day to day or colleague to colleague. Understanding the influences that give rise to the differences between people – and the same person at different times – is a key point of this book.

---

2 The abnormal frequency of achromatopic people on Pingelap followed a devastating typhoon in 1775, in whose aftermath and resulting famine only 20 people survived. Of these, one had an achromatopic gene that was certain to be passed on to any children. The result was an increase in the frequency of the condition from 1 in 40,000 to 1 in 20, so that today some 150 of the 3,000 inhabitants are totally colour-blind.

We will come back to this in a number of different ways. For now, let's continue by revisiting the huge impact of context that we introduced in Chapter 3 (Being framed). You see, context exerts a powerful effect not just on the decisions we make but on our lower-level perceptual systems as well.

Seeing things that aren't there

In 1955, the Italian psychologist Gaetano Kanizsa famously published a diagram showing a borderless white triangle clearly standing out from black 'pac-man'-shaped objects in the background.[3] The diagram was interesting because there was no white triangle in the picture. Instead, your brain constructs one for you.[4]

What you see are the results of your sense-making kicking in to help you understand what your eyes are picking up. In the process, your brain creates something that doesn't actually exist in the real world but is being presented to you as if it did. Our brains do this a lot.

Sometimes what we see is a contextual result of the way our eyes work. The neuroscientist Beau Lotto[5] produces novel illusions at his studio-cum-laboratory. In one of them, you stare at a white dot. To the left of the dot is a large green square and to the right is a large red square. After 30 seconds, you transfer your gaze to another pair of squares showing mirror images of the same desert scene. Disconcertingly, you find that your eyes have been learning that the left- and right-hand worlds are coloured differently, and this is now strikingly projected onto the new scene.

Lotto's effect works unless you are achromatopic or else you are one of the 8% of men or 0.5% of women who are red–green colour-blind.[6]

You can experience a contextual effect similar to Beau Lotto's red–green visual afterglow with your sense of touch. Place your left hand in very cold water and your right hand in hot water (not too hot!). After 30 seconds, transfer both hands to a bowl containing water at room temperature. The result seems impossible: two quite different temperatures from the same body of water.

You must be hearing things

What about audio confusions? In Diana Deutsch's tritone paradox, you listen to a pair of musical notes and try to say whether the second of the pair is higher or lower than the previous one. You can try it yourself at the BBC website.[7] It seems quite easy to do this task, because it appears to be obvious whether the second note is higher or lower than the first. But it's an illusion. The problem is that each note is a complex blend of different tones separated by an octave. This makes it impossible to say which of the two notes is higher. Since your brain can't tell, it makes the answer up. Interestingly, you have no insight at all into the fact that your brain decided for you, although it seems our brains are influenced

---

3 Kanizsa (1955, 1976)

4 You can see it for yourself at https://en.wikipedia.org/wiki/Gaetano_Kanizsa [accessed April 2017].

5 Beau Lotto gives a great TED Talk on his work here: https://www.ted.com/talks/beau_lotto_optical_illusions_show_how_we_see [accessed April 2017].

6 Men are red–green colour-blind much more commonly than women because the genes responsible for red–green pigment detection are on the X chromosome. Males have only one X chromosome, while females have two. Since the condition will not be present if at least one X chromosome is normal, it follows that women are much less likely to be affected.

7 http://www.bbc.com/future/story/20150420-the-strangest-sounds-in-the-world [accessed April 2017]

by the learned rhythms of the way we speak. According to Deutsch, who works at the University of California San Diego, British-accented people tend to choose the opposite of what Californians choose.

In the mid-1970s, Harry McGurk and his research assistant John MacDonald stumbled across a powerful illusion in which the exact same spoken sound is interpreted differently depending on how it is seen to be spoken. For example, a recording of someone saying 'ba-ba' will be interpreted as 'fa-fa' if the mouth of the apparent speaker is seen to be forming the latter sound. The effect is very powerful, because even when you know what the sound actually is, the visual cue dominates. The McGurk effect has been shown to affect whole words and to change the perception of spoken utterances given in evidence in court cases (so-called earwitness), with potentially dire consequences.[8] The illusion even works when the speaker and observer/listener are the same person![9]

What you see depends on who you are

We see objects when sufficient light from them falls on the retina at the back of the eye, causing receptor cells to fire. These cells are very sensitive. In unpolluted, completely still air, the human eye can detect a single candle at a distance of 14 miles (22 km). The vision of birds of prey is eight times sharper than that of the average human. Owls can track a mouse in an area the size of a football pitch with the equivalent illumination of one candle.

Cone receptors in the centre of the retina give colour vision, while more sensitive rod receptors either side of the cones register black, white and shades of grey. While the central cones are good for fine detail, the rods are much better for detecting subtle movement. It is the rods that allow you to notice something 'out of the corner of your eye', but not in sufficient detail to see what it actually is.

In every human eye there is also a blind spot. When retinal cells fire, the signal is passed down the optic nerve, located just off-centre of the retina. In humans, there are no receptors covering the optic nerve, and so this part of the retina is permanently blind. So why don't we see a blank spot in our field of vision? It's partly because our brains combine information from around the blind spot with information from the other eye to fill in the blank, and partly because we simply ignore it. If you want to 'see' your own blind spots, follow the instructions in Figure 6.1.

---

8 Wright & Wareham (2005) showed how the two phrases "*He's got your boot*" and "*He's gonna shoot*" were heard by many as "*He's got your shoe*". They also referred to the case of Derek Bentley, who, in 1952, was involved in a robbery in south London. Police earwitness testimony was that, when confronted, Bentley shouted "*Let him have it, Chris*" – whereupon his 16-year-old accomplice, Chris Craig, fired a weapon and wounded Detective Sergeant Fred Fairfax. A few minutes later, the cornered Craig shot and killed PC Sidney Miles before jumping from a roof and severely injuring himself. Craig, a minor, was imprisoned for ten years. Bentley was convicted of incitement to kill and, in 1953, aged 19 but with a mental age of 11, became the last person to be hanged in the UK. He was posthumously pardoned in 1998 after a long campaign arguing that Bentley was telling Craig to give up the weapon, not fire it. Although this is not strictly speaking an example of the McGurk effect, it is a powerful and tragic example of the power of context in earwitness interpretation.

9 Sams et al (2005)

Figure 6.1 How to see your own blind spot

Hold the page in front of your face. The box should be directly in front of your eyes and about three times as far away as the distance between the diamond and the circle. Close your left eye and look at the diamond. Move your head further away or closer to the page until the circle disappears. You've just seen your own blind spot!

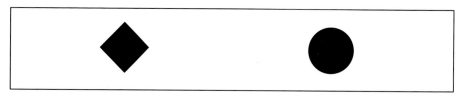

We expect a 3D world

In 2003, the Japanese designer Nobuyuki Kayahara created a video of a rotating silhouetted dancer.[10] It's easy to see the figure rotating clockwise in Kayahara's video. However, the person next to you is reasonably likely to see it rotating anticlockwise. Even more surprising, at any moment, as you stare at it, it will suddenly reverse direction for you! So which way is it actually rotating? The answer is that there is no correct answer to this question. The problem with a silhouette (like a radar dish or a person on deck at night) is that it contains no three-dimensional (3D) information and so your brain cannot tell which way it is turning. But your brain can detect movement and you understand what the silhouette represents. So your brain makes it up. And at any moment your brain can simply decide that it's turning the other way.

Note the oddness of this. It's not *you* that decides; it's your brain. And your brain doesn't bother to inform you that it made any choice at all. We will come back to the curious business of our unconscious life again in Chapter 7 (Being in the know – part II).

There are times when your brain makes no decision at all – even though the world may have changed dramatically. This can happen when things change sufficiently slowly that we can't detect the change. The extraordinary thing is how fast this change can be while still being too slow to notice. Professor Daniel Simons, a psychologist at the University of Illinois, provides a compelling example.[11] He presents a scene of shrubs and rockery in a country lane. As you carefully examine the scene, a large planted area in the foreground slowly changes into a bare rock. The change takes place gradually over just 12 seconds. Amazingly, at the end, well over 95% of us (including the authors of this book!) simply fail to see that any change at all has taken place, however diligently we've been scanning the picture. When the change is revealed, it is quite alarming to realise that we have missed something so big and obvious.

We live in a 3D world where there is a foreground and background, and objects are separated by distance. We are generally good at spotting sudden changes in this world, but, as Simons has shown, we are easily outfoxed by stealth. We can also be outfoxed by expectations of depth.

---

10 You can see the dancer for yourself at https://en.wikipedia.org/wiki/Spinning_Dancer [accessed April 2017].

11 Viscog Productions (2003)

In Figure 6.2,[12] Diagram A is a flat object drawn in two dimensions (2D) that many of us can't help but interpret as a representation of lines disappearing into the distance. We know that railway sleepers are all the same length, but that they necessarily look shorter as they recede into a 3D background.

Diagram B superimposes two red bars that are of exactly the same width. (They really are – go ahead, measure them.) However, such is the power of our 3D expectations that in the context of the 'railway sleepers', we experience the upper bar as slightly longer than the lower one.

Figure 6.2 Conflicting expectations

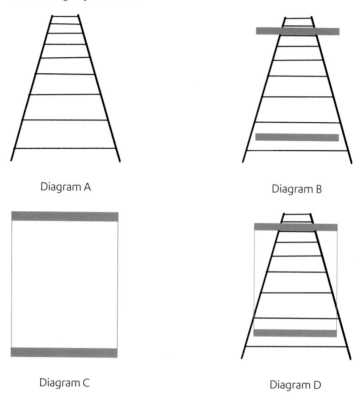

Diagram A   Diagram B

Diagram C   Diagram D

Diagram C removes the railway lines and draws vertical lines to prove the identical widths of the bars – and the illusion disappears.

Diagram D reintroduces the railway lines. But notice what happens! In an attempt to reconcile the conflict between our prior 3D knowledge and the reality of the identical red bars, we experience the vertical red lines as apparently bending!

Edward Adelson, Professor of Vision Science at the Massachusetts Institute of Technology (MIT), created the astonishing illusion in Figure 6.3. Look at the figure on the left. The grey shade in square A is clearly darker than the shade in square B. There can be no doubt – they are quite different. And yet they are the same shade! The common shaded bar in the figure

12 This a variation on the Ponzo illusion, first demonstrated by the Italian psychologist Mario Ponzo in 1911.

on the right shows this to be true. The illusion is caused by our prior understanding of the world of light and shade in which we live. In the context of the picture as a whole, square A should be darker, and so, as if under instruction from an invisible commander, we make it so.

Figure 6.3 The eyes don't have it

Edward H. Adelson

All our senses are in on it

Context and prior knowledge exert powerful influences on what our senses tell us. And it's not just our vision and hearing – it's true for all of our senses.

Taste has a very limited number of sensations: sweetness, sourness, bitterness, saltiness and umami. However, taste is inextricably tied up with the expectations provided by our other senses. If you hold your nose tightly and close your eyes, you will find it very difficult to tell whether it is an apple you are crunching on, or an onion. You are quite likely to report a lime flavour if you drink green-coloured cordial that is actually strawberry flavoured. If a caramel agent that has no actual taste is added to a drink, the drink is experienced as sweeter tasting than one without the caramel smell.[13] Many people report the smell of vanilla as sweet, yet sweetness can only be actually detected by our sense of taste.

Taste is also affected by temperature. For some people, placing a tasteless ice cube on the side of their tongue creates a salty sensation.[14]

In 2014, Charles Michel and his colleagues neatly demonstrated the power of context in an illusion involving sight, touch and taste. Michel, a trained chef, collaborated with Charles Spence, an experimental psychologist and Director of the Crossmodal Research Laboratory at Oxford University. First, the visual illusion. They made a box into which a participant inserted their tongue at one end. At the other end, the participant saw what they took to be their own tongue reflected in a mirror. In fact, the reflected tongue was a fake rubber one. Second, the touch illusion. When Michel stroked a wet cotton bud across both the real and rubber tongues simultaneously, 70% of participants reported that the rubber tongue they could see being stroked was their own. Even more interesting was that 40% of participants reported feeling their tongue being stroked when only the fake tongue got the cotton-bud treatment.

---

13 Cliff & Noble (1990)
14 Cruz & Green (2000)

Being Human in safety-critical organisations

What about the illusion of taste? Michel tried the experiment with the English celebrity chef Heston Blumenthal. This time he showed Blumenthal a lemon, into which he dipped the cotton bud. When he touched only the rubber tongue with the cotton bud, Blumenthal did not respond with *"I can't feel anything"*. Instead, he said *"I don't believe this is not sour"*. He was convinced he was tasting something, but it was not the taste he expected.[15]

All our senses can exert powerful influences on our mood. Smell, in particular, has an enormous impact on us through our emotions. This is because the five million smell receptors high up in our nasal passages are directly connected to the emotional centre deep in the brain. As a result, emotional responses are often activated long before we can name what we are smelling.

The influence of smell on our mood and expectations is powerful. Pleasant or unpleasant smells can lead us to rate people and products as more or less attractive than we would otherwise do. In an experiment in the Hilton casino in Las Vegas, people put significantly more money into slot machines when the gambling area was infused with a pleasant smell.[16]

The amount of information we derive from our senses is huge. Vision is the greatest source, accounting for two billion neuron firings per second in our brain when our eyes are open. This is two-thirds of our total waking brain activity.[17] We shouldn't be surprised. Vision is a high-bandwidth channel that has given us an evolutionary advantage in dealing with our threats, recognising food and taking care of our families. Hearing is our next-highest-bandwidth channel.

If both vision and hearing fail, our need to remain connected with the world means that our sense of touch can increase to unexpected levels of performance. We acquire the finger-tip sensitivity necessary to construct meaning from patterns of subtly raised dots printed on Braille pages. Usher's syndrome is an incurable genetic disorder afflicting around 1 in 25,000 people. It is characterised by profound deafness, which is usually followed later in life by blindness. Incredibly, people so afflicted have been observed to develop higher-order communication skills in which they can still understand sign language after they have gone blind. They gently cover each other's hands with their own and *feel* the signs that they previously only saw.

Imperfect channels

Our senses connect us with the world in which we move and live. But it should now be clear that they do not mirror it for us. Rather, they are imperfect channels that are vulnerable to context and whose central business is to help us in the process of constructing and maintaining meaning. And the bricks that they provide us with are used by higher brain functions to build and manipulate more layers of meaning. Some of these higher construction processes involve our conscious participation, but many don't. Together, they enable us to construct and share arbitrarily complex worlds.

Why is all this important to operators, managers, directors and regulators of safety-critical industries?

---

15 Michel et al (2014)

16 Hirsch (1995), replicated by Hancock (2009)

17 Fixot (1957)

The fact that our perception is both imperfect and vulnerable provides a major clue to the whole business of where responsibility for our decisions and actions does and doesn't lie. In turn, this clue informs the content of Chapter 12 (Being human) and begins to lay the ground for an approach to safety that starts by acknowledging what we are really like. This creates new demands and expectations of the organisations we work for, based on fair-minded accountability, rather than blame and retribution when things go wrong. And it creates new expectations of ourselves and each other, based on insight and mutual understanding, rather than division and conflict.

In Chapter 7, we take a further step towards understanding the responsibilities we all have by taking a closer look at what's involved in making sense of what passes between us and the world through our sense channels.

7 Being in the know – part II
where meaning comes from

Why can't we know everything there is to know?

Could we make better decisions without emotion?

Why are we forever looking for shortcuts?

What does memory actually remember?

Why do we miss obvious things?

Sense-making is construction, not reflection

At first glance, knowing things is about sensing what is out there, independent of us, and then learning what it means. But it is not like this. Perception is only partly a detection process. It is also fundamentally a construction process. Our brains do a lot of work making things up, and they do so by relying on what they already know.

In 1976, Ulric Neisser, a cognitive psychologist, upset many of his colleagues when he presented a new view of perception as a highly active cycle. His insights were a significant departure from views that even he had taken a decade before.[1] In his new view, perception operated as a continuous, proactive loop in which our current context and what we think we know *directs* our senses to *sample* our environment in particular ways, the results of which we then use to *modify* what we think we know. And so the cycle continues: directing – sampling – modifying.

Somewhat analogously, in the early 1970s, the Chilean biologist Humberto Maturana and his students introduced an exotic name – autopoiesis (pronounced auto-poy-eesis) – for a fundamental biological process of growth and development.[2] Think of autopoiesis as what a one-celled amoeba does as it moves slowly around its watery environment. Its current structure helps to determine its current capabilities. It can move just so far and so fast and reach out its 'arms' to embrace one particular morsel of nutrition rather than another. Having done so and digested the food, its capabilities are changed. It is now in a different place, is slightly bigger, can now move slightly differently, slightly more strongly, and reach out for morsels of nutrition that it couldn't reach before. Each cycle helps it to both reinvent itself and be open to different things.

---

1   Neisser (1967)
2   Varela et al (1974)

This dual principle of autopoiesis – organisational closure and informational openness – also describes how our brain, body and behaviour develop . Actually, it's a good model for just about every kind of organic development – including human organisations and complex, adaptive systems.

And, complementing Neisser's insights, it also has something to say about the process of perception. Our senses help us create understanding that changes our ability and our expectations about what to perceive next. Each perceptual interaction with our world is dependent on our current perceptual capabilities, and the results inform the next perceptual interaction.

Our senses are vulnerable to influences rooted in the way they work (eg blind spots, time dependency, and confusions between the content and sources of sensations). They are also vulnerable to the influence of context that comes from our prior expectations.

Our senses are not biological recording devices that document an external reality. Instead, they are channels that we use to create and maintain relationships that mean something to us. It is crucial to understand the vastness of this difference. We are not zombies. We are builders.

Is that why we can't know everything?

Yes. We have arrived at a key reason why we cannot know everything there is. Simply stated, we have no direct access to anything. Sure, we collect sense data, but then our brains immediately start working with it: filling in gaps, deciding how things should be, helping us to make sense of it all, and constructing the meaning of the situation we are in. And the more we look at this area, the more surprises there are.

In 2008, Chong Siong Soon and colleagues from the Max Planck Institute in Germany used functional Magnetic Resonance Imaging (fMRI) to discover that, in simple free-form decision-making tasks, our brains make decisions up to *ten seconds* before we consciously become aware of them. This has astonishing implications for free will, and adds perspective to the now hundreds of studies about unconscious mental biases.

It is also consistent with the ground-breaking work of neurologist Antonio Damasio and Nobel-winning psychologist Daniel Kahneman – as we shall see shortly. There is now plenty of evidence from several different quarters that our understanding – and our trade-off decision-making – is heavily influenced by what is going on in our unconscious brains.

 Read more about specific unconscious mental biases affecting risk perception in **Chapter 8**

Where does emotion fit in?

Before that, it is crucial to realise that what we know – or think we know – is also highly influenced by how we *feel* about it. Our emotional lives have a great deal to say about the sense we make of what our senses tell us. People routinely underestimate the influence of emotion or feelings on their decision-making.

 Get help with controlling your emotional response to stress in **Chapter 13**

Over hundreds of years of research, we had grown used to thinking of emotion and reasoning as two quite distinct things that brains do. The utility of basic emotions such as anger, fear, disgust, happiness, sadness, surprise, love and hate was that they prepared us physiologically for 'fight or flight'.

Humans are very good at rapidly and accurately identifying the emotional expressions on the faces of others. In fact, there is a specific part of our brain that is dedicated to recognising and processing facial information.[3] We do it very easily and very quickly (see the panel 'How did the man in the moon get there?'). We do it unconsciously by focusing on 37 lines around the eyebrows, eyelids and mouth.[4] The 'tells' that communicate many of our emotions (such as fear, anger and disgust) to others are universal across all human cultures.

How did the man in the moon get there?

Everybody knows about the man in the moon. Look at a full moon on a clear night and there he is, staring right back at you.

Throw a handful of beans on a flat surface and, likely as not, you'll spot a face in the resulting random pattern. On 23 November 2004, the BBC News Channel reported that a ten-year-old toasted cheese sandwich said to bear the image of the Virgin Mary had been sold on eBay for $28,000.[5] Whether you see the New Testament Madonna, the modern Madonna, Marilyn Monroe or just a toasted sandwich will depend on the things going on in your head and your culture.

Humans recognise faces very fast – so fast that scans show our brain registers them as faces faster than we are aware of it. We have evolved to do so, since faces bear valuable information about the emotional state of their owners, and therefore what action we might need to take to ensure our own survival. We are so good at it that we see faces even where there are none. Doing so is a constructive act with a name: pareidolia. We should remember, however, that 'normal' perception is no less an act of construction. The only difference is that in the case of pareidolia, it is easier for us to appreciate what we have created.

Meanwhile, we struggle to deploy our separate power of reason to create a more rational, civilised and purposeful world. If only we could set those emotions to one side in the world of rational business and decision-making! Wouldn't it all be so much more predictable, stable and, above all, *safe* if we could train ourselves to leave out the nuisance of emotion and deploy pure reason?

Well, no, it wouldn't. It turns out that without emotion and the feelings it generates, we can't function rationally. It may seem strange, but we need our feelings to make good decisions.

The curious case of Phineas Gage

Antonio Damasio is Professor of Neuroscience at the University of Southern California. In his book *Descartes Error*, he tells the story of Phineas Gage, a railway foreman from Vermont. One day in 1848, partway through preparing an outcrop of rock for demolition, the explosive

---

3   First described by Sergent (1992) and named as the Fusiform Face Area (FFA) by Kanwisher and her colleagues (1997)

4   Etcoff and Magee (1992)

5   You can see it for yourself at http://news.bbc.co.uk/1/hi/world/americas/4034787.stm [accessed April 2017].

charge went off prematurely. It blew a 1 metre tamping iron out of a hole excavated to take the charge. The iron rod entered Gage's head tapered end first, just inside the left cheek bone. Missing both upper and lower jaws, it shot upwards behind his left eye, permanently destroying vision on that side, through the left side of his brain, and out through the top of his head. The rod landed point first some 25 metres away.

Miraculously, Gage survived, but the damage to areas of his brain responsible for his emotional life brought about disturbing changes to his personality. The passage of the rod through Gage's head severely disrupted communication between the emotional and reasoning centres of his brain. Many documentary sources tell of a loss of ethical behaviour, and an increase in profanity and social disinhibition – all apparently examples of emotionally generated behaviour normally thought to be suppressed by higher faculties. Though he lived for 12 more years, he suffered increasing convulsive fits as time wore on, and died at the age of 38. Although there is evidence that some of his personality changes were exaggerated, the case established the importance of the interaction between emotion and intellect. But what was the relationship?

Damasio provides a much more recent story that offers further compelling evidence that emotion is actually essential to reasoned decision-making and normal social behaviour. As it turns out, without emotion, our rational behaviour becomes worse. Much worse.

Following an operation to remove a benign tumour, 'Elliot' suffered damage to a part of his brain similar to Gage's. The surgery left Elliot able to function in all areas of his life except when it came to making decisions. For example, Elliot would fully understand and accept the task of reading and sorting documents. However, he was likely to become absorbed in reading one of them to the exclusion of doing anything else for the rest of the day. Or he might become preoccupied with indecision about how the documents should be sorted, eg by date, size or relevance.

Damasio worked with Elliot over an extended period to identify the exact nature and source of the problem. It became clear that, while Elliot understood emotion and emotional response on an intellectual level, he could no longer feel it for himself. The inability to 'feel' turned Elliot into an observer of his own life – and robbed him of the 'gut feelings' humans need to choose some course of action over another. Tellingly, Damasio says that Elliot typically became caught in a never-ending loop of doing the task too well at the expense of never actually completing it.

In other words, the removal of emotional input to our reasoning brains results in a preoccupation with thoroughness at the expense of efficiency. Efficiency requires risks to be taken, and our emotional brains help us decide what risks are acceptable.

Damasio concluded that we use emotion in the form of positive and negative gut feelings to rapidly assess possible future scenarios. This vastly reduces all the effortful conscious reasoning we have to do in order to make decisions about our actions in an uncertain world. It also means that these 'gut feelings' are a major pre-conscious influence on our expectations and responses.

Animals deal with their worlds in something like this way. Sharks, dogs and bees appear to make sensible choices that ought to require knowledge, memory and goal-oriented reasoning. Leslie Real[6] has made a detailed study of bee behaviour. According to Real, in the absence of conscious reasoning, two fundamental preference rules must be present:

- High expected gain will be preferred to low expected gain.
- Low risk will be preferred to high risk.

Interestingly, the first rule is all about efficiency and the second is about safety, a key aspect of thoroughness. The efficiency–thoroughness principle is universal – a piece of biological wiring that is found in many species, and not least at an unconscious level in humans.

In fact, emotion and reason are intimately linked precisely because rational thought developed as an evolutionarily useful extension to emotional response as the world became more difficult to predict. Emotion allows us – and many other animals – to act smartly without having to think smartly. But for humans, reasoning gives us the crucial option of thinking smartly too.

Thinking fast and thinking slow

In his book *Thinking, Fast and Slow*,[7] veteran psychologist Daniel Kahneman characterises the way our minds work as if they were composed of two different, but parallel, systems. *System 1* is automatic and uses instinct, emotion and well-learned habit to try to respond to situations very quickly. *System 2* requires attention, mental effort and lots more time, but is able to apply reason and logic so that we can come to a much more considered decision.

As we noted earlier, when you glance at someone, you can often tell in a second what mood they are in and therefore how to prepare to deal with them. Many people have had the experience of driving a car in undemanding circumstances and suddenly noticing – miles later – that they haven't been paying attention to the task. If you learned your multiplication tables by rote in your early years, you immediately know the answer to 7 x 8. These are all examples of rapid, relatively automatic *System 1* responses that require little effort. *System 1* is also where shortcuts come from (see the panel 'Shortcuts to efficiency').

Shortcuts to efficiency

Shortcuts are enormously appealing to us. They create large efficiencies, allowing us to achieve what we think we need to, while freeing up our *System 2* brains for the new and difficult stuff. It is important to understand that while shortcuts are dangerous in complex system operations and are usually disallowed by our procedures, they are an embedded part of our evolutionary psychology. Devising them is what allowed us to survive, and the need to invent and deploy them will not go away.

Professor Gerd Gigerenzer is a psychologist and Director of the Max Planck Institute for Human Development in Berlin. He has studied our affinity with a particular type of shortcut usually known as 'rules of thumb', but properly called heuristics.[8] These are of central importance to human decision-making – and, indeed, survival.

6   Real (1991)

7   Kahneman (2011)

8   Gigerenzer et al (1999) and Gigerenzer (2008)

Consider, for example, the *recognition heuristic*. Faced with the question of guessing which US city – Detroit or Milwaukee – has the most inhabitants, 60% of US undergraduates get 'Detroit' right. Whatever that may say about general knowledge in the US, the interesting thing is what happens when undergraduates at a German university are asked the same question. Most Germans know little about Detroit and may never have heard about a place called Milwaukee. Yet virtually 100% of them correctly guess Detroit. Why? Because rushing into their knowledge vacuum comes the recognition heuristic, supplied by an eager and willing *System 1*. Expressed in words, the heuristic says: *'If you are faced with several choices, choose the one you've heard of most, since it is more likely to be bigger and more important than the ones you've never heard of.'*

Another heuristic is *take the best*, in which people choose answers based on a single fact that seems to be most relevant to the problem. It turns out that in real-life, time-limited decision-making, this is how groups such as police and airport security make choices.

Still another heuristic is *imitate the majority*, in which people do the same as the majority of their peers. As Chapter 11 (Being together) shows, this is a powerful force in group behaviour. And as psychologist Robert Cialdini[9] demonstrates, it is also what underlies the most powerful principle of human persuasion. For example, a campaign to persuade people to reduce their household energy consumption only worked when they were shown evidence that their neighbours had already done so.

Gigerenzer's work on heuristics provides some perspective on the many unconscious biases that this chapter samples. We agree with him that such biases are not irrational detractors from 'true' or objective knowledge. Instead, they form the contents of an 'adaptive toolbox' – the repertoire of all our evolved efficiency-centred heuristics. Rationality comes not from the (impossible) task of ridding ourselves of our *System 1* shortcuts. Instead, we must learn how to choose the heuristics that are most appropriate to the task in hand – including the choice not to deploy any at all. It follows that, together with our colleagues and managers, we must create a culture in which the fundamental nature of our evolved propensity to manage shortcuts in the interest of efficiency – both individual and organisational – is recognised fairly. We shall say more about this in Chapter 12 (Being human).

Read more about fair-minded organisations in **Chapter 12**

Get help with how to develop fair-minded organisations in **Chapter 14**

However, when you are counting basketball passes, or you instantly focus on the voice of someone who has just called your name in a crowded room, or you search a radar plot for a specific target, you are deploying *System 2*. And in so doing you are using up significant chunks of a precious and limited resource – attention.

---

9 Cialdini (1984)

According to Kahneman, both systems are running whenever you are awake, with *System 1* running automatically and *System 2* routinely operating at a low level to conserve resource. Moment by moment, *System 1* rapidly and effortlessly suggests a response. *System 2* either endorses the suggestion or else steps in with precious resource to make a more considered assessment.[10]

It should be obvious that this arrangement biases us towards the effortlessness and efficiency of *System 1*. The problem is that *System 1* is incapable of logic or the analysis of new situations, and is defeated by surprise. *System 1* can seduce us into believing that a situation is familiar, so causing us to miss something that is both new and significant. It beguiles us with uncritical efficiency when we should be deploying mindful thoroughness. But while we must use our effortful *System 2* to reason our way to thoroughness, we now know from Damasio that we need the spontaneous 'gut feelings' from *System 1* to actually make progress.

Exclusive use of *System 2*, as for 'Elliot', means that we remain stuck in a detailed intellectual understanding of the options without ever selecting one. Exclusive use of *System 1* means that we quickly succumb to the surprises that the complex interactions of our uncertain world throw at us.

For those of us with safety-critical operational lives to lead, the trick is to know when and how to question the low-effort suggestions our *System 1* generates. Getting this wrong gets us into trouble. Here's an example.

When *System 1* dominates

The authors were recently talking with a maritime accident investigator. He told us of an enquiry in which he had been trying to get to the bottom of the reason for the collision of a large tanker with a fishing vessel. The officer of the watch (OOW) had spotted the fishing vessel in plenty of time, and knew that the master's standing orders required the ships to stay 2 miles (3 km) apart. But instead of using that separation instruction, the OOW flashed the fishing vessel and did this repeatedly for 20 minutes until it was too late and there was no time to turn the large tanker.

Detailed questioning revealed the dominance of a *System 1* strategy in the OOW and a *System 2* that had failed to question the underlying assumptions. It turned out that the OOW had been a fisherman in those waters for many years, man and boy. His fishing experience was ingrained and told him that 1 mile (1.6 km) was easily enough for fishing boats to take evasive action from oncoming large ships – as he had done many times. While this may have been true, it did not work for a fishing crew who were themselves allowing too much airtime to their *System 1* and not paying sufficient attention.

One of the key points of a story like this is that it is one of a countless number that continue to be told, despite the operation of all the traditional approaches to human factors that we described in Chapter 4 (Being sufficient). The design of the ship, operating equipment and interfaces may be state of the art; the crew involved may have been through rigorous organisational selection and training processes; the level of automation may strike the perfect balance between what people and computers can, and should, be doing; the

---

10 Peters (2012) provides an entertaining alternative account of the same distinction by contrasting your 'inner human' with your 'inner chimp' – see the panel in Chapter 5 (Being in a state).

company's policies, procedures and rules may be clear, unambiguous and available. Yet it all fails when worlds collide – the different worlds of understanding that are constructed by different people using imperfect senses whose blind spots are unsuspected and whose effortless *System 1* efficiencies go unchallenged by conscious *System 2* mindfulness.

> **Read more** about the need to move beyond traditional human factors in Chapter 4

USS *Vincennes* – when worlds collide

And this is exactly what happened in the Combat Information Centre (CIC) of USS *Vincennes* in 1988.[11] *Vincennes* was a fast, lightly armoured ship built on a long, narrow destroyer hull. She was equipped with two 5-inch surface-to-surface guns, one fore and one aft, while her main battery of SM-2 anti-aircraft missiles were controlled by the advanced Aegis electronic fire-control system around which she was built. Aegis was state of the art – capable of processing the data from a complex air battle extending over hundreds of square miles, and displaying the results on a large central screen in the CIC. It could search, track and engage up to 200 targets simultaneously. As *Vincennes* patrolled the restricted waters of the Persian Gulf, tasked with enforcing the embargo of Iran, she represented the US Navy's most prized, high-technology warship.

And that was part of the problem. Fresh in the minds of the crew – and not least their captain, Will Rogers III – was the memory of the sinking of USS *Stark* in the same area in the previous year. Back then, *Stark* had been hit by two Exocet missiles fired from an Iraqi F-1 Mirage. The ship was severely damaged and 37 of the crew were killed. It would have been much worse had the first Exocet exploded as well as the second. It had been a tragic and embarrassing episode, for which the Iraqi and US governments both came to hold Iran accountable.

Now, at around 10.00 on the morning of 3 July 1988, and following apparently hostile behaviour, *Vincennes* opened fire on a group of gunboats crewed by the Iranian Revolutionary Guard Corps (IRGC). There was a heavy technology mismatch between *Vincennes* and the gunboats. As a commentator later put it, it was a bit like shooting at rabbits with a radar-guided missile. Partway through the engagement, *Vincennes* manoeuvred violently to bring both guns into play. In the CIC, high above the water line, books and loose equipment went flying off desks, and drawers flew open. Many of the crew had to grab on to something to prevent themselves from being thrown to the deck. The surface engagement ended less than 20 minutes after it had begun, with one of the IRGC gunboats sunk and the others sent into retreat.

But in those same few minutes, *Vincennes'* command team, supported by a flawlessly operating Aegis, had also detected, tracked, engaged and shot down a civilian Iranian Airbus, tragically killing 290 innocent people.

The state-of-the-art manned military system had mistaken a civilian Airbus on a scheduled flight plan for a hostile Iranian F14 Tomcat fighter that was thought to be descending towards the ship in an attacking dive. But how?

---

11 Barry & Charles (1992) and Cannon-Bowers & Salas (1998).

Context, of course, is everything. What was the context that suggested one interpretation over another? We have already mentioned the crew's determination not to be caught out as *Stark* had been. It didn't help that, while all the technology worked flawlessly, key members of the crew had difficulties in dealing with it. Meanwhile, other crew members were far too comfortable with the technology: some ingenious individuals had discovered that they could hack in to the command net to hear the action via their Sony Walkman® devices. With half the crew doing this, the power drained from the circuit and the volume faded. This caused the command team to switch to a new frequency every few minutes, losing vital information and adding to the confusion.

Key to understanding what happened that day, though, was that the crew saw what they expected to see and then worked hard to bend information to that belief. When the Iranian Airbus appeared on *Vincennes'* radar, the ship was already under attack on the surface. The hostile gunboats served to increase the expectancy of further attack. In turn, this increased the tendency for the command team to seize upon any information that could be used to support their expectancy, at the expense of ignoring the stream of contrary evidence that flowed from the ship's electronics.

When the Iranian Airbus was first picked up on radar, the Interrogation Friend or Foe (IFF) system correctly identified it as a commercial aircraft. But when it was later checked in the scheduled listings, it was not found. In the confusion of the ongoing surface battle, the crew overlooked that Aegis had assigned it a different track number after a data merge with a neighbouring US warship. A crewman wondered aloud if what they now saw was an Iranian warplane. Once uttered, this thought began to gain currency. Sure enough, a later IFF check returned a hostile signature. But this was because, in the increasingly charged atmosphere, the operator had neglected to reset the range of the IFF. He actually got a return from an Iranian military transport aircraft still sitting on the runway at the airport from which the Airbus had taken off several minutes earlier.

As the Aegis system showed the Iranian Airbus climbing away over the Gulf at 12,000 feet and a speed of 380 knots, *Vincennes'* crew interpreted the information in a different way. For them it was an Iranian F14 Tomcat accelerating towards them in an attacking dive. That's what they saw and that's what they fired at – with complete and devastating success.

How many brains do you have?

It is instructive to understand something about the way the brain has evolved, so that some light can be shed on observations by researchers such as Damasio and Kahneman.

Simply stated, there are three basic parts of a human brain. The oldest part is the reptilian, which first appeared over 300 million years ago. It is located in and around the brain stem, and regulates the vital functions that keep you alive. It is what generates your drive for food, sex and shelter. It works without reliance on conscious thought, which is why you don't need to spend any of your valuable mental resources attending to how often you need to breathe or make your heart beat. However, since all parts of the brain are connected, you can, with practice, take considerable conscious control of these normally automatic functions.

Next to evolve was the limbic[12] brain, which generates your feelings, emotions, memory, arousal, basic motivation, and instinctive judgements about value. First appearing in mammals over 200 million years ago, the limbic brain basically makes and remembers distinctions between pleasant and unpleasant experiences. It's what enables mice to be one-trial learners about poisoned food, so that if they survive, they never return to that food source. And, with an experimentally imposed low-voltage connection to the pleasure centre in their brains, it's what makes rats press a lever time and time again in preference to eating and drinking, until they eventually collapse from dehydration and exhaustion.

Unique to primates such as the great apes (including humans) is the third part – the neocortex (literally, 'new bark'). This evolved over millions of years, reaching its present form in humans when *Homo sapiens* first appeared in Africa around 200,000 years ago. The neocortex forms 75% of your entire brain and is the source of sensory perception, sense-making, reasoning, rational thought, planning, language and social relationships. The evolutionary psychologist Robin Dunbar has found that the size of the neocortex relative to the older part of the brain is highly related to the social complexity of its owners.[13] By his calculation, the human brain evolved to cope with a social group of around 150 individuals – about the size of many human clans and rural settlements, the average size of a village in the Domesday Book,[14] the smallest autonomous military unit (the Company) and many modern business units. Any more than this and we cannot sustain meaningful personal relationships with everyone.

While these three parts of the brain are separate, they are connected by rich networks of neurons, through which they constantly influence each other.

Different understanding, different response

The panel 'How many brains do you have?' outlines the basic parts and functions of our brains. From this, it is perhaps unsurprising that we have different, but connected, ways of understanding and responding to our world and each other. The fast, efficient *System 1* controlled by our limbic brain focuses on the familiar and offers us tactical, impulsive and rapid responses to the situation that it tries to persuade us we are in. The slow, resource-intensive *System 2* is controlled by our rational brain as it tries to eliminate and deal with surprise through considered, strategic response. And connecting them both is the evolved inevitability of our rational responses being informed by our emotional and reptilian brains.

Outside all of this is the overarching principle that whatever our brains are doing for us, they are doing so constructively and individually, making the best use they can of pre-existing knowledge.

What does memory actually remember?

Daniel Kahneman points out that there is a huge difference between the experiencing self and the remembering self. When you experience the thrill of a rollercoaster ride, or

---

12 'Limbic' derives from the Latin limbus, meaning 'edge' or 'border', because the limbic system borders the part that connects the left and right sides of your brain.

13 Dunbar (1998)

14 The Domesday Book was a survey of over 13,400 English settlements, published by William the Conqueror in 1086 AD.

the pleasure of a great job appraisal, or the pain of failing a vital qualifying examination, it is not those experiences that determine your later decisions. It is the memory of those experiences. And since your memory encodes feelings and meanings, not facts, what you remember is not the event, but how you felt about the event and what it meant to you. Furthermore, your memory changes with each remembrance, throwing away parts that no longer matter, and emphasising and embellishing the parts that do. The next time you remember it, you are remembering how you felt about it the last time you embellished it. The result may be a vivid and detailed memory of something that simply never happened the way you now remember it.

Accident investigators are aware of this, which is why they try to interview eyewitnesses as soon as possible. They need to hear people's stories while memories are still fresh and uncontaminated by the processing that goes on as people try to make sense of what happened and fill in the gaps with things that never occurred.

Huge concern has been raised about eyewitness testimony by researchers such as Elizabeth Loftus. Loftus, a cognitive psychologist, has spent her whole career investigating the nature of human memory.[15] In the 1970s, she showed that people's memories of events are significantly altered depending on how questions are put. For example, witnesses who were asked *"About how fast were the cars going when they* smashed *into each other?"* gave higher estimates of speed than those who were asked the same question but using words like *bumped* or *hit*. References to *"the broken headlight"*, rather than *"a broken headlight"*, were more likely to produce false memories of seeing broken glass. In other words, all sorts of embellishments were created to fit the wording of the question, rather than what actually happened.[16]

Loftus's studies led her to elucidate what is now one of the most widely known unconscious biases, the *misinformation effect*. As it turns out, our memories are soft, malleable things that can be significantly changed by suggestion after an event, without us being aware of it, or complicit in its alteration. This has had dire consequences for many. According to the Innocence Project in the US, *"Eyewitness misidentification is the greatest contributing factor to wrongful convictions … playing a role in more than 70% of convictions overturned through DNA testing nationwide."*[17]

Cognitive biases – mechanisms for greater efficiency

If you type *'cognitive bias'* into Wikipedia, you will be rewarded with a list of around 200 biases – including Loftus's misinformation effect – that have been systematically explored in countless scientific journals.

 Get help with approaches to allowing for human biases in **Chapter 13**

One of the most fundamental principles underlying several major cognitive biases is 'priming'. Priming refers to the influence of some event on what we think, attend to or

---

15 Loftus's expertise and insight into the malleable character of human memory has led her to serve as an expert witness at over 250 trials, some of them very high profile, including OJ Simpson, Ted Bundy, Oliver North, the Bosnian War trials and the Oklahoma City bombing.

16 Loftus & Palmer (1974)

17 http://www.innocenceproject.org/causes-wrongful-conviction/eyewitness-misidentification#sthash.TlhXziVR.dpuf [accessed April 2017]

decide to do next. The prior event may be quite subtle, may have nothing whatsoever to do with our subsequent action, and can exert its influence without any awareness on our part that it is doing so. Key to the power of priming is our need for context – even if we have to invent one in the absence of anything more obvious.

Let's see how priming works.

Consider the sequence of roughly drawn characters in Figure 7.1.[18]

Figure 7.1 Letters

Asked to describe these characters, most people find it easiest to report the letters F, G, H. Actually, to see the first and last characters as F and H involves a further perceptual trick we all have up our sleeves. 'Perceptual closure' refers to our ability to allow our senses to chunk separated things together to form more meaningful, more memorable objects that ease the strain on our memories. The F and the H in the diagram are formed of lines that do not meet. Your brain closes the gaps to make things easier for you.

But now look at the sequence in Figure 7.2.

Figure 7.2 Numbers

This time, most people report the numbers 5, 6, 7. Note, though, that the middle number (6) is identical to the middle character (G) in the previous sequence. In each case, the adjacent objects set a priming context for the way you interpret the squiggle in the middle. Move your eyes between the two sequences and just feel the priming happening somewhere in your brain!

---

18 Figures 7.1 and 7.2 are based on a concept discussed by Kahneman (2011).

Being Human in safety-critical organisations

So, priming relies on your brain making use of contextual cues. We already know about the power of context, but the extraordinary thing about priming is that while our brains use it, we, our conscious selves, frequently remain unaware that our brains have done so. This happens most dramatically when we are struggling to answer a question in the absence of relevant information. To help us, *System 1* is quite happy to seize upon something that seems at first sight to be relevant – and *System 2* is very often quite happy not to notice the shortcut.

In classroom conditions, the authors of this book presented the following problem[19] to a large number of our students over a couple of years:

- Californian redwood trees are the tallest living things on Earth.
- Think for a moment whether the height of the tallest redwood tree is more or less than [we said '50 metres' for some students and '250 metres' for others].
- Write down your best guess about the height of the tallest redwood tree.

The actual height of the tallest redwood tree is approximately 115 metres. But the average results we got from the 250-metre-primed students were clearly higher than those from the 50-metre-primed students.[20]

Amazingly, priming exerts a powerful influence even when the information *System 1* seizes upon is completely irrelevant. Dan Ariely is a professor of management science at MIT Sloan School of Management. He got his MBA students to participate in a mock auction in which they bid for a series of items (eg wine, chocolate and computers) that they did not know the value of. Crucially, he first had them write down the last two digits of their social security numbers. Clearly, these numbers had nothing to do with the value of the auction items. However, Ariely found that the half of the group who wrote down the higher numbers bid between 60% and 120% more than the other half of the group.[21] In the absence of relevant information, the students had unknowingly used the numbers as a reference for what they did next.

In many UK supermarkets, wine is displayed according to region of origin. Within their regions, however, very expensive bottles are often found right next to moderately expensive ones. The intention is not that you pick up an expensive bottle by mistake, but that the less expensive items seem affordable by comparison – even though they may cost more than you might otherwise have wanted to pay.[22]

Priming can be very subtle. The *Florida Effect* was coined after a much-cited study from the social psychologist John Bargh's laboratory in 1996.[23] Here, half the participants manipulated sentences involving words with meanings related to old age (eg wrinkle, grey, lonely, stubborn, retired, Florida[24]). The other half were given words that were unrelated to being

---

19 The problem was suggested to us by Kahneman's book (2011).

20 These are anecdotal results, since we could not use experimental conditions and statistical tests of significance.

21 Teach (2004)

22 There is nothing accidental about the arrangements in a modern supermarket. Shopping staples (eg milk and bread) involve a journey up and down several aisles, and then back through several others to pay for them; the smell of the in-store bakery on the way makes it difficult to resist those doughnuts and cookies; the reduced beat of ambient music slows people down in the aisles long enough to notice other products they might consider; roughened floors slow down shopping carts next to selected items; the ice in the fish department is unnecessary to product freshness, but it influences our perception of a key buyer value, which we then unconsciously generalise to the whole store.

23 Bargh et al (1996)

24 In US culture, Florida is well known as a popular retirement destination.

elderly. Immediately after the task, the participants in the elderly condition were observed to walk away from the lab more slowly than those participants in the control condition. The crucial thing about this study was that the participants were completely unaware that the words they had been using had any effect on their subsequent behaviour, or that they were behaving any differently from normal.[25]

What relevance do these findings have in the everyday world of safety-critical operations?

Here, there are plenty of opportunities for the automatic, effortless, primed responses that *System 1* offers us to produce tragic results if we allow them to go unchallenged by our more critical *System 2* thought processes. We described one earlier in this chapter ('When *System 1* dominates'). Here is another.

A tragic *System 1* miscategorisation

During the voyage of a general cargo ship, the officer of the watch (OOW) became worried that a deck officer had not been heard from for a while. He had last been seen near the ship's holds. Entering an enclosed space on a ship is notoriously dangerous without the right personal protective equipment (PPE) – in this case oxygen breathing apparatus – among other rigorous procedures. Concerned for his safety, the OOW alerted the rest of the ship and the deck officer was found unconscious inside one of the ship's cargo access areas.

The crew carried out an enclosed-space rescue but, tragically, their attempts to resuscitate the officer failed and he died. The cause of his death was the oxygen-depleted atmosphere in the area where his body was discovered. The vessel had been carrying a cargo well known to deplete oxygen in any compartment in which it was loaded.

The officer who died was known to have prior experience of this specific cargo and had been present at a health-and-safety meeting where the exact hazards were discussed in detail prior to loading. The enquiry concluded that it could be reasonably assumed that he knew the risks associated with it. It was never established why this experienced officer decided to enter an area where a mortal danger existed without the correct safety precautions necessary to sustain his life.

However, it was noted that the deck officer had put on a gas mask to enter the enclosed space. Donning a gas mask might have satisfied his *System 1*, but his *System 2* did not engage to tell him that it could not protect him from the depleted atmosphere. He needed an oxygen supply, not protection from noxious gases.

Priming happens everywhere, all the time. Advertisers, salespeople, politicians, supermarkets, confidence tricksters, social engineers[26] and stage magicians[27] use it deliberately. And in our everyday lives, our *System 1* sense-making is essential to our efficiency – much of the time without our conscious awareness.

---

25 Recently, some criticism of Bargh's 'Florida' study has emerged after failures to replicate it. However, there appears to be a lot of evidence for the general principle that recently used words impact subsequent behaviour without the hearer's conscious knowledge.

26 Social engineering refers to the deliberate manipulation of people, often using highly tuned social skills, so that they divulge confidential information. The aim is to get past otherwise impenetrable (usually high-tech) security systems – see Schneier (2008).

27 If you'd like an unusually clear description of how close-up magic makes use of a cluster of unconscious biases, including priming, you will enjoy Derren Brown's 2010 book *Confessions of a Conjuror*.

The curious problem of attention

The apparently effortless operation of *System 1* relies on priming – and indeed many of our unconscious biases. Why are these biases – and the *System 1* they underpin – so influential? The answer comes down to our need to conserve the enormously powerful, but effortful and highly limited, resource upon which *System 2* depends: attention.

As we said in Chapter 3 (Being framed), attention is like a pie. It only has so many slices – and once they have all been consumed, there is literally nothing left. If this happens, we will miss unbelievably large events, even though they are completely obvious to others. Chapter 3 described the problem we have with *inattentional blindness* and showed how gorillas can hide in plain sight if all our attention is being used up elsewhere.

Trafton Drew is a psychologist at Harvard Medical School's Visual Attention Lab in Boston, Massachusetts. In 2013, his team published[28] a fascinating follow-up to Simons and Chabris' original 'gorilla' studies. Drew wanted to know whether deep experts were as vulnerable to inattentional blindness in their specialist field as were naïve observers of basketball games. Drew's team embedded a very obvious outline of a gorilla in a series of lung images and asked experienced radiologists to examine them for lung nodules. Eye tracking revealed that although the radiologists looked directly at the gorilla shape for considerable amounts of time, more than 80% failed to recognise it as such. While they performed very well at the familiar recognition task for which they were trained, it seems that experts are also highly vulnerable to the beguiling limits of attention.

Operationally, it is easy to spend all of our available attention on the task under way, the task that must follow, the clear and present risks, the things we'd rather be doing, the family problem back home that's currently preoccupying us, the headache we've got, the fatigue we're feeling – and BANG! – where did that gorilla come from?

On top of a high level of technical competence, advanced motorcycling skills are centred on an explicit and highly tuned observational process. The trick is to always be conscious of the 'vanishing point' (also known as the 'limit point') of the road in front, beyond which is the unknown. An advanced motorcyclist seeks to make efficient progress while deliberately and continuously maintaining a position and speed that maximise the distance to the vanishing point and guarantee the ability to stop safely and in control before that point is reached. Everything on the road must be constantly interpreted and prioritised as a hazard that can redefine the vanishing point at any time. Such hazards are not just other vehicles, pedestrians and the weather, but also kerbs, bends, hill crests, junctions, road surfaces and road edges. Advanced motorcyclists also actively gather clues about the intentions and capabilities of other road users – for example, through observation of their gaze, trajectory, demeanour, positioning and their own apparent attentiveness (or, as is too often the case, their lack of it).

One observational technique that is useful when riding through busy environments is to look straight ahead but pay deliberate attention to what can be seen in your peripheral vision. This maximises your sensitivity to sudden or unusual movement to the sides, while attending in more detail to the space immediately in front. You've got this right when you become aware that you feel a relaxed alertness in which you are ready for anything. It is in this way that gorillas may be spotted before they step out and reduce your vanishing point to zero.

---

28 Drew et al (2013)

In safety-critical operations, something akin to a state of relaxed alertness needs to be maintained in one part of our *System 2* brains. We need to reserve a part of our attention in which we can step back to evaluate where the rest of our attention is being spent. If not, we will not be well placed to recognise that things are going wrong and that we need to reprioritise.

 Get help with managing your biases in **Chapter 13**

Such calamitous attention to the wrong things is precisely what happened in the case of *Royal Majesty* in June 1995.

The grounding of *Royal Majesty* – a case of misplaced attention[29]

On 9 June 1995, the Panamanian passenger ship *Royal Majesty* left Bermuda, bound for Boston, Massachusetts. On board were 1,509 passengers and crew. Thirty-four hours later, the ship grounded on shoals off Nantucket Island, 17 miles (27 km) from where the watch officers thought the vessel was. Fortunately, there were no deaths or injuries as a result of this accident. However, the repair bill was $2 million, another $5 million of revenue was lost while the repairs took place, and the corporate embarrassment was very large.

So how was it that the officers' attention became so misplaced, and remained unchecked over such a long period?

Just after 12.00, as the ship got under way, the navigator correctly calibrated the ship's GPS with a backup, radio-based navigation system, a LORAN-C unit. The more accurate GPS had been in use without incident for three years. The autopilot was set and, every hour for the next 30 hours, all fixes were plotted from the GPS.

At 12.52, however, the GPS disconnected. A flapping cable connector in a restricted space had come loose – possibly having earlier been inadvertently kicked by a passing crewman. Unnoticed, the GPS switched to dead reckoning (DR) mode. Unfortunately, the autopilot was not programmed to recognise the mode change and simply carried on using the now increasingly inaccurate GPS for its automated course instructions.

The GPS receiver was located in the chart room. When it disconnected, its internal alarm beeped for just one second and the tiny characters DR and SOL (SOLution, meaning calculated rather than actual) appeared in a corner of the display –small enough to be overlooked by the inattentive. The GPS external alarm repeater to the bridge had not been wired in when it was installed three years earlier.

At 16.00, the chief officer (CO) took over from the navigator. He continued hourly fixes using the GPS in line with established routine. Like the navigator, he regarded the less accurate LORAN-C system as a backup in case the GPS failed – which, as far as he was aware, it had not.

The watch changes and hourly fixes continued for 24 hours. At 20.00 the second officer (SO) took over from the CO; at midnight the navigator was back; and at 16.00 it was the CO's watch again. It was now 28 hours since departing Bermuda.

---

29 National Transportation Safety Board (1997)

Figure 7.3 Actual and plotted courses of *Royal Majesty*

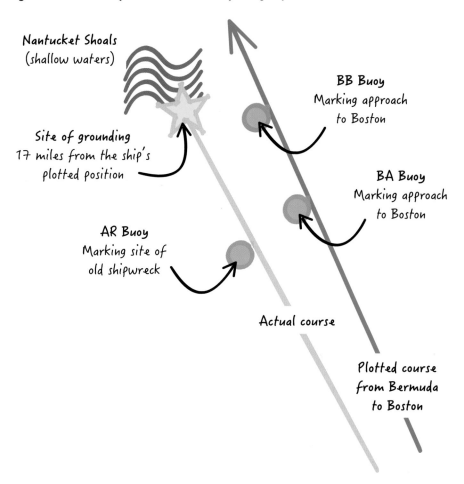

Nantucket Shoals
(shallow waters)

BB Buoy
Marking approach
to Boston

Site of grounding
17 miles from the ship's
plotted position

BA Buoy
Marking approach
to Boston

AR Buoy
Marking site of
old shipwreck

Actual course

Plotted course
from Bermuda
to Boston

At 16.45, the master telephoned the CO to ask when he expected to see the BA Buoy – marking the southern entrance to Boston traffic lanes (see Figure 7.3). The CO reckoned they were 2.5 hours away. Forty-five minutes later, the master visited the bridge and checked again, this time examining *Royal Majesty*'s progress on the position chart. The GPS agreed exactly with the position chart. This was unsurprising, since one had generated the other. What was unsuspected was that the GPS had been diverging more and more from the ship's real position.

At 18.45, the CO got a radar return off his port bow and concluded it was the expected BA Buoy. The return showed an object he was looking for at exactly the place and time he expected to see it. A feeling of certainty and security fell over the bridge. It did not occur to the CO that this was a return from the AR Buoy, marking a wreck at an entirely different spot (see Figure 7.3).

Forty minutes later, the radar said that the BA Buoy was 1.5 miles (2.5 km) away. The CO was a little puzzled that he couldn't see it, but he told himself it must be due to the glare of the setting sun.

At 19.30, the master telephoned the bridge and asked about the BA Buoy for the third time. The CO told him it had been ascertained by radar.

Half an hour later, at 20.00, the SO arrived on the bridge to take over the watch from the CO. The SO was new to the ship but not a novice mariner. The CO informed the SO of the vessel's course and speed, and discussed the traffic conditions. He did not explain that the BA Buoy had not been visually sighted.

The SO continued with hourly fixes by GPS. Like the CO, he had no reason to suspect the GPS, which appeared to be working normally, and so he had no reason to deploy the backup radio-based system.

Now in charge on the bridge, the SO was in a situation in which he had inherited a history of chart positions made and certified by a succession of senior officers over the past 32 hours, as well as by himself. What's more, the expected BA Buoy had been checked off by the CO and the ship was on course for the BB Buoy further north on their current course. What could go wrong?

Early in his watch, the SO received a channel 16 international distress transmission from a Portuguese fishing vessel. The English part of the message did not convey urgency. The Portuguese part, which the SO did not understand, questioned the location of a large cruise ship in these shallow waters. The SO told them to get off the emergency channel.

At 20.30, when *Royal Majesty* should have been halfway between the BA Buoy and the BB Buoy, the port lookout told the SO he had seen a yellow light off the port bow. The SO acknowledged the message but took no action. In the context of everything he took to be true, it made little sense.

A few minutes later, both port and starboard lookouts reported high red lights off the port bow. The lights were marking shallow waters off Nantucket Island, which should have been way off to the north-west. Again, the SO acknowledged but took no action. We don't know what the SO was thinking at the time, but it was clearly a lot easier to believe that the lookouts were confused, or wrong, or exceptionally long-sighted – anything rather than disbelieve the last 32 hours' work by the SO and his fellow officers.

Just then, the master came to the bridge. Both master and SO discussed the vessel's progress on the position chart. Both were satisfied that the vessel was on the right track.

The SO did not mention the red and yellow lights to the master. If the master wasn't asking about them, they couldn't be important – and why say something that betrays your own ignorance?

At 21.45, the master telephoned the SO to ask whether he had seen the BB Buoy. The SO said that he had. In fact, he hadn't, but he told himself that it must have been seeable due to the GPS track: maybe the radar had not reflected the buoy on this occasion.

At 22.00, the master came to the bridge and once again checked *Royal Majesty's* progress. Now fully sold on the convincing – but utterly wrong – context he was in, the SO again told the master that he had seen the BB Buoy. Happy, the master left the bridge.

At 22.15, the lookouts reported blue and white water ahead. The SO acknowledged the information but, once again, took no action.

Five minutes later, *Royal Majesty* grounded on the Rose and Crown Shoal less than 10 miles (16 km) from Nantucket Island and 17 miles (27 km) west of where the navigation team thought they were.

The official accident report found that the key problem was *"over-reliance by watch keeping officers on the automated features of the integrated bridge system"*. There have been many incidents of radar-assisted (more recently ECDIS[30]-assisted) collisions. Trust, awe and an inability to recover from the failures of complex automation have developed in recent years. And as they have done so, people have found themselves increasingly immersed in the window on the world that the technology provides, instead of looking out of the real window and mentally stepping back to consider things from a different perspective, informed by insights about the way people really work.

 Get help with how to become more mindful in **Chapter 13**

We don't know how far the SO on *Royal Majesty* was in a culture that allowed him to easily cast doubt on the accuracy of more than 30 position fixes by senior officers.[31] However, it seems certain that *System 1* efficiency heuristics were operating. In the context of a trusted technology, everyone felt they were in the same safe, familiar and shared story. No-one reserved part of their attention to properly consider the parts that didn't fit: the meaning of DR and SOL on the GPS display; the meaning of the missing visual on BA Buoy; the meaning of the channel 16 broadcast; the meaning of the missing BB Buoy; and the meaning of the yellow and red lights.

 Read more about team influence in **Chapter 11**

 Get help with how to challenge senior officers in **Chapter 13**

Priming was evident on board *Royal Majesty* that day in 1995. Part of it was tied up with the signals everybody was giving everybody else that all was OK. Part of it was embodied in the trust that the officers had for the modern, high-tech bridge, with the GPS at its heart. And part of it lay in the comfort offered by the procedurally required documentation of the many hours of position fixes.

But there was another cognitive bias operating that day. *Confirmation bias* refers to a common human tendency to look for evidence that supports what we currently believe to be the case. It doesn't take long to realise that this is another aspect of our constant leaning towards greater efficiency. It is, after all, easier to stick with all of the investments we've made in our current belief than to start from scratch with a new hypothesis. So, we surround ourselves with people who share the same views and favour information that is consistent with what we believe.

Psychologists have known about this bias for many years. Sixty years ago, the social psychologist Leon Festinger made a study of people who had survived a major earthquake

---

30 ECDIS – Electronic Chart Display and Information System

31 See Chapter 11 (Being together) and Chapter 13 (Being practical – part I) for more about the difficult business of challenging senior officers.

in India in 1934.[32] Contrary to his expectation, he discovered that survivors of the earthquake chose to believe fearful rumours about much worse events to come. He realised that believing the rumours was much more consistent with the shock that they felt as a result of the recent event. In essence, their beliefs about horrors to come justified the fear they felt today. People find it enormously stressful to hold two conflicting views at the same time and will seek to reduce their psychological discomfort by avoiding situations or information that might increase their *cognitive dissonance* (or 'thought inconsistency').

The real problem with this, however, is that we start to notice more things that match our views and, simultaneously, devalue or dismiss things that do not match. Have you ever learned a brand new word and then started noticing it being used around you? It's all part of the same bias. The word was being used with the same frequency all the time – it's just that you paid no attention to it before, since it had no meaning for you. Our brains are constantly directing our senses to search for information that appears to be relevant to the things we already know and the decisions we have already made. In so doing, we fail to notice the very large amount that appears not to be relevant.

The unconscious operation of the confirmation bias goes a considerable way to explain the puzzle of why the officers on *Royal Majesty* failed to act on the parts of the story that didn't fit. To avoid potential cognitive dissonance, they simply downgraded the potential significance of the information and so maintained the story they shared.

As we all accommodate and adapt our behaviour to each other, we must continuously resolve uncertainties to which we are variously sensitive. These uncertainties, combined with the dynamically changing influences on each of us (State, Understanding, Goals), mean that we are sometimes faced with a highly constrained set of options, none of which will end well.

The fact that we live constantly with more or less uncertainty to which we are more or less sensitive means that we are always dealing with some level of risk. This introduces a range of new safety issues since, as we will find out in the next chapter, our perception of risk is always changing.

---

32 Festinger (1957)

8

Being in the know – part III
why do we do risky things?

Can we live and work risk-free?
Why do we often overlook the risks in our actions?
Why do we sometimes deliberately take risks?
What makes something feel more or less risky?
Can we get better at assessing risks?

Risky business

In the previous chapter we discussed unconscious mental biases and described the case of *Royal Majesty*. The officers involved were no different from the countless other participants in the incidents and accidents that continue to characterise safety-critical operations in complex, adaptive systems. There is, therefore, an important further question about the operation of the biases that underpinned their *System 1* thinking.

Read more about Kahneman's *System 1* and *System 2* thinking in **Chapter 7**

The question is this: if people routinely construct and inhabit stories, and if those stories are capable of transporting them towards great danger, what is happening to their sense of risk and why doesn't it stop them? Why do they not see the inevitability of a calamity and do something to avert it?

To answer this question, we need to understand two things.

The first is that our perception of risk is ever-changing – moment by moment – and depends on the amount of confidence we feel in our ability to assess and respond to the situation we think we are in.

The second is that the hindsight we use to explain an event and its riskiness is an illusion. While hindsight analysis can do a great job of describing the precise (and often complex) timeline of an incident, it has no explanatory power unless it includes a participant-oriented analysis of the world at the time the participant was involved.

This chapter is concerned with the first of these two points. The second is the focus of Chapter 9 (Being in the know – part IV).

Perceiving risk

First, we need to understand what risk actually is. This turns out to be quite difficult, because the word represents a compound idea. Here's a straightforward expression of it:

Risk = Probability x Consequence

At first sight, this simple equation appears to be quite useful – and it has a tempting implication. If the probability of the risk can be reduced to zero, we can all relax. It won't matter how dire the consequence might be, since multiplying it by zero results in zero. A similar logic applies the other way: there can be no concern about the certainty of something happening as long as it has no consequence that we care about.

However, in the complex world of human operations, the values of both probability and consequence are usually something above zero. And that's where we hit two problems.

The first is that humans are not very good at understanding probability. The second is that we are not very good at predicting consequences – especially in complex, adaptive systems, which are inherently uncertain and constantly vulnerable to unintended and large consequences from the most innocuous of changes.

Why is it difficult to understand probability?

The problem with probability is that it produces results that are often counterintuitive. A roulette wheel has 36 numbers plus the 0. The 18 even numbers are red and the 18 odd numbers are black. The zero is green and always belongs to the casino. The gambler's fallacy is the belief that, as a run of consecutive red numbers on the roulette wheel continues to grow, there is an increasing likelihood that the next number will be black. The fallacy resides in the idea that somehow the roulette wheel – or the ball – retains a memory of its own history and will need to 'even things out' as time goes on. In reality, the only memory or sense of frequency is in the gambler. At each and every spin of the wheel there is slightly less than a 1-in-2 chance that the number will be red, with exactly the same odds that it will be black, and a 1-in-37 chance that it will be green.

The 2008 heist movie *21* featured a version of Monty Hall's 1950s TV game show puzzle. The scene is a graduate lecture theatre and Kevin Spacey's character, MIT Professor Micky Rosa, is on the lookout for mathematical talent for his Las Vegas casino card-counting scheme. He tells the class that behind one of his three chalkboards is a new car. Behind the other two boards are goats. He asks the class to choose a board. But before revealing either the car or the goat behind it, he eliminates one of the unchosen boards, which he guarantees was hiding a goat. He now asks the class whether they want to stick with their original choice or switch to the other unchosen board – and whether it makes any difference.

To most of us, there would seem to be no difference. Behind our board there is either a car or a goat, and the same is true for the other board. But the 'talent', senior math major Ben Campbell (played by Jim Sturgess), explains why it is very much in his interest to switch: his 1-in-3 chance of revealing the car then becomes a 2-in-3 chance. Counterintuitively, the professor's removal of one of the goats allowed its 1-in-3 probability to 'transfer' to the remaining unchosen board. Meanwhile, the board originally chosen by the students retains its 1-in-3 probability because those were the odds when they chose it.

Unconvinced? Practical experiments reveal probability theory to be spot on. Over 30 to 40 trials, if you always switch, you end up with the car roughly two-thirds of the time. If you never switch, you are successful one-third of the time.

Probability theory relies on formal logic, an intellectual discipline in which statisticians and insurance actuaries can become trained, but which does not come easily or naturally to the human brain.

A big part of our problem in comprehending probability is the very thing that evolution favoured our brains to find easy. It's that efficiency-oriented *System 1* at work again. Kahneman illustrates the impact of *System 1* with a real survey on the incidence of kidney cancer across all 3,141 counties within the 50 states of the US. The first results revealed that the lowest incidence of cancer occurred in rural, sparsely populated, Republican areas in the mid-west and south-western states. However, theories about wholesome lifestyles had to be abandoned when the results also showed that the *highest* incidence of cancer occurred in rural, sparsely populated, Republican areas in the mid-west and south-western states (albeit different ones). A new theory was suggested: perhaps the results reflected differing levels of medical screening and facilities in these counties?

It was, of course, neither. The real problem was that there were too few data points in these areas to allow any conclusions to be drawn. These data points were simply random outliers and there was nothing to explain.

System 1 is very good at seeing patterns and causality where there is just random variation. We are frequently only too ready to join up a few dots and jump to easy conclusions to make a highly plausible story. Having done so, our confirmation bias kicks in to protect the story we have now invested in. If we do anything, it is often just to search for confirming evidence, while discounting the value of any other kind of information.

The tendency of *System 1* to lure us into ever greater efficiency occurs even for highly trained professionals. One of the most common oversights affecting medical doctors is premature diagnosis (also known as 'premature closure'). Here, a doctor may quickly spot a pattern of symptoms but fail to ask questions that might disconfirm a diagnosis that has been reached too quickly. The mistake may be magnified through the operation of another of our largely unconscious influences – the availability bias. We tend to estimate a much higher probability than exists in reality for a condition that we have recently encountered. So, a doctor who has recently treated a rare but dramatic condition that ended badly may become overly predisposed to suspect the same condition in other patients and order unnecessarily specialised diagnostic procedures.

Our willingness to create patterns that don't actually exist can be further increased by the tendency of apparently extreme events to become less extreme over time through random variation. This is called 'regression to the mean' and it plays a part in explaining why football clubs that are at the top of their league at the end of one season perform rather more averagely in the next. Or why the installation of a speed camera at an accident black spot may be mistaken as the reason for a subsequent reduction in accidents.

For 25 years, since around 1990, speed cameras have proliferated throughout the UK. Designed to reduce accidents by enforcing speed limits, the cameras have collected over £100 million ($130 million) per year in fines. Meanwhile, the number of road deaths in the UK has stayed fairly constant[1] and the evidence for the effectiveness of the cameras has been argued to be of generally poor quality, with insufficient control for other factors that might have distorted the authorities' conclusions.[2]

Regression to the mean may play a part in convincing organisations that new safety procedures are having the desired effect. It seems quite sensible to address a spate of accidents involving trips and falls on stairs with new guidance and awareness campaigns. Sure enough, these may be followed by an observed decline in such accidents. The question is whether the new rate is any different from the old rate measured over a longer period of time. If not, then the spate was probably a random fluctuation. If a genuine change is produced that appears to be directly related to the safety campaign, then organisational attention might well be paid to other risk areas which may now be receiving less attention within a system that is operating with the same overall resources.

Why are consequences difficult to see?

Our ability to predict the flow of consequences from an event is just as hampered as our ability to understand how probability works. Safety-critical industries continue to tell stories of incidents and accidents played out by people who had absolutely no clue about the catastrophe that was about to befall them, their colleagues, their families, their employers and, in some cases, the planet.

Why?

There are some very good reasons. Some operate at an individual level, in the brains of those who suddenly find themselves at the centre of something bad and unintended. Others operate at an organisational and systems level. Let's look at both in turn.

Why do consequences surprise us as individuals?

We sense and manage risk in the moment. Practice and contingency planning ahead of time are obviously important, but in the end, it is the application of skilled performance and knowledge, high levels of situational awareness, and our sensitivity to changing priorities that are all brought to bear – in the moment – to perceive and mitigate risk. This is what we all do, at least implicitly, when we drive a car or ride a motorcycle. If you are an advanced driver or rider, it's what you have learned to do in a much more explicit, more conscious way.

The risks we perceive depend on our levels of knowledge and situational awareness. The more insight we have into our task and its context, and the more we understand its changing context and circumstances, the better calibrated we will be with its riskiness. However, research on the human perception of risk shows that our calibration is vulnerable to considerable distortion by some very particular mental – and often unconscious – biases. We are all vulnerable to these biases, whether we are riding a motorbike, watchkeeping on a ship's bridge, performing a surgical operation, or running a nuclear power station. Any one of them can make us seriously underestimate the amount of risk we are taking, or make us much more blind to the consequences of getting things wrong.

---

1   http://www.bbc.co.uk/news/magazine-10762590 [accessed April 2017]
2   http://www.roadsafetyobservatory.com/Evidence/Details/10716 [accessed April 2017]

Here are three key biases that particularly affect our perception of risk:

- Control bias – how much we believe we are calling the shots
- Value bias – how badly we want to achieve something – for ourselves, our families, our colleagues, our managers or our shareholders
- Familiarity bias – how comfortable and familiar the situation appears to be.

Bad calibrations

Here are real examples of each of the three influences at work on our sense of risk – and the blindness they produce in our ability to judge the consequences.

Losing control to motorway madness[3]

The M5 motorway is a six-lane highway in England that runs for 160 miles (260 km) and connects the South-West to the Midlands. Late in the day on 4 November 2011, 30 miles (50 km) north of Exeter where the motorway begins, it was dark, wet and foggy. As the evening traffic made its way northwards, a driver suddenly met a dense wall of fog just north of junction 25, near Taunton. The driver braked heavily and was hit by the vehicle behind. Within a few seconds, 34 cars, vans and articulated trucks had piled into each other. Some of the vehicles exploded, generating a large fireball and flames 20 feet high. The collisions, explosions and fires killed seven people and injured 51 others.

The horrific scene of twisted metal and burned-out vehicles was attended by 15 fire appliances and a fleet of ambulances. An air ambulance landed a surgeon who performed roadside operations to free and stabilise some of the victims. It was the deadliest accident on a British motorway for 18 years and it closed the road in both directions for two days. The accident involved 34 drivers who, seconds earlier, had all considered themselves to be in full control.

There was a further misunderstanding of control associated with this incident. At the time of the pile-up, 50-year-old Geoffrey Counsell had been operating a fireworks display at Taunton's rugby club ground, adjacent to the motorway. Soon after the accident, the police announced a criminal investigation into the contribution made by smoke from the display. Nearly a year later, in October 2012, the unfortunate Counsell was charged with seven counts of manslaughter. In January 2013, the manslaughter charges were replaced with a single charge that Counsell had failed to ensure the safety of others. His trial began on 19 November 2013 and finished a month later, when the judge concluded that there was no case to answer and instructed the jury to find the defendant not guilty.

Commenting after the case, the acquitted man said that, before his firework event on that fateful night, he had informed the Highways Agency, the local borough council and the police. No-one had raised an objection of any kind. Even if the smoke from the fireworks had been instrumental, these agencies had failed to object to an event with consequences that they, as safety experts, had themselves failed to foresee. Not only was the M5 drivers' sense of control badly calibrated with reality, but so, potentially, was the sense of control of the authorities who approved the fireworks. In the event, in April 2014, the coroner concluded that dense fog was the primary trigger and that the accident had little to do with firework smoke.

---

3 Wikipedia; BBC (2013a); BBC (2013b)

As a balancing example of the relationship between control and risk, Phillip Belcher revealed an intriguing finding in his study of collision avoidance behaviour among merchant ships in the Dover Strait.[4] The mandatory collision regulations (COLREGS) require that when two ships need to pass each other, one is the *'stand on'* ship (which maintains its course and speed) while the other is the *'give-way'* ship. Unless there is an explicitly made agreement to the contrary, the give-way ship changes its position so that the two ships pass each other on the port side.

The Dover Strait is the busiest international seaway in the world. It is transited by over 400 commercial ships every day. What Belcher found is that when they want to cross the Strait, officers adopt strategies that minimise their reliance on the other ship to resolve the risk of collision. This means that they will typically manoeuvre early in order to become the give-way ship – even if this means contravening the COLREGS to do so. The reason they do this is because they do not trust the other ship – especially fishing vessels – to manoeuvre correctly or in time. This is an example of people who actively take control because they are well calibrated to their risks, as opposed to assuming they are in control due to bad calibration.

The catastrophic value of punctuality[5]

On Sunday 27 March 1977, a bomb exploded at Las Palmas Airport on Gran Canaria, one of the Canary Islands and a popular sunshine resort. With a second bomb feared, incoming aircraft were diverted to Los Rodeos Airport on Tenerife, another of the islands in the archipelago, 62 miles (100 km) to the north-west. Los Rodeos (now Tenerife North) was a much smaller airport, with very limited passenger facilities, limited aircraft parking, and one runway. Among the diverted aircraft were Pan Am 1736 and KLM 4805, two jumbo jets fully loaded with holidaymakers.

Commanding the KLM 747 was Captain Jacob Veldhuyzen van Zanten. Not for nothing was he KLM's chief flying instructor. Aged just 50, he had received his commercial pilot's licence 27 years earlier. It was Veldhuyzen van Zanten who had gone to Seattle in 1971, shortly after qualifying on the new plane, to fly the airline's first Boeing 747 home. Now, sitting on the runway in 1977, he was widely regarded as the company's pilot expert on the 747, having notched up over 1,500 hours on the jumbo out of a career total of 11,700 hours on all aircraft types. Just recently, he had become the 'face' of KLM in a full-spread advertisement in the company magazine. The headline read: *"KLM: From the people who made punctuality possible"*. As they sat on the runway, there was a copy in the seat back of each of his 234 passengers.

Things were difficult at the tiny Tenerife airport. Planes were parked on the taxiways, hard decisions had to be made about whether and when to deplane passengers, and air traffic control (ATC) were stretched with the unusual amount of activity. In Captain Veldhuyzen van Zanten's case, he had finally been instructed to let his passengers off into the overcrowded terminal. He had decided to try to recover some time by refuelling while he waited for Las Palmas on Gran Canaria to reopen. That way, he could have a quicker turnaround for the long-haul leg back to Europe and thereby do what he could to live up to the value that he now headlined in the KLM magazine.

---

4   Belcher (2007)

5   Subsecretaría de Aviación Civil (1978)

Finally, the security problem at Las Palmas was resolved and the planes readied themselves for departure. The KLM was cleared to taxi the length of the runway and then completed a 180-degree turn in preparation for take-off. Meanwhile, the Pan Am was told to follow the KLM down the same runway and take the third exit off into the parallel taxiway. There, it would wait for its own take-off instruction.

Unfortunately, in the last few minutes, a dense fog had descended. This was quite common at Los Rodeos, due to the airport being 2,000 feet above sea level and frequently finding itself in the clouds. In the gloom, the Pan Am missed its intended exit, which in any case had no signs. Communication channels were crowded, radio traffic was confusing, and there was no ground radar available for ATC to see where the taxiing planes were.

Up at the beginning of the runway, the KLM cockpit crew could see the billowing fog coming towards them. They couldn't see the mighty Pan Am sitting across the runway in the middle of the same cloud. The KLM crew were more than ready to go. Aside from the organisational value of punctuality that he now represented, Captain Veldhuyzen van Zanten was only too aware that they were in danger of exceeding permitted flying hours. He started the aircraft forward. His co-pilot told him that ATC clearance had not yet been received. The captain responded, "*I know that. Go ahead, ask.*" There followed an exchange with the tower in which the KLM crew said they were ready for take-off and waiting for ATC clearance, and ATC issued post-take-off route instructions. The KLM co-pilot completed the read-back to the tower with the words "*We are now at take-off.*" Captain Veldhuyzen van Zanten then spoke the fateful words "*We're going.*"

ATC responded with a non-standard "*OK*", meaning that they acknowledged the status of the plane as being ready for take-off. But in the context of an afternoon of delays, and his heightened desire to be airborne, the captain interpreted "*OK*" as a response to his own statement of intent.

The next three seconds were filled with a whistling over the radio as simultaneous communications interfered with each other. The interference blocked two crucial messages. ATC was telling the KLM "*Stand by for take-off, I will call you*". And the Pan Am was broadcasting "*We're still taxiing down the runway!*"

With the KLM now rolling down the runway, the tower told the Pan Am "*Report when runway clear*". The Pan Am replied "*OK, we'll report when we're clear.*" As the KLM gathered speed, the flight engineer heard the exchange and asked "*Is he not clear, that Pan American?*" Captain Veldhuyzen van Zanten was now totally focused on getting his aircraft to where he wanted it to be. He emphatically replied "*Oh, yes*" and continued to accelerate the plane.

By the time they saw the Pan Am looming out of the fog, it was too late. The KLM pilots lifted off early in a desperate attempt to clear the aircraft in front of them. The Pan Am pilots increased power and tried to taxi out of the way. As the tail of the KLM scraped violently along the ground in an exaggerated climb, it sliced through the centre of the Pan Am, its right engines ripping through the upper deck behind the cockpit. Only briefly airborne, the KLM crashed back into the ground 150 metres down the runway. The 40 tonnes of fuel that had just been taken on exploded in a huge fireball.

All 234 passengers and 14 crew on board the KLM were killed, as were most of those on the Pan Am. Miraculously, 56 passengers and five crew members, including the Pan Am captain and two others on the flight deck, walked away.

In total, 583 people were killed in the worst aircraft collision that the world has ever known. The investigation was one of the first in which a systematic examination of human factors was conducted. Out of it came a new approach to decision-making by mutual agreement, called Crew Resource Management (CRM), a version of which is known in the maritime world as Bridge Resource Management (BRM) and which has recently been extended to Human Element Leadership & Management (HELM).[6]

Among these human factors is that a highly valued goal can come to dominate thinking, thereby masking the true riskiness of the actions and decisions taken.

Hoegh Osaka – when familiarity breeds disaster[7]

Hoegh Osaka is a modern car carrier. Constructed in 2000 and with a crew of 24, she is a very large steel box. At 180 metres long, she is the length of two football pitches. She is also very tall. Ten of her 12 cargo decks tower out of the water. Each deck can accommodate the equivalent of around 400 Land Rovers, but the lower decks have more headroom, so they can take trucks, cranes, bulldozers and other large plant. The design of the ship is a clue about basic physics. Heavier items are best placed towards the bottom if stability is to be maintained.

Hoegh Osaka had got into a rhythm. Every two months, the ship would load vehicles in Hamburg, then in Bremerhaven (just 150 km around the German coast) and finally in Southampton. She would then set off on the long haul to discharge her cargo of luxury cars and industrial vehicles in 11 Middle East ports, before returning to Europe for another cycle.

But as the ship arrived in Southampton on the afternoon of 2 January 2015, the itinerary had been changed not once but twice. The latest orders were to do things in the opposite order: Southampton–Bremerhaven–Hamburg, finally also taking on 2,000 tonnes of bunker (fuel) oil at Hamburg before the long voyage east.

That evening, the master received a copy of the pre-stowage plan. It had been prepared by the port captain,[8] who would use it to control the sequence and position of the 1,400 vehicles to be loaded the next day. The plan was much the same as for previous cycles.

Hoegh Osaka arrived at Southampton with a small, previously loaded complement of 200 Hyundai cars on the lowest decks 1 and 2, and 21 heavy vehicles on deck 6. The other decks were empty.

The following day at Southampton, she was loaded with 1,250 more cars, the majority of them high-end Range Rovers. The barcode on each vehicle contained its exact weight, but although each one was scanned, this weight information was not utilised. Instead, the port captain's plan assumed a 'rule of thumb' weight of 2 tonnes to make the calculations easier.

The Southampton stevedores also loaded 164 heavy road construction vehicles. Each of these carried a manufacturer's shipping note with its declared weight. In fact, these shipping-note weights were later found to be less – sometimes much less – than the vehicles' true weights when they were measured by accident investigators.

---

6 The contents of HELM were developed from an earlier examination of human factors in the shipping industry by the authors of this book (Gregory & Shanahan, 2010).

7 MAIB (2016a)

8 The port captain was a representative of the ship owner, with responsibilities for establishing and merging the cargo and loading plans at each of the three European departure ports.

The loading operation was supervised by the port captain in accordance with his plan. As the vehicles were driven on, the chief officer was at his position in the control centre high up on deck 13. From here he could operate the ballast system to keep the ship level as the loading continued.

When loading was finished, unknown to anyone, the combined actual weight was 5% more than the assumed weight. In fact, the rule of thumb would have worked out in the ship's favour had the port captain not decided to load additional plant without telling anyone. Had he stuck to the original plan, the total weight would have been 10% under the assumed weight.

What was critical, though, was that 92% of the cargo – over 5,300 tonnes – had been loaded on the highest decks 6 to 12. By comparison, the lowest five decks were virtually empty, with only 465 tonnes between them. What's more, the contents of the bunker oil tanks at the bottom of the ship were very low, making the ship even more top-heavy.

The combination of an inappropriate loading plan and the absence of an accurate stability calculation meant that, unknown to everyone, the ship's centre of gravity was now higher than her operational design limit.

At just past 20.00 on 3 January, with the pilot on board, *Hoegh Osaka* slipped her berth, let her tugs go, and began to sail up the main channel out of Southampton harbour. Some 20 minutes later, up in the ship control centre, the chief officer finally sat down to calculate the ship's actual departure stability. He had made some calculations before, but loading had been complicated, so he deleted all the data from the loading computer and began re-entering everything from scratch. As he did so, the master telephoned him with prophetic words: *"She doesn't feel right." "I'm working on it,"* the chief officer replied.

Of course, the departure stability should have been calculated before the ship sailed. Furthermore, the calculation was even more pressing for this sailing, since the chief officer and port captain had been working to a loading plan that had been devised for Southampton as the last port, rather than the first.

Hoegh Osaka survived the first major turn ordered by the pilot. It was a turn to starboard just before 21.00, and it was needed to set up the entry into the Solent before a second turn to port to head east out of the Solent, bound for Bremerhaven. These two turns would keep the ship in deep-water channels anticlockwise around the Bramble Bank in the middle of the Solent. The ship was making a speed of 10 knots. After the turn, things looked good and the pilot ordered a speed increase to 12 knots.

Up on deck 13 in the ship control centre, the chief officer's stability calculations were giving him a furrowed brow. It was becoming obvious to him that the ship was dangerously top-heavy. He was beginning to consider *en route* ballasting to try to reduce the ship's centre of gravity.

Five minutes after completing the first turn, the pilot ordered 10 degrees port to turn the ship east along the Solent. Less than a minute later, the pilot was worried too. He reduced the turn rate to 5 degrees. Forty seconds after that, he called *"Midships"* to reduce the turn rate to zero, followed by *"She's very tender, Captain."*

As all seafarers know, when a ship turns, she tilts the other way. It's called 'heeling' and it's physics. As the ship comes out of the turn, she rights herself to continue vertically in a straight line. *Hoegh Osaka*'s second turn was to port and she had started heeling to starboard as normal. The problem was that the heeling kept getting worse until it became a pronounced tilt. Even as the pilot ordered *"hard starboard"* to try to reverse the tilt, the starboard heeling became ever more severe. The ship was tipping over. Her massive rudder and propeller lifted out of the water and, at 21.15, she grounded on the very sandbank she had been trying to sail around.

The ship was on her side with a 40-degree list. The bridge team managed to wedge themselves between consoles, but no-one could reach the radio to raise the alarm. After a few minutes, the master managed to extract his mobile phone from a coat pocket and called VTS (the shore-based Vessel Traffic Services) to summon urgent assistance. An off-duty crewman suffered the only serious injury when he left his cabin only to fall 18 metres across a floor that wasn't there any more. He broke an arm and leg and had to await rescue in considerable pain.

On the upper cargo decks, luxury cars had crashed into each other. One of the heavy plant vehicles on deck 6 rolled across the tilted deck and punctured the starboard hull at a point that was now below the water line. Water started flooding in through the hole and down into the lower decks. Over a quarter of the total cargo was written off or damaged.

How was it that the loading plan devised for Hamburg–Bremerhaven–Southampton had been used for a passage plan that had been reversed, resulting in a top-heavy ship that simply keeled over when she turned?

The failure of the crew to understand the true extent of the risk they were taking was influenced by two variations of the familiarity bias.

First, the chief officer had allowed six years of familiarity with car carrier operations to seduce him into a false sense of security. In all that time, ship stability had never presented him with cause for concern. He had become comfortable with what had become a familiar practice of allowing the ship to sail before calculating her stability. After all, why hold operations up unnecessarily? A triumph of efficiency over thoroughness.

Second, the port captain's familiarity and sense of comfort with his own loading plan allowed him to overvalue the efficiency of sticking with it, rather than focus on the thoroughness that was actually required to understand the risk of applying it to circumstances that had radically changed.

So, what do we know about risk perception?

A lot of research has been done into how the human perception of risk is affected by these three biases. Here are the conclusions:

 Get help with dealing with risk and complacency in **Chapter 13**

Perceived control

- Younger and older people tend to underestimate risk. They also overestimate their ability to deal with it.

- Men tend to take more risks than women. They also underestimate the amount of risk they are taking relative to women.
- We perceive activities that we think are under our control as less risky than if they are being controlled by others.
- If we are engaged in an activity with an unknown level of risk, we perceive it as more risky than an activity where we think we understand the risk.

Perceived value

- Payment by piecework increases productivity, but it also increases risk-taking and accidents.
- We perceive decisions we think are unfair to be riskier than fair ones.
- We judge activities with negative, doubtful or unseen outcomes to be riskier.
- We think that activities that can lead to many simultaneous deaths (eg an air crash) are riskier than those with scattered incident patterns (eg seafaring).
- We judge things we fear or dread (eg exposure to carcinogens) to be riskier than activities that do not arouse such emotion (eg accidents at work).

Perceived familiarity

- More experienced people have a better awareness of risk, but they are also more vulnerable to complacency.
- We judge activities that are unfamiliar or not well understood as riskier than those with which we are familiar.
- If a risk repeatedly fails to appear, we perceive it as less risky than we used to.
- We underestimate the risks attached to our previous decisions.
- If activities have an accident history, we judge them as riskier than activities with no accident history.

Biases are sensitive to context

We started this chapter by saying that our perception of risk changes moment by moment. It is certainly dependent on the amount of confidence or control we feel we have, and this can change quite suddenly. If you've ever been involved in a road accident in which you have collided with a vehicle in front that has stopped suddenly, you may have noticed that for some considerable time afterwards you end up leaving too much room between your vehicle and the one in front (which generates further problems and risks). The only thing that has changed is your level of confidence, produced by a changed context for your activity.

Context has an especially powerful effect in changing the way you unconsciously value things.

How much do you value a new car radio versus a new car? The answer to most people is pretty obvious. The new car is obviously more expensive than a new radio, and 'more' is usually perceived as better than 'less'. What about having a new car next week as opposed to next month? Again, pretty obvious: next week would be best, because 'sooner' is usually perceived as better than 'later'.

What's interesting is that our perception of value, expressed as 'more' and 'sooner', is not rooted in cold logic, but depends instead on our old friend, context (see Chapter 3: Being framed).

Harvard psychologist Dan Gilbert[9] demonstrates this further. You decide you want a car radio and see that the shop on the corner will sell you the exact model you have in mind for $200. But then you discover that a store on the other side of town has it for $100. If you are like most people, you will choose to make the trip across town and thereby save yourself $100.

Now let's change the item we want to buy. The dealership on the corner will sell you the car you want for $31,000. The dealership across town will let you have it for $30,900. Most people will choose to buy from the dealership nearby.

Gilbert explains how illogical this is. The saving is the same and the value of the saving is the same. But it *appears* to be of less value because we are allowing ourselves to compare the saving with the price of the item being bought. Yet, as Gilbert says, when you go to the grocery store with $100 the next day, the money doesn't care where it was saved: $100 buys $100 worth of groceries. With the comparison gone, the money has now reacquired its rightful value in our perception.

Simply inserting and removing items of different comparative value into our consciousness will change our perception of the value of something that has nothing to do with the thing being compared. We have previously noted how supermarkets may use this technique to make products appear to be less expensive.

Behavioural economist Dan Ariely discovered that the presence of an option – even a deeply unattractive one – exerts a powerful influence on our other preferences. In a famously elegant study,[10] he asked his students to choose between one of three annual subscription options for The Economist. They could choose an online subscription for $59, a print-only subscription for $125, or an online-and-print option for $125. Faced with these choices, 84% favoured online-and-print. No-one (0%) wanted the print-only option. Why would they pay the same money for something less?

Then Ariely deleted the option with apparently no value whatsoever – the print-only option – and offered the remaining two choices. The results were spectacularly different. Now, two-thirds thought the online-only version was the best value. So, although no-one had wanted the print-only option, its presence in the mix made the online-and-print option seem like the best value for $125. Once the decoy option was gone, people felt they could not justify $125 for online-and-print when they could have the online option for half that price.

Why do consequences surprise systems?

We assess, avert and manage risk by sensing, behaving, thinking and communicating. We do this socially, personally, professionally, operationally and strategically, and we do it whether we are an operator, a manager or a member of the board.

---

9 Gilbert (2005)
10 Ariely (2009)

In our operational or managerial lives, we give ourselves tools to help make our risk-management strategies more systematic and more explicit. Such risk-management tools often take the form of lists of bad things that we think could happen, together with our assessment of how likely they are and how bad they would be if they did occur. Then we formulate measures that we believe will prevent or mitigate each risk and see to it that the resources are in place to support our measures. We also have different, scalable versions of this process – from cascading management spreadsheets to the toolbox talks on the deck just before a job starts. All good stuff, but is it job done?

Here are three systemic reasons why risk-assessment tools and procedures are not enough to prevent surprises in complex systems:

- **Too much variety** Whatever set of measures we put in place to deal with risk, they will never have the requisite variety[11] to deal with everything the world can throw at us. It's worse than this, though. It is not only the case that you are always at the decision point in the SUGAR cycle; everybody else is always at their decision point too. You can talk to some of them and you can attempt to bind everyone together with common procedures. But again, those procedures will never contain sufficient variety to deal with all the variety they may encounter. This is why procedures are, at best, aids to risk-reduced performance. They are as good as the assumptions we make for their conditions of use. If these assumptions fail, reliance on set procedures becomes dangerous.

  In 1979, the operators in the initial stages of the incident at Three Mile Island were locked into such a set of assumptions. These were not properly challenged until the relief crew arrived and applied fresh thinking – more variety – to the situation.[12] The answer here seems to lie in teamwork (which facilitates cross-checking), lots of creative what-if training and a culture that permits people to question each other – especially if things seem to be going too well.

- **Accidents are normal** In 1984, Charles Perrow invited us to consider that the events we call 'accidents' are simply part of the normal range of a system's behaviour – especially when that system is both complex (with lots of agents and variety) and tightly coupled (everything has been made very efficient, redundancy has been reduced, and things are highly interdependent).

  We need to remember that whatever happens is always in the repertoire of the system that produced it, as its components interact with each other. Since these interactions are too various to predict, the answer appears to lie in building resilience into such systems, so that they can detect fragility and brittleness, and maintain their plasticity.

- **Organisational standards drift** In the cut and thrust of operational life, and in the context of making progress and profits, standards can drift over time. Underpinned by our evolved human predilection for efficiency, whole organisations are seduced away from thoroughness and towards greater efficiency. In her account of the *Challenger* disaster (see Chapters 3 and 9), Diane Vaughan[13] called this the "*normalisation of deviance*". In the years leading up to the 1986 *Challenger* launch decision, NASA,

---

11 Ashby's (1956) brilliant exposition of the law of requisite variety showed that if a system is to maintain stability, it must be controlled by something that has an equal or greater number of possible states. As Ashby succinctly concluded, "*only variety can destroy variety*". Since a complex, adaptive system has infinite possible states, there is no way of assuring complete predictive control over it.

12 Kemeny (1979)

13 Vaughan (1986)

sensitive to Congressional scrutiny, failed to notice the degree to which they had been seduced. As the Chair of the Presidential Commission, Richard Feynman, later concluded, *"reality must take precedence over public relations, for nature cannot be fooled"*.

How do you notice organisational drift? In 2001, Karl Weick and his colleagues[14] noticed that dangerous places like aircraft carriers have far fewer accidents than you might expect. Weick described them as High Reliability Organisations (HROs) and was able to show that they were markedly different from the rest. For example, HROs refuse to simplify measures to just a few key performance indicators (KPIs). Instead, they acknowledge the complexity of their world for what it is and try to see as much richness as possible. Another difference is being preoccupied with failure – especially small failures. They use incident-reporting schemes to understand why lapses and near misses happen. Of course, this has fundamental implications for organisational culture. You won't find effective incident-reporting systems in cultures that are focused on blame.

 Read more about fair-minded organisations in **Chapter 12**

 Get help with what individuals and organisations can do about risk in **Chapters 13 and 14**

Our ability to better align our perception of risk with its actual reality will depend on both individual and organisational changes. These include changes in our understanding of the value and function of teamwork, a sea change from finding individual blame to the measurement of organisational resilience, and the development of the kind of fair-minded culture needed to allow these shifts of focus to flourish. These changes are the focus of later chapters of this book and are, in large part, the point of the tools set out in Chapters 13 and 14.

Before we leave the business of what we think we know, we need to spend a little time exploring the distorting impact of another major bias on our thinking. This is the double-edged sword of hindsight, which we explore in the next chapter.

---

14 Weick and Sutcliffe (2001)

9

Being in the know – part IV
how hindsight deceives us

Does hindsight tell us what really happened?

Why is hindsight and root-cause analysis so compelling?

Is human error an explanation, or something that requires one?

Can we use hindsight in a helpful way?

Seeing with hindsight

The forensic analysis of an event shows with the most wonderful clarity how the event unfolded over time. It documents the characteristics, qualifications and actions of the participants in the drama. It establishes the state and serviceability of any vehicles and equipment involved, together with the relevant prevailing environmental conditions. It creates a detailed narrative pinpointing the exact order of events in the simultaneous activity streams of multiple players.

Increasingly, narrative analysis is helped by closed-circuit television (CCTV) footage of the event – often from different angles. While this undoubtedly helps, great caution needs to be applied as to *how* it helps. Once again, the power of context comes to the fore (see Chapter 3: Being framed).

Eugene Caruso and his colleagues recently became concerned about the way CCTV footage was being used in the prosecution of criminal cases of robbery, assault and worse.[1] While the CCTV footage may show without much ambiguity a crime taking place, the punishment meted out to the perpetrators turns out to depend on the degree of presumed intent. Often, such footage is played to real jurors in slow motion so that they can see what's going on more clearly.

In a series of controlled experiments, Caruso and his colleagues showed more than 1,600 people actual surveillance footage of football violence. They found that those who watched it in slow motion were three times more likely to attribute deliberate intent than those who watched it at normal speed. It seems that when the action is slowed down, viewers assume that the perpetrators had more time to think about what they were doing – even though it is perfectly clear that the footage has been slowed down.

---

1   Caruso et al (2016)

Worryingly, this effect persists to a measurable degree even when viewers see both slow-motion and normal-speed versions. This is of high relevance to a number of inmates currently on Death Row in the US, convicted of first-degree murder. For example, the researchers highlight John Lewis, who murdered a policeman during an armed robbery in Philadelphia in 2007. Lewis's appeal against death by lethal injection on the grounds of slow-motion evidence was turned down when the appeal court ruled that jurors had seen both slow-motion and real-time footage.

With caveats about what we can conclude from it, narrative analysis is enormously helpful in describing what happened, once it has happened and now that we know the outcome of the sequence of events described. At the same time, the picture it reveals is mostly illusory for the people who were involved at the time. By definition, hindsight was simply not available to those who were struggling with the uncertainties, partial knowledge and unimagined outcomes at the time they were making their decisions.

Accurate timelines do a great job of retrospectively describing what happened. In accident investigation, such an analysis usually then goes a lot further by trying to establish causal links between actions and outcomes, ultimately arriving at a determination of a *root cause*, which is said to be the primary reason for the calamity. Blame attribution and court cases often follow. Penalties are paid. Personal careers and company reputations are lost. New procedures are issued. Rule books get bigger. And accidents continue to happen.

The problem with all of this is that, however accurate and fine-grained the description, there is no real explanation of what happened unless we consider two further pieces of the jigsaw:

- **The characterisation of the mindsets of those involved – and how it was that they had those mindsets** What did they know – or think they knew – at the time they used that information to act (or decide not to act)? How had they come to those beliefs and knowledge? How reasonable was it for them to construct and interpret the situation they thought they were in? What were the key influences on those interpretations? What options did they actually have? In Chapter 14 (Being practical – part II), we offer a mindset methodology to enhance timeline analysis.

- **The characterisation of the uncertain, complex, adaptive system in which those mindsets were deployed** What uncertainties were people struggling with? What were the wider priorities and goals of the system they were part of at that time? How hard were they – and the rest of the system – working to service those goals? How far had the norms and standards of the whole system drifted towards danger – and for what reasons? We will have more to say about the kind of organisational culture that is required for these questions to be properly considered in Chapter 12 (Being human). We suggest a methodology that organisations can use to characterise the resilience of their systems in Chapter 14.

Root causes are as illusory as the hindsight analysis that generated them. Jim Reason[2] defines a root cause as whatever the investigators had arrived at when they ran out of time and money.[3] One can always ask one more time: 'Why?'

One of the most unhelpful conclusions of root-cause analysis is when it points to some variation of human error. Humans make errors all the time. And most of the time they catch

---

2 Professor Reason is a veteran psychologist with many years of research and publications in human error, including *Human Error* (1990), which set the groundwork for the now widely known 'Swiss Cheese' model of accident causation.

3 Reason et al (2006)

Being Human in safety-critical organisations

their own errors – or those of others – before any real damage is done. The question, then, is what prevented the error from being caught on this particular occasion?

The question can become even more pressing. The fact is that many accidents involve well-practised, adequately qualified people who aren't doing anything very different from what they normally do, when things suddenly go wrong. So what is it that suddenly turns a routine human action into a catastrophic error? Very often, the answer is that the action is only recognised as a mistake when it leads to something bad, ie with hindsight. The unhelpful circularity should be obvious.

Reading accounts of accidents, it is easy to fall into the trap of thinking 'How could they do that?' and 'What were they thinking of?' The panel gives some examples.

What were they thinking of?

On 28 February 2004, the chemical tanker *Bow Mariner* left New York, bound for Houston, Texas. Twenty-two of her tanks were empty except for a potentially explosive vapour remaining from her previous voyage from Saudi Arabia. Six of the remaining tanks contained 13.5 million litres of ethanol. When they were out at sea, the highly experienced captain gave an order that doomed the ship. He told the third officer, on his first voyage as a licensed officer, to open the 22 tanks full of vapour to the air. The infusion of oxygen from the air turned the ship into a floating bomb. The ship exploded and sank 14 hours after sailing, with the loss of 21 seafarers, including the fateful captain. Showing great presence of mind throughout the unfolding chaos – including the sending of the ship distress signal – the third officer survived, along with just five other crew members.[4] How could the captain have done that?

On 13 January 1982, the crew of Air Florida flight 90, a Boeing 737, took off from National Airport in Washington DC in freezing conditions without turning on the engine de-icing equipment. The ice build-up on the wings meant that the aircraft could not gain height. After 30 seconds of laboured flight, it clipped the 14th Street Bridge, striking seven vehicles and killing five of the occupants before plunging through the ice on the Potomac River just 2 miles (3 km) from the White House. There were five survivors, including flight attendant Kelly Duncan, who was captured on TV cameras being dramatically rescued from the freezing river after she had given the only life vest she could find to a passenger. Seventy-six people died.[5] How could the cockpit crew have done that?

On 28 January 1986, in extremely cold conditions, NASA decided to launch the space shuttle *Challenger* even though they knew the O-rings that protected the integrity of the solid fuel were severely cracked. The shuttle broke apart 73 seconds into its flight, at a height of 48,000 feet. In their protected Orbiter craft at the top of the rocket, most of the seven crew survived the disintegration and the resulting three minutes of freefall. With no escape system (deemed too expensive for larger crews), they could not survive the 207 mph impact with the sea, which produced a deceleration force of 200 g.[6] How could NASA have done that?

---

4   Couttie (2014)

5   National Transportation Safety Board (1982)

6   Rogers Commission (1986)

On 8 January 1989, the crew of British Midland flight 92 turned to make an emergency landing at East Midlands Airport, near Kegworth in the UK, after losing an engine in their 737 twin-engine jet. The aircraft crashed into the M1, a major UK highway, just 475 metres short of the runway. The crew had mistakenly shut down the one remaining good engine instead of the one that had flamed out. Thirty-nine people were killed outright and a further eight died later of their injuries. Seventy-nine people survived the impact, including the pilots, although they suffered injuries.[7] How could the cockpit crew have done that?

How could highly qualified, experienced people make those decisions? Two years after the Kegworth crash, Captain Hunt, the senior member of the British Midland crew, asked the crucial question: *"We made a mistake – we both made mistakes – but the question we would like answered is why we made those mistakes."*

Whenever you find yourself thinking something like 'How could they have been so stupid?', you need to catch yourself. You have been seduced by hindsight bias. Those people certainly did not consider they were being stupid – and even less that the actions they took would lead to catastrophe. We need to find out why the actions they took – or thought they were taking – made sense to them in the light of the assumptions, knowledge and understanding they had at the time.

Hindsight makes it easy for us to believe that the things that are obvious now were obvious for those in the thick of the developing incident. It replaces all of the uncertainties and possibilities they were facing then with the crystal clarity we have now. And it permits a compelling, but fictitious, story of an inevitable, causal chain, rather than a series of trade-offs made with uncertain information and little or no control over the resulting interactions.

The second-to-worst thing that can happen

The worst thing that happens in an accident is that people get hurt or die. If we are interested in safety, the next worst thing is that the whole matter becomes a matter for criminal prosecution. The different parties become locked in a struggle to apportion blame, so that decisions can be made about who pays whom how much. As Sidney Dekker observes,[8] when the legal system becomes involved for such purposes, safety is often the first casualty.

The whole court becomes beguiled by assumptions of a deterministic world of simple systems as the search is made for a 'root cause' that can be pinned on specific people or companies. And since accidents in socio-technical systems always involve humans, it will not be long before human error is found. It is at this point that the search usually stops, the finger of blame is pointed and the opportunity to learn valuable lessons vanishes. (See the panel 'Hollnagel's *Safety – I* and *Safety – II*'.)

---

7   AAIB (1990)

8   Dekker (2012)

Hollnagel's *Safety – I* and *Safety – II*

Erik Hollnagel was responsible for the efficiency–thoroughness trade-off[9] idea at the centre of our SUGAR model. In a subsequent book,[10] he makes a compelling distinction between two quite different perspectives on safety.

Safety – I is what organisations, accident investigators and the courts are traditionally concerned with. Its focus is on 'things that go wrong'. When they do, it is assumed that something has caused the transition from normal, prescribed functioning to one where something has failed. In this perspective, it is natural to search for the responsible cause and fix it – for example, via penalties, a new or revised procedure, a new rule, more training, or perhaps by attempting to shock people into being more careful through the use of graphic posters or videos.

Hollnagel describes a number of beliefs inherent in *Safety – I* that, with proper scrutiny, turn out to be myths:

- The belief in differential causality – that things that go right have systematically different causes than things that go wrong, and (therefore) that the latter can be found and eliminated without interfering with the former.
- The belief in the accident pyramid (sometimes depicted as an iceberg) – that there is a one-to-many ratio describing the relationship between fatalities, major injuries, minor injuries, incidents and near misses, and that reducing near-miss events at the bottom of the pyramid will directly improve the negative outcomes higher up.
- The belief in the '90% solution' – that accidents are mainly explained by 'human error'.
- The belief in root causes – that there is a primary and absolute 'first' cause for accidents, which can be unambiguously identified and fixed.
- The belief in compliance – that safety is assured through adherence to procedures.
- The belief in defences – that increasing the quality of barriers will produce better safety.
- The belief in preventability – that 'zero accidents' is possible through the exhaustive identification and elimination of causes.
- The belief in the efficacy of accident investigations – that the logical and rational process they embody is sufficient for the identification of causes from an objective analysis of the facts.
- The belief in the relationship between causes and outcomes – that large and serious outcomes have large and serious causes, and vice versa.
- The belief in safety culture – that 'higher' levels of safety culture will improve safety statistics.
- The belief in 'safety first' – often expressed in the mantra that 'safety is paramount' and that it is non-negotiable.

---

9 Hollnagel (2009)

10 Hollnagel (2014)

Hollnagel presents powerful arguments that explode many of these myths. While he does not suggest jettisoning *Safety – I* thinking altogether, he argues for a new understanding of its effective range of convenience and proposes a major extension, which he calls *Safety – II*.

The focus of *Safety – II* is 'what goes right'. It starts with the realisation that things go relatively well most of the time, but that this is not because people follow laid-down procedures. The belief that safety is guaranteed by the application of prescribed procedures is mistaken. This view of operational life is 'work as imagined' by employing organisations, senior managers and regulatory bodies. Rather, things go well because people are good at sensing the dynamic demands of their complex operational lives, and constantly vary their performance as they make adjustments in the moment. Furthermore, they are successful more than 99% of the time.

These ideas are central to our SUGAR model, and some of the practical ways to facilitate and optimise the emergence of safety from 'work as done' are the concern of Chapter 14 (Being practical – part II).

The pointing of a single finger of blame at a single piece of behaviour that was judged singly responsible for what went wrong was the extraordinary conclusion of the investigation into the tragedy of Concorde flight 4590.

The tragic story of Concorde, Air France 4590

At 14.30 on 25 July 2000, Air France 4590, a Concorde supersonic passenger aircraft with a cruising speed of 1,350 mph, took off from Roissy Charles de Gaulle Airport in Paris. Its flight plan aimed to deliver its passengers to JFK Airport in New York just three-and-a-half hours later.

In the cockpit were Flying Captain Christian Marty, 54, First Officer Jean Marcot, 50, and Flight Engineer Gilles Jardinaud, 58. Ninety-six of the 100 passengers were German tourists on their way to join a cruise ship in Ecuador via a connecting flight from JFK. They were on the trip of a lifetime and were looking forward to a stylish service from the six Concorde cabin crew on this, the first major leg.

As the Concorde taxied towards its take-off position at one end of the runway, it weighed in at 186 tonnes. Half of that was fuel. In fact, Air France 4590 was 1 tonne above its certified maximum weight[11] and would need at least 3 km of the 4 km runway 26R to get airborne.

Shortly after 14.42, Captain Marty set the four huge Rolls-Royce Olympus 593 engines to maximum thrust. Forty seconds later, at V1,[12] the aircraft was at the point of no return. As it passed V1, travelling at a speed of 150 knots, there was an unusual and violent deviation to the left.[13] Down below, one of the eight huge main tyres had fragmented. A 4.5 kg piece

---

11 Rose (2001) claims that the aircraft was actually 6 tonnes above the maximum weight for the runway length, given wind conditions that had recently changed, producing a tail wind of 8 knots.

12 V1 is the aircraft speed beyond which the take-off cannot be aborted without exceeding the available runway.

13 The official accident report (BEA, 2002) says that the sudden veering to the left was because of uneven thrust from the right side when the left engines were damaged by the ingress of tyre debris. Controversially, Rose (2001) claims that a failure to reinstall a spacer in the landing gear produced several degrees of uncontrolled freedom, which were enough to twist the gear and cause a sideways trajectory. Rose bolsters his claim with skid-mark analysis and Concorde pilot testimony that engine loss does not produce uncontrollable yaw.

of rubber struck the underside of the left wing, just below the completely full tank 5. The resulting pressure wave inside the tank blew a hole in it, dumping a large amount of fuel on the runway. Fuel sprayed out of the ruptured tank at 60 kg per second, combining with sufficient oxygen to create a viable mixture for ignition. And just then, an ignition source was provided – probably by a short-circuiting power cable in the damaged landing-gear bay. The fuel erupted into a streak of flame 50 metres long and 3 metres wide that tailed behind the stricken aircraft.

The aircraft was now in a desperate no-man's land between V1 and VR,[14] and still veering towards a just-landed Boeing 747 that happened to contain Jacques Chirac and his wife, the President and First Lady of France, returning from the G7 summit in Japan. Aborting the take-off now would mean running off the end of the runway at over 70 knots (80 mph), the landing gear breaking up and the aircraft bursting into flames, with certain catastrophic loss. Captain Marty chose the most compelling option and gently rotated the aircraft off the ground. It was travelling at 183 knots (210 mph), 15 knots below its intended VR of 198 knots (228 mph).

Inside the passenger cabin, the crew noticed the unusual engine surges, the strange sideways movements, the sudden accelerations and the acrid smell of jet fuel being pumped into the air-conditioning system by the failing engines.

Captain Marty achieved take-off. Seventeen seconds into the flight, at a speed of 200 knots (230 mph) and a height of 200 feet, he called for the landing gear to be raised. Long flames extended from underneath the aircraft. The gear refused to retract, despite several attempts. Flight Engineer Jardinaud had already shut down engine 2. Engine 1 now lost thrust. The aircraft banked sharply to the left, went nose up, turned through 180 degrees, and finally dropped almost flat out of the sky, striking the back of the Hotelissimo in Gonesse. The impact demolished the hotel as the Concorde erupted into a huge fireball, instantly killing all 100 passengers, nine crew and four others on the ground.

Back on the runway, just where the aircraft's tyre had fragmented, was a thin titanium strip 43 cm long. It had fallen off a Continental DC-10 that had taken off five minutes earlier.

The strip was a piece of edging that had been fitted to the reverse thruster cowl of one of the DC-10's engines a few hours earlier, back at Continental's hub in Houston, Texas.

Concorde accident investigators examined the procedures involved in wear-strip replacement at Continental. They found inconsistencies and difficulties. For example, the aircraft manufacturer specified that the wear strips needed to be fabricated from steel, although the original 1979 design had been titanium.[15] Confusingly, their maintenance procedures contained a note stating that "alternative solutions can be used for tools, equipment and consumables recommended". The procedure for wear-strip maintenance was categorised as a "minor repair" involving no special tools and no post-repair inspection. Yet the procedure was difficult to complete using the manufacturer's original method and it had evolved over time in the interests of practicality and efficiency. Is this ringing any alarm bells?

---

14 VR is the aircraft speed at which the pilot flying moves the controls back to lift the aircraft off the ground (referred to as 'rotation').

15 Learmount (2000)

But there's more context to come. The very same wear strip that had been replaced in Houston and had now fallen off onto the Paris runway had been replaced six weeks previously by Continental maintainers in Tel Aviv. In that short time, it had become twisted and was protruding from the cowl, requiring a second fix. The Houston fix was allegedly made by John Taylor, a 32-year-old Danish-born fitter who had been living in the US since he was three. Once the accident report was published, French prosecutors got started.

In 2010, ten years after the crash, Continental Airlines and John Taylor were found criminally responsible for the disaster by a Parisian court. Others were prosecuted, but all except John Taylor were acquitted. The airline was fined €200,000 ($200,000) and ordered to pay Air France €1 million plus 70% of all compensation claims. Taylor was given a 15-month suspended sentence and fined €2,000. His manager, Stanley Ford, was acquitted, along with three French employees of Air France and the French civil aviation watchdog.

The conclusion of the case was that just one individual 4,000 miles (6,500 km) away in Texas had been solely responsible for the disaster. This was problematic to say the least. And two years later, even the French appeal court agreed: in December 2012, it overturned the criminal charges against both Continental and Taylor, leaving Continental to face the compensation claims under civil law.

One problem here is that while the court was fixated on the findings of the accident investigation, those findings – all based on hindsight – had little to say about the relevant mindsets of the individuals they subsequently blamed. We therefore don't know:

- Why the wear-strip repair in Tel Aviv did not work; how problematic wear strips were; how many times they fell off DC-10s in service; and, therefore, what was common thinking and practice among DC-10 fitters in the context of this 'minor repair'.

- Why the wear strip replaced at Houston was deliberately fabricated in titanium. Was it due to the inconsistent workshop manual that appeared to allow alternative materials, plus the fact that the part was originally fabricated in titanium? Or was it because the fitter was responsibly trying to achieve greater quality and longevity than had been achieved by his Tel Aviv colleagues?

- How fatigued, stressed or loaded was the fitter who did the job that day. Was there anything that he could have known about himself, and over which he had control, that would influence his performance? What about his supervisor and colleagues?

- What was the culture of the management and workers at the maintenance depot. How often were procedures violated at Continental? What was the supervisory attitude towards them? How much was productivity (efficiency) valued over safety (thoroughness)? What measures were in place for rewards and sanctions? Did the fitter do anything different from what any other fitter would have done on that day?

These and related questions move beyond hindsight, into the province of mindset. Mindset is all about establishing the narratives that those involved were using to explain their behaviour to themselves at the time. Mindsets are not concerned with the alien world of absolute rationality, where probability theory lives, but local rationality, where we find people's real purposes, priorities and reasons for doing things. Hindsight-based analysis encourages us to inhabit a world of 'work as imagined' by those who don't do it. Mindset-based analysis provides us with the opportunity to understand the world of 'work as done'. We describe our approach to Mindset Analysis in Chapter 14 (Being practical – part II).

Establishing mindset is not about avoiding accountability, but establishing fair grounds for it. If those in the thick of an incident or its precursors had genuine choices that they ignored due to indolence, malice or any other deliberate breach of professional standard, then they should be held accountable in accordance with those deliberate oversights. However, if their behaviour emerged from best intentions, lack of training, lax supervision or management pressure, then the search for accountability must continue. And if the behaviour turns out to be a locally rational adaptation of system components as they adjust to each other in the pursuit of multiple agendas, then the whole system must be examined to understand the extent to which it has drifted towards danger – and why.

 Read more about accountability and responsibility in **Chapter 12**

In December 2013, Taylor started a lawsuit against his old employer for $3.5 billion (three times the amount paid to the crash victims). His lawyer claimed that Taylor had never worked on the DC-10 and that he had been targeted due to his union activities.[16] At the time this book was published, the outcome was unknown.

An evolutionary perspective

Looking over these last four chapters on Understanding in the SUGAR model, it is helpful to take an evolutionary perspective. The genus *Homo* evolved over 2.5 million years, until *Homo sapiens* emerged on the African plains 200,000 years ago. Then, 70,000 years ago, we suddenly developed the ability to communicate whatever we could imagine. The migration of modern humans across the planet began and has been accelerating ever since.

 Read more about what it means to be human in a complex world in **Chapter 12**

But over these 70 millennia, little has changed about the way our brains work. In the context of our long evolution and our new understanding of the complex, adaptive systems of which we are all a part, punishing people for being human is misinformed at best. At worst, it achieves the opposite of what is aimed for – a crucial matter to which we shall return in Chapter 12 (Being human).

 Get help with how to increase safety and resilience in ways that acknowledge our evolved humanity in **Chapter 14**

---

16 Bouboushian (2013)

10 Being on target
managing purposes, procrastination, plans and practice

Why do you do the job you do?

What really motivates you and your colleagues?

Why do you put things off and what can you do about it?

What part do impulses, habits and willpower play?

How does a plan help – and what dangers can a plan create?

How can you go from being competent at work to being an expert?

Goals in the SUGAR model

In this chapter we come to the third class of human factors influencing our approach to job performance and safety: *goals*. 'State' is about what condition we are in, and 'Understanding' is about how we perceive and make sense of the situation we are in. 'Goals' is about what motivates us, what we want to achieve and how we energise ourselves to do it.

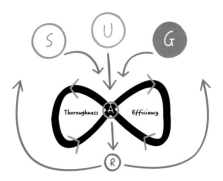

Read more about State in **Chapter 5** and about Understanding in **Chapters 6 to 9**

Motivation is a crucial ingredient to safety-critical operations. People need to be motivated to do the right thing and to remain committed to their objectives when the going gets tough, or even dangerous.

We all have many goals, of many different types. They are driven by several different kinds of motivation. Some of these drivers turn out to be surprisingly different from what we think motivates us. Sometimes, our different goals conflict with each other. And sometimes, the goals that we have are different from the goals that we *should* have.

In this chapter we explore goals and motivation, and how we balance them. We examine their influence on our trade-offs between efficiency and thoroughness and discover ways in which we can exert more control, so that we improve our ability to direct our activities effectively.

What gets you out of bed?

You are warm and comfortable in bed. The alarm on your smartphone goes off. Why should you leave your very pleasant situation and face the day and all the demands it is likely to bring? It's a working day and you should be at work in an hour and a half. You're tempted just to turn over and pull the duvet over your head. But you probably don't. Why not?

One obvious reason is that if you don't go to work, you won't get paid. You have a family to care for, food and clothes to buy, rent to pay; the monthly instalment on your car is due. And so on. Unless you come from a wealthy family or have just won the lottery, you don't have much choice: you need to work.

But you probably do have a choice about the particular job you do. If you looked around, the chances are that you could find other jobs to do – possibly jobs that would pay you more than your present one. You also have a choice about *how* you do your job. Are you fully engaged in your work? Do you go to work willingly or do you have to drag yourself there? When you are working, do you attend to every detail? Do you stick to the rules? When there are problems, are you willing to put yourself out to solve them? Do you sometimes act on impulse? Do you put off doing tasks you should do, building up difficulties for later? These are all issues of motivation.

What is motivation?

Motivation is what prompts you into action. You move, rather than just sitting there. It is the reason for your action. If someone asks *"Why did you do that?"*, your answer is likely to be in terms of your motivation:

Q: *"Why did you go to Barcelona?"*

A: *"I wanted to visit old friends/I wanted to watch Messi play football/I wanted to get some sunshine/My boss told me to go."*

Motivation has two aspects. First, as a reason for action, it determines what you are moving towards: your goal (visiting friends in Barcelona). Second, in conjunction with the decision to pursue this goal, motivation releases the energy you need to reach your desired goal (eg going online to buy tickets, packing, driving to the airport).

Where does motivation come from?

Motivation arises from a variety of needs and wants. Our most basic needs have to do with our *survival*. As we noted when discussing why you get out of bed, much of your motivation will come from your basic survival needs: to eat, sleep, be clothed, have a roof over your head, etc. These are rooted in your physiology and, as such, are needs you share with all human beings. We can also include here your needs for *health and safety*. You need to be protected from harmful agents and conditions. If these needs are not met, then quite simply you will not thrive and quite possibly not survive.

As we discuss at greater length in Chapter 11 (Being together), human beings are profoundly social beings. This gives rise to our *social* needs: warm, close relationships with family, friends and colleagues; love and affection; respect; status. In many societies, one of the worst punishments is ostracism – when a person is completely ignored by their community. Others behave as if you did not exist. In the old English phrase, the punished person is 'sent to Coventry'. In fact, our social needs are not so different from our health-and-safety needs. Recent neuroscientific studies have shown that the social pain of ostracism is registered in the brain in the same way as physical pain.[1]

So far, we have been talking about *needs*: things we must have to ensure our physical and social well-being. A need is something you cannot do without. Accordingly, much of our behaviour is driven by needs. But we also have *wants*. A want is something we desire, but we probably won't be harmed if we don't get it. A four-year-old in the supermarket may declare to her parents "*I need chocolate!*", but in most cases she won't die without it, whatever she says.

Needs are common to all human beings, in varying degrees, but wants are much more individual. You may want to get your master's ticket by the time you are 28, buy a Mercedes, or visit New York. You see your job as the means to achieving these wants. Even if I do the same job as you, my list of wants is likely to be completely different from yours.

All of these survival and social needs, and individual wants, may be good reasons why you do your job. They may be sufficient to motivate you to work really hard. But they have nothing to do with the work itself. The job is just a means to an end. You could be just as motivated doing another job if it paid the same or gave you an equally fast route to promotion. This type of motivation is known as *extrinsic*, since it is external to the job itself. Extrinsic motivation can often involve the fear of not having these needs and wants fulfilled – for example, the fear of being disciplined, losing one's job, or failing to earn enough to buy the desired house or car.

The income you get from your work is important because it enables you to meet your basic survival needs and, hopefully, at least some of your individual wants. How much you are paid is also likely to have an impact on your social needs, in terms of giving you appropriate status in your community. For these reasons, you may think of money as your primary motivator.

Following this reasoning, most managers think that if they pay more, then people will perform better. However, there is now a large body of evidence that says the relationship between money and performance is not so simple.[2] For straightforward, largely manual or 'piecework' activities (eg production-line tasks, picking fruit), rewarding greater productivity with more pay works. But if the work requires any degree of thinking, creative problem-solving and the like, performance suffers when higher financial rewards are at stake. Striving for more financial rewards damages mental work.

As we have noted, money is an extrinsic motivator: the work is just a means to an end. But there is also *intrinsic* motivation – reasons for doing a job that are integral to the work itself. A builder may choose his work because he loves working with his hands, the feeling of the materials, the satisfaction of creating something that did not exist before. A doctor may be drawn to her profession because she loves working with people and helping them get better. A person may become a scientist because of deep curiosity about the nature of the universe and an attraction to intellectual challenges.

---

1   Williams & Nida (2011)

2   See, for example, Barber (2010), Chamorro-Premuzic (2013) and Frey (1997)

Historically, managers in many industries have focused almost exclusively on extrinsic rewards, especially pay. Since the beginning of the Industrial Revolution in the late 18th century, work has become increasingly fragmented.[3] The division of labour, the breaking up of processes into smaller and smaller steps, has contributed to huge increases in productivity while simultaneously reducing the skills required of the worker, ie making labour cheaper. From the factory production line, the same principles have been extended to service industries (eg fast-food outlets) and to administrative work in offices.

In 1776, Adam Smith published *The Wealth of Nations*, which laid the foundations for the discipline of economics. Smith famously observed how productivity could be increased in the manufacture of pins by dividing between a number of workers the various tasks that had previously been carried out by one person: "*One man draws out the wire, another straights it, a third cuts it, a fourth points it, a fifth grinds it at the top for receiving the head; to make the head requires two or three distinct operations; to put it on, is a peculiar business, to whiten the pins is another; it is even a trade by itself to put them into the paper; and the important business of making a pin is, in this manner, divided into about eighteen distinct operations.*" By this arrangement, Smith calculated that productivity could be increased four thousand fold.[4]

The price paid for increased productivity and reduced labour costs has been the loss of most of the intrinsic rewards of work. It is hard to see what pleasure or satisfaction can be gained from sticking the heads on pins for many hours a day. In such circumstances, the worker has no reason to do their job other than for the pay. Even the pay is probably not sufficient to keep them fully engaged with their work for hour after hour. Hence in such workplaces there is a need for constant, strict supervision to ensure the worker sticks to their task. The result is that, all around the world, people are doing work that is boring and unsatisfying. Money to meet life's needs is the only reason for doing their jobs.

For many years, Gallup has carried out a global poll measuring engagement in the workplace. It uses three levels of engagement:

- **Engaged** employees work with passion. Because they feel a strong connection to the organisation, they work hard to innovate and improve.

- **Not-engaged** employees do the work expected of them, but they do not put in extra effort.

- **Actively disengaged** employees aren't just unhappy, but are spreading their unhappiness to other staff.

The figures from the 2012 global survey showed that only 13% of employees were engaged. Of the rest, 63% were not engaged and 24% were actively disengaged.[5] If these numbers are typical of employees working in safety-critical operations, they point to a major problem. Look again at the definitions of the three levels of engagement. It is highly probable that if systems are going to be safe, they need a workforce that is engaged. Only engaged employees are going to take that extra care, put in that extra effort that will prevent complex systems from sliding over their safety boundaries. This is borne out by a 2016 analysis of the Gallup workplace engagement data: organisations with the highest levels of employee engagement

3   For a highly readable account of how modern organisations have been influenced by the writings of Adam Smith and many of the ideas raised here, see Schwartz (2015).

4   Smith (1776), book 1, chapter 1, paragraph 1.1.3

5   Crabtree (2013)

have 70% fewer safety incidents than organisations with the lowest levels of engagement.[6] This is a finding of the greatest significance but it is questionable how many safety-critical organisations are aware of this connection and work actively to promote staff engagement.

It is also worth noting that a quarter of employees are actively disengaged. Attempts at intense control of these people are likely to provoke hidden acts of sabotage or even open rebellion.

Such a control strategy rarely works. Supervision might be effective while the supervisor is present, but as soon as their attention is turned elsewhere, standards will drop. Similarly, if someone is motivated only by money, and they are asked to do something extra for which they will not be paid, then they are unlikely to do it. Somebody might, for example, notice that another team member has not carried out some safety-critical task. If this person has only external motivation, they may well not take it upon themselves to do this task. *"It's not my job"* is the usual response. Does this seem unlikely in a safety-critical setting? It's exactly what happened on *Herald of Free Enterprise* when the bosun did not cover for the assistant bosun. The bosun's inaction was by no means the complete story, of course, but the ship left harbour with her bow doors open, she capsized, and 193 people died.[7]

> **Read more** about the *Herald of Free Enterprise* tragedy in **Chapter 4**

What is required is that staff are fully engaged with their work. Externally imposed controls – far from being effective – are in fact usually counterproductive. This is because engagement relies on intrinsic motivation and attempts at extrinsic motivation actually make intrinsic motivation evaporate.

Why should this be?

Organisations that seek to reduce safety-related incidents typically resort to a strategy of control. They try a mixture of financial rewards, competitions, league tables, ever more rules and regulations, closer supervision, performance assessment, and disciplinary action against transgressors. It should be noted that rewards and punishments are essentially the same when used to control. They both involve costs for the person who deviates from what the organisation demands (eg loss of bonuses, missing out on promotion).

But a large body of research concludes: *"Deadlines, imposed goals, surveillance, and evaluations ... undermine intrinsic motivation ... These events drain people's enthusiasm and interest."*[8] We can compare this to children's relationships with play and lessons. Play is an activity that the child is interested in and is fun. Children *want* to play. Lessons are what they *have to* do. Children learn far more from play than they do from lessons. Lessons are *work*, and work implies compulsion and control.

Adults may not think of themselves as playing, but they make the same distinction between things they want to do and things they have to do. What is it about situations that make people want to work in them, with minimal or even no need for external control?

---

6   Rigoni & Nelson (2016)

7   Sheen (1987)

8   Deci & Flaste (1996), p. 31

Deeper levels of motivation

Many organisations still adhere to the carrot-and-stick concept of motivation: go in the direction I want you to and you get a carrot; go in any other direction or go too slowly and you receive a sharp reminder. For many years, workers in many industries were referred to as 'hands'. This reflected a certain reality. They were employed to do the manual tasks that were too tricky or too expensive to be done by machines. Any deviation from the prescribed movements was forbidden.

For simple, repetitive, routine, algorithmic tasks, the carrot-and-stick approach can produce results. But increasingly – especially in complex safety-critical activities – the tasks performed by humans cannot be reduced to algorithms or simple procedures.

In the age of complex, adaptive systems, skilful hands are still often required, but in conjunction with clever human senses and brains. As we described earlier, it is the task of the human to constantly monitor and adjust their part of the system when it moves towards the boundary with danger. Most critically, it is the task of the human to come up with novel solutions when problems are encountered that were not – and probably could not have been – predicted by the system designers. This kind of work requires knowledge and expertise gained through experience. Extensive research has shown that where a task requires intellectual focus and inventiveness, the attempt to induce and maintain motivation by control is generally doomed. As it turns out, control damages those capabilities of people that are most important in ensuring that complex systems remain safe. We can compare the situation with parents who control their child's every move. While at home, the child may indeed be kept safe, but it never learns how to cope with difficulties and setbacks later in life.

 Read more about the nature of complex, adaptive systems and why they are important in **Chapter 12**

Read more about the difficulties of self-monitoring in **Chapter 7**

 Get help with these issues in **Chapter 13**

A recent study by Størkersen and his team,[9] examining the introduction of safety management systems (SMS) in the maritime world, makes some valuable points. The introduction of an SMS manifests itself in the form of greatly increased numbers of written procedures. Where these procedures are consistent with a seafarer's concept of seamanship, especially regarding personal injuries, they tend to be followed. But where they clash with the seafarer's idea of seamanship or are too distracting or time consuming, they tend to be ignored.

The function most negatively affected by SMS procedures is navigation. This has potential implications for ship accidents such as groundings. The Størkersen team found that most navigators "*are quite negative towards the effects of the International Safety Management (ISM) code, feeling that it may actually have worsened safety ... They describe the safety systems as a 'necessary evil', which improves safety in some ways but at the expense of good seamanship and practical attention and, therefore, might decrease safety in other ways.*"

---

9   Størkersen et al (2016), pp. 10–13

If the normal external controls of reward and punishment do not make people resourceful and creative, then what does? Research over four decades provides clear answers: *autonomy*, *mastery*, *purpose*, *belonging* and *fairness*.[10] Of course, individuals will have specific intrinsic motivations, but these five fundamental factors provide the foundations for the person's overall level of motivation.

Let's explain what they are and how they work.

Autonomy We all want a certain freedom in how we do our work. We want to be treated as responsible adults, able to exercise intelligent choices. Everybody thinks this way about themselves, but we often think that others need stricter guidance or control. Jobs are frequently designed to eliminate the opportunities for making choices. This leads to a lack of job satisfaction and underperformance. Of course, in most safety-critical work there cannot be total freedom of action. There has to be a framework that sets some limits. But as far as possible, the system should give the operator a 'space' within which they can move freely. Setting limits should be about encouraging the individual to act responsibly, not about trying to control or manipulate them.

Mastery The development of increasing levels of competence is in itself highly motivating. We not only want to do something of value (see *Purpose*, below); we want to know that we are getting better at our work. If the job is too simple or is overprescribed, this not only reduces the operator's sense of having autonomy; it also restricts the operator's opportunities to develop progressively higher skills, the acquisition of which is highly rewarding in its own right.

Purpose Human beings seek meaning. What we perceive to be happening depends very much on what we think it means. Attributing meaning is very much an individual affair, but in the world of work there are certain fundamentals. We want to know what the purpose of our work is. What is it for? We derive enormous value in knowing that our work is in pursuit of some larger cause. Such work is not just about making a profit, but in some way improving the lives of people, providing what they need, making the world a better place. Many psychologists and psychiatrists have demonstrated that a sense of purpose or meaning in one's life is essential for full mental well-being.[11]

Read more about how humans create meaning in **Chapter 7**

Belonging Humans are eminently social beings. At the heart of our social nature is a deep need to belong to families, groups, communities, nations. This has a direct motivational effect: a person is more likely to be committed to their work if they feel they belong in their workplace. It can also have an indirect effect: the person absorbs and adopts the motivations of their colleagues in the workplace. As we see in Chapter 11 (Being together), this can be for good or ill.

Fairness Humans need to be treated fairly. Most people are willing to accept the consequences if they know they have done something wrong. What will hugely demotivate

---

10 In his best-seller *Drive* (2011), Dan Pink covers the first three motivations, drawing on the work of Edward Deci and others. The need for fairness is discussed at length in Dekker (2012) and later in this book (see Chapter 12: Being human). Deci & Flaste (1996) discuss the need for belonging, as well as autonomy and purpose. A discussion specifically about belonging as a fundamental human motivation is also given in Baumeister & Leary (1995).

11 See, for example, Frankl (1959) and Allport (1955)

them is being blamed for something for which they were not responsible. Often, organisations blame individuals unfairly. Working with complex systems always involves an element of risk. A person may have made the best decision they could in a difficult situation and the outcome may still be bad – through no fault of their own. To fail to take account of the full context in which a decision was made is unjust. If a person feels they have been treated unjustly or have observed colleagues being treated unjustly, their commitment is eroded. This fundamental need to be treated fairly is one of the reasons why organisations must develop a 'just' culture as a vital element of resilience.

Read more about the importance of fair-minded accountability and the place of 'just' cultures in **Chapter 12**

Get help with developing resilience in **Chapter 14**

The organisations that are successful and that remain successful in the long term are those that have motivated and committed staff. Managers often ask *"How can I motivate my staff?"* Edward Deci has pointed out that this is the wrong question. A better question is *"How can I create the conditions within which others will motivate themselves?"*[12] Self-motivation will always outperform external sources of motivation. Creating the conditions in which the powerful motivators of autonomy, mastery, purpose, belonging and fairness can work properly is largely about providing opportunities and removing obstacles. We discuss how to do this in Chapters 13 and 14 (Being practical).

Motivational issues in high-risk environments

We have stressed that safety-critical operations rely on people who are highly committed and motivated. However, even with the best-motivated staff, problems can still arise. We now look at some of the issues that are particularly important in safety-critical activities.

We all have many goals: some professional, some personal; some long-term, some short-term. Some of your most obvious goals will be defined by your job. If you are a ship's engineer, your goal will be to ensure that the engines are working properly, as required by the master and the officer of the watch. If you work in healthcare, your goals will be to keep your patients healthy and to return them to health if they get ill. The organisation for which you work will expect you to achieve these goals. But sometimes there will be a conflict, or at least a tension, between goals – even ones that are an inherent part of your job.

The conflict between efficiency and thoroughness

In March 1967, the oil tanker *Torrey Canyon* was on a voyage from Kuwait to Milford Haven. After delays during a stop-over in the Canaries, the vessel was running short of time to reach her destination. As the ship approached the UK coast, the master decided to make up time by taking a shortcut through the Scilly Isles. He made this decision knowing that he would have to sail through a narrow channel, and even though he lacked a chart with sufficient detail for close navigation. While manoeuvring to avoid fishing boats, *Torrey Canyon* hit Pollard's Rock in the Seven Stones reef, and ripped open six tanks. Over the next 12 days, the entire cargo of 119,000 tonnes of Kuwaiti crude oil escaped. It polluted 270 square miles

---

12 Deci & Flaste (1996), p. 10

(700 square km) of sea and 170 miles (270 km) of the French and English coastlines. It remains one of the worst oil spills ever.[13]

Organisations involved in safety-critical work have a vested interest in both thoroughness and efficiency.[14] The metrics for efficiency, such as productivity, delivery to customers on time, costs of resources used, and so on, are very immediate and concrete. These metrics are at the front of managers' minds on a daily basis. Thoroughness, especially safety, is not so salient. Of course, most managers want to keep their staff safe and avoid damage to the environment, but these are concerns about things that *might* happen, and day by day usually do *not* happen. It is natural that managers tend to give their staff messages about efficiency more frequently and with greater emphasis than messages about thoroughness. Safety is a matter for monthly briefings, whereas getting the job done is a message continually repeated each day.

> **Read more** about the efficiency–thoroughness trade-off in **Chapter 4**

The likely effect of this managerial tendency is that staff will be motivated to favour efforts aimed at efficiency rather than thoroughness. This obviously increases the risk of unsafe acts – for example, shortcuts to speed up tasks or the omission of safety checks. One famous example of this is RMS *Titanic*, where the company and captain maintained a high speed in an attempt to break the record for crossing the Atlantic in spite of sailing through an area where icebergs had been reported.

Conflicts between competing motivations may also help to explain the behaviour of Captain Veldhuyzen van Zanten, the pilot of the KLM jumbo jet in the Tenerife airport disaster discussed in Chapter 8 (Being in the know – part III). The pilot tried to take off down a runway masked by fog before he had clearance from air traffic control. It is noteworthy that Captain Veldhuyzen van Zanten was both the public face of KLM's reputation for punctuality and its head of airline safety. Possibly as a result of all the frustration and delays he had experienced, the captain prioritised punctuality (ie efficiency) over safety, with disastrous consequences.[15]

Other motivational conflicts

Although the tension between thoroughness and efficiency is the most evident of the potential conflicts between goals, other conflicts can occur. A common source of conflict is when personal goals clash with professional goals. For example, you are coming to the end of your shift. You have nearly finished some maintenance tasks on an important piece of equipment. It probably won't be needed overnight but it just might be. Ideally you'd finish the maintenance. But you also have social plans for the evening.

Do you let your personal motivations influence your behaviour at work? This is an example of a short-term personal goal possibly influencing your behaviour, with potential safety implications. Other conflicts may involve long-term goals, perhaps to do with your career ambitions. Consider this dilemma. Your company offers you a posting that will be good for your prospects for promotion. But it will mean being away from your home and family for a year. What do you decide?

---

13 Cahill (1990)

14 Before Hollnagel (2009), James Reason (2000) expressed this thought with the remark that all organisations must strive to maintain a delicate balance between production and protection.

15 Subsecretaría de Aviación Civil (1978)

There is a particular risk where a person experiences two competing motivations equally strongly. Such a situation can result in inaction, the person acting on neither goal. This is illustrated by the ancient story of Buridan's ass. In this story, a donkey is equally hungry and thirsty, but it is standing between a bucket of water and a bale of hay. Unable to decide which way to turn, the donkey dies.

Motivation and values

We asked earlier where your motivation comes from. The two examples we've just presented illustrate that, at its deepest level, motivation is derived from your values – what really matters to you. Is it making money? Gaining status and power? Career progression? Or do you value work to provide goods or services that meet real human needs? Is it important to you that people are kept from harm and the environment from damage?

What will also be important is how well your organisation's values match your personal values. You are unlikely to be fully committed to an organisation whose values are fundamentally different from your own.

Procrastination

In 2002, the tanker *Prestige* was struck by a large wave off Cape Finisterre and sustained structural damage. This was followed by several days of struggles to save the vessel while negotiations/arguments continued between the ship operator and owner, various salvage tugs and companies, and the Spanish authorities. Eventually *Prestige* broke up, resulting in the worst-ever pollution of the Spanish and Portuguese coasts. The precise course of events remains unclear and responsibility for the disaster has never been assigned in spite of investigations and a court case (held only in 2012).[16]

At one point the Spanish authorities accused the master of *Prestige* of 'procrastination' over setting up a tow from one of the tugs. The master disputed the authorities' account, but even so, was this really a case of procrastination? He had chosen to remain in a position of great danger, trying to save his ship while grappling with legal and commercial issues over salvage, as well as trying to resist instructions from the Spanish authorities for the ship to be towed out to sea, rather than to a place of safe refuge (which would be the normal practice).

If the master took time to make a difficult decision over the tow, this seems understandable. This does not seem to us to be an example of procrastination. In everyday usage, procrastination normally refers to someone not taking action that is plainly necessary and obvious. The following is a clear-cut example of procrastination leading to undesired consequences.

A ferry had some internal piping protruding through the deck. It ran along the toe rail for several feet until it bent back below deck, and the crew would stand on it while handling lines during docking and undocking. The captain and owner were both made aware by an insurance surveyor that this was a trip hazard. There was also the possibility that a work boot could become lodged under the piping. It was one of those 'we'll fix it when we get time' deals. The fix was finally attended to $350,000 later, when a crewman twisted his knee and filed a Jones Act claim.[17]

---

16 Bahamas Maritime Authority (2004) and BBC (2012)

17 McKeever (2016)

We probably all procrastinate at some time or another. We know we have to do something, but we just cannot find sufficient motivation to act. This may be a particular example of conflicting goals – we want to do something other than what we are supposed to be doing. It may be that the task we have to do is boring, difficult, or anxiety provoking. Or it may be that we just cannot summon up the energy. It is tempting to say *"I'll just make a cup of coffee first."* Or *"I'll do it this afternoon or maybe tomorrow."* We are highly skilled at persuading ourselves that the task can wait. *"I checked this machine last week and it was fine."* *"I am sure George will have done this on the last shift – he always does."*

Ever-present social media pose a special threat of procrastination. Most of us have a smartphone, tablet or laptop within easy reach. *"I'll just check my texts/Facebook feed/ email/WhatsApp messages, then I'll do this task."* We think that this will just take a few seconds, and a very short delay in starting the task won't really matter. Contact with friends and family can give a little emotional buzz that is far more attractive than getting on with the task at hand. But then there is a message that we really have to reply to, and oh, they've replied at once to my reply, so I'll just text back. And suddenly the time to do the task is gone, and something else more urgent must be attended to.

We imagine that tomorrow we will feel more motivated, more energetic; we'll have more time. But the reality is that tomorrow will be pretty much like today. So the task doesn't get done, and the seed of an accident has germinated.

Impulses

We all sometimes act impulsively, although some of us may have a tendency to be more impulsive than others. At first sight, impulsiveness and procrastination seem to be opposites. When we procrastinate, we delay doing something we should do now. When we are impulsive, we do something without any delay. But both procrastination and impulsiveness are motivational problems. When I procrastinate, I am not motivated enough or I have conflicting motivations. When I act impulsively, I am too motivated. We often buy the item we see in the shop, only to regret it later. We regret the expense, or we realise that we had overegged its benefits or overlooked its drawbacks. We eat the cake on the table even though we don't really want it. We say a harsh word to a colleague or family member in a heated moment and later try to make amends.

Impulsive behaviour is obviously related to the *System 1* thinking[18] we discussed in Chapter 7 (Being in the know – part II). *System 1* is the fast, automatic thinking that we rely on much of the time. In his book *Impulse*, David Lewis[19] says that impulsive actions occur *mindlessly* rather than *mindfully*. We only think of an act as impulsive when we subsequently reflect on what we have done and see that it did not work out well. We should have used *System 2*, our more considered, deliberate, slower form of thinking. Why didn't we?

System 1 works a lot with associations. For example, we see a coat when we are out shopping. *System 1* immediately associates this coat with our memories of previous purchases: how warm previous coats kept us on snowy days, the pleasure we got from owning something fashionable, the compliments we received from family and friends when we first wore the coat. These associations translate into powerful desires, which we may act on immediately.

18 Kahneman (2011)
19 Lewis (2014)

Another reason for not engaging a full thinking process is that we are unduly influenced by the people around us. Maybe you are out for the night with friends. They are drinking heavily. You don't want to drink so much, but your motivation to belong, to be accepted by the group, is stronger than your desire to remain sober. (See also Chapter 11: Being together.)

Imitation of others can have a physiological basis. Neuroscience[20] has suggested the existence of *mirror neurons* in our brains. When we see someone else doing something (drinking, say), then the neurons in the parts of our brains that are active when we ourselves are drinking are themselves activated. Our brains mirror what we are seeing. Not only do we mirror others' actions; we mirror their feelings and intentions. This happens without our conscious engagement. Mirror neurons explain a lot about how we are so skilled at social interaction. We know what others are feeling and intending, because in parts of our brains we are feeling and intending the same things.

 Get help with becoming more mindful about *System 1* and *System 2* thinking in **Chapters 13 and 14**

Habits

In fact, much of our behaviour bypasses motivation: it just happens. By some estimates, up to 40% of our behaviour is habitual.[21] The alarm rings, we get out of bed, get ready and walk to the station, all with minimal thought and with little role for motivation. We can think of a habit as a self-contained chunk of pre-scripted behaviour. Some cue initiates the habit and off it goes.

Habits are valuable in situations where the behaviour required is frequent, routine and does not vary. Habits free our limited attention to concentrate on those aspects of the situation that are not predictable.[22] Once we have learned the basics of driving, the process of changing gear can be reduced to a habit. More of our mental resources can be devoted to the unpredictable features of driving: the behaviour of other drivers and pedestrians, roadworks, and the like.

Habits can be good and bad. A good habit, like always putting on your seatbelt when you get in a car, can save your life. A bad habit, such as not checking your mirror when overtaking, can cost you your life. But there can be a negative side even to good habits. This arises from the same source as the benefits of habits: namely, they do not require conscious thought. Habits are by definition fixed and unvarying. This is fine if the situation is reasonably close to one in which the habit was developed. If something in the situation has changed, the habit will proceed as usual although the behaviour is no longer appropriate.

We said earlier that there is a natural tendency at work to focus on efficiency rather than thoroughness. In safety-conscious workplaces, this tendency is countered through the use of methods such as toolbox talks and risk assessments. Ideally, these keep the goal of safety at the front of employees' minds. However, their very frequency carries risks. Such methods can become habitual: so familiar that people can carry them out with their brains 'in neutral'. With minimal thought the box can be ticked and the 'real' work begun.

---

20 Rizzolatti & Craighero (2004)

21 Burrell (2016)

22 See Chapter 7 (Being in the know – part II) for more about the curious business of attention.

Being Human in safety-critical organisations

Willpower and self-control

As we have just discussed, a rich mixture of competing motivations and goals, impulses and habits drives our behaviour. How well we can harness our behavioural tendencies comes down to our ability to regulate ourselves. Central to this ability is *willpower*. Until recently, the concept of willpower had a rather stern Victorian flavour. Human failings were felt to be due to defects of character. If you failed to keep to a diet, you blamed your lack of willpower and felt guilty. In recent years, psychologists have been able to put the idea of willpower on a more scientific footing.

To achieve anything significant requires you to find the motivation, set a clear goal, monitor progress towards the goal, and exercise willpower. One of the leading authorities on willpower, Professor Roy Baumeister, has said: *"It is difficult to identify any major personal problems that do not have some element of self-control failure."*[23] So, willpower is about self-control. But what is willpower? One good definition is *"the ability to resist short-term temptations to meet long-term goals"*.[24] Willpower turns out to be more important than IQ in predicting academic success. When they grow up, children who are high in willpower are healthier, get into less trouble, have happier relationships, and are more prosperous. They even live longer.

Willpower and self-control are plainly key human qualities in safety-critical systems. Self-control means staying with difficult or unpleasant tasks to make sure they get done. It also means not giving way to emotions when things go wrong or situations become dangerous. Self-control is closely connected to the capacity to make decisions when under pressure, as we discussed in Chapter 5 (Being in a state).

Modern research has shown that willpower – far from being some mysterious moral quality – is actually a very physical human characteristic. Physiologically, our impulsive nature largely resides in the evolutionary older parts of the brain. Our capacity to control our impulses is located in a much more modern part of the brain, the prefrontal cortex. This is where many of the qualities that most distinctively make us human are located.[25]

> **Read more** about our different brains in **Chapter 7**

It is tempting to think of the 'human' prefrontal cortex as reining in our more primitive urges, but this is probably an oversimplification. Psychologist Kelly McGonigal, who runs a highly popular course on willpower at the top US university Stanford, notes that we normally think of willpower as *not* doing something, eg *"I won't eat the last biscuit"* or *"I won't go out drinking tonight"*. McGonigal argues that willpower is actually three distinct powers, all of which can be located in your prefrontal cortex:[26]

● 'I won't' – the ability to resist temptation, as just described

● 'I will' – the ability to stick to the things you aim to do (eg *"I will go to the gym four times this week"*)

● 'I want' – the ability to 'find your motivation when it matters'.

---

23 Baumeister (2012)

24 American Psychological Association (2012), p. 2

25 The prefrontal cortex is part of the neocortex, the most recently evolved part of our *Homo sapiens* brain – see Chapter 7 (Being in the know – part II) for more details.

26 McGonigal (2012)

This view of willpower as a very physical capability has led to the surprising conclusion that in many respects willpower behaves like a muscle. Many studies have shown that willpower can get tired if it is exercised over an extended period. Willpower gets used up. If you have to perform a task requiring willpower for a time, you will perform less well on a following task that also requires willpower. Furthermore, Roy Baumeister and his colleagues found that a task requiring concentration didn't just lead to worse attention but to weakened physical strength. Exercising extended willpower to control emotions didn't just result in an emotional outburst later, but made people more vulnerable to spending money on unneeded items. And resisting tempting sweets didn't just produce a chocolate craving later, but also increased vulnerability to procrastination. The researchers concluded that *"It was as if every act of willpower was drawing from the same source of strength, leaving people weaker with every successful act of self-control."*[27]

The case of Captain Veldhuyzen van Zanten and the Tenerife airport disaster is illustrative here. This senior captain's many years as a successful pilot and instructor, and his position as the airline's head of safety, point to a man who had great self-control. But he had spent many hours dealing with repeated frustrations. First, the diversion to Tenerife; then having to remain in control and being seen to be in control in his dealings with the airport, his passengers and the crew. Even *his* large reserves of self-control had been eroded. When he finally manoeuvred his jumbo jet to the end of the runway (an activity that required still more self-control), and fog came down and there were confused exchanges with the air traffic controllers, his reserves finally ran out. He could not resist trying to take off, even though it would have been obvious to a pilot with his experience that this was dangerous.[28]

Read more about the Tenerife airport disaster in **Chapter 8**

Willpower has another very physical similarity to a muscle: it is dependent on glucose levels in the body. A person whose willpower has been depleted through protracted use can boost their willpower by consuming a glucose drink. Fatigue has also been shown to reduce willpower, so getting enough sleep can help to reinforce willpower.

We can connect what we know about willpower with our previous observation that intrinsic motivation outperforms extrinsic motivation. The American Psychological Association notes that *"People who felt compelled to exert self-control (in order to please others, for example) were more easily depleted than people who were driven by their own internal goals and desires. When it comes to willpower, those who are in touch with themselves may be better off than their people-pleasing counterparts."*[29]

There is one other way in which willpower can be compared with physical muscle: it can be built up through exercise. There is abundant evidence that regular practice of willpower leads to better self-control. You can do this by practising even small acts of willpower. This can mean doing something you want to do, but usually don't: going to the gym, getting up on time, keeping your admin up to date. It can also mean *not* doing something you want to do: not eating biscuits with your coffee, not making sarcastic remarks to colleagues, not checking your email every three minutes. Surprisingly, the regular practice of willpower in such ways builds up your capacity to exercise your self-control when it really matters. In this

---

27 McGonigal (2012), p. 57

28 Subsecretaría de Aviación Civil (1978)

29 American Psychological Association (2012), p. 6

way, you become better able to give your boss bad news about some threat to safety, stay on-shift so that you don't leave a problem for the next team to sort out, and go out of your way to check that equipment is working in the way it should.

Plans, goals and priorities

An important aspect of being on target is planning. In most working situations, we have more things to do than it seems we have time to do them in. Without a plan, we run the risk of drifting, focusing on the wrong thing or jumping erratically from task to task. Some people would argue that a goal without a plan for how to achieve it is not a meaningful goal, just a vague aspiration.

Human brains have the unique capability to imagine a range of future scenarios, choose the most desirable, and then consider how best to bring this about. To make a plan, you clearly need to decide how and when you are going to carry out a particular task. This can be considered tactical planning. But in addition to this, you need to consider how you are going to organise individual tasks into a higher-level, strategic plan that takes account of task priorities.

In thinking about priorities, it is helpful to distinguish between importance and urgency. A task may be important but not urgent – so it can wait. Another task may be urgent – it must be done now or very soon – but not important. The highest-priority tasks are those that are both urgent and important.

Scheduling must also reflect the dependencies between tasks. Some tasks may require the same resources, technical or human, or one task must logically be completed before another can begin.

We will not go into precise planning methods here; there are countless good books on planning your working day and the related topic of time management.[30] These days, there are also a variety of helpful apps for smart devices.

Setting goals and making plans are plainly necessary but some words of caution are needed. The military devotes huge effort to planning operations, but it also bears in mind the old adage *"No plan survives first contact with the enemy"*. When things start to go wrong, it is a matter of fine judgement whether to stick with the plan or to change. It can help if, in drawing up the plan, you have thought about things that could go wrong and have identified 'if–then' options.[31]

Within the complex systems in which safety-critical operations take place, it is always likely that the unexpected will occur, but the mental exercise of thinking about alternative actions will help you remain flexible. However, be aware that there are risks associated with having a Plan B. Research has shown that having a Plan B can cause people to not try their hardest to make Plan A succeed.[32] For example, you go to an interview for a job you want, having also arranged to go to an interview for another job elsewhere (your 'Plan B'). If things get difficult, it is easy to slip into the attitude *"Well, if I don't get this job (and maybe I don't want it so much after all), I always have this other possibility"*.

---

30 Some examples we like include Allen (2015), Covey (2004) and Peters (2012). We are concerned here with ways of increasing your personal performance, not with large-scale project management.

31 Gollwitzer et al (2004)

32 Shin & Milkman (2016)

Research also shows that having a plan with a clear goal makes you more sensitive to information relevant to this goal. However, the downside is that you become less sensitive to other information. This can be serious if the other information is trying to tell you about better ways to achieve your goal[33] or problems in achieving it.[34]

Read more about the range and power of our mental biases in **Chapter 7**

The setting of goals at the organisational level is especially important in view of the wide-ranging effects of goals coming from 'on high'. While setting clear goals has been repeatedly shown to improve performance, the Harvard Business School has highlighted possible dangerous side-effects.[35] One particularly striking example is that of the Ford Motor Company in the late 1960s. Ford in the US was under pressure from foreign car makers, mainly Japanese, who were selling many small, fuel-efficient cars. Legendary Ford CEO Lee Iacocca set the company the goal of producing a new model with precisely stated targets for size and price. It had to be ready by 1970. The Ford team delivered against Iacocca's targets, but safety was not one of the prescribed goals and this was neglected. The new car, the Ford Pinto, was designed with a badly placed fuel tank that had a propensity to burst into flames in a collision. The result was 53 deaths and many injuries, not to mention the cost to Ford of multiple lawsuits.

Another example is the ill-fated Enron Corporation, an energy, commodities and services company based in Houston, Texas. Among many other problems, Enron executives set their sales teams targets in terms of volume of sales. By focusing on turnover rather than profit, this target sowed the seeds of the biggest bankruptcy in US history at that time (2001). The subsequent attempts to cover up the problems led to members of the top management team being indicted on numerous charges.

On the basis of their review of cases such as these, the Harvard Business School offers the following warning:

"WARNING!

Goals may cause systematic problems in organizations due to a narrowed focus, unethical behavior, increased risk taking, decreased cooperation and decreased intrinsic motivation.

Use care when applying goals in your organization."

Plans are necessary, but you mustn't get so locked into your plan that you overlook other good ways of achieving your goal, or neglect other goals that may have become higher priority. This takes us to the subject of self-awareness.

Self-awareness

You can only improve your ability to deal with goal conflicts, procrastination, impulsive behaviour and other failures of self-control if you monitor yourself. This means taking a hard look at yourself with complete honesty, but also without judgement. Observe yourself when

---

33 Masicampo & Baumeister (2012)

34 Fishbach & Ferguson (2007)

35 Ordóñez et al (2009)

you procrastinate. What sorts of task do you typically put off until later? What is your state in such moments? Are you tired, stressed, bored, complacent, distracted? When do you tend to succumb to impulsive behaviour? Are you more impulsive when you are alone or with others? Are you depressed? Angry? Fearful?

Read more about how different states affect your decision-making in **Chapter 5**

It is important when observing yourself that you take a detached, objective view. Even if you see yourself doing something 'wrong', or something you regret, do not become self-critical or blaming. The aim is to learn and to be able to calibrate your own behaviour. If you know how you are likely to behave in different situations, you can take steps to ensure you are more likely to act in accordance with your highest-priority goals.

The attitude you need to cultivate is that of the scientist. For example, an entomologist systematically notes how ants behave in different situations and adds to the body of scientific knowledge. The entomologist does not criticise or blame the ants for what they do. Ants just do what ants do. Try to see yourself in the same spirit of seeking knowledge about yourself.

The words '*Know thyself*' were carved over the entrance to the temple of Apollo at Delphi. Greeks used to go to the temple to seek answers from the Oracle to the big questions of life. The philosopher Socrates said "*To know thyself is the beginning of wisdom.*"

Safety demands that the people working within the system have a deep knowledge of the system and an awareness of its current state and the ways in which it is likely to develop. If they are to successfully manage and control the system, they also need to understand themselves: their strengths and weaknesses, their tendencies and biases. And they need to do this at all decision-making levels throughout the system.

Get help with these issues in **Chapters 13 and 14**

We have focused so far on the people working in front-line jobs, but it is important that managers and senior staff also become aware of their own motivations and their own tendencies to procrastinate or act impulsively. Countless accident investigations have highlighted how management failures created the conditions in which disasters could unfold. The cases of Ford and Enron outlined above show how management failures can have financial and safety consequences. Here are two more examples from the aviation world, where a bit of timely reflection by managers could have saved many lives.

On 11 July 1991, flight 2120, a DC-8 operated by Nigerian Airlines, caught fire when taking off from Jeddah Airport. The fire eventually caused the plane to crash, killing 14 crew members and 247 passengers. The fire started when two underinflated tyres burst during take-off. This event was not noticed by the flight crew. The wheels scraping along the runway generated so much heat that a fire started and soon spread to the cabin. Shortly before take-off, a mechanic had noticed that the tyres were deflated but was instructed by his manager not to delay the plane's departure.[36]

---

36 Flight Safety Foundation (1993)

On 31 January 2000, Alaska Airlines flight 261 crashed in its home state. The horizontal stabiliser failed after the collapse of the jack-screw assembly, and 88 people died. This followed an initiative by the airline to double aircraft utilisation and extend service intervals. A maintainer had recommended that the jack-screw assembly be replaced but his managers overruled him. After the maintainer reported maintenance violations to the US Department of Transportation, he was suspended by the company.[37]

Stages on the road to expertise

This chapter is called 'Being on target'. So far, we have focused on motivation and goals. To be on target, you obviously need to know what the target is and want to achieve it. But this is not enough. You also need the knowledge and ability to reach the target. If we use the term *will* as shorthand for motivation and goals, and *skill* as shorthand for knowledge and ability, we can write the following equation:

Performance = Will x Skill

Now, if either *Will* or *Skill* is zero, then *Performance* will also be zero. In this last section of the chapter, we look more closely at skill (in particular, *expertise*) and how it can be developed.

Skill development is why training exists. Training is a vast topic, about which many good books have been written.[38] In most organisations operating in high-risk environments, training is about people becoming *competent*. For most purposes, competence is good enough. The person knows how to carry out their everyday tasks to a satisfactory standard. But safety-critical work is not about normal, routine operations. It is about keeping things going or bringing about safe and graceful degradation when they are going seriously wrong. Mere competence is no longer enough. Such situations demand deep levels of knowledge, understanding, insight and capabilities. This is the level of *expertise*.

The distinction between competence and expertise is detailed in a five-level model developed by two professors from the University of California, Berkeley. These professors are the Dreyfus brothers: Hubert, a philosopher, and Stuart, a computer scientist and industrial engineer. Before we take a look at their model, it's useful to briefly describe how it came about.

In the 1970s, the brothers were approached by a US Air Force captain, Jack Thorpe, who had a problem. Thorpe was in a struggle with his superiors about the best way to train pilots to cope with emergencies. Thorpe believed that skill acquisition was brought about by being faced with many different situations. But his superiors thought it was all about memorising rules, helped by printing them in bold-face type for emphasis.[39]

When the Dreyfus brothers studied the development of pilot skill, a radically different view emerged. According to this view, as skill develops, there is a shift from rule-based learning to situation-based learning.

This new view of skill development was taken up by others concerned with training professionals. One of these was Patricia Benner, a nurse and professor at UCLA San Francisco. In the same way that Captain Thorpe had concerns about the training of pilots, Professor Benner had concerns about the training of nurses.[40]

---

37 National Transportation Safety Board (2002)

38 Patrick (1992) is a particularly comprehensive and useful example.

39 Dreyfus, H.L. (1997), pp. 17–8

40 Benner (1982, 2004)

Benner saw the development of nursing expertise as a progression from abstract principles to the use of concrete experience. In her view, rather than being simply about the accumulation of knowledge, becoming an expert involved a fundamental change in how the learner perceives and experiences the learning domain. For example, the learner's perception moves *"from a situation as a collection of equally relevant pieces, to a complete whole in which only certain parts are relevant"*.[41]

Another quotation from Benner is particularly relevant in the context of this book: *"Nursing in acute-care settings has grown so complex that it is no longer possible to standardize, routinize, and delegate much of what the nurse does."*[42] This reinforces the point we make throughout this book: complex systems are always capable of surprising those working with them. There are just too many possible states to cover with rules.

We now describe in more detail the five levels in the Dreyfus & Dreyfus model. We draw here on several publications by the Dreyfus brothers,[43] as well as the works of Benner already cited.

Novice – student

In 1890, the pioneer psychologist William James described a new-born baby's impression of the world as *"one great blooming, buzzing confusion"*.[44] James probably underestimated the astonishing capabilities of human infants, but his description fits well with the experience of a novice confronted for the first time with a truly complex system: the engineering cadet on his first visit to an oil tanker's engine room, or the student nurse facing a real live patient for the first time. The authors of this book vividly recall the first time we entered a modern signal box controlling one of the big London stations and were faced with the overwhelming complexity of the series of large 'mimic' panels that railway signallers use to steer trains.

The novice is likely to be overwhelmed if they are asked to take in too much at this stage. By definition, novices have little or no experience of the situations that can arise with the system, so the instructor can only introduce the simpler attributes that can be recognised without situational experience.[45] These might be fuel levels and engine temperature for the novice engineer, or pulse rate and body temperature for the student nurse, or maybe track layout and signal aspects for the signaller.

The novice is taught rules based on the features that they can understand. These are typically if–then rules that specify the actions to be taken: *"If the pointer on the temperature dial goes into the red zone, then call the second engineer."* However, the novice lacks the big picture, which would make sense of the reading for a more experienced engineer: *"Oh, yes, the engine temperature always goes high when ..., but it should go down again as soon as ..."*. Since the cadet has experienced only a few situations, they don't yet know what is *normal*. The student nurse may be able to monitor a number of indicators (temperature, blood pressure, weight, pulse, etc) but they don't yet know which of these are most important for a given patient. Nor does the student yet know how to relate these indicators to one another to make an overall assessment.

---

41 Benner (1982), p. 402

42 Benner (1982), p. 402

43 Dreyfus & Dreyfus (1988); Dreyfus, H.L. (1997); Dreyfus, S.E. (2004)

44 James (1890), p. 462

45 Benner (1982), p. 403

Advanced beginner – new graduate

With time and experience, the novice becomes an advanced beginner. Benner categorises the new graduate nurse as an advanced beginner – a term that most graduates might think does not convey full recognition of their status. Over time, the novice begins to notice aspects of the wider situation that utilise prior experience.[46]

The advanced beginner car driver starts to notice, for example, whether the engine is racing or straining, and adjusts their actions accordingly. They may develop this awareness themselves or through the instructor pointing out these contextual cues. The instructor may give the learner *maxims* – general principles or truths. A maxim may give a pointer to what to do in the situation, but it is far less prescriptive than the if–then rule taught to the novice. When driving down a busy street, the trainee driver might, for example, be told to 'make allowances for parked cars and pedestrians'. This may be good advice, but exactly what an 'allowance' means in practice is left to the learner to decide.

Aspects and maxims cannot be totally objective. How, for example, could an instructor describe an engine racing or straining? Benner gives the example of a patient indicating they are ready to take care of some aspect of their treatment. The more senior nurse may say the patient indicates readiness by beginning to ask questions. But it all depends on what questions and how they are asked. This is something the learner has to figure out for themselves.

The advanced beginner is also likely to have difficulty assigning priorities. More experienced colleagues will need to help here.

Competence – one to two years in practice

As the advanced beginner progresses, they notice more and more features of the situation. The driver may notice the sound of the engine, the speed of the car, the state of the road surface, upcoming bends or junctions, time, and so on. They still have difficulty in deciding which features are relevant at any given moment; many situations may still be overwhelming and stressful. But as skill develops, the learner starts to develop a plan that helps them focus on the most important aspects of the situation.

The competent learner is still largely rule-driven and would like to discover rules that indicate what plan or perspective to adopt. But there are so many situations and they differ so much from each other that it is difficult, if not impossible, to find rules that specify what to do. It follows that the competent performer must begin to work out what to do without being sure that it will turn out well.[47] This state can be frightening, disappointing, discouraging and exciting. (See the panel 'A nurse becomes competent'.)

46 Benner (1982), p. 403
47 Dreyfus, S.E. (2004), p. 178

A nurse becomes competent

"I had four patients. One needed colostomy teaching, the others needed a lot of other things. Instead of thinking before I went into the room, I got caught up [with doing things] … Someone's IV would stop, and I'd work on that. Then I'd forget to give someone their meds, and so would have to rush around and do that. And then someone would feel nauseated and I'd try to make them feel better while they were sick. And then the colostomy bag would fall off when I wanted to start teaching. And all of a sudden the morning was gone, and no-one had a bed bath. Now, I know I have a couple of things that I have to do. Before I go in the room, I write down the meds I'm supposed to give for that day, and then walk in there and make sure that everybody's IV is fine … I know what I have to do, and I am much more organised."[48]

However, this emotional involvement turns out to be a necessary element of learning. Dreyfus notes a study of nurses[49] and comments *"unless the trainee stays emotionally involved and accepts the joy of a job well done, as well as the remorse of mistakes, he or she will not develop further and will eventually burn out trying to keep track of all the features and aspects, rules and maxims that modern medicine requires".*[50]

Read more about the necessity of emotion for decision-making in **Chapter 7**

We have said in this book that when dealing with complex, adaptive systems, rules are necessary but only work up to a point. In this context, Dreyfus's remark about the development of expertise sheds some light: *"In general, if one seeks the safety of rules, one will not get beyond competence."*[51] Competence is the first level at which a person can begin to feel personal responsibility for their actions. Indeed, feeling responsible is a necessary component of competence.

 Read more about responsibility, accountability and their place in a 'just' culture in **Chapter 12**

Proficiency

The move from competent to proficient is the biggest step on the road to becoming expert. Becoming proficient involves a fundamental shift to assessment and decisions based on the whole situation. This only becomes possible when a person has had direct experience of a large number of varied situations. The novice is looking for specific cues to trigger the application of rules and they are therefore missing a lot. Learners making the transition to proficiency become increasingly aware of the entire situation. In addition, they develop the capacity to discriminate between types of situation on the basis of subtle differences.

We can make a comparison with a child learning to read. The five-year-old has to painfully analyse the features that make up each letter D-O-G and then speak out the sounds of the

---

48 Benner (1982), p. 405
49 Benner (1984)
50 Dreyfus, S.E. (2004), pp. 178-9
51 Dreyfus, S.E. (2004), p. 179

letters until the child recognises the word 'dog'. The adult reader simply sees the word 'dog' and most of the time is unaware of the constituent letters.

Benner emphasises that the transformation from competence to proficiency is a 'qualitative leap' that is marked by a radical change in the problem-solving approach: from rules and look-ups to an approach based on experience.[52]

Another way to characterise this development is that novices and advanced beginners both experience themselves as being separate from the situation. They are observers looking at the situation from outside. Proficient learners experience themselves as being an integral part of the situation. They increasingly rely on intuition. At earlier stages, they have to *analyse* the situation and consciously think about how to act. As they become proficient, they increasingly *recognise* the type of situation and *know* what their goal should be, without extensive consideration of options. At this stage, however, they still have to deliberate about how to achieve the goal.

Expert

In contrast to the proficient person, the expert knows intuitively both what to do and how to do it. Experts can do this because they have a still greater capacity to distinguish between different situations. The chess grandmaster is estimated to be able to recognise more than 50,000 situations on the chessboard and can play at a rate of five to ten seconds per move without their performance getting worse. The grandmaster does not analyse the position of each piece, but can recognise the overall pattern and knows the underlying dynamics of the state of the game.

The subjective experience of the expert is that of 'being at one' with the situation. The competent pilot experiences that they are flying the plane. The expert pilot simply experiences they are flying. Concert pianists achieve a state where there is no longer the musician, the instrument and the score; there is simply 'the music'. At its peak, the expert achieves a state that the Hungarian psychologist Mihályi Csíkszentmihályi[53] has called *flow*. Royal Navy warfare officers talk of having 'the bubble' when they are totally in tune with the operational situation. Financial traders describe being in 'the pipe'. Air traffic controllers and railway signallers refer to the loss of flow as 'losing the picture'. Flow requires both that the person's skill levels are high and that the challenges are high to match.

Flow involves all the following experiences:[54]

- Intense and focused concentration on the present moment
- Merging of action and awareness
- A loss of reflective self-consciousness
- A sense of personal control or agency over the situation or activity
- A distortion or loss of the sense of time
- Experience of the activity as intrinsically rewarding.

---

52 Benner (1982), p. 406

53 See Csíkszentmihályi (1990) (He helpfully advises non-speakers of Hungarian to pronounce his name as Me-high Chick-sent-me-high.)

54 Nakamura & Csíkszentmihályi (2001)

Flow brings benefits for the organisation through increased quality and performance. For the individual, flow is highly satisfying and motivating. Notably, all of the means of achieving control that reduce intrinsic motivation (over-prescriptive rules and procedures, close supervision, external incentives) work *against* achieving a state of flow.

An important aspect of developing expertise is that the expert often cannot articulate the nature of their expertise. Their expertise has been absorbed through the course of experience with many practical situations. One consequence of this is that when experts are asked why they made particular decisions, they tend to revert back to the rules and principles they learned in the early stages of their careers. Because they were explicitly taught these rules and principles, the expert can readily put them into words – although in their actual professional practice they have long outgrown most of them. Benner quotes the chess grandmaster who, when asked why he made a particular move, could only answer *"Because it felt right."*

While experts may act without conscious deliberation, this does not mean that they always act without thinking. The best of experts will think before acting when time permits or circumstances demand. However, the nature of their thought process is not that of the non-expert. Typically, they do not try to apply rules to figure out their actions or goals. Instead, they think about the goal they want to achieve and let the possibilities for action emerge.[55]

Experts use analytical thinking when they encounter novel situations. While the expert relies heavily on intuition derived from many experiences, there will be occasions when intuition is wrong: the situation is not actually how it first seemed, or the chosen course of action is not working as expected. In such situations, the expert can always switch to analytical problem-solving. They break the problem up into its parts, explore local cause-and-effect relationships, identify and evaluate alternative courses of action, and finally make a deliberate decision.

How do you become an expert?

The Dreyfus model shows how expertise develops with experience. But most people have met highly experienced professionals who don't appear to be experts. They may be competent, but they don't demonstrate the very highest levels of performance that would mark them out as true experts. Benner observes that many nurses never rise above being competent. Is this because they just don't possess the talent to become experts? Benner also observes that, in most organisations, training is only ever designed to develop competence. So is it the lack of training that keeps people two levels below expert?

As it turns out, experience on its own is not enough for expertise to develop. To become an expert demands that people *learn* from experience. In this last part of the chapter we explore how to nurture experts and expertise. The leading thinker in this field is Anders Ericsson, a professor at Florida State University.[56]

Ericsson notes that it is popularly believed that to become an expert in some area of human endeavour – pilot, athlete, musician, doctor – you have to have been born with particular talents. The common example is Mozart. Mozart astonished crowned heads of Europe from the age of six with his virtuoso performances on the piano. He composed his first symphony

---

55 Dreyfus, H.L. (1997), p. 28

56 Ericsson et al (2006); Ericsson et al (2007); Ericsson & Pool (2016)

at the age of eight. He had the ability of *perfect pitch* and could tell precisely what note he was hearing: A flat, F sharp, C natural. How else could such a young boy achieve so much if his abilities were not inborn?

But experiments have shown that if you use particular training methods with very young children (under six), then nearly all children can have perfect pitch.[57] Detailed examination of Mozart's childhood shows that his ambitious father subjected Mozart and his sister to a rigorous musical training regime virtually from birth. More recently, László and Klara Polgár began intensively playing chess with their three daughters. All three became world-class players.[58] Many studies of experts in all sorts of fields have similarly demonstrated that experts are not born but *made*.

Now, with activities such as music and chess it is fairly easy for parents to begin early intensive training. It is not so common for parents to be able to give their young children access to the flight deck of an Airbus, the control room of a nuclear power station, or the bridge of a VLCC.[59] These are all complex, safety-critical systems in special need of highly expert operators and managers, so the question is how to develop expertise in the adults who work with such systems, or more specifically, how to turn competent staff into experts.

What separates the expert from the merely competent is largely the special nature of the practice they have engaged in over extended periods of time. Ericsson explains it this way:

"The journey to truly superior performance is neither for the faint of heart nor for the impatient. The development of genuine expertise requires struggle, sacrifice, and honest, often painful self-assessment. There are no shortcuts. It will take you at least a decade to achieve expertise, and you will need to invest that time wisely, by engaging in 'deliberate' practice – practice that focuses on tasks beyond your current level of competence and comfort. You will need a well-informed coach not only to guide you through deliberate practice but also to help you learn how to coach yourself."[60]

Again, we must emphasise the distinction between *experience* and *practice*. Experience alone does not guarantee the growth of expertise. Ericsson says you may have lived in a cave for years, but this does not make you a geologist. He also cites the example of doctors who have worked with patients for many years, but who have difficulty in diagnosing rare conditions. They may have learned about these conditions in their original training, but, because they have not encountered them in the intervening years, they have forgotten the signs and symptoms.

Organisations, especially those operating in high-risk environments, will naturally want to assess the degree of expertise among their staff. It is worth mentioning here a number of things to be aware of when evaluating expertise:[61]

- **Individual accounts of expertise are often unreliable** Evidence put forward in support of a person's supposed expertise is often anecdotal. Isolated examples are given undue weight. People's memories of past events are often unreliable and re-interpreted in the light of present concerns.

---

57 Miyazaki & Ogawa (2006)

58 Ericsson et al (2007)

59 Very Large Crude Carrier

60 Ericsson et al (2007)

61 Ericsson et al (2007)

- **Expertise has to be consistent and measurable** True experts achieve outcomes that are consistently superior to those of their peers, and this superiority can be demonstrated through objective measures.

- **Intuition can be misleading** Many people believe they can simply trust their intuition. This may work in routine, familiar situations, but for more challenging decisions, intuition has to have been developed via *"considerable practice, reflection and analysis"*.

- **Simply changing methods does not make you an expert** Expertise goes deeper than methods. The whole foundations of professional decision-making have to be developed through *"consistency and carefully controlled efforts"*.

- **Expertise is not captured by knowledge management systems** Knowledge management systems do not contain knowledge. They only contain data. Data can only be transformed into knowledge in the expert decision-maker's head.[62]

Read more about the nature of knowledge in **Chapters 6 and 7**

But what does Ericsson mean when he talks about 'deliberate' practice? And how does deliberate practice differ from normal practice?

"Not all practice makes perfect. You need a particular kind of practice – deliberate practice – to develop expertise. When most people practice, they focus on the things they already know how to do. Deliberate practice is different. It entails considerable, specific, and sustained efforts to do something you can't do well – or even at all. Research across domains shows that it is only by working at what you can't do that you turn into the expert you want to become."[63]

In his recent book *Peak: Secrets from the Science of Expertise*,[64] Ericsson presents an extensive list of the characteristics of deliberate practice. We can summarise these as follows:

- There must already exist a well-established body of know-how
- Effective training methods must already exist
- Practice must enable the student to build on top of existing skills
- There needs to be an instructor, teacher or mentor
- Practice must constantly push the student beyond their current limits
- There must be specific goals and a plan for steps leading to this goal
- The student must be able to see if they have improved
- Practice must engage the student's full attention
- Feedback must be provided so that the student can adjust their performance against the feedback
- The student must be able to form mental representations of their performance, so they can monitor and adjust what they do.

We should say a bit more about what a mental representation is. Ericsson says it's *"a mental structure that corresponds to an object, an idea, a collection of information or anything*

---

62 See Chapters 6 and 7 (Being in the know) for more on the true nature of knowledge.

63 Ericsson et al (2007)

64 Ericsson & Pool (2016), pp. 99–100

else, concrete or abstract, that the brain is thinking about".[65] He gives the example of Leonardo da Vinci's famous painting, the *Mona Lisa*. Say '*Mona Lisa*' to many people and they will form in their mind a picture (a mental representation) of the painting – although people will vary in their accuracy, level of detail, etc. You can then hold a conversation about this painting with someone who can form a representation, even though no physical copy may be available.

Chess players construct mental representations of the state of play on the board. As they become more experienced, they do not memorise the position of each piece, but instead see patterns and dynamics. These representations are efficient ways of storing the game position; the advanced chess player can manipulate them to rapidly identify and evaluate different moves and tactics. An important aim of deliberate practice is to increase and enhance these representations, so the expert can see and assess many more possibilities than the less advanced player.

It is probably fair to say that few organisations carrying out safety-critical activities are currently engaged in developing expertise via deliberate practice as described by Ericsson and his colleagues. Aviation and the armed services have probably led the way. More recently, healthcare has also made significant advances.

A problem with developing expertise in high-risk environments is that opportunities for learning are usually rare. When an incident does occur, there are limited opportunities to learn. The person managing the incident typically does their best in the moment. They may or may not have thought beforehand about how to deal with this particular type of incident. Afterwards, there may be opportunities to review what was done, and whether that was the best course of action. But such reviews are inevitably speculative, even if other experts are on hand to give their opinions. Nobody knows for sure whether the outcome could have been improved, unless there were glaring failures.

To get the most out of deliberate practice, the student, supported by their instructor, needs to identify an area to improve and set goals for a practice session. The student then needs to exercise their skills in an appropriate situation, get feedback on how they have performed, identify things to do differently, and then repeat the exercise, trying to apply the lessons learned and seeing whether the outcome is better. And then they need to repeat the process again. And again. For years.

Case studies and 'wargames' are two options for developing expertise in responding to incidents in safety-critical systems. Perhaps the most lavish approach to developing expertise is the 'Top Gun' model (see panel).

Top Gun and expertise[66]

Many people have enjoyed watching Tom Cruise in the film *Top Gun* without realising this was an actual US military training programme. In the Vietnam conflict, US Navy fighters were doing badly. In 1968, every Vietnamese plane shot down was at the cost of one US Navy plane also shot down. Many pilots did not survive their first dogfight. But if you did survive the first, you were much more likely to survive your second. If you survived 20 encounters, you were almost certain to survive subsequent dogfights. The question confronting US Navy trainers was how to help pilots survive long enough to become expert.

---

65 Ericsson & Pool (2016), p. 58

66 This account of the Top Gun initiative is based largely on Ericsson & Pool (2016), pp. 115–20.

The US Navy's response was to set up the US Navy Fighter Weapons School, which became known as Top Gun. The Navy chose its best pilots to be the instructors. The next best pilots became the first trainees. The instructors formed the Red Force: they flew planes similar to the North Vietnamese and adopted their tactics. The trainees formed the Blue Force, flying US planes and using US tactics.

Over and over, the Blue Force engaged with the Red Force. Although they were not using live weapons, in all other respects both forces pushed their planes, themselves and the opposition to the limit. Over weeks, the trainees were exposed to almost every situation they could conceivably encounter.

To begin with, the Blue Force would usually lose. After each battle, instructors and trainees would gather to review what had gone on. The instructors would interrogate the trainees ruthlessly, getting them to analyse every aspect of what they had done and to think about other things they might have done. With repeated practice, the Blue Force eventually learned to hold their own against the Red Force.

After their training at Top Gun, the trainees returned to their squadrons and taught the other pilots there what they had learned. The improvement was huge. By 1972, the US Navy pilots were shooting down an average of 12.5 enemy planes for each US fighter lost.

The elements of Top Gun – repeated experience of challenging situations, the opportunity to try out different courses of action, skilled instructors, prompt and thorough feedback sessions[67] – provide a template for using deliberate practice to develop expertise. Of course, the Top Gun programme was vastly expensive, demanding planes, fuel and time from skilled instructors, plus all the support personnel and facilities. But it was able to approximate actual wartime conditions to great advantage, so that situations could be repeated and opportunities for learning maximised.

Technological advances since the 1960s have meant that simulators often offer a more cost-effective approach to developing expertise. While simulators are now a standard tool in training, one study[68] of particular interest here examined the impact of deliberate practice on pilot decision-making in a once-in-a-career crisis scenario. Ericsson noted the study's main finding: if the crisis had been practised in a simulator, then pilots were reliably more successful in dealing with it in real life.[69] One other area where simulation is now being used extensively in training is healthcare[70] – and, in particular, in surgery[71] and nursing.[72] It is also of interest that a Top Gun-style competition has recently been used to motivate doctors on a surgical training course.[73]

---

67 Referred to as 'After Action Review' in some military circles

68 McKinney & Davis (2003)

69 Ericsson (2006), p. 693

70 For an overview, see Levine et al (2013)

71 See, for example, Trehan et al (2014)

72 See, for example, Chee (2014)

73 Enter et al (2014)

We discuss the merits of and approaches to simulation in Chapter 14 (Being practical – part II), in relation to decision-making under stress. The same arguments essentially apply here in relation to taking personnel from competent to expert. In particular, simulation offers four important capabilities:

- The ability to work in situations offering high psychological fidelity[74]
- The ability to expose students to abnormal and emergency situations that are serious but likely to occur only rarely in real life
- The ability to practise the same situations repeatedly while trying out different options
- The ability to record and replay training exercises, and generate descriptive statistics, so amplifying the value of review and feedback sessions. In some simulators, it is also possible to pause the training scenario, enabling the instructor to give instantaneous feedback, and then switch to play again.

Simulation does not have to mean expensive, ultra-high-fidelity simulators. What matters is that the fidelity of the aspects of the task in which people are being trained is good enough for the learning to be transferred to the actual task.[75, 76]

Ten years ago, leading researchers in the field of simulation observed that technological advances in simulation had outpaced our understanding of how to apply this technology to develop expertise. There has been much progress in the intervening years, but much still remains to be learned. We can sum up this situation by saying that safety-critical systems rely on expert people, and that simulation can be a powerful tool for developing expertise (especially in how to cope with rare and unexpected operational situations), but there are no off-the-shelf solutions. Each new application of simulation requires analysis of the expertise to be acquired, and detailed exploration and testing of how to meet the identified requirements, including the fidelity required for effective transfer of the acquired learning.

---

74 *Physical* fidelity is a property of the engineered simulation *equipment* and has no necessary relationship with training effectiveness. In contrast, *psychological* fidelity is a property of the trainee's *experience* of the simulation and is directly related to training effectiveness: the higher the psychological fidelity of the simulation, the better the transfer to the operational environment. High psychological fidelity does not necessarily entail high physical fidelity.

75 Known in training simulation circles as the 'transfer of training'

76 Ward et al (2006), p. 258

11

Being together
good teams, wicked groups and the need for diversity

> How do teams create safety?
>
> How do effective teams work?
>
> How does our intensely social nature sometimes work against safety?
>
> How can diversity both help and hinder effective teamwork?
>
> How can team leaders promote safety?
>
> What is 'social capital' and why does it matter?

Why does teamwork matter?

People make systems safe in the face of heavy or unexpected demands through a continual process of adjusting system operation. In contrast to many discussions about safety, which tend to focus on human error, the primary focus in this book is on how safety emerges from the trade-offs that humans make between efficiency and thoroughness. We have organised our description of how people behave in terms of our SUGAR model, introduced in Chapters 3 (Being framed) and 4 (Being sufficient). In this model, a person's decisions and actions arise from the interaction of their Understanding, State and Goals. Importantly, the trade-off point is also affected as the operational situation moves from routine, through non-routine, to emergency.

In most safety-critical work settings, of course, individuals do not work on their own. When a system needs correction to prevent a serious incident or to recover when something has gone wrong, it usually takes coordinated action by a number of people. Ensuring timely and effective action is the business of teamwork. Normally, teamwork is something we take for granted – so much so that we only notice it in extreme situations or when teamwork has gone wrong.

Two examples of good teamwork

Good teamwork prevents a VLCC from grounding[1]

In 1997, the UK's Marine Accident Investigation Branch (MAIB) reported an incident involving a very large oil tanker leaving the Fawley oil terminal on the British south coast. The pilot was on board and a tug was assisting. The tanker's planned passage required it to make a short turn into the main channel around a sandbank. At a critical moment in the turn, the vessel failed to respond in the correct manner. There was a real risk that the tanker would ground on the sandbank and pollution would result. Good teamwork prevented this malfunction from leading to a major environmental disaster.

First, the pilot carefully monitored the situation throughout. He had discussed the manoeuvre beforehand with the shore-based Vessel Traffic Service (VTS) operator, who was keeping an eye on the tanker on radar. Being aware of the situation and the intended plan, the VTS operator was able to assist the pilot by taking over some of his communication tasks. The pilot was free to communicate with the ship's bridge team and the tug. The members of the crew were informed what was happening and could all act accordingly. The master communicated with the engine room, the officer of the watch ran to the helm to investigate the steering problem, the deckhands prepared the anchors in case they were needed, and the engineers stood by in the steering flat (the compartment containing the steering gear).

Using the VLCC's engines and with help from the tug, the pilot regained control of the vessel within four minutes of the initial failure. The ship stopped short of the sandbank and a potential major accident was avoided. The MAIB noted that *"The successful outcome resulted from good communications between the pilot and the master of an escort tug experienced in the practice, together with a VTS operator working as a team"*. We could also include the members of the ship's crew, who all knew what actions they should take when facing an emergency.

Good teamwork aboard United Airlines flight 232[2]

In 1989, an explosion in the tail engine of a United Airlines DC-10 not only destroyed the engine but also took out all three hydraulic systems. The DC-10 was perfectly capable of flying on its two wing-mounted engines, but with no hydraulics, the pilots were unable to operate the plane's control surfaces. As the manufacturer's engineers had considered it impossible for all three hydraulic systems to fail at the same time, no emergency procedures had been developed. The chances of being able to fly the plane to an airport, let alone make a safe landing, were remote. What followed illustrated many aspects of good teamwork displayed by the flight crew and beyond.

The captain allowed the co-pilot to take control of the plane without insisting on his seniority. They were soon joined in the cockpit by a third pilot, a DC-10 instructor who happened to be on board as a passenger. The three pilots shared between them the task of trying to fly the stricken plane. The captain showed he was open to suggestions from the others, again demonstrating a willingness to put the safety of the plane ahead of concerns about his own status.

---

1 MAIB (1997), section 11. VLCC stands for Very Large Crude Carrier.

2 Based on Haynes (1991)

Critically, the quality of the communications by all those involved remained high throughout the incident. The air traffic controller the plane was communicating with continued the good teamwork, not least by remaining very calm throughout. The cabin crew also remained calm while informing the passengers what they needed to know. The passengers themselves cooperated in, for example, rearranging their seat positions to optimise access to the emergency exits.

Through skilful use of the throttles to vary power to the wing engines, the pilots managed to steer the plane to an airport and crash land. The plane broke up and caught fire. Although there were many deaths, 185 of the 296 people survived, including the pilots, when it had seemed probable that everyone would be killed. The high survival rate was helped by the prompt actions of the emergency services at the airport and the skilled care provided by the medical professionals at the hospital where the survivors were taken.

Unsurprisingly, this incident is widely used in Crew Resource Management (CRM) training in the aviation world. We will discuss what makes good teamwork shortly, but first we look at an example of bad teamwork.

Bad teamwork aboard USS *Vincennes*

USS *Vincennes* was the most modern cruiser in the US Navy. Despite being equipped with all the latest technology, it shot down an Iranian Airbus A300 by mistake, causing the deaths of 290 civilians. The subsequent investigation revealed that all the technology had functioned precisely as it was designed to do. What had failed was the teamwork in *Vincennes'* Combat Information Centre (CIC). The CIC was variously described as being in states of panic, confusion and disorder. As a result of this incident, a major research programme into teamwork, known as TADMUS (Tactical Decision-Making Under Stress), was set up in the US. This ten-year programme generated a clear set of findings about human teamwork, and we have drawn on some of them in this chapter.[3]

> **Read more** about the USS *Vincennes* incident in **Chapter 7**

Figure 11.1 shows a team as a number of individuals in a network of relationships. Each red circle represents an individual. As fellow members of a team, I am influenced by you, and in return, I influence you. If you and I are working together, my State, Understanding and Goals are influenced by your communications, including your actions, body language, facial expressions, tone of voice, and so on. All of these are an expression of the interactions of your State, Understanding and Goals. These interactions – both within us and between us – are powerful factors in how effective and resilient our teamwork is.

---

3   Cannon-Bowers & Salas (1998)

Figure 11.1 The team as a network of dynamic relationships

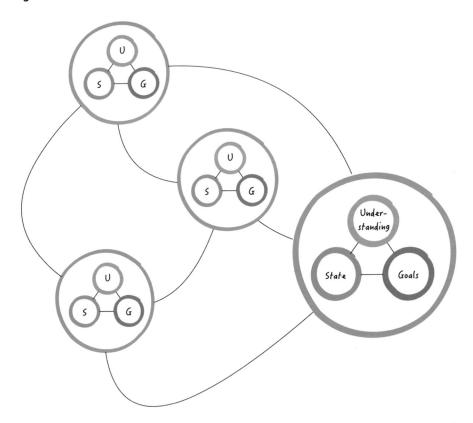

In this chapter, we look at how good teams are effective and how they create safety through their skills and, equally importantly, their attitudes. We also look at how sometimes social influences can put safety at risk. Lastly, we look at the role of organisations in promoting teams that are both effective and safe.

Ten ways good teams create safety

1. **Good teams communicate** An effective team's members know who needs to know what – and when. Information is not hoarded but shared. Keeping each other informed about what you are doing, planning to do, and have done is essential if others whose tasks are interdependent with yours are to be properly coordinated. Good teams use *closed-loop communications*. If I have told you something critical to safety or task performance, I don't just assume that because I have said something, you will have heard and understood me. I will expect you to confirm your understanding of what I have said. Then I can complete the communication by confirming that what you have understood is correct. Interestingly, really high-performing teams are likely to communicate less in an emergency. They trust each other to be doing what is really necessary and will not distract each other with non-critical messages.

2. **Good teams look out for each other** If you are a good team member, you will pay attention to what other team members are doing and how they are getting on. If another team member is struggling with a task, or is stressed or overloaded, you will notice and either provide what support you can or find someone else to help. In many workplaces, a common attitude is expressed in phrases such as *"It's not my job"* or *"It's somebody else's problem"*. In effective teams, everyone recognises that getting the job done safely is everybody's responsibility. In Chapter 4 (Being sufficient) we described the *Herald of Free Enterprise* disaster, a dreadful loss of life that could have been avoided if (among actions by several others) the bosun had paused to think through the implications that his assistant was not at his post.[4]

3. **Good teams back each other up** Knowing that a fellow team member is in difficulty is obviously important, but effective teams go further and act on this knowledge. Others step in and help. To do this requires not only a willingness to help, but enough knowledge of the other person's task to be able to relieve them of at least some of the load.

4. **Good teams listen to everybody** In bad teams, the most senior member or the pushiest person talks and everybody else listens. Good teams recognise that nobody has a monopoly on important information or good ideas. They also know that in confusing, complex situations, multiple perspectives are needed to find the best course of action. Inviting quiet, junior or less experienced members of the team to express their views is usually good practice.

> **Read more** about the nature of knowledge in **Chapters 6 and 7**

5. **Good teams challenge each other** Sometimes a person – often a person in authority – will undertake an action or give instructions for an action that somebody else perceives as inadvisable or dangerous. When the danger is imminent, somebody else must issue a direct challenge – possibly in forceful terms. Again, this is especially difficult when a junior or less experienced member of the team feels they must challenge a senior colleague.

>   **Get help** with how to challenge senior colleagues in **Chapter 13**

In 1893, Admiral Tryon of the Royal Navy was in command of two parallel columns of battleships on exercise in the Mediterranean. He gave an order for the columns to reverse course by turning inwards. Given the distance between them, this would inevitably result in ships colliding. Ten senior captains and a rear admiral on the other ships failed to question the order. Admiral Tryon's flagship, HMS *Victoria*, collided with HMS *Camperdown* and sank. Three hundred and fifty-eight sailors, including Admiral Tryon himself, drowned.[5]

After the Tenerife airport disaster in 1977,[6] the aviation world developed CRM training. Many other sectors, including the maritime world, have since introduced variations of CRM, such as Bridge Resource Management (BRM). A central element of CRM and BRM is the responsibility of all team members to challenge unsafe decisions and actions, even by their superiors.[7] So incidents like Admiral Tryon on HMS *Victoria* should not happen nowadays,

---

4   Sheen (1987)

5   Dixon (1976)

6   The Tenerife airport disaster is described in some detail in Chapter 8 (Being in the know – part III).

7   We give some clear guidelines on how to challenge seniors effectively in Chapter 13 (Being practical – part I).

right? Wrong. The failure to challenge leadership decisions effectively has continued to the present day. Several recent high-profile accidents in the maritime world and other sectors have resulted in loss of life, costs running into billions of dollars, and even criminal prosecutions. In 2015, the passenger ship *Hamburg* grounded on charted rocks off the coast of Scotland with 461 persons on board. Although there were fortunately no injuries in this case, the damage was considerable. Despite explicit training and an approved safety management system, the enquiry found that *"no actions or decisions taken at any stage on Hamburg's bridge, before or following the grounding, were questioned by any member of the bridge team."*[8]

6. **Good teams manage interpersonal difficulties and conflicts** Members of good teams know it is not necessary to like every other person in the team. Liking is not needed for effective teamwork, but good teams know that any ill feelings can get in the way of the rapid and smoothly coordinated actions needed when the system drifts towards its safety boundary. So they don't complain about someone behind their back, but address the problem openly. They also recognise that we all have a tendency to assume that if somebody does something we don't like, they have done it deliberately, when the truth is probably that they had no bad intention.[9] Or, maybe the people concerned just have different personal styles. (See the panel 'Using SUGAR to sweeten relationships that have gone sour'.)

 Get help with how to gauge and deal with different personal styles and how to approach difficult conversations in **Chapter 13**

Using SUGAR to sweeten relationships that have gone sour

The SUGAR model can help in managing problems with someone else's behaviour. By asking about the other person's State, Understanding and Goals, as well as our own, we can get a deeper perspective, rather than just blaming them. Were they tired or stressed? And does this explain what they did? Did it influence them to react out of proportion to the 'offence'? Did each person have a different understanding of the situation, perhaps because they had access to different information? What were they trying to do? Maybe each person's intentions were perfectly reasonable in their different ways?

It is also worth considering the other's personal style. Is one person highly social, while the other prefers to do things alone? Is one person loud and confrontational, while the other prefers to be quiet and reflective? Normal differences like these can be a source of tension and even conflict. Often, the person we think of as difficult is actually just different. Thinking through questions like these and, ideally, discussing them with the other person won't necessarily make interpersonal difficulties totally disappear, but they can be removed as obstacles to effective teamwork.

In Chapter 13 (Being practical – part I), you'll find a convenient tool to help assess and work with other people's personal styles, as well as get an insight into your own.

---

8   MAIB (2016b)

9   See the guidance on conducting difficult conversations in Chapter 13 (Being practical – part I).

7. **Good teams learn** Good teams know that when working within complex, adaptive systems, learning never ends. A complex system will always present the team with some new aspect of how it works, or maybe some new way in which it can go wrong. In a good team, everyone recognises that others may have had the chance to learn some important lesson. It may be that the newest recruit has discovered something that the old hands have not. A good team member isn't too proud to learn from any other member of the team, whoever they are. Equally, good teams are happy to share their knowledge of the system with newcomers. Through these learning processes, good teams promote safety by developing a deep knowledge of the system – knowledge that provides a shared basis for collective action, especially when prompt coordinated action is demanded.

This kind of learning can, of course, only happen in teams whose members stay together for some period of time. In many safety-critical situations, people have to come together and function as a team more or less immediately. Captains and co-pilots in airliners may not have flown together before, but in a very short space of time they have to coordinate closely to fly a jet with perhaps several hundred passengers. In a slightly longer timeframe, seafarers may join a ship on a short-term contract, perhaps for a voyage lasting only a few days.

In these situations, if a team is going to be effective, then the learning must have taken place beforehand. Robert Ginnett[10] has argued that in roles where the work is highly proceduralised, people need to have not only learned their tasks but also absorbed the organisation's values, norms, expectations, authority structures and boundaries. He uses an analogy in which team members have a 'shell' that enables them to fit together with the shells of their colleagues. The time they have to spend together before the work begins can be devoted to identifying any personal or situational factors that need to be taken into account in ensuring a good fit between their respective shells.

8. **Good teams trust each other** Trust is perhaps a good team's most valuable asset. Think what happens when you don't trust one of your colleagues in a safety-critical operation. You will always keep at least one eye on them, making sure they are doing things right (or at least what you *think* is right, which is not always the same thing, as we saw in Chapter 7: Being in the know – part II). This means you are doing extra work, in all probability distracting you from the things you should be doing. Meanwhile, your colleague will be aware of you scrutinising their every action, raising their stress level and probably increasing the risk of them making a mistake. They will almost certainly feel inhibited from taking any initiative, when that may be exactly the best thing they could do.

The issue of trust is even more important when it involves the leader in an emergency.

At the beginning of this chapter, we described how the crew of United Airlines 232 managed to save most of the people on board after an explosion destroyed the tail engine and took out all the hydraulic systems. A comparable incident involved Qantas flight 32[11] in 2010, when an explosion in one engine caused a fuel leak, a fire and widespread damage to other systems. By chance, there were five pilots on board: the usual three plus a check captain and a supervising check captain. Led by flight 32's captain, Richard de Crespigny, all five pilots worked together to safely land the plane in spite of the extensive damage and being heavily over the prescribed landing weight due to all the fuel that it had not been possible to ditch. Once landed, the crew and passengers faced another danger as the plane was surrounded by leaking fuel and the very high risk of a catastrophic fire. Thanks to Captain de Crespigny's

---

10 Ginnett (2010)

11 de Crespigny (2012)

calm and unhurried appraisal of the situation, all 440 passengers and 29 crew were able to get safely off the plane.

Later, Captain de Crespigny said that he had complete trust in his colleagues to do what was necessary. In return, the other pilots had complete trust in him. The passengers also reported that, although it was clear they were in danger, the way the captain and others reacted to the situation gave them complete trust that all would be well.

We say more about trust in the section on organisational responsibilities at the end of this chapter.

9. **Good teams are creative** In our world of complex, adaptive systems, human beings are continually *creating safety*. Conditions for 'normal' operations are paradoxically often suboptimal: the right tool cannot be found; essential materials are missing; a member of the team is off sick or absent; component subsystems interact in unexpected ways, and so on. And yet these 'normally abnormal' conditions rarely result either in performance stopping altogether or some disastrous outcome occurring.

Managing unpredictable complex, adaptive systems depends on creativity as a constant source of new degrees of freedom,[12] and only humans have the necessary creativity. Humans continually find ways of adjusting the system and finding workarounds that keep it functioning adequately, if not perfectly, while avoiding major risks. They routinely operate the system in ways never envisaged by its designers or senior managers.

While we can spot problems and come up with solutions as individuals, we tend to be far more creative when working as part of a team. As the old saying goes, 'two heads are better than one'. The examples of United Airlines flight 232 and Qantas flight 32 show how good teams can solve the most challenging of problems. Apollo 13, the space mission that nearly ended disastrously, provides another example.

In 1970, the Apollo 13 lunar mission was approaching the Moon when the crew heard an explosion and saw most of their oxygen supply venting into space. There was a real threat that the spacecraft and its three astronauts would be stranded in space for ever. To have the smallest chance of returning to Earth, the astronauts and ground crew had to solve a number of serious problems.

One of these was how to overcome failing carbon-dioxide filters. Back at Houston, the mission control engineer, Ed Smylie, got members of his team together, told them what was available on the spacecraft and issued the challenge *"Figure something out"*. They created a filter out of a plastic bag, a cardboard box, some duct tape and a sock. In the command module of the spacecraft, Jim Lovell, Jack Swigert and Fred Haise managed to construct the replacement filter. It worked and contributed to their safe return. Instead of being a total disaster, Apollo 13 became a *"successful failure"*.[13]

Captain de Crespigny of Qantas flight 32 describes the process well: *"We sucked the brains from all the pilots in the cockpit to make one massive brain and we used that intelligence to resolve problems on the fly because they were unexpected events, unthinkable events."*

---

12 We reference Ross Ashby's (1956) law of requisite variety a number of times in this book. The variety of a system can only be controlled by greater variety, ie the controller must have the same or greater number of degrees of freedom as the system controlled. This fundamental principle is complicated in complex systems since the controller is part of the same system and is therefore contributing to the degrees of freedom of the system as a whole.

13 Lovell & Kluger (1995)

We say more about team creativity later in this chapter.

10. **Good teams read each other's minds (up to a point)** Many animals are social, but only human beings *think* about being social. (Maybe other primates do a little bit, but to nothing like the extent that humans do, nor with the same sophistication.) As individuals, we are conscious that we have ideas, feelings and intentions. In other words, we can reflect on our State, Understanding and Goals. But as humans, we can go further: we know that others have ideas, feelings and intentions too. Crucially, we take these insights into the minds of others into account when we ourselves act. Listen to celebrity chef Alain Bourdain as he describes the extraordinary nature of the bond between him and his sous-chef: "*In our glory days together ... I could look across the room at Steven, raise an eyebrow, maybe make an imperceptible movement with my chin, and the thing – whatever the thing was at the time – would be done.*"[14]

We think about mind-reading as a stage act, but in fact we are engaged in reading the minds of others all the time in our families, at work, in the street. It is something that even very young babies begin to learn. By having some clue about what another person is thinking, feeling or intending, we can better predict what they are likely to do. We can then adjust our actions accordingly.

(It is worth noting that this kind of mind-reading can get complicated: 'I can predict what you are going to do because I know what you predict I am going to do'. It is the key to playing many types of game. If I can predict what you are likely to predict that I am going to do, then I can wrong-foot you by doing something different. However, you may predict that I will try to wrong-foot you, so you try to do something different yourself.)

It is this kind of wordless communication that is so critical in an emergency, although here of course – unlike in a competitive game – you want your predictions about your colleagues and their predictions about you to be accurate. The more you can achieve this, the more integrated and coordinated your actions will be.

A word of caution

As human beings, we have an unsurpassed capacity for mind-reading. It is this ability – imagining the imaginations of others – that is considered responsible for the success of our race in building civilisations and achieving our dominant position on the planet.[15] But while we are good, we are not as good as we think we are. Even long-standing colleagues, or husbands and wives who have been married for decades, are often wrong when they make assumptions about what the other is thinking, feeling or intending. There is only one way to be (reasonably) sure and that is to *ask*. The reason why one can never be totally sure is that, as well as a capacity for mind-reading, humans have a related talent for deception.

Mind-reading and deception are both obviously related to trust, and we say more about this later. Many of these points are related to our capacities and limitations in making sense of things – see Chapter 6 (Being in the know – part I).

---

14 Epley (2014), p. xii

15 Harari (2014)

Taskwork training versus teamwork training

Most professional training focuses on *taskwork*, the technical knowledge and skills needed to perform a particular job. The requirements for *teamwork*, the knowledge and skills needed for working with others, are often left for the individual to pick up informally on the job. Over the past 10 to 20 years, organisations engaged in high-risk operations have recognised that a more systematic approach to developing teamwork is necessary if their systems are to be safe. But this demands the right kind of team training.

Traditionally, team training took the form of team-building events that involved sending members of a team on some physically demanding activity, such as designing and building a raft to cross a river. The aims were for team members to get to know each other, especially their strengths and weaknesses, and to build a somewhat mystical quality – 'team spirit'. While team building undoubtedly had some benefits, it did not necessarily develop the specific skills that research such as the TADMUS and CRM programmes has shown are the key to high-performance teamwork.

A range of different teamwork training approaches have now been developed, including training based in the classroom, simulator and live workplace. The content includes communication, coordination, assertiveness and challenging, decision-making, problem-solving, cross-training (learning about other roles in the team) and so on. It is important that team training is not simply about giving information, but about opportunities for direct experience and practice, coupled with feedback on performance.[16]

How our social nature can create threats

Human beings are supremely social animals. We spend our lives in groups. We evolved to be in groups. Our well-being and very survival depend on being part of groups, which is why we want to be in them. Many students of human evolution see our underpinning ability for shared work in groups as the main factor in the emergence of *Homo sapiens* as the dominant species on the planet. Our capacity for imagination, cooperation and coordination has let us do increasingly complex and ambitious things. But the importance of groups in our lives means that sometimes groups have an influence that can be harmful. Here are some examples.

Compliance with group norms and organisational drift

Think back to when you started a new job, possibly your first ever job. How did you feel? Probably a little nervous. But what were you nervous about? You may have been confident about your ability to engage with the job, but you were probably a bit worried about your new colleagues. Would they accept you? Would you fit in?

In such situations, you are naturally sensitive to any clues about what the group norms are. How does this particular group think and act? What opinions and attitudes are acceptable – or not? What do they find funny? Objectionable? How will you have to behave to become one of the group?

---

16 For more information on techniques for team training, see Cannon-Bowers & Salas (1998).

In 2011, a young man joined the crew of a ferry in Woolwich, near London, England. Not long after he joined, he became entangled in the ropes during a mooring operation. Tragically, he was dragged overboard and drowned. The accident investigation concluded: *"A number of the working practices used on board clearly demonstrated an erosion of the best practices the crew members had been taught ... it would have been very difficult for him to adopt working practices that were at variance to those followed by his more experienced and senior colleagues. Hence he is likely to have complied with the custom and practice on board."*[17]

The danger of compliance in this case arose because of the erosion of best practice. If the crew had been following best practice, it would have been in the young seaman's safety interests to comply.

It is common for work groups operating largely on their own to develop local practices that, over time, increasingly deviate from best practice. This tendency is known as 'organisational drift'.[18] These local practices are usually examples of operators finding their own balance between efficiency and thoroughness – typically biased towards efficiency at the expense of thoroughness. For much of the time, these local practices work. However, when something changes – for example, the group has to interact with other parts of the organisation that do not know about these local practices, or, as in the tragic case of the young ferryman, a newcomer to the group follows what the others are doing out of a social need to be accepted by them – then disaster can follow.

The bystander effect

Consider two situations you may find yourself in.

No smoke without fire

You are early for an appointment and are sitting on your own in an unfamiliar waiting room. As you wait, you smell smoke. Shortly afterwards you notice smoke coming under the door. What do you do? You react of course. You do whatever you can to find out what is happening and if necessary look for a safe way out.

But what happens if you are not alone, and there are other people also sitting in the waiting room? If they don't react, you probably don't react either. The more other people there are in the room, the longer you take to react. In fact, you are likely to wait four times longer to react when others are present than when you are on your own.[19]

Would you walk on by?

As you emerge from a busy railway station on your way to an appointment, you see a man in his late 20s lying on the steps. He is scruffily dressed and seems to be asking for help, although you can't quite make out what he is saying. This station is in a run-down area of town that you know is frequented by many down-and-outs. Do you stop and see if you can help the man? Or do you keep on walking to your appointment?

---

17 MAIB (2012)

18 See Chapter 12 (Being human)

19 Latané & Darley (1968)

We all like to think we would be the Good Samaritan and stop to help. But again, your behaviour is strongly influenced by the presence of others. If you are on your own, you are more likely to try to help. But if there are other passers-by and they are all hurrying about their business, then – regrettably – you are likely to do the same. This phenomenon is known as the *bystander effect*. It has been well substantiated by research and by numerous real-life incidents.

Research into the bystander effect was triggered by a notorious murder in New York in 1964. Kitty Genovese was a 28-year-old bar manager who was attacked by Winston Moseley on her way home. Moseley feared he had been spotted and left the scene. He returned half an hour later to attack Kitty again, this time wounding her fatally. The murder became notorious when it was later reported that 38 people had witnessed the attack but had done nothing to help.[20]

More recent – and more thorough – investigations have shown this to be a distorted account of the incident, possibly deliberately created by a police chief wishing to distract attention from the police's failure to respond to at least one, and possibly two, emergency calls from witnesses. Nonetheless, many people were at least partially aware of what was going on and yet did nothing.

Many incidents similar to the Kitty Genovese case have now been well documented – and in some cases captured on video. One recent case is that of Walter Vance, who collapsed with a heart problem in a busy store on Black Friday in 2011.[21] Shoppers continued to walk around the stricken man, some even stepping over him in their pursuit of bargains. Eventually a nurse found Walter and began CPR, but her intervention was too late and Walter died.

Even more shocking is the case of Wang Yue in 2011.[22] Wang Yue was a two-year-old girl in China. She was hit by a van. Bystanders left her lying in the road. She was then run over by a large truck and again left in the road. Eighteen people passed by without doing anything. She was eventually rescued by a rubbish scavenger but later died. The whole of the incident was captured on CCTV.

How can people be so callous? In fact, they are probably not so callous, but are following a powerful principle of social behaviour. That principle is 'do what others do'. Many social situations are ambiguous: it is not clear what is going on. Is the young man on the ground ill (in which case we will probably help) or is he drunk (in which case we don't want to get involved)? When we don't have enough information to resolve the ambiguity, then a reasonable strategy is to do what others are doing. They may well know things we don't know. So if they ignore the man on the ground, they may know for sure he is drunk, and we do the same. There is also an element of compliance with group norms here. If we intervene and the man is a notorious drunk, then we may look foolish in the eyes of the others. This is painful.

The risks associated with not reacting to signs of a problem when carrying out safety-critical operations are obvious but hard to avoid. When people around you are doing nothing, it takes courage to stand out from the crowd and do something. You may look foolish if you are wrong about there being a problem. But it is better to look foolish than to let a potential disaster develop unchallenged.

---

20 Darley & Latané (1968)

21 Kelly (2011)

22 Foster (2011)

Groupthink

Usually, decisions made by a group of people are better than those made by a single individual. This is true whether the group makes the decision collectively or whether one person makes it but in consultation with others. Sometimes, however, groups that make a decision get it horribly wrong. This is due to the phenomenon known as *groupthink*.[23]

The first well-documented instance of groupthink involved the US military fiasco known as the *Bay of Pigs*. In 1961, US President Kennedy and his cabinet decided to back an invasion of Cuba by Cuban exiles with the aim of overthrowing Fidel Castro. The invading force landed at the Bay of Pigs and was quickly defeated by Castro's army. The invasion was always doomed to fail, and afterwards Kennedy berated his colleagues and himself: "*How could we have been so stupid?*"

The thing was that Kennedy was far from stupid. He was probably one of the most intelligent US presidents. His cabinet included many of the brightest people in the US. Studies of this disastrous decision have found that the problem wasn't stupidity but group dynamics. Groupthink occurs when the primary focus of the group is on maintaining consensus, rather than on making the best decision. Groupthink is especially likely when there is a strong or highly charismatic leader. Group members either do not dare to oppose the leader or wish to avoid embarrassing the leader.

 Get help with how to challenge other people in **Chapter 13**

Typically, some members of the group sit there thinking "*This is a mistake*" or "*The boss is wrong*", but say nothing. And because nobody says anything, each thinks that nobody else agrees with them. All it takes to destroy the 'spell' of groupthink is for one member of the group to speak out. One person saying what they really think gives courage to the others. Soon it is obvious that the apparent consensus does not exist, and the chances of finding a good decision are greatly increased. Avoiding groupthink is obviously closely connected to the issue of challenging we discussed above.

In-groups versus out-groups

One of the many things our membership of a group gives us is *identity*. We all need a sense of identity, knowledge of who we are, what kind of person we are, what we do, who we are connected to. In fact, our identity arises from our membership of lots of different groups: family, occupation, gender, nationality, religion, interests, cause. Our membership of a group gives us status, values, a code of conduct, and much else.

For a group to be a group, its members must know who is in the group. This automatically means knowing who is not in the group. There is thus an *in-group* and an *out-group*. The tribal mechanisms favoured by human evolution mean that we have a deep instinct to perceive members of out-groups not just as *different* in some respect but as *threats*. We see our in-group as good and the out-group as bad. We help and protect fellow members of our in-group, but avoid or even attack members of out-groups.

---

23 Janis (1982)

Perceived group membership can appear anywhere and can be highly arbitrary. A car driver may be deeply hostile to a cyclist, perhaps even shouting abuse when their paths cross on the road. But when the same two people meet at work, their shared profession (engineers, say) may cause them to join together in shared hostility to another profession (managers, say).

In a famous experiment in the 1950s,[24] 12-year-old boys from very similar social backgrounds on a residential summer camp were divided at random into two groups. The boys gave their groups names: the Eagles and the Rattlers – a common means of creating a group identity. The groups were given competitive tasks to perform. As usually happens, the boys glorified their own group (they were the best and most honest, courageous, loyal, etc) and denigrated the other group (as the worst, cheats, cowardly, etc). The rivalry rapidly escalated into violence. The behaviour became so bad that the experiment had to be terminated early.

On a more serious scale, the same group dynamics underlie much prejudice, discrimination, and worse phenomena such as ethnic cleansing and genocide. Tribalism still runs deep in our evolutionary psychology.

In adult workplaces, in-group/out-group rivalries do not usually manifest themselves in violence, but they do create barriers between the groups, which can get in the way of full cooperation. Of course, it is precisely in those moments when safety is at risk that full cooperation between everyone is demanded. Any hesitation or reluctance in responding to requests for assistance, information or resources could mean an opportunity for system recovery is lost.

The safe organisation recognises the dangers that can arise from in-group/out-group dynamics, as well as groupthink, the bystander effect, compliance with inappropriate practices and norms, and other distortions of behaviour arising from social forces. In the next section, we look at the growth of diversity in the workplace. As people working together come from more and more different groups, the scope for separating into different in-groups and out-groups increases. Avoiding these dangers requires proactive initiatives across the organisation – in particular, the development of what has become known as *social capital*. We discuss this vital topic in the final section of this chapter.

Diversity is not a political aspiration – it's a practical need

To state the obvious, people are varied. We are all different from each other. Human beings come in various shapes, heights, colours, ages, genders, sexual orientations and nationalities. There are many different types of personality. Some of us are outgoing by nature, whereas others are more withdrawn. Some people tend to be happy and optimistic; some tend to be gloomy and pessimistic. Some of us like to take risks; others prefer caution.

All of these are aspects of who we *are*. We don't (as a general rule) choose our gender, skin colour, personality, nationality, and so on. These characteristics are usually constant through our lives. But we also differ from each other in terms of who we *become*. As we go through life we have different experiences and make different choices. Our educations vary. Some of us follow very practical paths; others take more academic routes. We choose different jobs and professions: mechanic, electrician, engineer, seaman, pilot, air traffic controller, doctor,

---

24 Sherif (1988)

nurse, system designer, programmer, farmer, fisherman, manager, trainer … Our personal lives vary. We may marry, raise children, divorce. We may have lots of money or struggle to get by. Most of us will experience good times and bad times, challenges and crises.

All of the characteristics we are born with and all our life experiences, whether these are the results of our choices or just what life brings us, shape who we are at this stage in our lives. In Chapter 5 (Being in a state), we looked at some aspects of state, such as fatigue and stress. These are (hopefully) temporary states – we get tired or stressed for a time, but with luck, we recover. Here, we are concerned with our more fundamental states – aspects of ourselves that are fixed or at least change very slowly.

It is these deep differences between people that are captured by the term *diversity*. Diversity matters. These differences affect our behaviour at work and especially how we interact with the people around us. As we discussed just now, they can provide the basis on which people divide into in-groups and out-groups, with all their associated dangers.

In terms of our SUGAR model, diversity means that different people in the same situation will have different States, Understanding and Goals. All of these are heavily influenced by the background that each person brings to the situation: their nationality, ethnicity, religion, culture, gender, age, disability, etc.

In this section, we look at how these differences are important for safety, both as potential risks but also as essential resources that can promote safety. We focus mainly on cultural differences – especially those rooted in ethnicity or nationality – since these are increasingly factors in the globalised workplaces of today and tomorrow.

There are two important points we must stress here. First, there is no suggestion that members of any group are better or worse than members of any other group. They are, however, likely to differ in certain aspects of their beliefs, attitudes and behaviours. Second, individuals vary in the extent to which they are representative of the various groups to which they belong. An awareness of group characteristics is important, but it should never obscure the particular nature of the individual.

A double-edged sword

Workforces in organisations of all types are increasingly diverse. There are a number of good business reasons for this. A recent study by McKinsey[25] found that companies that were diverse in terms of gender, race or ethnicity outperformed competitors with more homogeneous workforces. The authors point to an increased ability to win talent and improved customer orientation, employee satisfaction and decision-making. They note that other forms of diversity, such as age, sexual orientation and experience, probably also bring similar benefits.

The need to attract skilled personnel is leading to increased diversity. There is stiff competition to find staff with sought-after qualifications and skills. Advances in technology create the demand for new professions. For example, the new focus on 'big data'[26] has created jobs that did not exist a few years ago, such as data scientists with a combination

---

25 Hunt et al (2015)

26 'Big data' refers to the storage, rapid processing and analysis of very large data sets via specially designed algorithms, usually involving machine learning. The data sets can potentially be integrated from many different sources, including the 'internet of things', via data fusion techniques. Big data is characterised by its *volume* (quantity), *variety* (type and nature), *velocity* (speed at which it can be processed), *variability* (relative (in)consistency) and *veracity* (quality).

of computing and statistical knowledge. Demographic trends play a part too, as many populations in Western countries have fewer young people and more old ones. Companies must look beyond their traditional recruitment profiles, realising that there are major human resources beyond their traditional recruitment pools that have not been fully tapped. Recent years have also seen large movements of population towards the developed world as people leave their homelands to escape wars, drought, famine, poverty and unemployment. The McKinsey report presents figures showing that there remains much scope for finding new pools of talent. Over half of the senior executives of a large sample of major companies surveyed by *The Economist*[27] say that they strongly promote diversity and inclusion.

While diversity brings many benefits, it also brings problems. These problems include *"tensions, poor communication, reduced job satisfaction, higher turnover levels and stress"*.[28] As we shall see later, whether the effects of diversity are positive or negative depends largely on the quality of *leadership*.

Cultural diversity and culture shock

The double-edged sword of diversity is particularly significant in the context of safety-critical activities. We concentrate here on cultural diversity, since this is the dimension that is most relevant to high-risk enterprises. To be even more specific, we focus mainly on national culture. However, much of this discussion about national culture also applies to other types of culture, notably professional and organisational.[29]

The term 'national culture' is often used to refer to a nation's artistic heritage: its music, paintings, literature, and the like. That is not what we mean here.

When you go to a country you have not visited before, you are likely to notice that people dress differently, they eat different foods, they inhabit different houses, visit different places of worship and so on. These are all *artefacts*: physical objects that give outer expression to the local culture. But the things people *do* are likely to be different too. Maybe they drive on the opposite side of the road. They eat at different times of the day. They may address each other with more or less familiarity. Some people nod their head to indicate agreement; others shake their head. You may unwittingly give offence through some gesture that is perfectly acceptable at home. You may feel uncomfortable because when you talk with them, they stand 'too close' to you. They may use their hands a lot when they talk. What they say to you may seem vague and incomplete. You eventually realise that they assume you intuitively understand much more of what they say than you actually do. They expect you to 'read between the lines', but this is challenging.

All these types of custom and practice are deeper expressions of the culture. But there is a still deeper level of culture: the beliefs about the nature of people and the world, and the values they hold dear. These are facets of culture that we assimilate as we grow up. For us, this is just the way the world is. We hardly ever think about these beliefs, assumptions and values. We tend to take them for granted until we meet somebody who holds different beliefs, makes different assumptions, acts in accordance with different values. This can be profoundly unsettling and is captured in the term 'culture shock'.

---

27 Economist Intelligence Unit (2009)

28 Starren et al (2013), p. 7

29 See Helmreich & Merritt (2001)

Culture can be viewed as the different answers that societies come up with in response to various universal challenges.[30] Different theorists have defined these challenges somewhat differently, leading to different dimensions for describing different cultures. The most well-known of these is the scheme developed by Hofstede.[31] This is summarised in Table 11.1. Hofstede's methodology has sometimes been criticised[32] but his cultural dimensions are the ones most used in research. We only consider here the four dimensions in Hofstede's original model as a later, fifth, dimension is of limited relevance here.

Table 11.1 Hofstede's value dimensions[33]

Dimension		Description	Example countries
Individualism v Collectivism	Individualist	People should look after themselves and their family. It is easy and normal to move between different communities and groups.	US, Canada, Australia, UK
	Collectivist	People should be responsible/loyal to the community into which they are born. Community protects members.	Japan, South Korea, Mexico, Brazil
Power-Distance	High	People accept and respect inequality in power and status. Juniors should not disagree. Seniors should not consult.	Malaysia, Guatemala, India, Arab countries
	Low	People do not accept differences in power and status. They expect more autonomy and make their own decisions.	Denmark, Israel, New Zealand, Sweden
Uncertainty Avoidance	High	People are uncomfortable with situations that they perceive as unstructured, unclear, ambiguous, or unpredictable. They have absolute beliefs and strict codes of behaviour.	Greece, Japan, Portugal, Uruguay
	Low	People are more comfortable with uncertainty and ambiguity. Fewer formal rules and guidelines.	Jamaica, Sweden, Hong Kong, Denmark
Masculine v Feminine	Masculine	People value success, assertiveness, competition, earnings, and material acquisition.	Japan, Austria, Italy, Mexico
	Feminine	People value a friendly, caring atmosphere, security, good physical conditions, and cooperation.	Denmark, Finland, Norway, Sweden

---

30 For example, Schein (1985) defines culture as "...a pattern of basic assumptions – invented, discovered or developed by a given group as it learns to cope with its problems of external adaptation and internal integration – that has worked well enough to be considered valid and, therefore, to be taught to new members as the correct way to perceive, think and feel in relation to those problems".

31 Hofstede (1991 & 2001)

32 See, for example, McSweeney (2002)

33 Adapted from Taras et al (2011)

Cultural variation in the workplace

Using the Hofstede value dimensions, Taras et al[34] identify a number of ways in which people belonging to cultures with different combinations of values differ in the workplace. Table 11.2 shows some examples of these differences.

Table 11.2 Examples of different cultural preferences in the workplace[35]

Workplace issue	Culture	Preference
Leadership styles	Individualist + Low Power-Distance	Want participative leadership
	Collectivist + High Power-Distance	Want directive, charismatic leaders
Group dynamics	Collectivist	Want to work in a team
	Individualist	Less keen to work in a team
Communication style	Masculine + Individualist	Prefer directness, self-promotion and openness
	Feminine + Collectivist + High Power-Distance	Prefer indirectness and modesty
	Individualist	Use words primarily to convey meaning
	Collectivist	Much meaning is conveyed by body language, tone of voice and other non-verbal cues, including what is not said
Compensation	Individualist	Person who contributes the most should get the largest reward
	Collectivist	Rewards should be distributed equally, regardless of who did what
	High Power-Distance	Most senior person should get the biggest reward
Decision-making and authority	Individualist + Feminine	Want to be involved in decision-making. Tend to respect authority less
	Masculine + Collectivist + High Power-Distance	Prefer top-down decision-making. Tend to respect authority more
Conflict handling	Collectivist + Feminine	Concern for interests of other. Keen to use mediator. Want to maintain harmony
	Individualist + Masculine	More outspoken. May quit the group if believe they are treated unfairly
Work design	Individualist + Low Power-Distance	Want autonomy, flexibility, personal contribution, quality time off
	Collectivist + High Power-Distance	Want structure, clear directions, closeness with supervisor, tradition. Do not want to show initiative

---

34 Taras et al (2011)

35 Adapted from Taras et al (2011)

The problem with diversity

Certain cultures tend to be vulnerable to certain types of accident.[36] Perhaps the best-documented ones are those concerning flight crews from high power-distance cultures, notably cases where the co-pilot was too in awe of the captain to intervene even when it was obvious the plane was headed for disaster. The following are examples from both the aviation and maritime sectors:

- In 1977, a cargo plane crashed shortly after take-off in Alaska.[37] The pilot was American, but the other two crew members were Japanese. Neither crew member challenged the pilot over the fact he was drunk.

- Avianca flight 52 crashed near New York in 1990 after running out of fuel.[38] The Colombian crew failed to warn both the pilot and air traffic control about the dangers of the situation.

- Korean Air flight 801 crashed in Guam in 1997.[39] The flight encountered a number of problems and the pilot was suffering from fatigue. The pilot ignored warnings from the flight engineer that the signal he was following was not the correct one.

- In 1996, the bulk cargo ship MV *Bright Field* lost power and collided with a shopping mall in New Orleans. The American pilot could not understand the communications between the bridge and the engine room, as they were in Chinese. Furthermore, he did not take account of the cultural tendency for the Chinese crew to be reluctant to say 'no' to an authority figure such as a pilot.[40]

- In 2004, the chemical tanker *Attilio Ievoli* ran aground in the West Solent. The second officer, a Ukrainian, tried to tell the master, an Italian, that the vessel was off course. However, the master was using his mobile phone at the time and did not reply. The second officer did not try again. This has been interpreted as a result of the reluctance of East European subordinates to challenge their seniors.[41]

- In 2008, *Sichem Melbourne*, a product carrier, struck mooring structures as she was leaving the Coryton oil refinery on the River Thames estuary. The English pilot who was on board did not explain his plan to the Russian master. Apparently, the pilot feared that the master would take this as an insult to his professional competence. Due to the lack of a shared understanding of the planned manoeuvre, confusion arose, resulting in heavy contact with the mooring assembly and a near miss with an oil tanker.[42]

There are a number of research studies that give other views of the relationship between culture and safety. For example, one examined the surprising discovery that Danish workers on the Øresund Bridge between Denmark and Sweden had four times as many accidents as the Swedish workers on the same bridge.[43] The Danish and Swedish cultures are similar in many respects but, as a result of a number of differences (education, apprenticeship

---

36 For a detailed account of research in this area, see Helmreich & Merritt (2001).

37 National Transportation Safety Board (1979)

38 National Transportation Safety Board (1991)

39 National Transportation Safety Board (2000)

40 US Coast Guard (1997)

41 MAIB (2004)

42 MAIB (2008)

43 Spangenbergen et al (2003)

systems and pay for sick leave, among others), the Swedish workers had a more careful attitude to safety.

Another area of relevant cultural difference is risk perception. It turns out that Chinese people take more risks than Americans in their investment decisions but not in other areas.[44] This may be due to the fact that China is a collectivist culture, and people are more likely to receive financial help from others if they get into difficulty.

> **Read more** about the perception of risk and how it affects human decision-making in **Chapter 8**

In a study of national culture and safety in the oil and gas industry, groups of workers from the UK, US, US (Hispanic), Australia, Philippines and Malaysia were compared.[45] Workers from the UK and Philippines reported taking the fewest risks, while workers from Malaysia reported taking the most. The same study noted an interesting difference between Norwegian and UK workers on offshore installations. Norwegians had more 'fatalistic' attitudes, eg *"accidents just happen, there is little one can do to avoid them"*. UK workers believed that production had a higher priority than safety, eg *"rules and instructions relating to safety make it difficult to keep up with production targets"*.[46]

Although members of a given culture may have a tendency to express certain attitudes and perceptions related to safety, the risks are much greater when members of different cultures have to work together. It is readily apparent from Table 11.2 that different preferences in terms of leadership, communication, decisions, risk and so on can translate into threats to safety when people from different cultural backgrounds work together in high-risk environments.

And Table 11.2 does not even include the most obvious multicultural obstacle to safety: people speaking different languages. It is common for many workers in multinational organisations to be speaking a language that is not their mother tongue. Add in noisy workplaces and a variety of accents and there is immense scope for misunderstanding. In a large-scale study of communication errors on the UK railways,[47] the authors found that the most dangerous misunderstandings are where the people speaking to each other think they have correctly understood each other, but haven't. One manifestation of this is the well-known 'nod-and-grin' phenomenon, in which one person doesn't like to admit they have not understood, but tries to give the impression they have.

Aviation provides numerous examples.[48] The area naturally brings together people of different cultures, but the universal use of cockpit voice recorders provides communications data that is not so readily available to safety-critical operations in other sectors.

---

44 Hsee & Weber (1999)

45 Mearns & Yule (2009)

46 Mearns & Yule (2009), p. 782

47 Gregory Harland Ltd (2006)

48 See, for example, Orasanu et al (1997)

There are, however, a number of well-documented incidents and studies in the shipping sector.[49] In particular, there is an increased risk of communication problems when the pilot is on the bridge. A well-known example is *Cosco Busan*, the container ship that hit a span of the San Francisco-Oakland Bay Bridge, resulting in serious oil pollution. There were a number of factors in this incident, including the Chinese-speaking captain and crew, and the English-speaking pilot. Here the problem was not so much miscommunication as non-communication[50] between two very different cultures. While the American pilot behaved in a way that was to him, no doubt, normal and businesslike,[51] it came across to the Chinese captain as *"cold and adversarial"*.

Barry Strauch[52] cites a Canadian study[53] of 273 accidents involving ocean-going vessels when a pilot was on the ship with a multicultural crew. Of these accidents, 200 involved misunderstandings between the pilot and the captain or other bridge officers. Most of the misunderstandings were attributed to 'deficient language skills'.

All these cultural differences pose considerable challenges for the team leaders and managers who are responsible for culturally diverse teams and workgroups. But it is not all bad news, as we shall now see.

The need for diversity

While governments, companies and researchers have largely focused on the problems caused by multicultural workplaces, the sector with perhaps the most experience in this area provides a much more positive picture. This is the world of maritime operations. By the nature of their trade, seafarers have had to manage multicultural experiences for centuries. Two-thirds of the world merchant fleet have multinational crews and a significant proportion of ships have crews that include five or more nationalities. In 2002, a major study of the multinational aspects of the wider seafarer community concluded optimistically that *"multinational crews are not only viable but can operate extremely successfully. Multinational crews are popular with both companies and seafarers. A number of unanticipated advantages were associated with their introduction"*.[54] These advantages included improved cooperation and collaboration as the number of nationalities increased, greater awareness and avoidance of cultural sensitivities, and the disappearance of stereotyping of other nationalities.

There is another positive aspect of diversity that is very important to emphasise in the context of this book. We have repeatedly made the point that it is in the nature of complex systems to generate novel states that were never foreseen by the system designers, and which pose fundamental threats to safety. These states require operators on the front line to come up with novel solutions – and that demands not only deep expertise but also

---

49 See, for example, Strauch (2010)

50 National Transportation Safety Board (2009)

51 As is usual in major incidents, multiple factors played a part. In addition to the negative cultural issues, the pilot, John Cota, was found to be operating under the influence of a cocktail of prescription drugs, which he had declared to the US Coastguard, but without response. As a result of the investigation, the pilot became the first in US history to go to prison for his part in a disaster. He was sentenced to ten months in federal prison.

52 Strauch (2010)

53 Transportation Safety Board of Canada (1995)

54 Kahveci et al (2002), p. iii

creativity. Thomas Malone notes from his work on collective intelligence[55] that having a female team member makes a team more creative, and there is now lots of research evidence that diversity in general makes teams more creative.

A recent article in *Scientific American* concluded that diversity makes us smarter.[56] Katherine Phillips observed that while we might expect greater creativity to result from bringing together people with different knowledge and skills, a number of studies have shown that simply having more social diversity – nationality, race, gender, or even political affiliation – has the same effect. Being in a diverse team makes us think differently. We also listen differently. When trying to come up with solutions to a problem, more information is shared and more options are generated. Importantly, information and options get better consideration.

A key point from Chapter 6 (Being in the know – part I) is that humans have no access to an independent 'objective' world. Instead, we work with each other to construct a shared meaning, which we then use to ask more questions. The development of this shared knowledge depends on the different questions that spring from the different perspectives that we bring to each other. Our continued progress *requires* the diversity of these different perspectives as they challenge, inform and cross-fertilise each other – as they have done ever since we suddenly found within ourselves the capacity for imagination some 70,000 years ago.[57]

While the ancient expedient of tribalism evolved to provide sanctuary, familiarity, protection, comfort and survival from day to day, it seems that our creativity, development and survival in a world of complexity need something different: diversity, openness and a celebration of the power that different perspectives bring.

It is, of course, the case that it is more difficult to achieve a consensus in a diverse group than in one that is homogeneous. It should be expected that diversity leads to conflict, whose benefits must then be harvested via 'constructive debate'.[58] The key factor is agreement on the goal.

Diversity can be thought of as an antidote to *groupthink*. It is also a key source of the variety that Ross Ashby[59] showed us is essential to deal with the variety that complex, adaptive systems present us with.

In the end, variety is our only way of dealing with complexity, so we need to revere and use it. But how?

Managing diversity

The conclusion here is that diversity in workgroups and teams brings both risks and benefits. The potential risks are mainly due to conflict and miscommunication. The potential benefits are due to increased creativity and innovation. In the everyday functioning of safety-critical systems, it is probably the risks that loom largest. But when the perennial risk of unexpected system behaviour gives rise to a threat, then the better problem-solving capabilities of a diverse team may become paramount.

---

55 Malone & Bernstein (2015)
56 Phillips (2014)
57 Harari (2014)
58 Stanford Business School (1999)
59 Ashby (1956)

It is clear that both team leaders and team members need to be prepared for working with diversity. Diversity initiatives in organisations often seem to be aimed at obscuring the differences between people. This is done with the good intention of avoiding prejudice and discrimination. However, there is a risk that it can seem as if the organisation is trying to achieve a more uniform workforce. Individuals' sense of their identity can feel under threat, leading to loss of morale and motivation. Team leaders in particular must have the skills to ensure that each individual is treated fairly while their identity is respected.

Organisations need to develop policies and strategies designed to achieve both diversity and inclusion. Training and education is needed for team leaders and managers at all levels, but also for all front-line workers.

Network Rail provides a good example of a diversity strategy. This is, in fact, a *diversity and inclusion* strategy – and it is worth noting how Network Rail describes these terms:

"We use 'diversity' to describe our commitment to recognising and respecting the differences between people whilst valuing the contribution everyone can make to our business. 'Inclusion' means creating safe, welcoming workplaces with fair cultures that encourage innovative and fresh ways of thinking and allow people to speak up, especially to suggest where things could be done better. Diversity is about getting a mix, and inclusion is about making sure that the mix works well together." [60]

It is the responsibility of senior managers to create an organisational culture that can accommodate and value national, ethnic and religious cultures and other sources of diversity (gender, age, disability, etc) without suppressing individuals' sense of personal identity. We say more about this in Chapter 12 (Being human).

Leadership and safety

Leadership is a very large topic. There are countless books on how to be a leader, written by management theorists, academics, retired generals and captains of industry, sports coaches, and many more besides.[61] Here we limit ourselves to a rather briefer look at leadership through the lens of our SUGAR model.

In the SUGAR model we depict how what a person decides, does or says is determined by the interaction between their State, Understanding and Goals. In the diagram at the beginning of this chapter, we showed a team as a network in which each person's decisions, actions and communications influence what other team members decide, say and do. Each person is striving to find the optimal balance between efficiency and thoroughness for that moment, against a backcloth of needs, beliefs and objectives.

The primary task of the team *leader* is to ensure that the team as a whole finds the right efficiency–thoroughness balance, getting the job done on time, but safely. To do this, the leader has to make sure – as far as they are able – that each individual:

---

60 Network Rail (2014), p. 7

61 For a highly readable overview of the main current theories of leadership, we recommend Avolio et al (2009). We also recommend the excellent publication from the International Association of Oil & Gas Producers (2013). The purpose of this highly readable document is *"to raise awareness among leaders in the oil and gas industry of the way their leadership shapes Safety Culture. It explains what Safety Culture and Safety Leadership mean, and specifically describes the leadership characteristics that can influence Safety Culture"*. A third recommended publication is *Leading for Safety: A practical guide for leaders in the Maritime Industry*. This is produced by the UK Maritime & Coastguard Agency (undated) and focuses on ten core safety leadership qualities. All three publications are available online (see the references in Chapter 15).

- Is in a productive state (eg is not too tired or stressed)
- Has appropriate understanding (ie has the correct information and can make useful sense of it)
- Is acting in accordance with the agreed (or appropriately reprioritised) goals
- Is communicating effectively and accurately with other team members.

To achieve this, the team leader must get to know the team as individuals but also understand the team dynamics: who influences the others (for good or ill), who has the most experience or expertise, who has a tendency to disturb or annoy the others, who is the natural peacemaker, who likes others to do their work, who is willing to take charge when things get difficult, and so on.

The leader needs to think about their role in terms of the following areas:

- **Selection, training and rehearsing** This means ensuring that the leader has the right person for each role in the team, and each person knows how to do their work properly, both individually and collectively. This should include rehearsing for non-routine and emergency situations.

- **Creating the team climate** This reflects the motivational factors we discussed in Chapter 10 (Being on target).

  - *Autonomy* As the leader develops trust in the team, they must resist the temptation to over-control or 'micro-manage'. Each team member must be allowed the maximum autonomy that the working situation and their level of competence make acceptable.

  - *Purpose* The leader must make the work of the team meaningful, demonstrating by actions and words that the work 'makes a difference'.

  - *Mastery* The leader should always be looking for ways in which the individual and the team as a whole could be improving, acquiring new knowledge and skills and better ways of working together.

  - *Belonging* The leader should aim to create an atmosphere in which team members feel they belong. This means attending to the needs of newcomers to the team, making sure any team member from a minority does not feel excluded or discriminated against, and resolving any conflicts between team members that might compromise safe working.

  - *Fairness* As the team leader is likely to be the first in line in any disciplinary action or investigation of things that go wrong, they should not jump to conclusions; they should ensure that facts are gathered and then considered objectively. The leader should ensure that team members are not only treated fairly but *feel* they are treated fairly.

- **Review and learning** The team leader should create opportunities for the team to regularly review its performance. This should not be just about the leader evaluating the team (although of course they can express their observations and opinions). All team members should be encouraged to give constructive feedback with a view to helping the team to learn and improve as a whole.

- **Representation** The leader stands in a pivotal position between the organisation and the team. They represent the organisation to the team, but also the team to the organisation. The leader must recognise and articulate clearly and firmly the interests of the one to the other.
- **Role model** Lastly, the team leader must demonstrate to the team – through their own actions and ways of being – what team members should be aiming for.

The team leader is likely to be the person in the team with the deepest knowledge of the system. This means they are likely to take charge in any high-risk operational situation. The team leader should seek out opportunities to deepen their expertise (as described in Chapter 10: Being on target) and to develop their capacity to work effectively under severe pressure (see Chapter 5: Being in a state). The leader must also be willing to let another take charge when it is clear that the other person has knowledge or skills that are better suited to the developing situation.

 Get help with dealing with stress in **Chapter 13**

In Chapter 13 (Being practical – part I), we describe a tool (Tables 13.5 and 13.6) that helps leaders and managers to get the most out of their teams.

The magic and mystery of social capital

In 1995, the Japanese city of Kobe was struck by a massive earthquake. Approximately 6,500 people were killed and 300,000 were made homeless. The cost was estimated at $180 billion. Ten years later, in 2005, Hurricane Katrina hit New Orleans, killing 1,600 people and making 250,000 homeless. Within a year of the Japanese quake, Kobe was functioning again at 80% of pre-disaster levels. By contrast, a year after the New Orleans disaster:

"Some neighborhoods remained apparently untouched from the time waters struck, less than half of the schools, restaurants, and stores were open across the city, and employment hovered at less than two-thirds its pre-storm level. In some fields, such as public transportation, hospital openings, and child care centers, rebuilding all but ground to a halt." [62]

Why did Kobe recover quickly while New Orleans struggled? It wasn't that Kobe was more wealthy than New Orleans. Per capita income in Kobe was actually slightly less than in New Orleans. Nor was it that Kobe received more government support. The US government provided $16 billion to New Orleans, but the Japanese government operated a 'no compensation' policy and gave Kobe nothing.

So what made the difference? What made Kobe recover faster than New Orleans? Many studies have shown that what is more important than financial and material resources in such circumstances is the level of *social capital*. Social capital refers to the network of relationships that bind together the people in the community. Social capital depends not only on the number and density of the connections between people, but also on the *quality* of these relationships: how do people feel about the others they are connected to? How willing are they to help others? How much do they trust each other?

---

62 Aldrich (2010)

Large-scale natural disasters such as earthquakes and hurricanes may seem very different from the systems accidents we mainly talk about in this book. So let's look again at something on a more relevant scale, something we talked about earlier in this chapter: teams and creativity.

Social capital and teams

A popular theme in crime movies is the mastermind who brings together experts in the skills needed for the 'heist': the safe-cracker who can open any lock, the alarms wizard, the ace driver, and the rest. Such a brilliant team can surely come up with a creative plan to rob Fort Knox, the Tower of London, the Louvre ... But what actually makes a truly creative team? Margaret Heffernan describes a creative team she brought together when she was CEO of a software company:

"You could argue that we had a lot of brains in the room – and we did. But we also had something more important. We had social capital: the trust, knowledge, reciprocity and shared norms that create quality of life and make a group resilient. In any company, you can have a brilliant bunch of individuals – but what prompts them to share ideas and concerns, contribute to one another's thinking, and warn the group early about potential risks is their connection to one another."[63]

Heffernan also points to a programme of research at the Massachusetts Institute of Technology (MIT) in the US. This sought to identify the factors underpinning the performance of exceptionally creative teams – teams that demonstrated very high levels of *collective intelligence*.[64] One factor that was *not* very important was the IQ level of the individuals in the team. What mattered much more was:

- The team gave everybody nearly equal time to talk.
- Team members displayed high levels of social sensitivity – they were acutely aware of the State, Understanding and Goals of the others.
- There were women in the team – this may be because female members increased the diversity of the team or because women tend to be more socially sensitive than men.

From time to time, people try to create a Super World XI football team, usually to play in some special event. They bring together star players from the top clubs around the world. In spite of the huge talents of the individuals, the performance of these world teams is surprisingly mediocre.

What they lack is social capital – the quality of the relationships that bind people together on a deep level.

A case occurred recently in the English Premier League. Unfashionable Leicester had risen to the top of the Premiership in spite of bookmakers offering odds of 5,000-to-1 against them winning the title at the start of the season. In a key match, Leicester beat highly rated Manchester City at City's own ground. The total value of the Manchester team on the transfer market (an indicator of individual skill) was over £220 million ($290 million). The value of the Leicester team playing that game was less than a tenth of this, at £16 million ($21 million). Claudio Ranieri, Leicester's manager, attributed their success to mutual trust

---

63 Heffernan (2015)

64 Malone & Bernstein (2015)

and respect. One of the players, Leonardo Ulloa, said *"[The secret is] we all play for each other. We are a team."*[65] The *collective performance* of the Leicester team was far too good for the *collection of talent* that comprised Manchester City – as it was for all the other teams in the 2015–16 Premier League.

For teams, the 'whole' minus the 'sum of the parts' equals social capital.

The *Harvard Business Review*[66] has pointed to the value of social contracts for effective teamwork.[67] Such a contract aims to answer questions such as *"What expectations do team members have of each other? What is working well within the team? What is not working well? What should the team keep doing, start doing, and, as importantly, stop doing?"* Importantly, the team leader or the organisation should not impose a contract on the team. The members themselves must draw up the contract, with all feeling ownership of it.

The contract can emphasise qualities such as cooperation rather than competition, helping others and asking for help. It can also highlight negative behaviours to be avoided, such as speaking negatively about others in their absence. The contract should specify how violations will be dealt with.

The team needs to revisit the contract regularly to evaluate how well it is working. This review process will also reinforce the terms of the contract, reminding the team members about what to do and what not to do.

Social capital and trust

Think about the people in your life. Whom do you trust? The chances are that the people you trust most are the ones you have known the longest – family members or friends from childhood. Following close behind are likely to be colleagues you have worked with for years. The best foundation for trust is direct personal experience over an extended time. If someone has repeatedly proven reliable – they do what they say they will do and deliver on their promises – then you will trust them.

But often at work you have to collaborate with someone new, a person in whom you have not had time to develop trust. Nonetheless, you will have to trust them much of the time, since you cannot watch over them every minute of the working day. Your ability to trust someone at the beginning of a working relationship will depend on the trust you place in your organisation's recruitment, selection, training and job assignment systems. You hope that the organisation will only assign to work with you someone who is competent and reliable.

The primary focus of most organisational systems is professional competence. However, trust has to go deeper than this, to an individual's personal qualities: what really motivates them, the source of their integrity, how they will react under pressure. Somebody may have the best CV possible, but something about them means you still don't fully trust them. One way you can begin to develop this personal trust is through someone you do trust. If a friend or colleague in whom you already have deep trust recommends somebody to you, this is a good start. Having connections like this is one aspect of an organisation's social capital.

---

65 Nursey (2016)

66 Riordan & O'Brien (2012)

67 In fact, all working situations are underpinned by a 'psychological contract': the implicit, unwritten understandings and expectations that govern how people work together. The trouble is that, because it's implicit, different people may actually have different understandings. By making the 'contract' written, the Harvard article is attempting to remove the scope for misunderstandings.

Another way to develop trust is getting to know someone outside work. Time spent in social or maybe sporting contact provides opportunities to chat and to share details of leisure interests, family life, aspirations and so on. You are likely in such settings to meet the other's friends and colleagues. These other perspectives allow knowledge of personality and a wider network of relationships to develop. For most of the time, these connections may have purely social value. But in times of emergency, it may be precisely these relationships that give access to information or resources that may influence how well recovery can be made from a serious incident.

Some years back, the authors of this book held a workshop that was attended by UK train drivers and railway signallers. We asked them to share experiences where one of these groups had been affected by the actions of the other. For example, one young driver graphically related what it was like to be driving a train at 100 mph when a signal was changed to red right in front of him, too late for him to stop. It was a revelation to many who had not thought before about how their actions would be experienced by others. The 'old hands' who had worked on the railways for a long time told how, in the days before the privatisation of British Rail, drivers and signallers would share the same mess rooms. Over meals and refreshments, the two groups chatted and got to know each other and learned about each other's jobs. After privatisation, drivers and signallers worked for different companies and no longer shared mess rooms. The opportunity to develop social capital had been lost.

As individuals, we appreciate our personal relationships. On a larger scale, organisations are realising that the richness of the network of relationships within the organisation and with the world outside is a huge source of value. However, people's willingness to trust and help each other can only arise in an organisation that operates in accordance with the fundamental human principle of fairness – a crucial point which, among other matters, we turn to in Chapter 12 (Being human).

 Get help with how to achieve a fair-minded, 'just' culture at a deep level in **Chapter 14**

12 Being human
how organisations get the opposite of what they want

What's the difference between 'complicated' and 'complex'?
Why is hindsight not enough – and what can be done to fix it?
Why is a 'just' culture important – and why is it not enough?
What makes humans 'human'?
What is operational resilience and how can it be increased?

Mere complication

Imagine that you are standing in front of a sleek, brand new, modern automobile.

Underneath its beautiful high-tech paint are a host of integrated subsystems: the advanced braking and anti-wheel-spin system; the hybrid power plant that shuts down petrol combustion when the car is stationary, and harvests braking energy to recharge the advanced battery; the all-round airbag, collapsible components and force sensors of the collision protection system; the video- and radar-assisted manoeuvring system; the forward anti-collision system that engages the brakes if the car approaches something too fast; the dynamic, real-time suspension system that suitably stiffens one side of the car when it goes around the opposite corner; the automatic proximity access system that opens the car when the key fob gets close enough, imparts all the car's service data to the fob when it's docked on the dashboard, and refuses to lock the car if the fob is accidentally left inside; the driver's head-up displays and passengers' entertainment system. And so on.

The myriad of integrated, interdependent, interacting subsystems that make up this car are barely short of miraculous to non-engineers. Nevertheless, the whole car really has been engineered. Its millions of possible states are finite and knowable. Sure, a rather large look-up table would be needed to document them all, but it is possible in principle to do this, to trace through all possible interactions, debug problems and fix them.

So far, we have in front of us a system that is merely *complicated*. It is only when we introduce drivers into cars and let them loose on the road that things radically change. The system goes from being complicated to being *complex*.

The nature of complexity

Complex, adaptive systems are quite different from systems that are merely complicated. Here's how they are different:

- **Complex systems have no central control** There is no-one sitting in a command centre, issuing prescriptive instructions to dumb components. Instead, the components are smart agents (ie decision-makers) who communicate and negotiate with each other autonomously over time and space in order to service their own agendas and fulfil their own terms of reference.

- **Complex systems have many interacting agents who are tightly connected** The leaner, the more just-in-time, and the more efficient such systems are required to be, the tighter the connection between all the components. The tighter the connection, the bigger and more rapid the effects across the whole system of even minor adjustments in the behaviour of any one agent.

- **Complex systems produce behaviour whose specific consequences are unpredictable** This is because the precise behaviour required by agents is always underspecified ahead of time, due to the inherent uncertainty of a system in constant, multidimensional oscillation. Agents must necessarily 'complete the design'[1] moment by moment. The variation in their performance is not just normal, but is inevitable. Sometimes the consequences are good (new efficiencies and processes are created) and sometimes they are bad (accidents, loss and damage occur). Either way, the outcomes emerge from the same source: the necessary performance variability of the agents, who, despite relatively unchanging agendas, can suddenly find themselves at the centre of a constellation of circumstances that has never before occurred.

- **Complex systems can 'drift' over time** This happens because interacting, autonomous agents adapt to each other as they work locally to achieve their goals. Sometimes agents find themselves working harder to fulfil their terms of reference in a system that has been disturbed in some way. Maybe new demands have been placed on the system as a whole from outside. Or perhaps the locally optimising behaviour of agents in one part of the system has made things more difficult in another part. Whatever the source, if the amount of additional work or stress experienced by one or more agents becomes chronic, then the system becomes increasingly brittle and will eventually break – with potentially catastrophic results. The fracture rapidly promulgates across the whole tightly interconnected system like a stone hitting a windscreen.

- **Complex systems can arise even when their agents have relatively few degrees of freedom** Shoals of fish and flocks of birds move, change direction, divide and re-form in astonishing and quite unpredictable ways. Yet each agent (fish or bird) is simply trying to keep itself facing the same way, close to its neighbours and as near the centre as possible. Complexity rises exponentially when the agents are humans with a large number of degrees of freedom that are constantly influenced by the dynamic constellations of factors that comprise their State, Understanding and Goals at any moment in time.

Interestingly, car drivers don't have to be human to create a road system that is complex. There is currently a lot of work going on to develop robotic cars and great hopes for their future are being expressed in some quarters. Such systems will be complex if they

---

1   Dekker (2005)

rely on driver robots making local, on-the-fly adjustments as they negotiate each other's manoeuvres. The different question of how safe such systems are will depend on the law of requisite variety that we discussed in Chapter 8 (Being in the know – part III). If the number of things that can go wrong is greater than the number of degrees of freedom available to the robot, then self-driving cars will still be involved in accidents – just as is the case now for cars driven by humans.

There is increasing talk in shipping circles about the potential for unmanned ships. Based on the law of requisite variety, the same warnings apply: what happens when the ship's controlling software is faced with a unique set of rapidly developing circumstances that are being generated by an arbitrarily large collection of other ships' crews (or robots), which are all trying to pursue their own agendas, adapting to each other and the environment as they go?

The work that is done in safety-critical complex, adaptive systems such as ships, nuclear facilities, construction sites, operating theatres, aircraft cockpits, and road and railway networks depends upon people who constantly vary their performance as they negotiate locally optimal ways of executing their tasks. This means that it is perverse for organisations to automatically construe this variation as non-compliance or as a violation of laid-down procedure. Such perversity tends to happen when gaps open up between the realities of operational life and management expectations. Such gaps appear when there is confusion between 'work as it is imagined', and 'work as it is done'.[2] The difference is that 'work as imagined' is free of the grey, noisy, physically, emotionally and cognitively biased, multi-purposed, ever-changing compromises that characterise dynamic operational environments. The procedures that look so clean and crisp on the office printer are a different matter on the high seas, with badly designed or broken equipment, time-pressured and fatigued crew, incomplete knowledge, uncertain communications, inaccurate assumptions and competing goals that suddenly seem difficult to prioritise in the middle of a force 9 storm.

It is also true, of course, that the behaviour of those same HQ folk must be equally understood as the result of 'grey, noisy, physically, emotionally and cognitively biased, multi-purposed, ever-changing compromises' that characterise their own 'work as done'. No-one is immune from the reality of the complex, adaptive system of which they are a part – wherever they happen to be carrying it out. Difficulties can arise, however, when the assumptions and norms of one operational environment (eg the office) are imposed upon another (eg the ship at sea).

Why do we favour efficiency over thoroughness?

Most pressures to act in the workplace – wherever the workplace is – tend to bias operations towards greater efficiency and, therefore, away from thoroughness. This pressure towards efficiency arises from two sources: *business economics* and *human evolution*.

As agents of the organisation that employs us, we have both a commitment to, and a personal interest in, being productive. Business economics means that our jobs and prospects depend on it, and the organisational measures of our pay and competence are very often geared to the value and tempo that we are able to deliver. It is in our interest to do so.

---

2 Hollnagel (2014)

From the point of view of human evolution, our brains have developed over 2.5 million years to deploy barely conscious, seemingly effortless gut feelings and rules of thumb (also known as 'heuristics'). We favour *System 1* shortcuts over the resource-intensive attention of *System 2*,[3] and we are often quite happy to jump to conclusions from minimal information in order to reserve our limited and precious reasoning abilities as far as possible. We constantly search for efficiencies of time and effort. It is in our nature to do so.

 Get help with dealing with unconscious biases in **Chapter 13**

The 'brakes' of thoroughness, why they fail and how to understand it when they do

The decisions that people are faced with in their operational 'work as done' lives are always trade-offs between efficiency and thoroughness. While people are constantly being nudged towards efficiency by their organisations and their own psychology, thoroughness 'brakes' are imposed by training, professional standards, supervisors, regulators, fellow team members, rules, procedures and the 'common sense' of self-preservation. Trade-offs are made in the moment, and moment by moment. The actual trade-off made in each moment is influenced by the inter-related presence of three very large sources of human factors:

- **State** – which constrains our physical, attention, reasoning and prioritisation capabilities, and colours our interpretation
- **Understanding** – which influences the meaning and context we create and maintain, the expectations we generate and seek to confirm, and our perception of the extent of the risks we think we are taking
- **Goals and motivations** – which govern our needs to survive, to belong and find purpose, to maintain the standards that help define us, and to trust and cooperate with one another.

It follows, therefore, that people's actions and decisions at work need to be evaluated in the light of all the above. It is only ever half the story to apply the narrative of hindsight to try to explain why people did what they did. The other half comes from placing ourselves in the minds of those who suddenly found themselves at the centre of something bad.

What were their beliefs and expectations, and how had these come about? What were the options that they believed they had at the time – and why? What was the status of all the SUGAR human factors for all those involved – not just those directly involved, but all those in other parts of the same connected system – and how had they come to pass?

To the extent that State played a part, how was it that they came to be in that state and to what extent was it avoidable? To the extent that their Understanding turned out to be flawed or misapplied, how was it that it came to be so, and how was it that they were unable (or did not think) to fix it in the time they had available? To the extent that their Goals were flawed or mis-prioritised, what line of thinking led to this, and how was this line of thinking set in motion?

How did all of these factors combine to produce the situation that they constructed for themselves? How far were they in control of those factors? How far was this situation

---

3 Kahneman (2011)

shared? How far was it a function of local optimisations by different people across the system that combined in an unintended, unique way? And how far was it the unintended consequence[4] of perturbations introduced into the system from outside, eg by newly imposed targets, resource changes, new regulations, new rules or changes to working practice, and new priorities?

As a complementary technique for accident investigation, the authors of this book have developed a protocol called Mindset Analysis, based on the SUGAR model.

 Get help with Mindset Analysis in **Chapter 14**

However, Mindset Analysis and the kind of conclusions that it is designed to generate will not be attractive to organisations unless they can see the value of moving beyond blame-based models of productivity, to business models that accommodate the principles of complex, adaptive systems as described above.

In particular, this means developing a culture that is 'just' because it embodies *fair-minded accountability*.

A 'just' culture is a means – not an end

In a 'blame' culture, people are often the targets of suspicion – if they survive – as a result of being close to the action when something goes wrong. A common organisational consequence is that people try to cover up their mistakes and conceal near-misses, which makes everything less safe. Seeing the unfairness or counterproductivity of blaming people, some organisations have tried to develop a 'no-blame' culture to promote a more open flow of safety information. But the problem here is that 'no-blame' cultures can be as unfair as 'blame' cultures when people are not held to account when they should be.

As a result, quite a lot has been written in the last decade or so about the need for a 'just' culture.[5] Tools have been developed as well. For example, the Baines Simmons FAiR® 2 system[6] uses a human-factors examination of incident investigation results to operationalise earlier ground-breaking work for Shell that was done by Professor Patrick Hudson.[7] In fact, the Baines Simmons methodology shares some insights with our Mindset Analysis methodology, which was mentioned above and is described in detail in Chapter 14 (Being practical – part II).

While we agree with much of what has been developed in support of a 'just' culture, we wish to emphasise that the real driving need for a 'just' culture is not simply that it is a prerequisite for the kind of open incident reporting that is required for organisations to learn about their fragilities. Nor is it that it happens to be highly consistent with the way complex, adaptive systems work. Rather, it is that, most importantly of all, it plays to a need that is deeply

---

4 Early thinking about the law of unintended consequences was documented by Robert Merton in 1936. Merton's thesis was that predictions about an intervention based on the premise of 'other things being equal' were flawed because other things are not equal, having been changed in unknowable ways by the existence of the prediction itself. This insight has parallels in quantum physics and the story of Schrödinger's cat, made famous by the Austrian physicist Erwin Schrödinger a year earlier, in 1935.

5 For example, Hudson (2004), Dekker (2012), Eurocontrol (2016)

6 Baines Simmons (2015)

7 Hudson (2004)

embedded in the human psyche, irrespective of national culture or ethnicity: 'being human' entails a shared and deeply felt sense of *fairness*.

Organisational cultures need to be 'just' because people require fairness before they can consistently behave in ways that deliver what complex organisations actually need to be safe.

Let's see how.

What is 'accountability', how is it different from 'responsibility' and how can it be made fair?

Responsibility is having a duty to get something done. If you are responsible for a task, then you have undertaken to deliver it to an agreed quality and by an agreed date. If anything arises during the task that threatens the agreed delivery, then it means that you have accepted that it is your place to fix the problem – or, if you can't, then you will use a sensible process to escalate it, ultimately bringing the problem, its insolubility and the process by which you have established its insolubility to the party to whom you have undertaken delivery.

Accountability is having a duty to justify the way responsibility is discharged. It is the process by which someone is judged to be responsible for their responsibility.

Fair-minded accountability is a process that:

- Clearly establishes agreed responsibilities, made on reasonable and mutually agreed grounds
- Clearly establishes any differences between the responsibilities as agreed and as carried out
- Clearly establishes where the responsibility lies for any differences so observed.

In a 'just' culture of fair-minded accountability, people are only held accountable for those matters for which they had reasonably accepted responsibility, and over which they had the means of control.

This description does not minimise blame as some 'just' culture models propose. For example, Eurocontrol's model wants only to blame people who fail to report a mistake.[8] Yves Morieux, a Director of the Boston Consulting Group's Institute for Organization in the US, wants to reserve blame for people who fail to help or ask for help.[9]

The problem is that while people may behave with honesty, integrity and due diligence much of the time, there are occasions when some may *avoidably* fall short of the standards they have agreed to and which everyone else expects. We are not talking here of times when a constellation of human factors combine to produce substandard performance despite good intent. Nor are we talking of deliberate 'violations' that were nevertheless well intentioned (if misguided or wrongly informed, in which case we want to know why). We are referring to deliberate, avoidable mal-intent, malpractice or malingering.

If malicious violations go unblamed, they deeply violate people's sense of fairness and undermine the very culture of openness that is necessary for accountability to work across the whole organisation. While deliberate malice is quite infrequent, we noted in Chapter 10

---

8 Eurocontrol (2016)
9 Morieux (2013)

(Being on target) that less rare are those workers who turn out to be 'actively disengaged', ie who are not just unhappy at work but actively find ways to let others know it.[10] Folk such as these are legitimate targets for a fair-minded accountability process, since their behaviour is both avoidable and under their control.

Since 2014, the UK Rail Safety & Standards Board (RSSB) has been running a project aimed at supporting the development of a fair culture[11] within the UK railway system. The project is focusing on improving the robustness of the rail incident investigation process in order to "provide the opportunity for improvement, corrective or, where appropriate, disciplinary action for staff members, depending on the severity of the operational incident and the underlying root cause". This positions 'blame' in a way that is highly consistent with fair-minded accountability, though it retains the terminology of 'root cause'. As we have argued elsewhere in this book (Chapter 9: Being in the know – part IV), root causes are often political judgements that frequently land on some form of human error, which is where the investigation then typically stops. And if you are looking for human error, then you will most certainly find it.

In order to be open and honest about their involvement in incidents, people need to trust that their organisations will use the information fairly to make things safer and better for all. They need to know that people – including themselves – will only be blamed for behaviour that is found to be reprehensible by investigations that have been fully informed by an insightful Mindset Analysis. But they also need to know that where behaviour is fairly determined to be blameworthy, then it will be treated as such. People will not be open and honest if they believe that they will not be treated in a way that appeals to their intrinsic and very human sense of fairness.

Of course, a strong sense of fairness is not the only quality that defines what it is to 'be human'. In other chapters of this book, we have described how humans evolved as inherently social, imagining beings capable of representing and sharing conceptual thought. Human brains appear to have developed to support deep personal relationships within communities of up to 150 others. Chapter 11 (Being together) talked about the powerful bonding processes that underpin group cohesion. As we saw in Chapter 10 (Being on target), this supports our need to belong to something – anything – and to be recognised by others as having a status that is collectively valued. This need to belong is so powerful that it may not matter how much a group's activities are regarded as aberrant or dysfunctional by the vast majority.

Chapter 10 describes the importance of other highly motivating elements that help to define what it is to be human. These include autonomy – in which we find ourselves able to direct our own activities; purpose – in which we come to know and find expression for a deeply meaningful value; and mastery – in which we derive huge satisfaction (and often respect from others whom we value) by becoming expert in some area.

A further defining factor is cooperation. As we all know from our own experience (and as illustrated in Chapter 11), people who trust each other enough to work in coordinated teams can succeed in tasks that are quite beyond any one individual. What has recently come to light, however, is that our brains have physically evolved to predispose us to such cooperative behaviour.

---

10 Crabtree (2013)

11 RSSB (2016)

Oxytocin is a hormone that is made in the pituitary gland in the centre of the brain. Discovered in 1952, it is released when we are stressed and its effect is to make us want to seek out and place trust in the support of others. And as we engage in trusted, cooperative behaviour with them, oxytocin latches onto receptors in the emotional centre of the brain (the amygdala), making us feel relaxed and less fearful. Oxytocin is released by virtually all vertebrate brains and research has shown that the higher the density of oxytocin receptors in a species, the more that cooperative behaviour occurs.[12] One study found that in humans the hormone even increased the extent to which individuals were prepared to lie for the benefit of their group.[13]

Why do organisations need to care about these qualities?

We have been talking about qualities that define us as humans. Their relevance to organisational safety is that they turn out to be crucial for organisations to recognise and harness. This is not because doing so is a nice or mature thing to do (though, of course, it is). Organisations need to properly take account of:

- Our sense of fairness and need for fair-minded accountability within a 'just' culture
- Our strong need to belong to something that has a purpose we can relate to
- Our drive to be socially connected with others
- Our need to self-direct what we do, to develop and deploy expertise, and to be trusted to do so
- The intense satisfaction we feel when cooperating with others.

But it's not because these defining qualities, like the openness and honesty that they help produce, are ends in themselves.

It's because they are all prerequisites for what organisations actually need to safely manage and mitigate the complex, adaptive systems in which they operate – *operational resilience*.

What is resilience?

Complex, adaptive systems get disrupted all the time. Very often, the disruption comes from within as people work to achieve their local objectives. For example, someone may reprioritise an action for reasons of personal efficiency, and this then interferes with the timing of a task being carried out by someone else, requiring an adjustment on their part – and so on. Sometimes the disruption comes from outside as new challenges are made on the system as a whole – for example, when USS *Vincennes* found herself having to deal with external threats, both real and imagined.[14]

Resilience is the quality of a system that allows it to maintain its stability in the face of constant disruption.[15] The irreducible uncertainty of complex systems creates the need for people to 'complete the design'.[16] In recognising this, resilience engineering does not set itself the impossible goal of 'zero accidents' based on safety campaigns, management declarations, root-cause analysis of human error and an ever-thickening rule book. Instead, it seeks to put in place organisational indicators capable of signalling the 'breakability' of an operational system as it organises itself and operates in its environment.

12 Benkler (2011)

13 McNamee (2014)

14 Barry & Charles (1992)

15 See Hollnagel (2006)

16 Dekker (2005)

To work, these indicators must have something to say about one or another of the properties of complex, adaptive systems that make them vulnerable to increasing brittleness. Examples of such vulnerabilities are given in Table 12.1.

Table 12.1 Ways in which complex systems are vulnerable[17]

	Complex system properties	Complex system vulnerabilities
1	**Buffering** The size or kinds of disruption the system can absorb or adapt to without breakdown	Overly lean manning or 'just in time' processes and operations that result in insufficient contingency
		Insufficient knowledge of disruptability, its consequences and realistic contingencies
2	**Flexibility** The system's ability to restructure itself in response to external changes or pressures	Too many rules, procedures and processes focused on the past, rather than adapting to the present
		Over-prescriptive operational practices that are insufficiently sensitive to changing operational circumstances
		Insufficient insight or ability to break outdated or inappropriate rules
3	**Margin** How closely or how precariously the system – or a specific component – is currently operating relative to one or another kind of performance boundary	Chronically too much to do in too little time with too little resource (numbers, quality or both) – perhaps due to an over-demanding organisational, management or appraisal culture, or else harsh economic realities
		Insufficient knowledge of performance limits, their proximity, or the damage that can arise from exceeding them
4	**Tolerance** How a system behaves near a performance boundary – whether it degrades gracefully as pressure increases, or collapses suddenly when pressure exceeds adaptive capacity	Insufficient fall-back positions in the event of sudden changes to demands or circumstances
		Insufficient knowledge of what will happen – and the speed and extent of its spread – as performance limits are approached
5	**Divergence** The degree to which a system is working at cross-purposes with itself, ie behaviour that is optimal at one level or location may produce maladaptive behaviour at another	Downwards, operator resilience may be degraded by senior mismanagement of goal conflicts, or poor automation design leading to unfair (and counterproductive) demands for responsibility: a product of 'work as imagined'
		Upwards, management resilience may be degraded by local adaptations of operational staff, leading to unworkable management expectations of compliance with industry standards: a product of 'work as done'

Reproduced from *Resilience Engineering: Concepts and Precepts* (Hollnagel et al, 2006: Ashgate) with kind permission

---

17 Based on Woods (2006)

An example of an organisational indicator that could indicate a growing vulnerability in the area of system buffering might be the amount of time an organisation needs to recover from a disruption. If the recovery time for such disruptions starts to increase over time, it will indicate a system that has started to approach its performance limits and is now prone to increased risk-taking and safety violations as people struggle to maintain productivity. More about organisational indicators can be found in Chapter 14 (Being practical – part II).

Measuring resilience

When soldiers march over a bridge, they break step to prevent damage caused by the resonance of their harmonised footfall. In just the same way, unwelcome resonance between components in complex systems must be detected and damped before it compromises their resilience. The resilience of a system is most cost-effectively addressed in the early stages of disturbance. In the later stages, the system may be oscillating too far out of control to intervene without enormous cost and effort – if at all. This means that resilience indicators should be *leading* indicators that sense increasing fragility (ie brittleness). Such indicators are very different from *lagging* indicators like lost-time-injury (LTI) statistics. Lagging indicators tell us how long it has been since the last accident, but they give no clue about what might happen today, or give any insight into the extent to which complacency might have set in – something that tends to increase as the 'time since the last injury' increases.

 Get help with understanding and mitigating complacency in **Chapter 13**

The aim of resilience indicators is to indicate what is increasingly likely to happen in the future. They create the possibility for informed organisational intervention before brittleness gives way to catastrophe. An example of a resilience indicator is the reaction of managers when someone takes a decision to sacrifice productivity for safety. The maturity with which such decisions are made and responded to is a good indicator of the organisation's inherent resilience. Another resilience indicator is the time taken by organisations to recover from disruptions. The longer the recovery time, the more the system may have eroded its safety margins.

In Chapter 14 (Being practical – part II), we describe these and other resilience-based leading indicators in more detail and give an example of a resilience-based operational review process that we developed for a shipping company.

Another way in which resilience detection can be approached is to estimate the propensity for unwelcome resonance in a system. One method for doing this is Hollnagel's Functional Resonance Analysis Method[18] (FRAM). We outline this in Chapter 14.

Resilience can be addressed at an individual level as well. In Chapter 13 (Being practical – part I), we give guidance on how resilience can be developed by operational staff for their own benefit.

---

18 Hollnagel et al (2014)

Two views of safety

In the familiar, traditional view of safety, the focus is on things that go wrong. Hollnagel[19] characterises this as *Safety – I* and we outlined his view in some detail in Chapter 9 (Being in the know – part IV). One way of using our SUGAR model is via Mindset Analysis (described in Chapter 14: Being practical – part II) to examine the world of work retrospectively (ie post incident) in terms of the many human factors that influenced our choices, moment by moment, and the trade-offs we made between efficiency and thoroughness. Doing so leads us to appreciate – with new, human-factors insight – why a deckhand got dragged overboard by a mooring rope, why a doctor amputated the wrong limb, why a cockpit crew became obsessed with an inconsequential green light, or why a port captain permitted the catastrophic overloading of a car carrier.

Understanding the human-centred reasons for how and why things go wrong leads us to more human-centred considerations and a reinterpretation of the place of blame. In turn, this creates a demand for a different kind of organisational culture – a 'just' culture – based on fair-minded accountability, in which openness and honesty can flourish, and organisational contexts can be established for why people do the things they do.

This is all OK as far as it goes.

A more recent view of safety focuses on the things that go right in the face of complexity. Again, as we saw in Chapter 9, Hollnagel calls this *Safety – II*. So, the other way of using our SUGAR model is to focus on the world of work, proactively, as it is routinely carried out. Here we see people at any and all levels of safety-critical industries engaged in successful, normal, everyday operations in which they are doing their best to get things done despite the distractions, unexpected demands and uncertainties that define and characterise most of their trade-off decisions. In this complementary perspective, the focus is on how it is they get it right most of the time, and how far the human factors represented by SUGAR typically constrain – and enhance – their freedom to operate (ie their performance variability).

Both of these perspectives – but especially the latter – naturally focus attention on the need to increase the *resilience* of both individuals and organisations. In particular, they lead to a consideration of practical guidance, tools and techniques inspired by the disciplines of resilience engineering and human factors, each informing the other within the reality of complex, adaptive systems.

 Get help with creating and measuring operational resilience in **Chapter 14**

Together, the aim of both of these views of safety is to achieve an effective, practical approach to the harnessing of human behaviour to make safety-critical operations as safe and resilient as our uncertain world permits them to be.

---

19 Hollnagel (2014)

The real source of safety

In the end, safety is not found in a poster on the wall, in the pages of the company Safety Management System or Disciplinary Code, in the lost-time-injury records, or in the proclamations and promises of senior management at company Safety Days. Instead, it emerges moment by moment, in the interdependent, everyday, pressurised behaviour of everybody in the organisation – at all levels – as they go about the task of getting things done in a fundamentally uncertain world.

The emergence of behaviour that is the safest it can be will depend on the extent to which the organisation is focused on creating and measuring operational resilience in the face of complexity. In turn, that will depend on how far the organisation's operators and owners understand the challenges, demands and necessity of 'being human'.

And that is down to you.

13

Being practical – part I
how can you increase your own resilience?

About this chapter

In the first 12 chapters of this book, we explored many of the main influences on everyday human behaviour at work. We saw how such influences are rooted in our evolution and our psychology, and we examined the difficulties that inevitably flow from our active participation in complex, adaptive systems.

Inexorably, we are drawn to the conclusion that while rules, procedures, hindsight and other trappings of deterministic systems have their place in our complex world of work, what we actually need to optimise the safety of safety-critical systems is increased *resilience*, rooted in a deep understanding of the factors that make humans 'human'.

In these final two chapters, we gather together some practical approaches and measures aimed at achieving just that.

This chapter focuses on what *individuals* can do to increase their own resilience, while the next one focuses on what *organisations* can do.

Do you have trouble with tiredness?

In Table 13.1 you will find a questionnaire about tiredness. Read each statement and indicate how much the statement applies to you. Do the topics in the statements ever affect you? Sometimes? Often? Or always? For the moment, leave the column headed 'Improvement ideas' empty.

Then read the next section, 'Dealing with fatigue'. As you read, note down any ideas you get for improving any problems with fatigue that you might have. You don't need to limit yourself to suggestions we make. You may well have ideas that are right for you that we haven't thought of.

> **Read more** about fatigue and how it affects our behaviour at work in **Chapter 5**

Table 13.1 Fatigue questionnaire

Do you have a fatigue problem?	Never	Sometimes	Often	Always	Improvement ideas
I feel tired even before I start work					
I need several cups of coffee (or similar) before I can start work					
I lose concentration at work because I am tired					
I forget things at work because I am tired					
I am bad-tempered with colleagues because I am tired					
I sometimes catch myself nodding off while working					
When I am working, I work without a break					
I work at night					
My hours of work change					
I work right up until I go to bed					
If I wake during my sleeping time, I find it difficult to go back to sleep					
I drink alcohol or take drugs to help me sleep					
I drink coffee (or similar) during the two or three hours before I sleep					
I have a full meal during the two or three hours before I sleep					
I use my phone, tablet or laptop shortly before I try to go to sleep					
I have little routine about when I go to sleep					
When I do get to bed, I find it difficult to go to sleep					
I can only sleep three or four hours at a time					
I sleep less than seven hours a day					
I am disturbed by noise during my sleeping hours					
It is too light during my sleeping hours					
It is too hot during my sleeping hours					
It is too cold during my sleeping hours					
My bed is not comfortable					
I am woken by colleagues with questions or problems					

Assessing your tiredness

Count how many statements you have rated 'often' or 'always':

- Less than 3: You sleep like a baby.

- 4–8: Fatigue is probably not a big problem for you, but you need to keep an eye on things that can stop you getting enough sleep.

- 9–12: You probably suffer from a lack of sleep. You need to find ways to improve your situation.

- 13 or more: Your level of fatigue probably makes you a hazard to yourself and the people around you. You need to find improvements and you will probably need the help of others in making these happen.

These scores are only for general guidance. You must use your common sense in looking at the statements you have marked 'often' or 'always'. Even a 'sometimes' could be serious at the wrong time or in the wrong circumstances. We recommend that you review your ratings with a trusted friend or colleague. If the problem is located in your place of work, you may need the active support of your team leader, supervisor or manager. If the problem lies in where you live (outside of work), then you may need the cooperation of members of your family, housemates or even neighbours. Confront these problems. Fatigue is dangerous!

Dealing with fatigue

In the end, the only thing that cures fatigue is good-quality, restorative sleep. For most humans, that means seven continuous hours every day, during which the individual goes through five distinct phases:

- **Stage 1** Dropping off – short-lived, accounting for less than 5% of your sleep

- **Stage 2** Light sleep – accounting for 50% of your sleep

- **Stages 3 and 4** Deep (and deeper) sleep – where the truly restorative benefit occurs

- **Stage 5** Rapid Eye Movement (REM) sleep – where you dream. REM sleep is deep enough for your muscles to be suppressed, so you are less likely to act out your dreams. REM sleep is critical for your memory, learning and mental health. If you are sleep-deprived, you usually recover your sleep debt on the first night and your REM sleep debt on the second night.[1]

During a normal seven-hour period of sleep, an individual will go through several cycles of phases 2 to 5.

Sleep is inevitable, but there are some temporary measures that can be used to delay it a little.

The most commonly available short-term measure is caffeine. Caffeine starts to help after about 15 to 30 minutes, and its effects can last for 3 to 4 hours. So, coffee works in the short term, but some care is needed. Too much coffee causes some people to become nervous or jittery. If it is taken three or four hours before going to bed, coffee can prevent deeper, restorative sleep from occurring, making the problem of fatigue worse the next day.

---

1   Murphy (2002)

The other most available remedy for fatigue is the nap. A short sleep – during a meal break, say – can replace a couple of hours of normal sleep. A nap shortly before starting a night shift is particularly helpful. It is important that the nap is brief, typically 15 to 20 minutes. If you nap for longer, you start to go into the deeper stages of sleep, and hormones are released that cause you to feel thick-headed or groggy when you wake. Going back to work in this state can be dangerous, as your level of alertness will be seriously degraded. In Chapter 5 (Being in a state), we saw that the captain of Air France 447 was asleep in the cabin behind the cockpit when he was summoned by the co-pilots as the Airbus went out of control. His ability to grasp the situation was compromised while he struggled to become fully alert.

Caffeine in combination with a nap is a particularly powerful way of fighting fatigue. At the start of your break, drink a cup of coffee. Then nap for 15 to 20 minutes. (Setting an alarm is desirable.) You will wake up and start work again as the caffeine takes effect. For a time you should be free from the worst of fatigue. Remember: this will only help you for three hours or so.

If your work requires you to sit much of the time, getting up and moving around at intervals will have a short-term benefit on your tiredness. Sometimes it might seem as if a bout of exercise will dispel fatigue. However, the effects of exercise on tiredness are very short-lived (up to 30 minutes) and there is evidence that, in the longer term, exercise makes you feel more drowsy than before.

Where possible, try to maintain a regular rhythm in your wake/sleep patterns. This may be difficult if you work in a changing shift regime. Moving from days to nights or vice versa is likely to result in extra fatigue. If you normally work days, there may be a temptation to stay out late at weekends or on days off. Maintaining a good social life is important but it needs to be balanced against the increased fatigue when you start work again. More generally, life is not only about working and sleeping. There are lots of other domestic and personal tasks that have to be fitted in. Where you can, try to do these tasks in the daytime. Keep as many of the night hours as possible for sleeping. Sleep at night will always be more valuable than sleep in the day.

You also need to take care in your choice of activity before sleeping. Avoid eating a large meal too soon before going to sleep. In the age of ever-present laptops, tablets and smartphones, it is very easy to find yourself writing reports, replying to emails and so on right up to the time you go to bed – or maybe even while you are in bed. The risks are even greater if you are in online contact with colleagues, friends or family who are in a different time zone. Such activities make our brains highly active and often provoke strong emotions at a time when we should be unwinding.

A particular problem arises from the nature of electronic screens. If you read from electronic devices before sleeping, it generally takes longer to get to sleep – and you will have a worse quality of sleep, and feel less alert the next day. The wavelengths of light from these screens suppress the body's production of melatonin, the hormone that prepares us to sleep. If you must use your device at these times, there are now filters and apps that reduce the level of blue light – the wavelength that is most damaging to melatonin production.[2]

---

2   Some devices now provide the option of a night-time setting, which automatically shifts the display illumination from blue to yellow after sunset. This produces less screen glare and makes it easier to get to sleep afterwards.

If you are having trouble sleeping, avoid using alcohol or sleeping pills. Alcohol might seem to work, causing you to fall directly into a deep sleep. However, as the alcohol wears off, you tend to miss out the REM sleep phase and wake up, producing the so-called 'false dawn' from which it is difficult to get to sleep again. Overall, you are likely to have much less recuperative REM sleep, which means you wake up earlier, still feeling tired. If this happens repeatedly, you will build up an operationally dangerous 'sleep debt'.

We are all poor at estimating our level of fatigue. We tend to carry on working long after we should have stopped or been replaced. Good teamwork is important here. In Chapter 11 (Being together), we saw that members of effective teams monitor each other and back each other up when required. So, if you see a colleague yawning excessively, making simple mistakes, their head dropping, their communications becoming less coherent, or other signs of fatigue, do not assume they are aware of their state. If you can, get them to take a break, with yourself or another colleague taking over their tasks for a time. If this is not possible, remain as engaged with them as you can. Talking with someone else will normally help a person remain tolerably alert – for a time, at least.

In a number of safety-critical sectors, workers must frequently travel long distances before starting work soon after their arrival. Jetlag is a condition that arises from your body clock being out of sync with the time of day. The additional fatigue it produces makes it a significant risk factor for safety-critical operational staff. The following are some anti-jetlag recommendations from the *Maritime Accident Casebook* (2016):

- Be fully rested before you travel. Don't make the mistake of making yourself tired so you'll sleep on the flight.
- Gradually adjust your meal and sleep patterns to fit those of your destination. Often, this may not be a practical option for a seafarer – but if you can do it, it will help.
- Your travel arrangements may not be yours to decide, but if you can, try to arrive in daylight. On arrival, stay awake until your normal sleep time, local time.
- Once on the aircraft, set your watch to the time at your destination: it's a psychological trick that may help.
- Stay well hydrated during the flight and avoid alcohol or coffee if you can.
- Stretch your legs, walk up and down, exercise during the flight. This is good practice anyway because it will help reduce the chances of deep vein thrombosis (DVT) – dangerous blood clotting caused by lack of blood circulation in the lower limbs.
- If the flight is long enough, sleep on the aircraft at the same time as you would sleep at your destination.
- On arrival, get as much daylight as possible and get some exercise.
- Taking doses of melatonin, the so-called 'sleep hormone', may help but it does have some risk, so only take it under medical supervision.
- Do not take sleeping pills for the flight.

Dealing with stress

Stress causes problems both in the world of work and in people's private lives. As a result, there are large numbers of courses, books and articles giving advice on how to manage stress. Many of these give valuable guidance on how to manage 'normal' stress, but are of limited applicability to the highly acute problems of stress confronting people having to respond to potentially life-threatening incidents involving safety-critical systems. The following blunt statement was made by a police psychologist working with the Chicago Police Department:

"What quickly became apparent is that the kinds of stresses experienced by police officers don't lend themselves very well to the kinds of fuzzy-wuzzy techniques that are often taught in traditional stress management courses and books. As an officer you live in the real damn world. You need to know how to use your brain as a tool to survive and prevail in a critical encounter, not sit around and sing Kumbaya."[3]

> **Read more** about stress and how it affects our behaviour at work in **Chapter 5**

Being able to make decisions even when under severe pressure is one of the main attributes of individual resilience.

Unsurprisingly, it is the military who have been most concerned with understanding what makes resilience and how it can be increased among service personnel. In one recent initiative, the US Air Force (USAF) established an Air Force Resilience Office. The USAF definition of resilience is *"the ability to withstand, recover and/or grow in the face of stressors and changing demands"*.[4] This definition covers how people cope after experiencing stress (eg dealing with PTSD – Post Traumatic Stress Disorder). Here, our major focus is on resilience as the ability to make decisions and perform when actually under severe pressure.

Some people are naturally more resilient than others. One recent book about performing under pressure[5] identifies ten characteristics of a person who is likely to be resilient when under threat:

- Not defensive when criticised
- Stays calm under pressure
- Handles setbacks and failures effectively
- Manages anxiety, stress and fear in pursuit of a goal
- Utilises feedback and criticism for growth
- Recognises how own behaviour affects others
- Remains positive despite trying circumstances
- Maintains a sense of humour when under pressure
- Tries to see things from another's perspective
- Airs grievances skilfully.

A self-assessment quiz based on these characteristics is available online.[6]

Most of us don't score maximum points on all of these aspects of resilience. Here, we look at what you can do to increase your resilience under pressure. We assume that you know how

---

3 Miller (2008)

4 Meadows et al (2015)

5 Weisinger & Pawliw-Fry (2015)

6 http://www.pressurebook.com [accessed April 2017]

to do your job. The question is: can you carry on doing it when something really bad is going on? And even more extremely, can you solve problems you have never encountered before when both your own life and the lives of other people depend on you finding a solution?

The guidance given here draws on a number of sources, including the training of US Navy Seals[7] and the US police,[8, 9] advice to business executives,[10, 11] tips for any of us on how to survive any major disaster from a forest fire to a terrorist attack,[12] and help with any situation in which we may experience extreme fear.[13] We divide this guidance into things you can do to prepare yourself before you find yourself in a highly challenging situation, and the way to behave when you are actually in the situation.

Your experience with stress

In Table 13.2 is an exercise concerning your experience with stress. It asks you to think about an experience you have had of being under stress or pressure. The more recent the example, the better. Just write a line or two against each question. If you want more space, you can use a separate page.

This exercise will help you see how you could apply the various ideas described in the next section, 'How to prepare for stress'. We suggest that you don't answer the last question in the exercise until you have read that section. Once you *have* read it, we recommend that you list at least four or five ways you think you could help yourself prepare for stressful situations.

As with all the exercises in this chapter, you will get more value if you discuss your results with somebody else who is familiar with you and your working situation, and with whom you can have an open conversation.

Table 13.2 Stress questionnaire

Do you have a problem with stress or pressure?	Think about a recent situation or event in your work where you felt under stress or pressure. Write brief notes about it against each question.
What was the situation and how did it arise?	
What were you supposed to do?	
How did the situation develop and what was the final outcome?	
Were you unsure what you had to do?	
Did you feel that lack of time was the problem?	
Did you know what you had to do but doubted whether you could do it?	

---

7   Carter (2015)

8   Miller (2008)

9   Sharps (2009)

10 Thompson (2010)

11 Weisinger et al (2015)

12 Ripley (2009)

13 Wise (2009)

Do you have a problem with stress or pressure?	Think about a recent situation or event in your work where you felt under stress or pressure. Write brief notes about it against each question.
Did the situation require you to make difficult legal or moral judgements?	
Did you feel lack of support from others?	
What was your main drive? Fight back? Run away? Just disappear?	
Did you feel physically at risk?	
Did you feel your job or career prospects were at risk?	
Did you feel your self-esteem was at risk? For example, you might look foolish?	
How did your body react? For example, shaking, rapid breathing, feeling faint, frequent visits to the toilet?	
Do you feel you made the wrong decisions or took the wrong actions?	
Do you feel your emotions got out of control?	
Did other things in your life add to your feelings of stress? For example, relationship issues? Financial worries?	
Had you practised dealing with situations like this?	
How would you like to have managed the situation better?	
How would you like to have managed your emotions better?	
How can you prepare yourself for situations like this in the future?	Read the next section for ideas

How to prepare for stress

Get rest when you can Fatigue is a major enemy of good decision-making. When you are tired *and* under stress, your ability to make sound decisions or find creative solutions is greatly weakened.

Get fit Being fit is an essential ingredient of resilience. This includes being an appropriate weight. Being in good physical shape will help your thinking stay clear when heavy demands are made on your body. This will be especially important if an incident lasts for many hours or even days. If you have to evacuate, being fit will also help you. When the World Trade Center towers (the 'Twin Towers') were struck by two planes on 9/11, people in poor physical condition were three times more likely to be hurt in the evacuation or fail to escape altogether. Furthermore, many staircases and emergency exits were not designed for people with today's common body sizes and weights. Large, unfit people may obstruct others who are trying to escape, as well as reducing their own chances of survival.

Familiarise yourself with the layout and safety procedures Only 10% of the people working in the Twin Towers on 9/11 had ever entered the emergency stairwell as part of a safety drill. Passengers on planes who have looked at the safety leaflet and followed the safety briefing have a better chance of surviving in the event of an emergency. In a state of great fear – and especially if visibility is poor (eg smoke, failed lighting) – it can be impossible to find the exit, even though at normal times it seems obvious where to go and what to do. Ironically, research by the US Federal Aviation Administration (FAA) shows that frequent flyers tend not to attend to the safety briefings and are especially at risk in an emergency.[14]

Assess the risks, make a plan and conduct a mental rehearsal – beforehand While you're at work, or even sitting in your seat on a plane, think about what the risks could be. Work out how you would handle the different emergencies that could arise. For example, where is the nearest exit and what is your route to it? Do you really know how to operate the oxygen mask? Many passengers don't. Think about what could go wrong (for example, if the passenger seated between you and the aisle will not move) and work out what you would do then. In 1993, terrorists exploded a large bomb in the underground car park at the World Trade Center in New York. In spite of the shock waves felt throughout the building, the head of security at Morgan Stanley could not get the office staff to take any notice. Finally, he jumped on a desk and shouted *"Do I have to drop my trousers to get your attention?"* This worked.

Expect the unexpected War is perhaps the most unpredictable of all human activities. The 19th-century Prussian general Helmuth von Moltke the Elder is credited with the principle we mentioned in Chapter 10 (Being on target), *"No plan survives contact with the enemy."* But you need a plan, even a short-term one (see above). In drawing up your plan, try to imagine all the things that could happen. However much time, effort and imagination you devote to planning, the chances are that something you didn't think of will occur. This could give you a severe jolt, impeding your ability to think and act. The more you can prepare yourself for the unexpected, and accept such events as normal, rather than the actions of a malign fate, the less likely your thinking will be thrown into disarray.

Get to know the people around you These could be colleagues, neighbours or just the people who work down the corridor. Build relationships with them. Know who they are and how to contact them. In a critical situation, they are likely to come to your rescue before the emergency services. You may of course do the same for them.

Prepare performance aids Do not assume that in an emergency you will remember anything, even the most familiar aspects of your job. The chances are that your mind will go blank. It is probable that your job already includes a number of performance aids: checklists, maps, key telephone numbers and so on. Think about what else you might need when everything seems to be going wrong, and produce your own performance aids to cover these possibilities.

Practise the core skills of your task over and over again Overlearning the core tasks in your job is the best way to stress-proof much of your performance. Overlearned skills do not place demands on your attention or decision-making capacity. They just happen. This means they are relatively immune to the effects of pressure. Royal Navy operations teams learn well-rehearsed threat response procedures called zippos. When a zippo code is announced, everyone knows exactly what to do without thought, question or discussion.

14 Flight Safety Foundation (2000)

Gain as wide a range of experience of working situations as you can Gary Klein is a world-leading expert on making decisions in tough, real-life situations. He found that individuals such as experienced fire chiefs and military commanders rarely make decisions in the way that economists and management theorists used to believe they did. Instead, decision-makers look for familiar patterns in the situation confronting them. This will normally rapidly indicate to the decision-maker the best course of action. Only if they cannot find a match for the present situation will the decision-maker revert to more detailed analysis and consideration of options. Klein has found that this way of deciding, known as the recognition-primed decision (RPD) model, is resistant to the effects of stress.[15] In some respects, RPD is similar to an overlearned skill.

Put yourself under pressure and learn how you react It is in the nature of complex systems to throw up problems you will not have met before. In these cases, overlearned skills and RPD, while important, will not suffice. You have to find a new way of managing the situation in the face of pressure. If you have been in a highly stressful situation in the past, and have observed how you reacted, this will help you act in a more effective manner when you are again in such a situation.

Practise the things to do when in the pressured situation Next, we describe the things to do when you are actually in the potentially dangerous situation where you have to make decisions and act when under stress. Some of these can be practised before you find yourself involved in a safety-critical incident.

What to do when disaster strikes

So the worst is happening. Your industrial plant is about to release clouds of radiation or highly poisonous chemicals on an unsuspecting community. Your ship or oil rig is about to discharge thousands of gallons of oil into an environmentally sensitive area. Your train has derailed and scores of passengers are trapped in the wreckage. Or, like Captain Chesley Sullenberger, your plane has hit a flock of geese and your engines have stopped (see the panel 'Cooking your goose – and eating it').

Cooking your goose – and eating it

On 15 January 2009, Captain Chesley Sullenberger[16] took off from LaGuardia Airport, New York. US Airways flight 1549 was the highly reliable Airbus A320, bound for Charlotte, North Carolina. Soon after take-off, the plane collided with a flock of geese. Both engines stopped and the left engine caught fire. Without any power, there was no possibility of returning to LaGuardia or reaching any alternative airport. All around were the skyscrapers of New York, offering no chance of a crash landing.

Captain Sullenberger quickly decided that the only option was to ditch in the River Hudson. This was highly dangerous. Not only was the landing itself difficult, but even if the plane landed relatively intact, there were 155 passengers to evacuate before the plane sank. The water temperature was only just above freezing.

---

15 Klein (1996)

16 The 2016 feature film *Sully*, directed by Clint Eastwood and starring Tom Hanks as Captain Sullenberger, is based on this famous incident.

The captain warned his passengers and crew, and guided his gliding plane to the river. He had the presence of mind to choose a location near boats to maximise the chances of rescue. The plane successfully ditched at a speed of 130 knots. As the cabin started to fill with water, the cabin crew supervised all the passengers safely out of the plane. Captain Sullenberger twice walked the length of the plane to make sure no-one was left behind. He was the last to leave. All the passengers and crew were rescued safely and only two were kept in hospital overnight.

What can you do to keep performing effectively in a situation like the one faced by Captain Sullenberger?

Accept the situation Many incidents become disasters because the people involved cannot accept there is a problem. This includes complacency (see later in this section), but it goes beyond this to become *denial*. In denial, the existence of a major threat is just too much to accept. The person's brain shuts out the possibility. Victims of fires are sometimes found dead in their chairs, having made no effort to escape. In some cases, they just couldn't accept there was an emergency until it was too late.

Breathe! Under pressure, our emotions can run away with us. In the language of Peters' Chimp model (see Chapter 5: Being in a state), our inner Chimp takes over control from our Human. One way we can regain control over our emotions is to breathe slowly and deliberately. Breathing is an oddity among the body's usual automatic and unconscious functions. Normally we don't think about our breathing; it just happens. But we can become aware of our breathing and take conscious control of it. Breathing serves as a bridge to our emotions, letting us bring them back under control. Breathing deeply lowers levels of the stress hormone cortisol, resulting in the evaporation of anxiety. To slow down your breathing, breathe in for a count of seven, hold your breath for a count of seven, then breathe out for a count of seven. Do this four times. Other variations are counts of 5/6/7 and 4/7/8. Try each one to see which you prefer. Slowing down breathing is a highly effective way of controlling panic.

> Read more about the way our emotions work and how they affect our behaviour in **Chapters 5 and 7**

Make short-term plans This is one of the US Navy Seals' key principles of mental toughness. You need goals, as well as plans for achieving these goals. But in a safety-critical situation, your goals should be very short term. These keep you focused and stop you becoming overwhelmed by all the things that will have to be done in the long term.

Focus on what you can control In a critical situation, it is very easy to let your mind wander to things, people and events you cannot control. Practise thinking about what you can and can't control. If, in a tight spot, you catch yourself thinking about something you can't control, park that thought and switch back to the things you can.

Slow down When under pressure, the temptation is always to speed up, to stop looking for information about the situation, to not ask for advice, to act before you are ready. Of course, the developing incident will help to determine the timescale in which you have to act. But make use of whatever time you have. Remember that, under stress, your working memory cannot handle as much information as usual. Take as much time as you prudently can to make sure your decisions and actions are the right ones.

Don't rely on technology Many computer-based aids are provided these days to help decision-makers. In an emergency, these may not be available. If you normally rely on such aids, their loss is likely to be an additional source of stress in its own right. Take opportunities to practise with alternatives (eg simulations you run in your head) and low-tech aids (eg pen and paper) that you can test in parallel with your normal aids.

Speak positive encouragement to yourself You can help manage the pressure by keeping positive. This means not only having positive thoughts but actually saying them to yourself. Remind yourself that this situation will come to an end. Tell yourself how tough and capable you are. Remind yourself of similar critical situations you have been in before, and which you managed to come through OK. Many others have coped with situations like the one you are in. Tell yourself not to give up. Remind yourself that being dominated by anxiety is just betting against yourself. If you make that bet, you lose, whatever the outcome – so refuse to bet!

Swap fear for anger Fear tends to undermine our belief that we are in control of the situation. It renders us powerless. When we get angry about something, we believe we have control. We become powerful. Try to reframe the situation you are in as one that makes you angry, not fearful.

Share your emotion We experience pressure literally as a build-up of strong forces within us. If there is someone you can talk to and share your feelings with, this relieves a lot of the inner pressure, helping you regain control of your thinking and emotions.

Act If you can take some action, then do so (subject to the 'slow down' advice above). Doing something – anything – reinforces the feeling that you have some control over the situation and are not totally controlled by it. Feeling that you are capable reduces your stress and helps you find the way to overcome the difficulties confronting you.

This is quite a long list of things you can do to help you make good decisions and take the right actions at the right time when under pressure. You cannot expect to remember all these the next time you are in a tough situation. What you can do is practise two or three of these ideas when work or life gets a bit stressful, but is not life-threatening. For example, you could try to become aware of any tendency to deny that a problem exists. In an argument with your boss or partner, you could practise deliberate breathing. Watch to see if your emotions take over in a certain situation. Do you say or do things, in the heat of the moment, that you later regret? Can you help by consciously holding back or slowing down your usual reactions?

As in so many aspects of life, experience and practice make the difference. Speaking of how he managed to ditch his Airbus A320 in the Hudson with no loss of life in 2009, Captain Sullenberger put it rather nicely like this:

"One way of looking at this might be that for 42 years, I've been making small, regular deposits in this bank of experience, education and training. And on January 15 the balance was sufficient so that I could make a very large withdrawal."[17]

17 Newcott (2009)

Dealing with complacency

The problem with complacency is that the word packs a negative punch without leading anywhere useful. The meaning needs to be unpacked a bit. When we do, we find that there are three key reasons why we might become 'complacent'. These reasons have little to do with being idle or lazy, and lots to do with overlooking some basic aspects of being human in a complex world.

- We tend to think the world is more stable than it is – because we overlook the fundamental uncertainty of the complex, adaptive system we are part of.
- We tend to miss things we are not looking for – because we overlook our limited capacity to pay attention.
- We tend to take risks we are not aware of – because we overlook our ever-changing perception of risk.

Read more about the nature and sources of complacency in **Chapter 5**

Read more about our limited ability to pay attention and our ever-changing perception of risk in **Chapters 7 and 8**

Read more about complex systems and why they matter in **Chapter 12**

There are a number of things we can do to help ourselves prevent these reasons from dominating our behaviour, as follows:

- **Expect the unexpected** (You'll already be doing this as part of your preparation to counter stress.) When everything seems to be going well, become suspicious and look for what you may have overlooked. Use your imagination to picture things that could be going wrong.
- **Observe your train of thought** Notice when your train of thought drifts away from your task. Gently bring it back on track. Conversely, notice when you have been too immersed in one line of thinking. Step back and look around. Getting up and moving around may help by literally giving you a different view.
- **Keep thinking about risk** Without making yourself anxious, keep reminding yourself of the risks you might be running, especially when doing an unfamiliar task. On the other hand, take extra care when doing a task that you are highly familiar with. The risk of switching to autopilot is high and you may miss something today that is critically different from the many times you have done this task before.
- **Try to avoid routine** Do tasks in different ways, in different sequences and at different times, as far as the working situation permits.
- **Do risky stuff first** When you can, do safety-critical tasks early in your watch/shift, when you are likely to be more alert and less tired.
- **Beware the witching hours** If you can, avoid doing safety-critical tasks between midnight and dawn. This is the time when we are naturally at our least vigilant – even if we are used to working nights.
- **Recognise when you are tired or stressed** These are the times when you are especially likely to miss something, so take extra care.

- **Take notice of colleagues** They are better placed than you to know when you are starting to suffer from fatigue or stress. In return, tell them if you observe them transmitting signs of stress or fatigue.
- **Remind yourself of your family, friends and colleagues** They are relying on you to keep them safe and to keep yourself safe.

There is a training film on the identification and prevention of complacency that dramatically illustrates some of these factors. The authors collaborated on the making of this film, which is available from KVH Media (2015).

Dealing with boredom

There are a limited number of things you can do as an individual to prevent yourself from becoming bored if you are given a necessary but boring task. For example, being the lookout on a ship in the middle of the night and in the middle of the ocean is inevitably boring a lot of the time. But the task is vital to prevent a life-threatening collision.

One thing you can do is to make sure you are not already tired when you start your shift. This will at least reduce the risk that you fall asleep on the job.

Remember that humans respond to boredom by finding things to do – either to kill or utilise time, or else to make the task more interesting. Most of the things you can do (depending on your place of work), such as catching up with administration or reading something (even memos from head office), run the risk of distracting you from the task – which can often change much faster than you think, especially if you lose track of the time you are spending on your diversion. This is a common occurrence. We noted, for example, in Chapter 5 (Being in a state) that problems arise when air traffic controllers don't have enough to do and allow themselves to experiment with alternative transits of light traffic through their sector, producing situations that can quickly escalate.

Dealing with risk

Some of the ways to deal with risk are covered in the section above, on dealing with complacency. One of the main reasons why we can become apparently complacent is that our sense of risk becomes badly calibrated with the amount of risk we are actually taking. As we pointed out in Chapter 8 (Being in the know – part III), such miscalibration is often down to one or more of three particular mental biases to which our natural overconfidence makes us vulnerable. Fortunately, forewarned is forearmed. Knowing about these common sources of bias offers us the means to continuously recalibrate ourselves during our operational work.

- **Control** How far do we feel in complete control of the situation? Why is that? Is there some aspect of the situation we have missed? Are we sure of the currency and accuracy of the information we are using? What assumptions are we making and when did we last check they were still valid? What are the most critical assumptions we are making? What is the worst thing that could happen if they turned out to be wrong?
- **Familiarity** How comfortable and familiar are we with the situation? Why is that? Are we sure there is nothing different about the situation this time? How far are we focused on those aspects that are familiar, thereby ignoring any unusual or different features? What can we see when we refocus on these differences? Are we able to ask another team member to do a cross-check of our thinking for us?

- **Value** How much are we focused on our current goal to the exclusion of everything else? How much do we want to get where we have decided to go? Why do we think it's really the most important thing we should be aiming for right now? What else is happening around us that might completely change our priorities?

Mental alarm bells should ring if, at any time, we find ourselves satisfied with our feelings of control, familiarity or value. Learn to listen for these alarm bells on a regular basis. They will remind you to recalibrate yourself with the real world in which you and your colleagues are actually operating.

Dealing with your unconscious biases

There are two basic problems with unconscious biases. First, they are real, numerous and powerful influences on what we do, the way we think and what we are predisposed to attend to. Second, they are ... well, they're unconscious – and therefore rather difficult by definition to attend to in their own right.

> **Read more** about the extent and impact of our unconscious biases on our behaviour in **Chapters 6 to 9**

Simply becoming aware of their existence and their everyday influence on us is a great help. We explored where they came from and what some of them are in the chapters on 'Being in the know'. Knowing that they are a fundamental part of what it is to be human is important for two reasons. First, it helps to nudge organisations into more appropriate ways of dealing with the human nature of their operational staff. Second, it helps us as individuals to become more resilient if we are aware that our interpretation of what is going on is something rather different from a reflection of a presumed reality 'out there' and independent of us. Rather than a mirror image of the world, our interpretations are, instead, hugely embellished constructions of our own making. Again, forewarned is forearmed.

Recently, an increasing amount of research has been focused on the notion of 'mindfulness'. The roots of mindfulness lie in Zen Buddhist philosophy, but it has grown in the West from the work of Jon Kabat-Zinn, now a Professor of Medicine Emeritus, who founded the Mindfulness-Based Stress Reduction programme at the University of Massachusetts in 1979. Kabat-Zinn defines mindfulness as *"paying attention on purpose, non-judgmentally, and in the present moment"*.[18] Mindfulness therapies have been shown to be clinically effective for conditions such as stress, anxiety, pain relief and drug addiction.

Our interest here is not in mindfulness as a clinical therapy, but rather in the sense of the 'relaxed alertness' to which we referred in the context of the advanced motorcyclist in Chapter 7 (Being in the know – part II). Using this approach, the operator not only becomes engaged moment by moment with the surrounding environment, but, crucially, is conscious of this immersion. In other words, the motorcyclist is aware that they are aware, consciously reserving a precious bit of their attention to monitor the rest of their attention. This is important because it allows continuous monitoring of the risk-evaluation process, ensuring they are ready to switch their attention, priorities and goals to those that may be more appropriate to the dynamically changing situation.

---

18 Kabat-Zinn (1994)

This kind of mindfulness is a habit that can be learned and improved with deliberate practice. You can begin just by choosing to become aware of yourself as an operator, making particular decisions and taking particular actions. The awareness you have created is a place within your mind from which you can challenge and critique your decisions and priorities. Sometimes, skilled work may require you to become more immersed in what you are doing for a while, but as your mindfulness habit develops, you will become an increasingly regular visitor to that special place of awareness where you can direct yourself in ways that will be more resilient.

Mindfulness is a habit that can help with our unconscious biases by preventing total immersion in our situations, thereby increasing the opportunities for Kahneman's *System 2* to prevail over *System 1*[19] when we really need it to.

Dealing with motivation

In Chapter 10 (Being on target), we asked *"What gets you out of bed in the morning?"* Manley Hopkinson[20] was a skipper in the Round the World yacht race and a participant in the Polar Race to the North Pole. He asks a similar question: *"What lights your fire?"* The heroine of Graham Swift's novel *Mothering Sunday*[21] says: *"We are all fuel. We are born, and we burn, some of us more quickly than others. There are different kinds of combustion. But not to burn, never to catch fire at all – that would be a sad life, wouldn't it?"*

> **Read more** about what motivation is and where it comes from in **Chapter 10**

It is clear that many people smoulder fitfully throughout their working lives, never bursting into a blazing fire. A quick search on the internet reveals countless websites and books dealing with self-motivation.[22] The popularity of this topic is strong evidence that many of us find motivating ourselves a problem. The danger is that we go along with what others want for us or from us. Parents, partners, teachers, friends, bosses and others may – with the best of intentions – all have strong ideas about what we should be doing. It is very easy to go along with these expectations and demands, possibly even convincing ourselves that they are what we actually want.

A few people discover what they want to do early in life. But for most of us there is no simple way to find out what motivates us. Often, this process of discovery works in reverse. We start on various careers and begin a number of different jobs. This may serve to make us aware of the jobs we do *not* want to do. But we are still left with the question of what we *do* want.

In Table 13.3 ('Are you in the right job?'), you will find a list of nine reasons why you might do a job. In the column '*In your ideal job*', take two or three minutes to rank these reasons why you would choose to do a job. Read through them all and then give the reason that is most important to you a rank of 1, the next most important a rank of 2, and so on. In the next column, about your current job, rank the same nine reasons again to reflect how likely you are to achieve each goal. So, if you think the goal you are most likely to achieve in your

---

19 Kahneman (2011)

20 Hopkinson (2014), p. 151

21 Swift (2016), p. 102

22 The best online resource we have found for helping with self-motivation is on the website mindtools.com. See https://www.mindtools.com/pages/article/newLDR_57.htm [accessed April 2017].

current job is to 'Work with like-minded people', give this a rank of 1. If you think the goal you are least likely to achieve is to 'Become rich', give this a score of 9. Rank all the other goals between these two extremes.

Once you have put rankings in each of these columns, calculate the difference between the two numbers for each goal and put the result in the final column. So, if you gave 'Become rich' a rank of 1 in your ideal job and a rank of 9 in your current job (how likely you are to achieve that goal in your current job), then you put a difference of 8 in the final column. (Ignore the fact that some differences may be positive and some negative: treat them all as positive.) Add up the differences. You should have a score between 0 and 40.

A score of zero indicates a perfect match between the goals you would like to achieve in your career and the probability of achieving them in your current job. A score of 40 indicates that you estimate a very low chance of achieving your preferred goals and you are probably in the wrong job – which may explain why you are finding it hard to leap out of bed in the morning.

This is a fairly simple tool and you should not take the specific scores to mean specific things. But generally speaking, if your score is low (less than 15) you are likely to find your job motivating. It lights your fire. If your score is high (above 25) you may find it difficult to stay motivated. Your fire may flicker and, one day, go out. In the meantime, you may not be paying as much attention as you should be to the risks you are exposed to.

Table 13.3 Are you in the right job?

Your career goals	In your ideal job	Likelihood of achieving goal in your current job	Difference in ranks (ignore minus signs)
Become rich			
Become famous			
Obtain power			
Acquire latest knowledge and skills			
Work with state-of-the-art technology			
Work with like-minded people			
Improve the lives of ordinary people			
Change society for the better			
Make my family proud			
		Total	

However good the match between your personal goals and what your job may provide, as we discussed in Chapter 11 (Being together) there are a number of factors to do with how your organisation functions that also determine how motivated you are. These are the subject of the next questionnaire, in Table 13.4 ('How could your job become more motivating?'). Just indicate how much you agree or disagree with each of the 20 statements with a tick in the relevant column. Again, this is not a scientifically validated tool, but is designed to help you to think about the various aspects of your job that may increase or decrease your motivation. Note down any thoughts or feelings that the statement triggers in you.

Whatever your job, it is unlikely you will agree with all these statements. However, if you disagree or strongly disagree with more than half the statements, then your fire could be blazing a lot more brightly in another job. You may want to use this tool on your own to prompt your own thinking, but you will get more value if you can discuss it with a friend or trusted colleague. If you identify any organisational obstacles to your motivation that you think could be removed, talk to your team leader or manager, if you feel comfortable doing so.

Table 13.4 How could your job become more motivating?

Rate how strongly you agree with the following statements	Strongly disagree	Disagree	Agree	Strongly agree	Comments
It was my own choice to take on this job					
I have a good understanding of my company's values and goals					
I generally agree with my company's values and goals					
My work provides something of real value to customers or colleagues					
My bosses and co-workers treat me with respect					
I respect my bosses and co-workers					
I am clear about what is expected from me					
I am clear about what I want to achieve personally in this job					
I am fairly paid for my work					
More pay would not make me work harder					
My work gives me a good level of interest and challenge					
My supervisor or manager regularly asks my opinion					
I am listened to if I make a suggestion					
I have a sense of belonging (in a good way) to this company					
I am free to make my own decisions in key areas of my job					

Being Human in safety-critical organisations

Rate how strongly you agree with the following statements	Strongly disagree	Disagree	Agree	Strongly agree	Comments
Rules and procedures are generally helpful					
I have good opportunities to acquire new knowledge and skills					
I can see how this job fits into my overall career ambitions					
I am willing to do more if there is an incident or emergency					
If I do something wrong, I will be treated fairly					

Dealing with your seniors

Whatever their experience or seniority, human beings are capable of making mistakes on one occasion when they wouldn't on another. The inevitability of these mistakes and their roots in a vast collection of interacting human factors is a key story in this book, as seen through the lens of the SUGAR model. Chapters 6 to 9 (Being in the know) showed why every individual has a different perspective, constructed dynamically from continuously varying influences, cues, attention and interpretations. As we saw in Chapter 11 (Being together), this is one of the key benefits that a team, as a collection of different perspectives, can offer.

The first safety-critical industry to realise the importance of harnessing all available team-member perspectives was aviation. Following the Tenerife airport disaster in 1977 – still the worst air crash in history – a new initiative got under way. What started as Cockpit Resource Management came to be extended more widely to Crew Resource Management (CRM). CRM training is now compulsory for all airline pilots and has been extended into other industries. Bridge Resource Management (BRM) training is becoming more common in the shipping industry and programmes have also been developed for fire-fighting and health teams in the US. In the UK, a further development of BRM is the HELM (Human Element Leadership and Management) course, which is now mandatory for all UK merchant officers. HELM's content is based on the topics of a previous publication by this book's authors.[23] Part of the point of CRM, BRM, HELM and their equivalents is to encourage more junior team members to speak up when they see something going wrong, and for more senior team members to listen to them when they do.

This can be rather difficult in practice, of course. There is a natural reluctance among many less experienced people to challenge their seniors. They may see such challenges as potentially career-threatening (especially if they are wrong), or else they may simply fall victim to a variation of the bystander effect,[24] in which they are psychologically cued by the inactivity of others to not intervene themselves. In many industries, there is still a failure

---

23 Gregory & Shanahan (2010)

24 See Chapter 11 (Being together)

among senior people to see themselves as vulnerable to failure, and they conduct themselves in a way that deters challenge. And in some cultures, the loss of face associated with challenge to a senior presents a high barrier.

> **Read more** about the bystander effect and the power of groups in **Chapter 11**

In the absence of an enlightened culture in which challenge is both expected and accepted, what is needed is a means of approaching it in a way that is safe for those involved as well as increasing the resilience of the system as a whole. One approach, based on established CRM practice, was developed by the authors of this book for very junior officers (cadets) in a major shipping company.

Freshly out of training in how to carry out safety-critical tasks, and newly on board, officer cadets may well see something in their operational duties that worries them as potentially unsafe. In such cases, we advise them to 'Head EAST' through the following four stages:

- **Engage** with the party they want to challenge. Get their attention via physical positioning, eye contact, body language, preparing to speak, or asking *"Excuse me, Captain ..."*
- **Ask** the party a question about the activity of concern. Juniors can use their lack of experience to great effect here. *"Chief, I haven't seen this procedure before – could you explain it please?"* or *"Captain, I don't think I understand the priorities here – do you mind explaining them?"*
- **State** the concern in direct terms. *"Officer of the Watch, do we have clearance to pass the ship on the starboard side?"* or *"Is the Captain aware that everyone is well over their working hours?"*
- **Tell** them or someone else. If something is going wrong, it will usually be the case that an earlier stage of EAST will be enough to enable mistakes to be noticed and corrective action taken. Or else, there was no mistake and the cadet has been able to capitalise gracefully on a learning opportunity. However, if there is no corrective response after the previous 'state your concern' stage, or the cadet's anxiety about what is happening has not been calmed, they should tell the other party what they think needs to happen – or, if there is time, they should consult someone else to ensure that the concern is shared and discussed.

The EAST procedure is not restricted to shipping or officer cadets, or even the most junior staff, but should be useful to everyone who would like a phased approach to an escalating concern.

Dealing with difficult people and difficult conversations

Most of the time, most people get along with each other. When they don't, there are two common sources of conflict. One is that the other person is perceived as difficult. They may appear to be uncooperative, difficult to approach, have an awkward way about them, or are generally 'hard work'. The other is that an issue has arisen that seems very difficult to confront with them. Perhaps it is embarrassing, personal, or a matter of their professional conduct.

> **Read more** about teams and their crucial role in the creation of safety in **Chapter 11**

Let's deal with difficult people and difficult conversations in turn.

Difficult people

Very often, difficult people are just different from us. And the way they are different means that they might have quite different personal styles, communication preferences and social needs. In the end, most differences are equally legitimate. The difficulty comes because other people are just different from us. It helps to understand what these differences can be, what different preferences they lead to, and how to cope with them. Doing so will lead to much more resilient operations, since not only can you understand better where others are coming from, but you can also adjust your own style when dealing with them to get more out of your relationships.

A very good framework for understanding and working with personal differences was developed by the psychologist Robert Bolton.[25]

The aim of the Bolton Behavioural Inventory is to give you a chance to understand more about how others see you, based on your behaviours. The results may or may not match your self-image!

The self-assessment is very quick and easy to do, and gives a lot of insight into the type of person you are in terms of your emotional tendency and your assertiveness. There are no right or wrong answers, and there are pros and cons to each style. After assessing yourself, what's particularly useful is to assess someone else whom you find difficult. It will almost certainly be the case that their dominant style is different from yours.

Bolton provides useful guidance on how to deal with people whose behavioural style differs from yours. For example, if the other person is very analytical, showing little emotion or assertiveness, it is best to prepare to meet with them by being very thorough, good on the details and listening carefully to them. It is also best to avoid appearing casual, or failing to follow through on something you have agreed to do. On the other hand, if the other person is very expressive, with high levels of emotion and assertiveness characterising their style, it is best to leave plenty of time for socialising, making sure you ask for their ideas and goals, and avoid too many details, impatience or being dogmatic.

Difficult conversations

A difficult conversation is any conversation that you dread having. Even the thought of having it fills you with apprehension or even fear. You may be a supervisor who needs to address someone's bad performance, or a master who needs to give bad news to a crew member, or perhaps a team member in serious dispute with a colleague. Whatever the circumstances, it helps to know that there are three similarities underlying all such difficult conversations:[26]

- **The situation is always more complicated than it looks – so listen for new information** Quite often, we assume we know all there is to know about another person or situation. We therefore think the challenge is to get our own message across, or to get the other person to admit their mistake and take the blame. The reality is that there are always two sides to the story, and that both sides will have made assumptions that

25 Bolton & Bolton (2009)

26 Stone et al (1999)

usually need to be corrected. An important opening objective is therefore to understand all perspectives and how they have interacted to produce the present situation. This is something that you should try to do together in the first part of the difficult conversation. Such an approach already takes some of the heat out of the situation.

- **The situation always involves emotions – so allow people to express them** By their very nature, difficult conversations always involve emotion. Very often, we try to avoid talking about our own and other people's feelings, or else confuse our feelings with the issue at hand. The trick is to acknowledge and include feelings without allowing them to determine the response that the situation needs. Sometimes, feelings on both sides may have to be properly exposed before they can then be set aside in order to find a way forward.

- **The situation always threatens our sense of who we are – so lighten up!** When faced with a difficult issue, such as a judgement that we have made badly, we often feel that something fundamental is being challenged about the kind of person we are. This makes us defend an image of ourselves that we have usually oversimplified into black or white. However, if you can cultivate a more complex (and therefore more realistic) self-image, you are much better able to achieve a balanced view of the impact of the threatening issues you are facing.

So how is your difficult conversation best approached? Consider each of these points:

- **Don't put it off** It's something that you need to deal with, and everybody will think more of you in the end for taking the first step in fixing the problem.

- **Think about what each of you contributed** It is almost certainly the case that you do not know all the relevant things about the circumstances of the other party. It may not change what needs to happen in the end, but it will certainly help by establishing the context for it. So, resist blaming and approach the conversation in a spirit of investigation of how each of you came to be where you are.

- **Distinguish between intent and impact** It may be that you have been deeply affected by what the other person did or said. Aside from the fact that the other person feels the same, remember that the effect on you both may be very different from what was intended. So assume positive intent until you know different.

- **Be clear about your objectives** Are you seeking fair treatment? A problem to be resolved? A relationship to be repaired? By being clear about what you want to have achieved by the end of the conversation, you can stay focused and will be better able to calmly return to the purpose of the conversation if it gets off track or threatens to be hijacked by emotions.

Being able to get past difficulties that threaten relationships between people who are on the same team is an important ingredient in the resilience of complex, adaptive systems. As we saw in Chapter 11 (Being together), such systems cannot function without teamwork, and as we saw in Chapters 6 and 7 (Being in the know), the perspective we happen to have is only ever a partial view that we created from incomplete information and parochial concerns. Other perspectives are vital pieces, and without them, the entire safety-critical project is threatened to the detriment of us all.

Dealing with teamwork

In Chapter 11, we described the skills and characteristics of effective teams. On the following pages we provide two questionnaires on teamwork. The first of these allows you to assess yourself as a team member (Table 13.5: 'How could you improve your team skills?'). Note your comments on any problems and any ways you could improve your own contribution as a team member.

Wherever you have scored an item as 'rarely' or 'never', you should ask yourself why this is the case. It may be something you can deal with yourself. But if an improvement is only possible with the involvement of other team members, you need to discuss this with your team leader or manager to agree any actions they or you need to take.

> **Read more** about the distinction between teamwork and taskwork in Chapter 11

Table 13.5 How could you improve your team skills?

Rate how often you personally score on the following	Never	Rarely	Often	Always	Comments
My goals are the same as my teammates'					
My understanding of the work situation is the same as my teammates'					
I use closed-loop communications for safety-critical messages					
I check on how my teammates are coping					
I back up my teammates if they need support					
I listen to my teammates					
I encourage quiet or junior members of the team to speak up					
I challenge senior members of the team if I think they are wrong					
I deal with any conflicts with teammates openly and constructively					
I am willing to learn from all my teammates					
I am willing to teach my teammates					
I trust my teammates					
My teammates trust me					
I am willing to find new ways of working					
I know what my teammates are thinking, feeling and planning					
I take extra care to help new team members fit into the team					

The second questionnaire, in Table 13.6 ('How could your team do better?'), is for you to assess your team as a whole. We especially recommend you complete this questionnaire if you are a team leader, supervisor or manager of a team.

Again, wherever you have scored an item as 'rarely' or 'never', you should ask yourself why this is the case. And again, note any ideas for actions you could take to improve the performance of your team as a whole. The following list contains some possible improvement steps you could consider:

- Do you have team briefings, including risk assessments, to prepare for safety-critical tasks – especially tasks that are out of the ordinary?
- Do you have team debriefings after completing a safety-critical task to review how it went and to agree any improvements that might be needed?
- Do you have contingency plans for things that might go wrong, and does the team *regularly* rehearse these plans?
- Does the team hold regular sessions to discuss team goals and priorities, to agree ways of working, and to resolve any conflicts or other issues that could degrade team effectiveness?
- Do you address *as a team* any new training needs and ways of working arising from changes in team members, technologies, and operational policies, procedures and rules?
- Do you engage with senior management to ensure the team gets the technical and human resources, clear directions, and training opportunities it requires to be safe and effective?

Table 13.6 How could your team do better?

Rate how often your team scores on the following	Never	Rarely	Often	Always	Comments
Team members work towards the same goals					
The team share a common understanding of the work situation					
Team members use closed-loop communications for safety-critical messages					
Team members check on how their teammates are coping					
Team members back up teammates if they need support					
Team members listen to each other					
Team members encourage quiet or junior members of the team to speak up					
Team members challenge senior members of the team if they think they are wrong					
Team members deal with any conflicts with teammates openly and constructively					

Rate how often your team scores on the following	Never	Rarely	Often	Always	Comments
Team members are willing to learn from each other					
Team members are willing to teach each other					
Team members trust each other					
Team members are willing to find new ways of working					
Team members know what each other is thinking, feeling and planning					
Team members take extra care to help new team members fit into the team					

This chapter has been concerned with practical ways in which operational individuals can improve their resilience at work. In the next chapter, we turn to ways in which senior managers can improve the resilience of the whole organisation in which they work – through strategic and enterprise-level initiatives.

14

Being practical – part II
how can you increase your organisation's resilience?

About this chapter

In Chapter 13 (Being practical – part I), we gave guidance on how you can improve your personal resilience.

In this final chapter, we give guidance for improving resilience if you have responsibilities for others, whether that means a team, a department, a unit or a whole organisation.

Both individual and organisational action is needed – in concert – to allow humans to create the safety required by the complex, adaptive systems in which we work.

Dealing with fatigue

If organisations are going to be resilient, they need to be managed by personnel who are themselves resilient. Resilience demands a high level of alertness. And yet fatigue remains a pervasive problem in many areas of safety-critical work. While managing fatigue is the responsibility of the individual, effective management can only take place if employing organisations – supported by the overarching industry legislators and regulators – create the right conditions.

Read more about fatigue and how it affects our behaviour at work in **Chapter 5**

Managers drawing up work rotas need to give consideration to:

- Length of shift
- Time of day/night
- Intensity and demands of the job
- Scope for colleagues to take over from each other when a break is desirable
- Number of shifts worked without at least one rest day
- Interval between longer periods away from work
- Changes from day to night work and vice versa
- Impact of moving between different time zones, where this happens
- Arrangements for leisure-time activities
- Adequacy of sleeping arrangements
- Time spent travelling to and from work.

A failure to consider factors such as these has been cited as a cause in several recent maritime and aviation accidents. Fatigue has also been a reason for experienced staff leaving their industries, contributing to a dilution of expertise. In most safety-critical industries there are regulations governing working hours, but wise managers see these as stipulating the basic minimum requirements and they go beyond these requirements as far as they are able.

Increasingly, organisations engaged in high-risk operations are extending the widely accepted principles of risk management to fatigue. In the maritime,[1] aviation[2] and healthcare[3] sectors, more and more organisations are developing and adopting a Fatigue Risk Management System (FRMS).[4] An FRMS is a systematic way of collecting, analysing and utilising data on fatigue-related safety risks. It is part of a continuous performance improvement process.

The US Federal Aviation Administration's (FAA) guidelines[5] cover the following elements of fatigue management:

- Hours-of-service limits
- Scientific scheduling
- Napping strategies
- Training and education for aviation maintenance technicians and inspectors
- Training and education for supervisors and planning staff
- Excused absences
- Medical treatment for sleep disorders
- Self-assessment
- Fatigue detection technology
- Work breaks
- Work environment
- Careful use of caffeine
- Fatigue-proofing of task procedures
- Task scheduling interventions
- Progressive restrictions of work responsibilities.

In the field of healthcare, a good FRMS provides for the following:[6]

- Education and training on the effects of fatigue for all organisational levels
- Strategies to increase alertness and mitigate fatigue
- Opportunities to identify and treat any medical conditions that may affect alertness or fatigue, such as sleep disorders
- Scheduling policies
- Investigation of errors, incidents, near misses and injuries.

---

1   IMO (2001)

2   Hobbs et al (2011)

3   Dubeck (2014)

4   In Chapter 5 (Being in a state), we refer to a number of fatigue management guidelines from a range of safety-critical sectors.

5   Hobbs et al (2011)

6   Queensland Health (2009)

An additional feature of an FRMS can be the use of computer fatigue prediction models, such as MARTHA, which was developed in Project HORIZON.[7] MARTHA is an acronym derived from 'a Maritime Alertness Regulation Tool based on Hours of work'. Another model validated for aircrew is SAFE (System for Aircrew Fatigue Evaluation).[8]

While the organisation should establish an FRMS that lays down the principles and framework, the way that the FRMS is implemented should be defined locally. Each department, team or unit can assess their own fatigue risks and agree how these risks will be controlled. The Resource Pack from Queensland Health (2009) gives a good account of how to set up an FRMS.

Dealing with stress

Organisations engaged in high-risk activities have both a responsibility and a major stake in doing what they can to help staff under stress.

Reducing stress in the workplace

By its nature, safety-critical work is bound to involve some stress. But organisations that are serious about safety try to identify and remove unnecessary sources of stress. These can include excessive noise levels, poor lighting, bad workspace layout, equipment designed without full consideration of ergonomics, excessive bureaucracy, and so on. Organisations can also review manning levels, work schedules, jobs requiring long spells in social isolation, and policies for – and ways of – handling complaints, harassment and bullying.

These days, many organisations provide some form of counselling support for staff who may be experiencing stress, whether inside or outside work. The source of an individual's stress may lie outside the workplace, but he or she will bring those stress levels to work, reducing their reliability and effectiveness, and making their efficiency–thoroughness trade-offs less than optimal.

> **Read more** about stress and how it affects our behaviour at work in **Chapter 5**

Designing for resilience

The way an interface, a control, a tool or a procedure is constructed can either help or hinder our ability to use it. This makes design a fundamental driver of resilience. In 1979, the psychologist James J Gibson created a new but self-evident word to describe what matters functionally about design. 'Affordance' refers to the possibilities that an object or environment suggests in an obvious way to those who encounter it.[9] Crucially, affordance is not an objective property of the object or environment, but is always relative to the capabilities and needs of those who engage with it. For example, a body of water affords swimming for a seal, support for a water bug, and recreation for a human. A rocker-style light switch affords the operation of pressing it in a particular direction. A drag-and-drop computer interface with a trash icon affords the dispatch of an unwanted file.

---

7   Warsash Maritime Academy (2012)

8   Eurocontrol (2012)

9   Gibson (1979)

Read more about the place of traditional human factors in the context of this book in **Chapter 4**

Even when a design has worked well, there can still be problems. As we know from Chapter 6 (Being in the know – part I), our perception depends not just on the capabilities of our senses, but also on the context we are in and what expectations we have. As humans, we can all instantly recognise the affordance of the light switch. However, American culture expects that 'up' means the light is on, while those from a British culture expect the opposite: they will assume the switch must be set to 'down' to be on. Such 'population stereotypes' matter since, under stress, people tend to revert to what they learned first and best.

Getting design right is not a trivial matter. These days, a great deal of what is known about human behaviour and operational purposes is increasingly – and wisely – deployed in the development of new working environments. It is imperative for organisations' safety, productivity and finances that they insist on user-centred and work-centred design in their procurement activities wherever possible.

That being said, the focus of this book is on operational behaviour at work as it is done right now. The general problem with design is that whatever it has delivered to us in the workplace, it is too late and too expensive to change anything much. Everyone is operating with legacy equipment and job designs – even if their equipment and tools were installed today.

As they develop their expertise and workarounds with the tools they have been given, people will evolve their own efficiencies and trade-offs – and hopefully this evolution will be informed by the insights contained within this book. Whatever effort an organisation has expended on user-centred design for its operational systems, increased resilience is best served by ensuring that experienced users help to optimise the design of supporting procedures, working practices, future upgrades and replacement programmes.

Since this book is principally about human behaviour at work, we will not spend any more time on the (nevertheless) essential precursor of good design. If you would like a comprehensive introduction to the human factors of design, as well as pointers to key source documents, please see Gregory & Shanahan (2008), pages 25–51.

Selecting for resilience

Organisations can try to select recruits for their capacity to stand up to the demands of extreme stress and pressure. Historically, however, it has not been easy to identify candidates with high levels of resilience or toughness – see the panel on Audie Murphy for a case in point.

Audie Murphy – when the going gets tough ...

When the US entered World War II, the young Audie Murphy tried to join the Marines. Audie was of scrawny build and almost pathologically shy. Unsurprisingly, the Marines rejected him. Eventually he was accepted into the US Army. His early instructors and officers were deeply unimpressed with Audie. They couldn't see him standing up to the rigours of combat, and recommended he be made a cook. But Audie persevered and finally joined an infantry regiment in North Africa. From here, he participated in the invasions of Sicily, Italy and then France, fighting through all these countries, right up to the German border.

During these 27 months, Audie won 31 medals for bravery. By now promoted to Lieutenant, Audie found himself engaged in a fierce battle. 102 of the 120 officers and men of his company had been killed or wounded. The survivors were subjected to an attack by a much larger force of tanks and infantry. Audie regrouped his men and called in artillery fire, but the attack continued. Audie climbed onto a disabled and burning tank that was liable to explode at any moment, and took over the turret-mounted machine gun. He killed a number of enemy infantry and the tanks began to fall back. When he ran out of ammunition, although wounded in one leg, Audie ran back to his small band and led them on a successful counter-attack. For this action, Audie Murphy was awarded the Medal of Honor. He returned to the US as the most decorated US soldier of the war.[10]

Nowadays, recruiters are armed with a battery of psychometric tests and assessment methods that mean they may do better than the instructors and officers of World War II did when assessing Audie Murphy. However, successfully predicting able and resilient individuals takes a lot of time, effort and money, and even then it is not guaranteed. It is only worth going to these extremes where the post to be filled really deserves it. One such example is the commander of a nuclear submarine – see the panel on 'The Perishers'.

The Perishers

The Royal Navy's Submarine Command Course (SMCC) is known as the Perisher course. To be allowed to take this course, you have to have reached an advanced level in the submarine service and demonstrated high levels of ability. If you fail the course, not only do you not get command of a submarine, your career in submarines is over. Full stop. Hence the name 'Perisher'. During the final month of the five-month course, students take turns commanding a real submarine at sea. They have to make instant decisions while subject to intense simulated attacks of all kinds. The course costs millions of pounds a year to run, and probably produces a maximum of four new nuclear-submarine commanders.

---

10 This account is based on Wise (2009), pp. 89–91. The story of Audie Murphy is well known, not least because it was made into a Hollywood film, in which Audie starred as himself. He went on to make further successful films, but even as a star he remained painfully shy.

In most safety-critical industries, it is probably unnecessary, unaffordable or impractical to subject candidates to this kind of assessment. The thing about serving in the armed forces is you are likely to find yourself in situations where other people are trying very hard to put you under pressure to make the wrong decision or do the wrong thing. In most civilian jobs, hopefully the people around you are trying to help you make the right decisions. But nonetheless, as the incidents we have described in this chapter show, there is always the chance when working in a high-risk environment that you will have to make life-or-death decisions, for which effective training is vital.

Training for resilience

While it is, of course, sensible for organisations to do what they can in terms of selecting new recruits for resilience, and to carry out ongoing on-the-job assessments, a more fruitful approach is likely to be found in measures to enhance resistance to stress and pressure among all staff working in high-risk environments.

Gary Klein's work has shown that the recognition-primed decision (RPD) model is resistant to degradation under pressure.[11] The problem with RPD is that it requires experts. People need repeated exposure to many real-life situations before they can learn to recognise underlying patterns and develop a repertoire of possible courses of action. This is viable for, say, fire chief commanders, who attend fire emergencies almost every day. It is less viable for decision-makers in many safety-critical industries, since, thankfully, emergencies are quite rare. Fortunately, there are ways to accelerate things. We now look at several approaches to giving decision-makers the opportunity to experience and learn from acting in operationally demanding situations.

Exercises in the operational setting

Historically, training people in how to respond in emergencies relied largely on exercises set up in the real working situation. For example, NATO conducts regular naval exercises in the Atlantic. A number of ships from various NATO countries form a task force, and are then subjected to 'attacks' by friendly aircraft and submarines acting as the enemy. Exercises of this general kind are carried out in most safety-critical industries, allowing staff to rehearse different emergency scenarios. Such exercises take a lot of preparation, are expensive to run, are difficult to evaluate, and disrupt normal operations. Various attempts have been made to develop more cost-effective approaches to promote the ability to act under stress, and we outline some below.

Table-top exercises and tactical decision games

At its simplest, training has taken the form of table-top exercises[12] or tactical decision games (TDGs). A TDG is essentially a low-fidelity simulation of an emergency. The idea is that it contains enough fidelity to demand and rehearse relevant decision-making skills. For many decades, the military have employed the 'sand table' to train commanders in tactical decision-making.

TDGs present a scenario to a decision-maker and team, describing a puzzle they have to solve. A session typically lasts 90 minutes. A facilitator plays a key role, providing information

---

11 Klein (1996)

12 Such exercises are examples of 'constructive' simulation, so called because most of the simulation is constructed inside the heads of the participants as they manipulate simple physical tokens or objects in the external world.

(usually incomplete) and driving the tempo of the scenario. The facilitator raises the stress level of the participants by, for example, suddenly reducing the time available for a decision or introducing an unexpected event. Another important role played by the facilitator is in providing feedback and especially encouraging the participants to analyse and evaluate their own decisions.

Stress exposure training

Exercises in operational settings, table-top exercises and TDGs all have value in giving staff opportunities to practise decision-making. However, they do not necessarily generate strong emotional responses in the participants. In contrast, a form of training has been developed that has the primary and explicit aim of producing near-real-life stress in people. This is known as stress exposure training (SET), sometimes called stress inoculation training.

Early in their careers, both of the authors of this book spent time at sea with the Royal Navy. This sometimes meant travelling from ship to ship by helicopter. The Navy insisted that if you were going to make regular flights, you had to go to the Dunker.[13] This is the body of a helicopter suspended over a large tank of water. After classroom training on how to escape, you strap yourself in the Dunker, which is then dropped into the water. And you have to get out. You do this a number of times. Each time, the helicopter is dropped at a more and more difficult angle, finally being dropped in upside down.

What was important was not only learning the practicalities of getting out, but also experiencing the extreme emotions (terror!) and learning how to be prepared for them. Learning the escape methods without the accompanying emotions would have had little value. It is this emphasis on the emotions associated with stress that distinguishes SET from conventional training. Without SET, skills learned in conventional training often do not carry over to performance when under stress.[14] Further guidelines on SET have been developed by Homeland Security in the US and are freely available on the internet.[15] Although these guidelines relate to training for law enforcement officers, the principles can be readily applied to SET for other sectors.

SET typically uses a simulator of some kind. Many organisations engaged in safety-critical operations already use simulators for conventional training, eg learning and rehearsing task skills. These do not necessarily include the features that are likely to be present during a critical incident. In contrast, a simulator for SET provides many of the stressors likely to be present in an emergency. Perhaps the largest, most expensive and most sophisticated simulator in the world is the US Navy's USS *Trayer*. *Trayer* is a 210-foot replica of a guided-missile destroyer and is installed in a 90,000-gallon tank of water.[16]

"Designed to recreate the intense environment of an attack at sea, the $56 million USS Trayer prepares recruits to deal with situations such as missile attacks, fires and flash floods.

---

13 In the merchant navy, there are a number of facilities offering training similar to the Dunker, known as HUET – Helicopter Underwater Escape Training (aka Helicopter Underwater Egress Training in the US).

14 The relevant carry-over of performance from the training environment to the operational environment is called 'transfer of training' and can be calculated to measure the effectiveness of different approaches to training.

15 Wollert et al (2011)

16 It is beyond the financial capability of many commercial enterprises to build such sophisticated simulators as *Trayer* on their own. Perhaps, though, groups of companies operating in similar fields could come together to provide such facilities on a joint basis. The companies, manufacturers and others engaged in providing offshore helicopter services who have joined forces to set up HeliOffshore to address safety issues of common concern provide a good model here. (But also note the discussion below on the need for simulator fidelity.)

The simulations provide stress inoculation so when sailors encounter a real-life catastrophe, they'll be better trained to handle it ... On the pier, fans are used to recreate wind; wave machines transform the calm pool into rough waters; scent machines recreate the smell of the sea; and there's even artificial guano spattered here and there, to offer that extra touch of realism. On board, smoke machines pump out an aerosol of glycol that looks like smoke but doesn't damage the lungs; strobe lights mimic the flickering of electrical fires; sub woofers vibrate under the floor to simulate explosions; heating pads simulate the high temperatures caused by raging fires; and electrically heated oils produce the smell of burning wires."[17]

Selecting the right simulator fidelity

The approach adopted in developing USS *Trayer* was to go for very high fidelity. *Trayer* looks and behaves like a ship at sea. As far as possible, every feature likely to be found in an emergency at sea is incorporated: compartments filling with smoke or water, the sight and sounds of seriously injured crew members, smells, noises of twisting metal, and so on. This level of fidelity comes with an expensive price tag. Fortunately, as in the case of simulations for individuals, it is not always necessary in terms of the cost-effectiveness of stress training to provide ultra-high fidelity. Nor is it desirable. If the stress experienced is too high, there may be little chance for the trainees to complete the task and there will be little learning to transfer to the real operational setting.

There are three principal types of simulator fidelity:

- *Physical fidelity* – how far does the simulator look and feel like the real working situation?
- *Functional fidelity* – how far does the simulator behave like the real working situation?
- *Psychological fidelity* – how far does the simulator provide a convincing experience for the trainees?

Of these, psychological fidelity is the most important for SET. This is because it provides a good emotional match between the training experience and the intended operational experience. Anyone who has observed teenagers in a bedroom playing, say, *Assassin's Creed* on a PlayStation or Xbox will know how totally absorbed the players can become in the game and how strong the evoked emotions can be. This is achieved even though the typical teenager's bedroom has little resemblance to the city streets of 15th-century Italy.

Virtual reality

An alternative to simulator-based SET or low-fidelity TDG that has become increasingly available in recent years is virtual reality (VR). VR offers the flexibility of TDG and an even more psychologically immersive SET experience without the cost of developing physical simulators. The use of VR for decision-making under stress has been explored in healthcare,[18] surgery,[19] homeland security,[20] fire-fighting,[21] mining,[22] train driving,[23] and the emergency services,[24] among others.

17 High Tech Edge (2016)

18 Bauman (2012)

19 Marescaux et al (1998)

20 Hedge (2011)

21 Bayouth (2011)

22 Van Wyk & de Villiers (2009)

23 Tichon et al (2006)

24 Bacon et al (2012)

VR is an artificial environment created by software and presented to the user via a variety of displays and other sensory devices. In advanced VR systems, the user can see, hear, touch and even smell the environment. The user can interact with the virtual environment, which appears to respond in a realistic way. All these features create a highly immersive experience for the user, in which they can readily suspend disbelief, and experience the environment and their interactions with it as if it were real.

PANDORA is an EU-funded project that developed a VR system for training police and fire-fighting strategic commanders, with an emphasis on the emotional aspects of their decision-making. VR appears to offer an exceptionally powerful means of helping decision-makers learn how to remain effective when under intense pressure. It is of particular value when the real-life operational setting would be too dangerous, difficult or expensive to use for training purposes, and there is a need to prepare decision-makers for crises that are very rare but which demand the high creativity that only humans can provide.

As a final note on the use of VR, we restate a plea made by an unnamed Greek ship owner at an international symposium in 2011. He had recently lost an entire ship and made the case for stress training in realistic crisis scenarios. It turned out that, under the stress of the situation facing them, the crew involved had abrogated their responsibility, preferring to defer decisions to insurers and politicians ashore. Amidst the resulting confusion and remote management, the ship foundered, resulting in an ecological disaster.[25]

Additional benefits of training to cope with pressure

A significant benefit of all forms of training for decision-making under stress is that decision-makers develop more confidence, a key ingredient in resisting the demands of stress and pressure. By presenting unusual and unexpected scenarios, TDGs, SET and VR in particular can also help counter two hidden dangers.

First, there is the danger of *blocked creativity*. Normal training teaches established routines and 'good practice'. These are often overlearned – which can be an advantage in emergencies, in that overlearned skills are resistant to stress. The danger is that in novel situations the decision-maker only considers standard responses, and fails to look for the creative course of action that may in fact be the solution to the problem.

The second danger is *reversion to type*. Under stress, we often revert to the ways of operating that we first learned in basic training. Training to cope under pressure, especially with good feedback from the instructor or facilitator, helps the decision-maker to be aware of – and thereby avoid – this danger. Of course, such overlearned reversion can help save the day – as it did for Captain Burkhill, the pilot flying British Airways' stricken Speedbird 38 into London Heathrow back in 2008 (for the full story, see Chapter 2: Being at work).

Dealing with motivation

An organisation that employs people to work in a high-risk environment needs to pay special attention to their motivation. Most managers still think mainly in terms of extrinsic motivators (especially money), although extensive psychological research has pointed clearly to the limits of extrinsic motivation.

---

25 Bacon & MacKinnon (2012)

Probably no-one is more aware of the need for a motivated force than the military commander. More than 500 years ago, Machiavelli, who knew quite a bit about the psychology of motivation, wrote about the difficulties of the prince who relied on mercenaries – soldiers who sold their services for pay.[26] Machiavelli described mercenaries as *"useless and dangerous"*. The prince who relies on them *"will stand neither firm nor safe"*. He goes on: *"[Mercenaries] have no other attraction or reason for keeping the field than a trifle of stipend, which is not sufficient to make them willing to die for you. They are ready enough to be your soldiers whilst you do not make war, but if war comes they take themselves off or run from the foe."*

We should note here that motivation cannot be forced by leaders. Motivation must always have its source in the individual, although organisations can very effectively suppress this source by placing unnecessary obstacles in the path of the truly important factors, such as purpose, autonomy, mastery, belonging and fairness. Edward Deci puts it well when he says: *"'How can people motivate others?' is not the question. Rather they should ask 'How can people create the conditions within which people can motivate themselves?'"*[27]

Leaders and managers are often not very good at assessing the motivation of their workforce, believing that money is the key reward. Sure enough, this often appears to be true. But it's not because they are good students of human nature. Rather, it's because they have not spotted that many jobs are designed in a way that leave little room for the real, deeper reasons why people work.

If there are questions about motivation in your organisation, we recommend you carry out regular surveys of workforce motivation. The questionnaire provided for use by individuals in the previous chapter (Table 13.2) can be readily adapted for organisational use.

In Chapter 10 (Being on target), we said that, worldwide, only 13% of employees feel really engaged with their work. In most responsible safety-critical organisations, selection and training processes probably mean they have a higher proportion of engaged staff. But how much higher? And can you be sure without actually asking? If your survey indicates that motivation levels are not as high as they could be, identify the obstacles and remove them.

Let's look again at the five factors underpinning motivation we discussed in Chapter 10, to see what practical guidance can be offered.

- **Purpose** The antidote to mercenary motivation is given by the author of the best-seller *Drive*, Dan Pink. *"Animate with purpose, don't motivate with rewards."*[28] Purpose is most powerful when it is a worthy cause, especially if this cause is shared with many others. As Machiavelli knew, princes are best served by their own forces – people who are fighting to defend their own families and homeland. An important leadership task is to articulate the organisation's purpose or cause. This often takes the form of agonised efforts to produce a mission statement. Difficult though this usually is, a successful mission statement works to the extent that it captures the shared cause for everyone in the organisation.

---

26 Machiavelli (1532), chapter 12

27 Deci & Flaste (1996), p. 10

28 Pink (2011), p. 168

- **Autonomy** In safety-critical systems, there will always be some things that have to be done in a prescribed manner. But around this fixed core of tasks, there will be other tasks where some degree of flexibility is either possible or essential. Most people who choose to work in safety-critical roles are mature, sensible individuals. But to what extent are they hemmed in with unnecessary rules and regulations that deny their full professional status, and prevent the deployment of the performance variability required by complex system behaviour to 'complete the design'?[29]

- **Mastery** Mastery is about continuing to get better at your work. Are people stuck doing the same things over and over again? Are there missed opportunities for employees to do new tasks, acquire new skills and knowledge? Usually, there are many such opportunities in the workplace itself, although these may need to be complemented with formal training courses. Team leaders and managers should look for such opportunities and encourage individuals to take advantage of them. Managers should find any additional resources that might be needed; for example, arranging cover for a person while they are away on a course.

- **Belonging** To develop a sense of belonging, a person must feel that they are an accepted part of the organisation, that the organisation is aware of their existence, and that it respects them whatever their age, seniority or experience. To put it rather grandly, belonging depends on a sense of a common destiny with the organisation and the other people working in it. Being employed on a short-term contract works against a sense of belonging. Similarly, divisions into us and them (often managers and workers) make a sense of belonging difficult to achieve. Sharp differences in pay and working conditions promote this feeling of us and them. Being a member of a racial minority or a woman in a male-dominated organisation does not necessarily undermine a sense of belonging, but this will depend on the attitudes and practices prevailing throughout the organisation.[30] As noted above, a sense of shared purpose is a key factor in promoting a sense of belonging, but it is important that all senior personnel 'walk the talk'. Any impression that executives say one thing but do another will rapidly destroy any feeling of belonging.

  Perhaps the greatest contribution supervisors and managers can make to developing a sense of belonging is to involve staff in decision-making – delegating the actual decision where possible, but at least genuinely consulting staff for their opinions. Some senior staff may feel they are giving up some of their authority if they involve their staff in decisions, but in reality they increase their standing through such actions.

- **Fairness** Fairness means not blaming people for things that go wrong over which they have no control. Some years ago, when we started working on safety in the shipping industry, an old seafarer said to us that the standard practice when something bad happened was to blame the most junior seaman who was standing nearest to the incident. We discuss at length why this is counterproductive in Chapter 12 (Being human).

Dealing in social capital

Chapter 11 (Being together) made it clear that a crucial determinant of safety in high-risk environments is team performance, and that, in turn, team performance is underpinned

---

29 Dekker (2005)

30 We discuss the more general issue of diversity in Chapter 11 (Being together).

by *social capital*. Social capital is the sum of shared values, goodwill, and sympathetic cooperation that enables a collection of individuals to trust and work with each other.

So, how can an organisation build social capital? And why don't all organisations engaged in safety-critical work do this? Here are some pointers:

- Recognise that a rich network of connections is called social *capital* for a reason. Like other forms of capital – financial, equipment and other physical assets – social capital has *value*. Research has shown that social capital influences safety in settings as diverse as the construction[31] and steel[32] industries and road safety.[33] Research also shows that social capital brings improved productivity and competitive advantage.[34]

- Don't focus purely on financial rewards as the way to improve performance. Recognise the importance of the social dimension of work in motivating staff (see also Chapter 10, Being on target).

- There are many commercial pressures that make managers adopt a very short-term view. Allow time for relationships, trust and social capital to develop.

- Invest in team training programmes, as described earlier in this chapter.

- Ensure managers and team leaders understand what social capital is and how it underpins performance, safety and resilience.

- Assess policies and practices for allocating staff to teams. The aim is to identify any causes of unnecessarily rapid turnover of team members. There is abundant research showing the longer a team has stayed together, the better, safer and more resilient its performance will be.

- Review organisational structures and physical work layouts to identify unnecessary obstacles that prevent staff in different areas from coming into contact and developing relationships.

- Provide spaces for social activities (even if it is only drinking coffee), where people can meet away from their work. Make arrangements so that staff use these spaces at a time when others are also there. Similarly encourage sporting activities, especially team games. The British armed forces have long recognised the role of the mess and the sports field in developing a strong collective identity.

- Recognise that when safety-critical activities are becoming dangerous, rich social networks are often key in getting rapid access to vital resources, advice, information and help. Understand the distinction between *strong* and *weak links*. You have strong links with the people you are most closely connected with, typically colleagues with whom you have contact every day. However, these people probably have much the same knowledge as you, and access to the same information, resources, etc. Weak links are with the people you know but have a more distant relationship with. These people are likely to be sources of knowledge, resources, and so on, to which you and the people around you don't have immediate access. They are also likely to provide further connections to other people you don't know, thus widening the pool of available help. *This makes weak links valuable.* Resilient organisations provide ways to develop

31 Koh & Rowlinson (2014)

32 Watson et al (2005)

33 Nagler (2011)

34 Nahapiet & Ghoshal (1998)

weak links: short-term exchanges of staff, workshops and conferences, and the like. Key connections may be with individuals outside the organisation, eg suppliers of critical equipment or the emergency services. These days, social media can also promote the development of weak links.

- Recognise that social capital underpins a *just* culture (see Chapter 12: Being human). A 'just' culture is usually mentioned in the context of something having gone wrong. It is normally taken to mean an organisational culture in which people are not blamed for things beyond their control. But in an organisation with a high level of social capital, a just culture permeates all aspects of everyday work. It is about people feeling that they are treated fairly: their views are listened to, any complaints are taken seriously, their working conditions and remuneration are satisfactory, and so on.

Dealing with complacency

Concluding that staff are 'complacent' is a poor explanation for accidents and does not lead to any useful way forward. Telling people not to be complacent in the future is an instruction that is unlikely to be effective since it ignores where complacency comes from and where organisational responsibility for it lies.

In the preceding chapter, we gave guidance to individuals in dealing with the sources of 'complacency'. Senior personnel and managers can assist their staff by arranging working hours and shifts to ensure people doing safety-critical tasks are as alert as they can be. Senior staff also need to recognise the dangers of asking bright, motivated people to undertake tasks that are unstimulating, uneventful and intrinsically boring.

> **Read more** about the nature and sources of complacency in **Chapter 5**

More generally, for organisations to deal effectively with the problem of complacency, there needs to be a 'sea change' in understanding where safety comes from and what it means to operate within a complex, adaptive system. Much of this book is concerned with this issue. Safety-critical organisations that fail to comprehend that their staff spend most of their operational lives 'completing the design'[35] of an uncertain, underspecified system are doomed to be chronic – and perhaps terminal – victims of 'complacency'. By contrast, those enlightened organisations that reward those who report problems, that seek to implement fair-minded accountability, and that are clear about the distinction between 'accountability' and 'blame'[36] will be well placed to avoid the catastrophic results of what others choose to dismiss as 'complacency'.

Dealing with boredom

Organisational solutions to the problem of boredom are best found in the original design of the system and the way in which tasks have been arranged to form jobs or roles. By combining a number of compatible responsibilities into a single role, it may be possible to ensure that there is enough stimulation in the work to avoid the worst of boredom.

---

35 Dekker (2005)

36 See Chapter 12 (Being human)

Read more about the nature of boredom in **Chapter 5**

Sometimes it will not be possible to avoid roles that involve boredom. It is then up to managers planning the work rosters to ensure that no one person is allocated to a boring task for too long. It may be possible to rotate two or three people through several boring tasks. Even if someone is moved from one relatively boring task to another, the change of task is better than being stuck in the same role for too long. If the task requires a high level of vigilance, then the time on the task should only be about 30 minutes, and certainly not longer than 90 minutes. After that, people will simply miss things. It's not their fault – it's how their brains evolved to work.

Dealing with incidents

Many organisations and safety-critical industries have come a long way in their approach to accident investigation. Systematic procedures for learning from how things go wrong are a vital part of the organisational governance that helps to control the difference between sustainable profitability and catastrophic collapse. As a shipping brand, Townsend Thoresen did not survive the *Herald of Free Enterprise* disaster in 1987,[37] and Exxon did not survive its 1989 Alaskan oil spill.[38] In space, the explosion of the space shuttle *Challenger* shortly after launch in 1986 set back NASA's programme for years,[39] and in aviation, the crash of Air France 4590 in 2000 was one of the final straws for Concorde.[40]

Read more about the nature of accidents and human error in **Chapters 2, 7, 8, 9 and 12**

Despite the advanced systematic analyses now carried out by modern accident investigators, the results are very often declared to point to causal factors such as 'human error', 'fatigue' and 'complacency'. While organisational problems are also often identified, the whole emphasis of such investigations is based on the premise that there is a 'root cause' – often a 'rogue' human factor – to be found. This cause is assumed to be a pathological element that has somehow crept into normal operations, and which must now be identified, and designed out or legislated against via some new rule, procedure or management instruction.

From what we know about human behaviour in complex, adaptive systems, this is misleading. Instead of a 'root cause', we need to discover how the constellation of dynamic, adapting behaviours of all the system parts combined to produce a negative outcome on this specific occasion, noting that the same system had managed to avoid this outcome previously.

Consistent with the themes and explanations in this book, it is our view that the existing approach to accident investigation needs to be enhanced with something we call *Mindset Analysis*.[41]

---

37 See Chapter 4 (Being sufficient)

38 See Chapter 5 (Being in a state)

39 See Chapter 3 (Being framed)

40 See Chapter 9 (Being in the know – part IV)

41 Mindset Analysis is © gs partnership ltd

Mindset Analysis

A mindset is a person's predominant set of attitudes, beliefs and expectations, all wrapped up in their theory about the way the world works. It is their mindset that helps people expect particular events, directs their attention to what seems to be important, and makes sense of what their senses tell them. Mindset Analysis is the name we have given to a four-step process (described shortly) designed to throw light on the influences on people at the time they take a decision that, with hindsight, is subsequently found to be significant.

Read more about the limitations of hindsight in **Chapter 9**

At the point of a decision, hindsight is (by definition) never available to the decision-maker who is immersed in the flow of operational activity. What is available is the decision-maker's ongoing sense of the 'story' they have created to provide meaning to the events around them and the role they are carrying out. Mindset Analysis is a systematic process for eliciting and understanding the decision-maker's 'story', how that story came about, what alternatives (if any) there were to the decision taken at the time, and what the learning implications are for the organisation.

Mindset Analysis involves using the three sources of influence on human behaviour described at some length in this book (State, Understanding and Goals) to generate questions designed to tease out the context of the decision-maker at the moment a key decision or action was taken. Key decisions can usefully be established by a hindsight-based narrative analysis of the sort that is usually created as part of a typical accident investigation. Ideally, the target for the questions should be the person who made the decision or action. Tragically, this will not always be possible; in these circumstances, mindset questions should be discussed with other key colleagues, witnesses and/or experts who are able to immerse themselves in the prevailing scenario. Scenario immersion requires personnel who not only have a similar level of technical expertise to that of the original decision-maker, but who are also (able to become) familiar with company practices and culture, and are able to use the mindset questions to gain an insight into the dynamics of the situation faced by the original decision-maker.

The output of Mindset Analysis is a rich picture of the reasons and purposes for each significant decision or action. The picture is rich because there may be several reasons and purposes for each decision. But it is even richer than this, because Mindset Analysis captures the reasons for the reasons and the purposes of the purposes and so on. In this way, the rationale for each decision is established in terms of the decision-maker's basic assumptions, resources, beliefs and values at the time.

Examining these assumptions for their organisational implications produces opportunities to go beyond the traditional recommendations of incident investigations. Instead of new rules, procedures, training and information campaigns, opportunities are revealed to address areas of *organisational brittleness*, where margins of manoeuvre have been eroded and the system is operating with insufficient degrees of freedom.

Such areas generally require interventions aimed at increasing resource or reducing demands somewhere in the system – but not necessarily at that point in the system occupied by the decision-maker at the time of the incident.

The four steps of Mindset Analysis

Step 1 *Narrative analysis* The first step is to create a narrative – the story – of the incident. This step is already a normal part of current incident investigation procedures and involves interviews with as many witnesses as necessary, together with other investigations (eg of equipment and environmental conditions), in order to develop a comprehensive and factual account of the incident's timeline. The output from narrative analysis is the set of decisions or actions that, with hindsight, appear to be significant to the development of the incident.

Step 2 *SUGAR analysis* Each of the significant decisions identified in the narrative analysis can now be subjected to a SUGAR analysis. With the focus on each of these decisions in turn, the relevant witness (or their stand-in) should be asked questions designed to establish the context and rationality of their thinking at the time. As will be clear from Chapter 7 (Being in the know – part II), the actions and decisions of people engaged in work may not seem rational in an absolute sense to an outsider who uses hindsight. However, they are almost always rational to the people involved at the time, with respect to what they knew, thought they knew, and were trying to achieve. The goal of Mindset Analysis is to determine *local rationality* relative to their assumptions, and, thereby, the reasons why those assumptions made sense to them. If people were making assumptions that proved to be patently false after the event, the Mindset Analyst will want to know why it made sense for them to make these assumptions at the time.[42]

Examples[43] of such questions are:

- How far did you believe you had the knowledge and skills to solve the problem at the time – and why (not)?
- What were your goals at the time, how clear-cut were your priorities – and why (not)?
- How safe did you feel at the time – and why (not)?
- What sense of obligation did you feel at the time – to whom, and why (not)?
- How pressing did the problem seem at the time – and why (not)?

For each response to a question (or a supporting probe), the witness should be asked why they have answered in that way (so as to provide rationale or evidence for their stated answer). See the panel 'Two kinds of why?' for further information.

The output of SUGAR analysis is a set of answers to the 'why?' questions – the trail of reasons and purposes – for each significant decision or action explored. A good way of capturing this information is in the form of a mindset picture, such as an influence diagram[44] or a mind map.[45]

---

42 It is important that the analyst understands the difficulty that true experts may have in describing their reasoning and logic. As we saw in Chapter 10 (Being on target), experts differ from those who are simply proficient, often deciding on courses of action 'because it felt right'. Careful and insightful probing will be needed to get to the bottom of such responses.

43 We give here just a few examples of SUGAR questions designed to tease out the State, Understanding and Goals of the witness in order to establish their local context at the time of the incident and how this context came about.

44 Forrester (1975)

45 Buzan (1974)

Two kinds of why?

It is important to distinguish between two kinds of 'why?' question. One kind is concerned with reason in the sense of 'because'; for example, *"I checked the PPE because the daily orders said so."*

The other is concerned with purpose in the sense of 'in order to'; for example, *"I checked the PPE in order to ensure I would be safe in the enclosed space I was about to enter."*

SUGAR analysis is interested in capturing both. Reason-type answers indicate witness preoccupations with, and responses to, pre-existing cues, conditions and circumstances, while purpose-type answers point to witness considerations of plans, ideas, expectations and goals.

Whenever the witness can answer a 'why?' question (of either type), they should be asked 'why?' again until further answers are unforthcoming. Pursuing *purposes* reveals more and more about witness values, while pursuing *reasons* reveals more and more about witness assumptions and situational context.

Step 3 *Resilience analysis* Studies of adverse incidents arising in complex, adaptive systems show that they occur due to increasing brittleness – in which the organisation loses its ability to flex, or fails to retain sufficient degrees of freedom to deal with normal variations in performance between its interacting parts.

Such brittleness can arise for several reasons. Here are three main ones:

- *Loss of coordination* – in which different parts of the organisation pursue different goals, but there is insufficient coordination between them – resulting in different parts of the organisation working at cross-purposes.

- *Loss of margin* – in which a part of the organisation runs too short of essential resource to meet the expectations of its other parts – finally resulting in overwhelming pressure and burnout.

- *Loss of adaptability* – in which part (or all) of the organisation finds itself operating according to assumptions, rules and practices that were once pertinent, but from which the world has moved on – resulting in anachronistic (and often considerable) activity of dubious relevance.

The output of the previous Step 2 (SUGAR analysis) is a picture of witness mindsets expressed in terms of purposes and reasons, which show how these mindsets are connected to the organisational contexts that helped produce them.

Now, in Step 3, these mindsets must be reviewed in terms of at least the three sources of brittleness just outlined. Understanding the brittleness of the organisational contexts that produced the witness mindsets examined in Step 2 (SUGAR analysis) allows the organisation to focus on how resilience in these areas can be restored or increased.

To do so, the mindset picture produced from the witness interview data should be considered in terms of the questions in the panel 'How can your organisation increase its resilience?'.

How can your organisation increase its resilience?

Here are 12 questions that arise out of three key sources of organisational brittleness. Answering them may point to weaknesses in the resilience of your organisation with respect to a specific incident.

Loss of coordination

1. To what extent was this incident due to the failure of different parties to understand each other's objectives?

2. What were the coordination and communication failures that led to this incident? Where, when and why did these arise?

3. In what ways could the organisation change to eliminate the kind of coordination and communication problems that occurred in this incident?

Loss of margin[46]

4. To what extent was this incident due to one or more parties operating at the edge of their ability?

5. How routine is it for these parties to operate in this way?

6. What are the sources of this pressure – how did they develop and over what period of time?

7. What action would senior management have taken about this loss of margin had it been pointed out before the incident occurred?

8. What is a safe and acceptable level of margin for these parties, and in what ways could the organisation change to create or restore it – without reducing the margin of manoeuvre for other parties in the system?

Loss of adaptability

9. To what extent was this incident due to the violation of everyday assumptions or common expectations?

10. How much of a surprise was the incident – to whom, and why?

11. How well established are these assumptions and expectations – and how have they become so?

12. In what ways could the organisation change to both stimulate and listen to challenges about commonly-held assumptions and beliefs?

 Get help with how to develop a strategy for increased organisational resilience towards the end of this chapter

---

46 'Margin' here refers to the amount of slack available before an operating limit is reached.

Step 4 *Accountability analysis* The result of Step 3 (Resilience analysis) should be a clear view of the degree of brittleness associated with the witness mindsets produced by Step 2 (SUGAR analysis), together with the identification of strategies for improving organisational resilience.

The purpose of Step 4 is to use the insights revealed by the preceding analyses to help consider how to apportion accountability for the incident. Apportioning accountability fairly is both a key purpose and a critical output of Mindset Analysis. If this is done unfairly, it is entirely counterproductive to the development of an effective reporting culture that adapts towards safer behaviour. Instead, people simply learn how to protect themselves from blame and unjust punishment by developing defensive behaviour that masks the complex dynamics that are really responsible.

Unfair accountability happens when someone has responsibility, but insufficient authority to control the outcomes for which they will nevertheless be sanctioned. A common example is when a person does not follow all the rules and procedures imposed by senior management because to do so will mean not getting the job done. In the event of an incident or failed safety inspection, they are then sanctioned for not following the rules. See Chapter 12 (Being human) for more on fair-minded accountability.

If people are made unfairly accountable, they will often respond in one of two ways. Either they try to transfer the responsibility to others, eg by working strictly to rule even when it's clearly inappropriate or unhelpful (thereby transferring the responsibility to the rule-makers); or else (and more commonly), they operate two different work systems, much like a tax-dodging business might run two sets of accounts. Here, they may appear to be working according to laid-down procedures by completing all the right paperwork (for example, working-hours logs, mandatory checklists), but actually carry out the work in a different, unauthorised way. If sanction threatens, they will seek refuge in the documentary evidence that they have created to mask their actual activities, and the organisation is blocked from real learning. More than this, the organisation is prevented from foreseeing the coming disaster.

Fair accountability needs to take into account all those reasonings – and how they came about, as exposed by SUGAR analysis – that created the prevailing mindsets significant to the incident. This is achieved by considering the degree of responsibility exercised by the witness in making the assumptions they did. Some of these assumptions will relate to witness trust in technology, or trust that their colleagues, managers and directors would carry out (or had carried out) their own responsibilities to the witness.

Judgement of witness responsibility comes down to these three considerations:

- How consistent were all the witness assumptions with each other?
- How far was it reasonable for the witness to fail to challenge or repair assumptions that were knowably inconsistent at the time?
- What did the witness actually elect to do, given the inconsistencies known to them at the time, and how equitable was this decision?

Judged this way, all those witnesses implicated in the incident are held accountable by reference only to what it was they were reasonably responsible for, *given their mindset at the time.*

When accountability has been fairly made, any sanctions that follow will be seen by everyone in the organisation to be fair and justified. It will frequently be the case, however, that much responsibility for the incident cannot be laid at the door of specific agents and witnesses. This is because it is in the nature of complex, adaptive systems that adverse events arise due to unintended and unwanted consequences of unforeseen combinations of normal variations in performance, rather than causal chains involving failed components.

It follows that much accountability for an incident may land on the organisation's failure to notice increasing brittleness and its resulting drift towards danger. We give some guidance on how to prevent – or at least mitigate – such a failure in the last section of this chapter, on dealing with prevention.

As a key enhancement to incident investigation, Mindset Analysis is aimed at bringing about a regime of fairer accountability, more open reporting, better organisational learning, increased resilience and improved safety. Furthermore, by focusing attention on areas of brittleness that are produced by variations in normal performance, the use of Mindset Analysis will help to sustain more fitting systems of governance that support the establishment of an intrinsically safer culture.

Dealing with prevention

Safety indicators

Mindset Analysis (see previous section) is all very well as a means to understand weaknesses in resilience (either individual or organisational) once an accident has occurred. What would be better is some way of detecting existing operational resilience levels and fixing any problems before something bad happens.

The most common organisational safety initiatives use various kinds of indicator to try to figure out how effective they are. These indicators tend to divide into two types:

- *Lagging indicators* provide safety information that is essentially historic. These include lost-time injuries, days since last accident, injury severity, and compensation costs. They precisely describe safety trends over time in terms of how many people get hurt and how badly. However, they have nothing to say about what is being done to prevent accidents, nor how likely an accident is in the future.

- *Leading indicators* provide information about factors that are known (or confidently assumed) to be associated with safety vulnerabilities. Examples are the frequency of safety audits, employee surveys, number and frequency of safety training courses and attendees, number of safety deficiencies or near misses reported per week/month/ quarter, and the speed with which safety deficiencies are dealt with.

While leading indicators are essentially proactive, their effectiveness obviously depends on the degree to which they are genuinely predictive of operational safety, and on the degree to which operational staff are serious about them. In turn, staff engagement will depend on the prevailing organisational culture, and in particular, the degree to which it is perceived to accommodate fair-minded accountability (see previous section and Chapter 12: Being human). Near misses will tend not to be reported if people fear what may happen to them or their colleagues if they 'blow the whistle'. The success of the UK Confidential Reporting Programme for Aviation and Maritime (CHIRP) is down to the fact that it operates independently of any employing organisation, keeps names confidential and deletes them once a report is closed.

A third kind of indicator identified by resilience engineering is the *resilience marker*. These are leading indicators that research has shown to be highly related to the operational resilience of complex, adaptive systems.

Organisations need to develop the resilience indicators (markers) that make the most sense to them. One good place to start is in Chapter 12 (Being human), where Table 12.1 presents a number of complex system vulnerabilities. Each of these vulnerabilities can be used as a starting point for developing indicators that could reveal the dynamic state of such vulnerabilities. Resilience indicators can also be reverse-engineered out of the 12 questions set out in the panel in the previous section, where we saw that loss of resilience can result from loss of coordination, margin or adaptability.

Other resilience indicators that have emerged from organisational resilience studies include the following:[47]

- **Sacrifice decisions** This refers to the ability of people to make 'sacrifice' decisions, and the reaction of their peers and managers when they do. A sacrifice decision is one that gives up immediate profit or efficiencies for the additional thoroughness, safety or standards considered appropriate by the decision-maker – whatever their seniority level. The maturity and insight with which sacrifice decisions are made and responded to provides a good indicator of the organisation's inherent resilience.

- **Differences between 'work as imagined' and 'work as done'** Large differences indicate that organisational leadership is ill-calibrated to the challenges and risks encountered in real operations. For example, there may be a large gap between checklist-based, procedure-driven processes mandated by management, and the work practices developed by the workforce to get around real-world problems and so get the job done within the available time. Revealing metrics here are how quickly productivity disappears or how suddenly targets become unreachable if everyone works to rule.

- **What people do when all seems OK** This refers to how far the organisation continues to scrutinise its risk models even when things seem safe. Some organisations do this by insisting on a constant state of edginess and investigation, or by increasing suspicion when 'things seem too quiet around here'. Other organisations adopt a 'pinging' process, in which factors that could herald a systemic change in risk are identified and sampled (pinged). Such factors include a sudden need for more people, stalling of expected progress, higher reported workloads, common tasks (eg getting permits) not performed or performed late, a decline in communications (eg unreturned calls or emails), and slowing or stoppage of routine maintenance. Importantly, the pinging process returns high benefits when it becomes part of everyday practice for all staff. This can be contrasted with an approach in which a Safety Department is created to carry out the process – an approach that may send an inappropriate message in perhaps seeming to transfer the responsibility for safety from everyday operational decision-making to a specialist department.

---

47 Derived from work by Woods (2006) and Hollnagel (2014)

- **Increasing time to recover from disruptions** This has been shown to be a good indicator that a system is failing to adapt any further because it is close to its performance limits and therefore may be close to collapse.

- **Maintenance of, and commitment to, professional standards** Insistence on adhering to professional standards – and management support for doing so – is a key protector of resilience in the presence of economic or production pressures.

- **Paying attention to the effectiveness of what is learned** This refers to evidence that the organisation is not only collecting feedback about its operations and initiatives (sometimes known as 'single loop learning'), but is also analysing what the pattern of learned lessons means. This kind of 'double loop learning' is essential to an organisation's ability to recognise how effective its learning is, and how urgently it may therefore need to learn new ways to work and adapt in a context of changing pressures and opportunities.

Resilience indicators in action – the Teekay initiative

When ships collide, founder or run aground, people get hurt, vast expense is incurred, and serious environmental damage can result. In its annual report, Allianz Global[48] reported that, across the world, 75 large[49] ships were lost in 2014 – around three ships every fortnight – and 2,773 people lost their lives. With the launch of MSC *Oscar* in January 2015, a new trend for super-sized container ships was begun. *Oscar* is longer than four football fields. Fully loaded, she packs over 19,000 containers. Further ships are planned, with capacities for 22,000 and 24,000 containers.

Allianz has calculated that if one of these container ships is lost, the industry needs to prepare itself for a loss of $1 billion.

Generally speaking, when ships are lost or damaged, something has gone badly wrong on the bridge, from where ships are navigated and manoeuvred.

It therefore makes sense for shipping organisations to pay serious attention to what goes on there.

But how?

Very recently, Teekay Shipping has gone live with a company approach that is firmly and explicitly rooted in measures of operational resilience.[50] Teekay operates a large fleet of some 200 oil and shuttle tankers, including some Very Large Crude Carriers (VLCCs), and Liquid Natural Gas (LNG) ships.

The Teekay approach places a highly experienced reviewer aboard each of its ships to carry out a structured observation of the bridge team under differing operational demands over a week or two. The reviewers are all ex-masters with a deep knowledge of bridge-team tasks, company expectations, the safety management system and international legislation.

---

48 Allianz (2015)

49 Defined as over 100 GT. When yachts and smaller fishing vessels are counted, ship losses are more like two per week.

50 Teekay (2016), reproduced here with permission

The review is organised in four main stages:

1. **Pre-review meeting** Here, the reviewer meets with the entire bridge team to explain the scope and format of the review. In particular, the reviewer explains that they will not interfere during critical operations or pilotage unless they feel the vessel is in grave or imminent danger. The reviewer emphasises that their objective is to provide opportunities for feedback on best practice and operational issues by the reviewer to the crew, as well as by the crew to Teekay via the reviewer. It is explained that key navigational scenarios are of particular interest and will be observed as many times as practicable during the review period. These scenarios include:

   a. Preparing for, accepting and handing over a navigational watch at sea

   b. Conducting an independent navigational watch

   c. Bridge-team operations with a pilot on board

   d. Bridge-team operations without a pilot on board

   e. Navigating in difficult conditions.

2. **Technical baselining** Here, the reviewer uses a checklist approach to record the availability and condition of the technical infrastructure and library resources required or recommended for the safe and effective navigation of the ship. Where such technical resources are found to be unavailable, the reviewer establishes the effectiveness and timeliness of the remediation that is under way to normalise the situation. If no remediation has been started, the reviewer questions the responsible officer(s) to establish the reason and its acceptability. This is also an opportunity to ensure that crew members are happy with the serviceability of the resources and associated training provision. The outcome of technical baselining is a clear picture of the equipment, procedures and knowledge available to the crew, and their deployment for that voyage.

3. **Resilience analysis** Here, the reviewer observes bridge operations to assess crew behaviour in terms of the team's ability to contribute to the resilience of navigational operations. For each navigation scenario (as above), the reviewer uses a five-point scale to assess the whole navigation team on each of seven resilience factors, as follows:

   1. Task achievement

   2. Effectiveness of communications

   3. Quality of teamwork

   4. Use of technical resources

   5. Impact of disruptions and distractions

   6. Appropriateness of changes to plans and priorities

   7. Management of pressure.

Importantly, the reviewer justifies the score they choose on each of the scales by documenting the evidence they observed for their choice. This evidence may be discernible from many different sources, including deployed crew-member technical knowledge; technical, social, management, communication and team skills; fatigue, stress, personality, attitudes and ship culture; plans, goals and expectations; equipment and procedural issues; and external conditions and traffic.

The seven actual Teekay resilience scales used by reviewers are shown below.

Resilience Scale 1	Task achievement			
How effectively, efficiently and correctly was the task achieved?				
1	2	3	4	5
The task was abandoned and never completed	The task came close to success, but failed	The task came close to failure or running out of time, but succeeded in the end	The task was achieved on time, with all risks being kept to a minimum	The task was achieved in a highly creative and unusually effective manner that dealt with all foreseeable risks

Negative indicators	**Positive indicators**
Crew become unduly distracted by other tasks or incidents	Crew follow procedures appropriately
Crew fail to follow procedures when they should	Crew respond creatively and successfully to unusual circumstances that require them to deviate from usual procedures or rules
Confusion or lack of agreement over the plan	Other tasks dependent on this one are able to start promptly
Lack of coordination among crew	

Observational evidence for score given

Resilience Scale 2	Communications			
How effectively, efficiently and correctly were the communications achieved?				
1	2	3	4	5
One or more critical communications were not made, or else misunderstood, resulting in an incident or near-incident	Critical communications were not made at all or made in ways that risked misunderstanding, although no incidents occurred	Communications revealed some weaknesses, such as not following correct protocols or using wrong channels	All necessary communications were made and confirmed at the right time and in the right manner	The timing and clarity of all communications were exceptional in terms of maintaining task momentum, risk aversion and overall safety

Note: These indicators apply to safety- or task-critical communications within the ship and with other vessels, port staff, etc

Negative indicators	**Positive indicators**
Failure to communicate, late or misunderstood communications result in a reportable incident	Receiver confirms receipt and understanding of message
Communications have to be repeated	Speaker uses language and jargon appropriate to receiver
Crew member has to request information they should receive without asking	Speaker makes allowances for receiver being busy, stressed, in noisy environment, etc
Communication channel is used that is less than optimal for message to be relayed	Clear, comprehensive and timely briefings are given to all relevant crew members
Communications are ignored or dismissed	Crew members ask questions when necessary and the questions are answered appropriately

Observational evidence for score given

How effectively, efficiently and appropriately did team members work with each other?

1	2	3	4	5
Teamwork was largely absent, putting at severe risk safety, task performance or both	Teamwork was generally poor, creating a level of risk to safety, task performance or both	Teamwork was adequate; the task was completed but not without some delays or risks	Teamwork quality was good enough to result in satisfactory task performance and standards	Teamwork was outstanding, leading to highly coordinated task performance that was significantly better than good, with all foreseeable risks being anticipated well and unforeseeable risks countered effectively

Negative indicators	**Positive indicators**
Crew members behave as individuals with separate agendas Crew members fail to coordinate and cooperate when required Crew members show little understanding of the tasks and roles of others Crew members do not take account of the needs and work of others Crew members do not assess the impact of their actions on others Nobody demonstrates any leadership	Crew members share and review their common goals Crew members keep an eye on each other and back each other up when needed The crew adapts to changing conditions by re-allocating tasks and roles as needed Crew members are open to learning from each other regardless of rank Leadership is clearly demonstrated by the member of crew who is most suited to take this role given the operational situation at the time

Observational evidence for score given

How effectively, efficiently and correctly were the available technical resources used?

1	2	3	4	5
The available equipment and/or procedures were ignored or misused, to the serious detriment of safety or task performance	The available equipment and/or procedures were substantially underused, creating unnecessary risks to safety or task performance	The available equipment and/or procedures were not generally well used, although safety and task performance were not obviously put at risk	Technical resources were used appropriately to get the task done	Technical resources were used in imaginative ways that showed deep technical understanding and significantly enhanced efficiency without compromising safety

Negative indicators	**Positive indicators**
Crew members do not use technical resources when appropriate Crew members show signs of lack of familiarity with technical resources or difficulty in operating Crew members use technical resources incorrectly or in an unsafe manner (eg without doing risk assessment or taking shortcuts)	Crew members use the appropriate technical resources for the task Crew members are efficient in their use of technical resources Crew members demonstrate they know how to use technical resources safely

Observational evidence for score given

Resilience Scale 5	Disruptions and distractions			

How effectively and efficiently were disruptions and distractions managed?

1	2	3	4	5
Performance was completely disrupted by otherwise normal operational events. Safety was put at severe risk	Disruptions were (or would have been) handled poorly, resulting in potential risk to safety and the success of the activity	Disruptions were not handled very well, with some hiatus and the need for time out for reconfiguration	Disruptions were handled with only minor disturbance and delays to the ongoing task and without compromising safety	Crew members prioritised and managed disruptions with insight and expertise that maintained optimal task efficiency and full attention to safety

Negative indicators	Positive indicators
The crew are taken by surprise by disruptions The crew disproportionately shift their attention to disruptions, to the detriment of the primary task The crew display confusion and disarray in the face of disruptions There is shouting and discussion that does little to help with disruptions There are unnecessary delays in responding to disruptions	The crew are aware of disruptions in a timely manner The crew understand the nature of disruptions and their implications with minimal discussion The crew have a collective understanding of how to adjust their tasks and roles in the face of disruptions The crew respond to disruptions without delay and without losing focus on the primary task Crew members remain calm and organised in the face of disruptions

Observational evidence for score given

Resilience Scale 6	Changes to plans and priorities			

How effectively, efficiently and appropriately were plans and priorities changed in the face of emerging demands?

1	2	3	4	5
The need to change plans and priorities was poorly managed, putting at severe risk own ship and crew or other ships or personnel on shore. Ship performance was severely degraded	The need to change plans and priorities was met poorly, putting own ship and crew or other ships or shore personnel at some risk. Ship performance was degraded	The need to change plans and priorities was barely adequately managed, possibly compromising safety or performance	The need to change plans and priorities was managed, avoiding undue risks to safety and performance	The crew rapidly adapted plans and revised priorities in ways that were highly innovative while maintaining or even improving safety and performance

Negative indicators	Positive indicators
The crew is slow to recognise the need to alter plan or priorities Changes in plans or priorities are acted on reluctantly When the plan changes, crew members are confused, slow and uncertain how to respond Crew members do not express any reservations about the change in plan Crew members do not ask questions to clarify any areas of uncertainty	The need to change plan or priorities is recognised and accepted in a timely manner Senior crew members share their intentions and plans as they develop Senior crew members give revised instructions clearly and in a timely manner, taking account of the tasks the crew is currently undertaking Questions and suggestions from crew members are encouraged, listened to and responded to with respect Crew members voice their ideas and views confidently but with respect Crew members respond to changes in plans promptly, smoothly and efficiently Tasks, roles and resources are re-allocated as necessary, with minimum discussion

Observational evidence for score given

How easily and smoothly did the team cope with the pressures of the situation?

1	2	3	4	5
The team collapsed under the pressures of the situation and safety was severely compromised, as was productive performance	The pressures of the situation were poorly handled, resulting in substantial underperformance and potential impact on safety, although no incidents resulted	The crew members responded satisfactorily to the pressures but were at the edge of their comfort zone	The pressures of the situation were normal and were handled confidently, competently and with due regard to safety	The pressures of the situation were particularly challenging, but handled confidently, competently and with due regard to safety

Negative indicators	Positive indicators
Safety-critical tasks are omitted or done badly	Crew members are aware when they are under pressure and respond accordingly
Emerging risks are ignored	
Coordination of crew members breaks down	Crew members take extra care, especially over safety-critical tasks
Safety-critical communications are not made or get lost in the confusion	Crew members remain calm, acting promptly but without undue haste
Crew members freeze under pressure, unable to act	Crew members monitor each other for signs of stress and provide additional support to anyone who appears over-stressed
Levels of shouting, aggression, destructive criticism increase with pressure	
	Crew members eliminate unnecessary communications, but when they communicate they speak clearly and precisely

Observational evidence for score given

Reproduced with kind permission from Teekay

4. **Improving resilience** In this final fourth stage, after the bridge team[51] has been observed and scored in all the different navigational scenarios, the reviewer brings the team members together for a debrief meeting. The scales have been designed such that a score of 4 indicates that performance was as expected, demonstrating normal levels of resilience. If the team executes the task beyond expectations, ie demonstrating (possibly new) best practice, then this would attract a score of 5 and merit special attention in the reviewer's report. If crew performance on any of the resilience scales was awarded a score of less than 4, the debrief discussion with the crew probes for the reasons and context for their observed behaviour.

The probe questions are all concerned with uncovering the deeper influences on human behaviour. Together, they build a picture of the mindset of the crew during the task. They fall into three groups, organised by the SUGAR model:

Key probe questions about State

- How pressing did things seem at that time to you – and why?
- How much rest had you had in the previous 24 hours – and why (not)?
- How were you feeling at that time (bored? excited? tired? afraid? stressed? overloaded?) – and why?

---

51 In practice, different people will be in the bridge team at different times, depending on the watch pattern. This is acceptable, since the reviewer is trying to establish the characteristics and relationships of the crew in different circumstances and to see if there are any repeating patterns of behaviour.

- How comfortable did you feel about challenging someone about the way things were going – and why (not)?

Key probe questions about Understanding

- How far did you believe you had the knowledge and skills to solve the problem at that time – and why (not)?
- What were your assumptions and expectations at that time – and why?
- What was your main focus of attention at that time – and why?
- How safe did you feel at that time – and why (not)?
- How much in control did you feel at that time – and why (not)?
- What did you think was the worst thing that could happen at that time – and why?

Key probe questions about Goals

- What was most important to you to achieve at that time – and why?
- How clear-cut were your plans and priorities at that time – and why (not)?
- How far do you feel your team shared a common sense of purpose – and why (not)?
- What sense of obligation did you feel at that time and to whom – and why?

Using a combination of the checklisted state of the ship infrastructure, the evidenced resilience scores over several scenarios, and the behavioural probe questions, the reviewer establishes how typical the observed behaviour is for this crew. Wherever appropriate, the reviewer passes on best practice to the crew. Equally, the reviewer can collect new instances of apparently effective practice to pass on to senior company levels. By collating reviews across all its ships, Teekay is able to establish how far the navigational issues observed with this crew are particular to them, or else have more general significance, requiring more systematic or strategic attention, eg via adjustments to its training programmes.

Teekay's overall aim is to quantify and improve its levels of operational resilience. It is possibly the first shipping company to directly confront the reality of operating within complex, adaptive systems.

Detecting resonance with FRAM

Resonance occurs when something that is activated starts to synchronise with its source in a way that amplifies its response. Sometimes this can be bad, which is why soldiers break step over a bridge so as not to destroy it with the vibrations produced by their lockstep marching.[52] But sometimes it can be good, as when any competent musician plays their wind, string or percussion instrument, or an expert vocalist activates the harmonic resonance in their vocal chords to sing.

In the operational life of a safety-critical organisation such as a hospital, airline or ship, unwelcome variability (resonance) can build up if (for example) the recruitment and training functions do not provide the necessary expertise and resources to meet the external demands placed on operational staff. The affected staff will be forced to adjust their own

---

52 In 1831, British soldiers marching over Broughton Bridge in Salford, near Manchester in the UK, produced sufficient resonance for the iron-chain suspension bridge to break apart under them, pitching them into the water. In June 2000, the new Millennium Bridge over the River Thames in London had to be closed for repairs designed to dampen a similar resonance produced when pedestrians fell into step with the bridge's vibrations, thereby amplifying its swaying to the point where people fell over.

performance via shortcuts, fatigue-based mistakes, failure to meet targets, and non-reporting of safety issues.

In line with his work on *Safety – I* and *Safety – II*,[53] summarised in Chapter 9 (Being in the know – part IV), Erik Hollnagel realised that looking for causes in complex, adaptive systems is misplaced effort, since the same performance variability that sometimes apparently causes bad things to happen is also necessary to prevent them from happening the rest of the time. Hollnagel reasoned that a more productive approach is to try to figure out where and when a system is likely to experience resonance. If that resonance is likely to lead to something bad, then it should be possible to see how to dampen it. Conversely, if the resonance is leading somewhere unexpectedly beneficial, then it should be possible to see how to enhance or repeat it.

The result of this line of thought was *FRAM – the Functional Resonance Analysis Method*.[54] Hollnagel's method is only summarised here, since the details are easily obtained (see the reference in Chapter 15). Free, downloadable FRAM software is also available from the same source.

The method comprises four steps:

1. Important system functions are identified and characterised in terms of six aspects, as illustrated in Figure 14.1, which shows just one function. In a medical example, such a function might be 'Assess the patient' and another might be 'Respond to test result'.

Figure 14.1 Structure of a function in a FRAM model

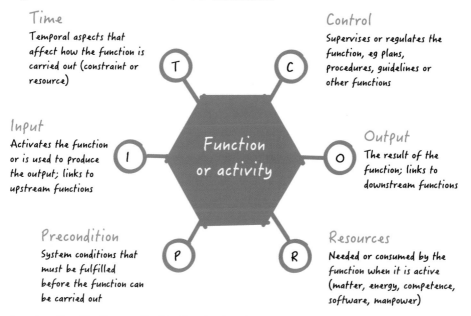

Time
Temporal aspects that affect how the function is carried out (constraint or resource)

Control
Supervises or regulates the function, eg plans, procedures, guidelines or other functions

Input
Activates the function or is used to produce the output; links to upstream functions

Output
The result of the function; links to downstream functions

Precondition
System conditions that must be fulfilled before the function can be carried out

Resources
Needed or consumed by the function when it is active (matter, energy, competence, software, manpower)

Reproduced from *The FRAM Handbook* (Hollnagel et al, 2014) with kind permission from Kring and Hollnagel

53 Hollnagel (2014)

54 Hollnagel et al (2014)

2. The potential variability of the functions needs to be characterised. This is done by considering each function in turn, using the experience of the people who do the work. Stock must also be taken of which functions are handled by technology, which by humans and which by organisations. The FRAM ground rule here is that technological functions are assumed to provide relatively stable outputs, human functions will tend to vary their outputs with high frequency and high amplitude, and organisational functions will generally vary their outputs with low frequency but high amplitude. This means that the output variability of human and organisational functions should receive the most attention in FRAM.

The potential couplings between functions can be found by matching the aspects that have been described. This makes clear how, for example, the output from one function provides the input of one (downstream) function, or the precondition of another, and hence how variability may propagate as an activity is carried out.

Outputs can vary in terms of time (too early, on time, too late) or in terms of precision (precise, acceptable, imprecise). If outputs are on time and precise, downstream functions that use them will not need to vary their own activities very much. Conversely, if outputs are not received on time or are imprecise, they will create considerable downstream variability, requiring more resources and time to execute.

3. Based on all the couplings between functions, the possibility of functional resonance needs to be determined. Functional resonance is assessed by considering all the ways in which the functions are coupled, the extent to which these can vary, and how control might thereby be lost.

4. Conclusions can be drawn about how to monitor and dampen the variability that may lead to undesirable results. Here, ways to attenuate the variability with indicators, barriers and design modifications are considered. If variability that leads to positive results is detected, recommendations can be made about how to amplify the variability to increase the benefits.

FRAM is not trivial to get to grips with, but it is a unique tool for addressing some of the central realities of modelling and understanding complex, adaptive systems. It can be used both prospectively as a risk-assessment tool, and retrospectively to understand what happened after an adverse event. It is not concerned with discovering causes, but rather helps to visualise what happens in everyday conditions when nothing goes wrong. Once visualised, it becomes possible to see how the variability of the functions may combine to produce unexpected results.

Creating a strategy for organisational resilience

The need for a unifying strategy

Resilient organisations pay attention to all of the topics described in this chapter. Paying attention to any of them should help to increase the ability of the organisation and its staff to become more resilient. However, advocates of any one topic should always be aware of Le Chatelier's principle that any change to a system leads to a new status quo as the other elements adapt. Care must be taken to consider a systemic approach, so that the overall result is a net gain.

Organisations carrying out safety-critical activities will already have various forms of training, development and policy programmes. Often, these programmes are 'owned' by different organisational departments – for example, operations, safety, engineering, or human resources.

We advocate gaining maximum benefit from these programmes by integrating them into a unifying strategy for explicitly developing resilience.

The aim is to deploy resources that support and complement each other systemically, and which are able to make the most efficient use of expensive training resources (eg simulation – see earlier in this chapter).

How could such a strategy be developed?

In this last part of the book, we give three different strategic approaches, as follows:

- A systems approach describes a stepwise methodology based on the formal principles of the Systems Approach to Training (SAT).[55]

- An organic approach follows a more formative methodology designed to accelerate the natural growth of a resilient safety culture at all levels of the organisation.

- A performance approach relies on the forensic identification of those operational performance areas that the data shows are most vulnerable. With the application of organisation-wide safety enablers, staff at all levels seek to improve accuracy and attention to detail in all those areas with respect to clearly defined goals.

Readers are invited to consider which of these may work best in their own organisations. In the end, however, they are only different starting points and elements of each can be used as the opportunity permits and your strategy unfolds.

Fundamental to all three approaches is the view that resilience is the key to safe operational performance at all levels – from front-line operators to board-level directors.

What they also share is that:

- Humans are crucial to safe performance in complex systems.

- Our strengths are vulnerable and our weaknesses need to be supported.

- Safety is not compromised by root causes, but by inherent uncertainty.

---

55 The steps described here are based on the good overview of SAT provided by Flin et al (2008), chapter 10. A very comprehensive description of SAT is also given by the US Department of Energy (1994).

- Safety does not reside in deterministic procedures, but instead emerges out of mindful behaviour.
- Sanctions must only be made on the basis of fair-minded accountability.

Here are the three approaches in a little more detail.

1 – A systems approach

The systems approach deploys the principles of the Systems Approach to Training (SAT) to create a training-centric strategy aimed at increasing the resilience of safety-critical task and teamwork behaviour among organisational staff. There are three key steps:

1. **Identify the needs**

   1.1 *Assess needs* This step first identifies those tasks that are most critical to safety in routine, non-routine and emergency situations. For each task identified, front-line staff and managers, supported by specialists as necessary, assess the knowledge, skills and attitudes (KSAs) required. This step should examine the KSAs in terms of team members and leaders, including any particular requirements to deal with issues of diversity and multicultural working. It should also seek to identify tasks and situations where leadership and deeper levels of expertise are likely to be required, over and above normal levels of competence. The process for assessing the resilience of current operational behaviour, as we developed for Teekay Shipping,[56] could provide an important input to this step.

   1.2 *Set objectives* For each training need identified (ie KSAs for each critical task), the objective for the training must be defined. This step entails assessing how well the required KSAs are being met by current staff and training arrangements. Where there is a gap between current provision and the task requirement, this identifies a training objective. For example, it might be discovered that an emergency task requires high degrees of expertise, which no-one has and for which no training currently exists. With respect to Step 3 (below), consideration can also be given to how the effectiveness of the training will later be assessed. For example, has knowledge been gained, and can it be used to more mindfully manage task performance in key scenarios?

2. **Meet the needs**

   2.1 *Choose methodology* This step translates the training requirements into the actual means of training. The main methods are information-based, demonstration-based, and practice-based training. While information- and demonstration-based training will be required, developing resilience also depends heavily on practice-based training – especially practice involving simulators. Resilience training must prepare personnel for the 'once in a career' incident, and such training can only really be effectively delivered via simulation. Recall Captain Sullenberger's comment after surviving his landing on the River Hudson: that he had made a massive withdrawal from a bank of experience into which many deposits had been made, over many years. We described the main issues in developing and using simulation earlier in this chapter.

---

56 See earlier in this chapter

Being Human in safety-critical organisations

2.2 *Deliver training* This step takes the objectives and matches them to particular methods and personnel, to form a coherent plan based on sound instructional principles of the sort noted by Flin et al.[57] There are many approaches to resilience training, and these are described in the Crew Resource Management[58] programmes in the aviation industry, Bridge Resource Management[59] and HELM[60] training in the shipping industry, and TeamSTEPPS[61] and CARMA[62] in healthcare. All these sources provide good templates and starting points for developing a bespoke programme. Other types of training that could be included in the strategy include cross-training, team self-correction training, event-based training, and team facilitation training.[63]

3. Evaluate the results

Once the training has been implemented, it is obviously important to evaluate what has been delivered to assess how effective it has been. Effectiveness can be assessed at a number of levels. How did trainees react to the training? Have individual KSAs changed? Has behaviour changed? Can individuals and teams perform their tasks more effectively? Is the organisation more resilient?[64] The resilience scales developed for Teekay and the resilience indicators described elsewhere in this chapter provide good starting points for the important business of measuring resilience and its trends over time.

2 – An organic approach

Figure 14.2 depicts an organic approach to growing organisational resilience. Since open reporting is at the heart of a resilient safety culture, one way to start is by focusing on your organisation's current incident reporting and investigation process. Consider how it can be enhanced with a Mindset Analysis component (see earlier in this chapter). Once this is done and greater insight is available into the mindsets of those involved in incidents, then the new information can be utilised to increase one or more aspects of resilience.

For example:

- *Organisational barriers* to resilience can be overcome by, for example, refining the staff appraisal system to detect and measure the behaviours and attitudes that mitigate the risk of incidents. Organisations tend to get the behaviour they measure – so be sure your organisation measures the behaviour that it wants!

- *Alertness to risk* could be addressed through, for example, the development of a self-audit risk-awareness tool or app based on the risk research presented in this book (see Chapter 8: Being in the know – part III)

---

57 Flin et al (2008)

58 See, for example, Kanki et al (2010), Marcellin (2014)

59 See, for example, Parrott (2011), Penn (2012)

60 Human Element Leadership & Management, a more comprehensive development of Bridge Resource Management

61 *Team Strategies & Tools to Enhance Performance and Patient Safety*. For a comprehensive description and materials, visit http://www.teamsteppsportal.org/teamstepps-materials [accessed April 2017].

62 *Crisis Avoidance Resource Management for Anaesthetists* – see Flin & Maran (2004)

63 See Flin et al (2008), pp. 250–1 for further description of these training methods and guidance on their use.

64 For a fuller account of the evaluation of training, refer to Kirkpatrick (1998). For a useful summary, see Flin et al (2008), chapter 10.

- *Expertise and responsibility* could be increased by, for example, ensuring that management communications are optimised in terms of style, content and consistency. The training requirements identified by the previous systems approach could also play a significant part here.

Figure 14.2 An organic approach to developing a safety culture based on resilience

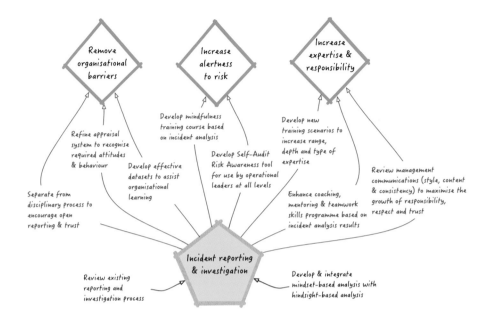

The blue lines in Figure 14.2 indicate other suggestions for action. In this organic approach, no specific order is recommended for the steps: it's a matter for opportunistic development in the operational context of the organisation and the available human resources and their interests. The upshot is a diffusion throughout the organisation – crucially, at all levels – of new values and codes of conduct that create greater resilience.

It should be noted that Teekay's development of a resilience-based strategy began with a diagram like this. In their case, John Adams (Teekay Glasgow Managing Director) led efforts to operationalise these human-element themes. Teekay's senior management amended their incident investigation process, which led to a focus on 'alertness to risk' via a behavioural review of operational bridge teams (described earlier in this chapter). Together, these pragmatic changes are helping to underpin the company's Operational Leadership initiative, which creates a clear, human-factors-informed line of sight from the board to the front line – and back again.

3 – A performance approach

When Gretchen Haskins was Safety Director at NATS Ltd, the organisation responsible for UK national air traffic services, she oversaw an initiative that produced some remarkable results. By identifying the key incident event types, and then the day-to-day functions that the human/machine system needs to perform well to help prevent these events, the company was able to create a proactive safety performance improvement strategy. This enabled a set of performance improvement goals to be set, and a clear view of where to invest resources in those areas where enhanced performance would reduce incident rates.

NATS' approach to its safety strategy explicitly embraces the thinking in Hollnagel's *Safety – II* and *Resilience Engineering*, and is fully committed to the use of leading resilience indicators, the idea that people create safety, and the analysis of what goes right as well as what goes wrong.

Haskins is now CEO at HeliOffshore, the international association for the safety of the offshore helicopter industry. Under her guidance, HeliOffshore has adopted the same principles of performance-based safety that were developed at NATS.

Key to this approach is shifting the organisational perspective: from reducing error, to improving accuracy and effectiveness; from responding to negative events, to mindful attention of senior decision-makers to those investments and actions that will enhance front-line results within organisations and across the industry. The approach is not focused on the management of risk, but rather on the improvement of operational and managerial performance in those areas with the greatest potential to enhance safety.

Figure 14.3 shows that, analogous to the NATS approach, HeliOffshore has created a safety performance model that first identifies the most serious *accident event types*. The model then defines a series of *accident prevention goals* that provide focus for the *safety enablers* and tools available to address them.

Figure 14.3 HeliOffshore Safety Performance Model (top level)

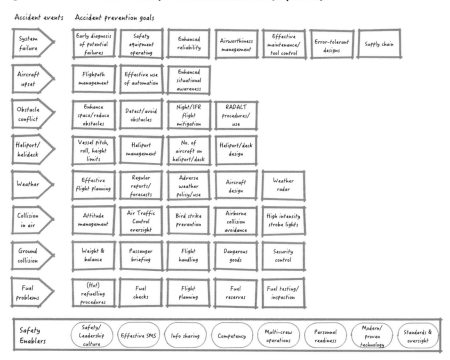

Reproduced from *HeliOffshore Safety Strategy* (2016) with kind permission from Gretchen Haskins

Safety enablers – the potential for 'big data'

Several of the safety enablers indicated in the HeliOffshore safety performance model entail resilience indicators of the sort identified earlier in this chapter. Measurement in day-to-day (and even minute-by-minute) operations, via recent developments in technology, makes it easier than ever to extract the important safety data.

Human-wearable biometric, fitness and activity-monitoring devices are both affordable and commonplace. Active RFID (Radio Frequency Identification) tags are able to store data about the performance and maintenance status of the equipment in which they are embedded. Tiny, low-power wi-fi modules are able to connect any component to the 'internet of things'. Inexpensive long-range (LoRa) routers are able to communicate without line of sight over distances measured in miles (kilometres). Arbitrarily large numbers of these smart, connected objects and agents are able to transmit performance data in real time to servers where artificially intelligent fuzzy logic and 'deep learning' neural-net-based algorithms are able to detect and analyse system-wide performance patterns.

These technologies hold out the possibility for a new type of dynamic, real-time resilience indicator based on 'big data' analysis. Such indicators could help detect the status of whole systems as they drift into danger, identify problems where parts of the system are starting to work unsustainably hard to achieve their objectives, measure the changing degree of stress being experienced by the system as a whole, and examine the changing degree to which the system is able to recover from such stresses over time.

The performance approach to resilience has already generated significant safety benefits and insights for NATS and HeliOffshore. The application of big-data techniques to large-scale, real-time monitoring of suitable resilience indicators has the potential to move safety creation within complex systems to a new level. In particular, the integration of data-driven human performance using behavioural contexts, patterns and indicators based on the SUGAR framework with other real-time data sources seems an especially promising line of development.

SUGAR ingredients

Whatever strategic approach is adopted for the development of organisational resilience, the following guidelines elaborate on some of the more important ingredients from the SUGAR model:

- **The assessment of current KSAs** Any attempt to develop competence in resilience needs to be informed by the current state of knowledge, skills and attitudes relating to teamwork, leadership and expertise within the organisation. The resilience indicator system developed for Teekay (described earlier in this chapter) includes scales for assessing teamwork that can be used by any safety-critical organisation. To do so, the resilience scales would need to be extended to address leadership and expertise. While the Teekay system is a formal process conducted by a reviewer, we recommend that organisations adopt a wider assessment process that team leaders, supervisors and all team members can carry out on a regular but informal basis.

- **The nature of leadership** Training for resilience needs to cover two different types of leadership. There is the 'normal' vertical leadership that is required during routine, day-to-day operations. This is the traditional role of the team leader or supervisor, and is concerned with setting goals and priorities, allocating tasks and resources, creating a safety climate, coaching and mentoring, adjudicating in conflicts, and so on. The other type of leadership is situation dependent, and is required in non-routine and especially emergency situations. In these situations, the person with the most relevant expertise should exercise leadership. This will often not be the formal leader or the most senior person. Leadership here is about taking charge of the developing situation. Training should be given to all operators, supervisors and managers who may find themselves having to lead when an emerging crisis demands. Formal leaders may have to be trained to allow authority to be passed to another for the duration of the incident.

- **The nature of expertise** This refers to technical expertise: deep understanding of the system and its behaviour. Complex systems will always have the potential to throw up novel, unexpected problems. Even the person with deep expertise may be confronted by situations they have never experienced before. But the person with a wide range of advanced training and operational experience, coupled with extensive deliberate practice (as discussed in Chapter 10, Being on target), has the best chance of correctly diagnosing the problem and finding a solution that works. Again, as discussed in Chapter 10, while there are other possibilities (such as case studies and role plays), the most effective practice is likely to be via simulation (discussed earlier in this chapter).

- **The focus of teamwork training** Analysis of research indicates that the most effective team-training initiatives focus on coordination and communications.[65]

- **The locus of learning initiatives** To complement a formal teamwork programme, team leaders, supervisors and managers should be encouraged to look for informal opportunities to learn about teamwork and the technical system in the workplace. This might be as simple as getting two team members to discuss the nature of their jobs over a cup of coffee. What are their biggest challenges? What experiences have they had of the system 'misbehaving'? Where and when do they depend on each other? What can they do to help the other do their job even better? Sometimes it may be possible for one team member to shadow another, observing, questioning and learning. Ideally, a newcomer to the team should have the chance to shadow all the other jobs in the team. When the person has sufficient competence and it is safe to do so, they can take over from the other for a time.

- **The importance of review and feedback sessions** Team leaders, supervisors and managers should be encouraged to hold review and feedback sessions with their teams. The aim is to discuss how they are working together, to identify any weaknesses, and to look for ways to improve. This is essentially the same as the reviewer-led debrief session in the Teekay resilience assessment process described earlier in this chapter, but is less formal. The team leader may initially facilitate these sessions, but as the team members become clearer about what they define as good work, the need for a facilitator will diminish.

- **The need to train for diversity** Many organisations have diversity training programmes, often conducted by somebody from the human resources department or an external consultant.[66] These programmes typically cover the legal requirements arising from equality or anti-discrimination legislation. They usually also aim to change attitudes and break down barriers between different groups. Diversity courses are

---

65 Salas et al (2007)

66 See, for example, McPherson (2007), Clements (2008)

undoubtedly important in creating a positive climate for multicultural teamworking, thereby contributing to increased safety and resilience.

- **Integrating diversity with teamwork and leader training** In many organisations, diversity training is run largely in parallel with more safety-oriented teamwork training programmes. But team-training programmes need to directly incorporate the issues of multicultural team members. For example, how should a team leader give due attention to differences between team members from different cultures while seeming to treat all members in the same way? Or how should the leader cope with team members who have culturally different attitudes towards, and expectations of, a leader? These kinds of difference can give rise to tensions and uncertainties, which may hinder prompt and effective action when a serious incident looms.

Last word

The guidance and tools set out in this final chapter have been included for their ability to increase human-centred resilience in the complex, adaptive systems that characterise safety-critical operations.

In the last part of this chapter, we have presented three approaches to developing organisational resilience: systems, organic and performance-based. These are quite rich descriptions and are not intended as prescriptive, stepwise procedures, but rather as three different starting places. Choose whichever one seems to have the most appeal for your organisational context. Think about what the approach would mean for you, and see where it takes you – just as Teekay and HeliOffshore are already doing with their resilience initiatives.

We strongly encourage you to consider any and all of the techniques, tools and approaches that we have set out in this chapter. Their development and creative enlargement through use at both the individual and organisational level will help to encourage the development of resilience. And with an explicit focus on increasing resilience, you will be taking an approach to safety that is consistent both with the reality of complex system dynamics and with the reality of being human.

Like the complex, adaptive systems we are part of, human beings are an endless source of variety – and as Ross Ashby showed us 60 years ago,[67] you can only 'kill' variety with variety. That is why, in the end, the safe operation of complex, adaptive systems depends on our collective, creative ability to facilitate and sustain what most human beings are continually trying to do: to understand and manage the variability of everyone – and everything – else, with sufficient variability of their own.

---

67 Ashby (1956)

15 References

AAIB (1990) *Report on the accident to Boeing 737-400 G-OBME near Kegworth, Leicestershire on 8 January 1989*. Department of Transport, Air Accidents Investigation Branch. London: HMSO.

AAIB (2010) *Report on the accident to Boeing 777-236ER, G YMMM, at London Heathrow Airport on 17 January 2008*. Department for Transport, Air Accidents Investigation Branch, January 2010.

ABC News (2015) *Los Angeles schools closed after threat*. http://abcnews.go.com/GMA/video/los-angeles-schools-closed-threat-35776108 [accessed April 2017].

Adelson, E.H. (2000) Lightness Perception and Lightness Illusions. In *The New Cognitive Neurosciences* (2nd ed.), Gazzaniga, M. (ed.), Cambridge, MA: MIT Press, pp. 339–351.

Akerstedt, T., Mollard, R., Samel, A., Simons, M. & Spencer, M. (2003) *Paper prepared for the ETSC Meeting to discuss the role of EU FTL legislation in reducing cumulative fatigue in civil aviation*. European Transport Safety Council, Brussels, 19 February 2003.

Aldrich, D.P. (2010) *Fixing Recovery: Social Capital in Post-Crisis Resilience*. Department of Political Science Faculty Publications, Paper 3.

Allen, D. (2015) *Getting Things Done: The Art of Stress-free Productivity*. Piatkus.

Allianz Global Corporate & Specialty SE (2015) *Safety and Shipping Review 2015: annual review of trends and developments in shipping losses and safety*. Munich, https://www.allianz.com/v_1427190309000/media/press/document/other/Shipping-Review-2015.pdf [accessed April 2017].

Allport, G.W. (1955) *Becoming*. Yale University Press.

American Board of Thoracic Surgery operative requirements. Available at https://www.abts.org/root/home/certification/requirements/operative-requirements.aspx [accessed April 2017].

American Petroleum Institute (2010) *RP 755 – Fatigue Prevention Guidelines for the Refining and Petrochemical Industries*.

American Psychological Association (2012) *What You Need to Know about Willpower: The Psychological Science of Self-Control*. APA.

Ariely, D. (2009) *Predictably Irrational. The Hidden Forces That Shape Our Decisions.* HarperCollins.

Ashby, W.R. (1956) *An Introduction to Cybernetics.* Chapman & Hall.

Association of Anaesthetists of Great Britain and Ireland (2014) *Fatigue and Anaesthetists.*

Atkin, R. (1981) *Multidimensional Man: Can Man Live in 3-dimensional Space?* Penguin Books.

Avolio, B.J., Walumbwa, F.O. & Weber, T.J. (2009) Leadership: Current Theories, Research, and Future Directions. *Annual Review of Psychology*, 60, 421–449. Available online at http://digitalcommons.unl.edu/managementfacpub/37 [accessed April 2017].

Bacon, L. & MacKinnon, L. (2012) Using Virtual and Augmented Reality to Create Realistic Training Events. *Compass: The Journal of Learning and Teaching at the University of Greenwich,* Issue 6, 2012.

Bacon, L., Windall, G. & MacKinnon, L. (2012) The development of a rich multimedia training environment for crisis management: using emotional affect to enhance learning. *Research in Learning Technology*, [S.l.], v. 19, January 2012. ISSN 2156–7077. http://www.tandfonline.com/doi/full/10.3402/rlt.v19s1/7780 [accessed April 2017].

Bahamas Maritime Authority (2004) *Report of the investigation into the loss of the Bahamian registered tanker "Prestige" off the northwest coast of Spain on 19th November 2002.*

Baines Simmons (2015) *FAiR® 2 System: a behaviour-based system for supporting and sustaining a Just Culture.* Baines Simmons Ltd.

Baker, D.B., Day, R. & Salas, E. (2006) Teamwork as an Essential Component of High-Reliability Organizations. *Health Services Research*, 41:4, Part II (August).

Barber, N. (2010) Is money the main reason we go to work? *Psychology Today*, 2 December 2010. https://www.psychologytoday.com/blog/the-human-beast/201012/is-money-the-main-reason-we-go-work [accessed April 2017].

Bargh, J.A., Chen, M. & Burrows, L. (1996) Automaticity of social behavior: Direct effects of trait construct and stereotype activation on action. *Journal of Personality and Social Psychology*, 71, 230–244.

Barry, J. & Charles, R. (Lt. Col. Retd) (1992) Sea of Lies: USS Vincennes shootdown of Iran Air Flight 655 on July 3, 1988. *Newsweek*, 13 July 1992.

Bassett-Jones, N. (2005) The Paradox of Diversity Management, Creativity and Innovation. *Creativity and Innovation Management*, 14 (2).

Bauman, E.B. (2012) *Game-based teaching and simulation in Nursing and Health Care.* Springer.

Baumeister, R.F. (2012) *Willpower: Self-control, decision fatigue, and energy depletion.* London School of Economics Public Lecture.

Baumeister, R.F. & Leary, M.R. (1995) The Need to Belong: Desire for Interpersonal Attachments as a Fundamental Human Motivation. *Psychological Bulletin*, 117 (3), 497–529.

Bayouth, S.T. (2011) *Examining fire fighter decision-making process and choice in virtual reality.* Iowa State University.

BBC (2012) *Spain Prestige oil spill disaster case in court*. http://www.bbc.co.uk/news/world-europe-19952329 [accessed April 2017].

BBC (2013a) *Manslaughter charges dropped in M5 crash case*. http://www.bbc.co.uk/news/uk-england-somerset-21024902 [accessed April 2017].

BBC (2013b) *Geoffrey Counsell cleared over M5 fireworks deaths*. http://www.bbc.co.uk/news/uk-england-25316055 [accessed April 2017].

BBC (2015) *Los Angeles schools shut over email threat to students*. http://www.bbc.co.uk/news/world-us-canada-35102954 [accessed April 2017].

BBC (2016) *FlyDubai crash pilot 'was due to leave job over fatigue'*. http://www.bbc.co.uk/news/world-europe-35855678 [accessed April 2017].

BEA (2002) *Accident on 25 July 2000 at La Patte d'Oie in Gonesse (95) to the Concorde registered F-BTSC operated by Air France*. Minsitère de l'Equipement des Transports et du Logement – Bureau d'Enquêtes et d'Analyses pour la sécurité de l'aviation civile – France, January 2002.

BEA (2012) *Final report on the accident on 1st June 2009 to the Airbus A330-203 registered F-GZCP operated by Air France flight AF 447 Rio de Janeiro – Paris*. Ministère de l'Écologie, du Développement durable, des Transports et du Logement – Bureau d'Enquêtes et d'Analyses pour la sécurité de l'aviation civile – France, July 2012.

Belcher, P. (2007) *Rule Following Behaviour in Collision Avoidance: a study of navigational practices in the Dover Strait*. PhD Thesis, Cardiff University.

Benkler, Y. (2011) The Unselfish Gene. *Harvard Business Review*, July–August 2011.

Benner, P. (1982) From novice to expert. *American Journal of Nursing*, March, 402–407.

Benner, P. (1984) *From Novice to Expert: Excellence and Power in Clinical Nursing Practice*. Reading, MA: Addison-Wesley.

Benner, P. (2004) Using the Dreyfus Model of Skill Acquisition to Describe and Interpret Skill Acquisition and Clinical Judgment in Nursing Practice and Education. *Bulletin of Science, Technology & Society*, 2004, 24, 188.

Benton, G. (2005) *Multicultural crews and the culture of globalization*. International Association of Maritime Universities (IAMU) 6th Annual General Assembly and Conference.

Bolton, R. & Bolton, D.G. (2009) *People Styles at Work… And Beyond: Making Bad Relationships Good and Good Relationships Better*. NY: AMACOM Books.

Bouboushian, J. (2013) *Last Victim of Concorde Crash Sues United*. Courthouse News Service, 2 December 2013. https://www.courthousenews.com/last-victim-of-concorde-crash-sues-united [accessed April 2017].

Brickman, P., Coates, D., Janoff-Bulman, R. (1978) Lottery winners and accident victims: Is happiness relative? *Journal of Personality and Social Psychology*, 36 (8), 917–927.

Brown, D. (2010) *Confessions of a Conjuror*. Channel 4 Books. London: Random House: Transworld.

Burrell, T. (2016) Force of habit. *New Scientist*, 16 January 2016, pp. 30–34.

Buzan, T. (1974) *Use your head*. London: BBC Books.

Cahill, R.A. (1990) *Disasters at Sea: Titanic to Exxon Valdez*. Century.

Cannon-Bowers, J. & Salas, E. (1998) Individual and team decision-making. In Cannon-Bowers, J. & Salas, E. (eds) *Making decisions under stress*, American Psychological Association, p. 19.

Carotenuto, A., Molino, I., Fasanaro, A.M. & Amenta, F. (2012) Psychological stress in seafarers: a review. *International Maritime Health*, 63 (4), 188–194.

Carter, G. (2015) *The Navy SEAL Mindset: Strength, Confidence, Control, Power* (2nd ed.).

Caruso, E.M., Burns, Z.C. & Converse, B.A. (2016) *Slow motion increases perceived intent*. Proceedings of the National Academy of Sciences of the USA, 10.1073/pnas.1603865113. http://www.pnas.org/content/early/2016/07/27/1603865113.abstract [accessed April 2017].

Chabris, C. & Simons, D. (2010) *The Invisible Gorilla: how our intuitions deceive us*. Random House: Crown.

Chamorro-Premuzic, T. (2013) Does money really affect motivation? A review of the research. *Harvard Business Review*. https://hbr.org/2013/04/does-money-really-affect-motiv [accessed April 2017].

Chee, J. (2014) Clinical simulation using deliberate practice in nursing education: A Wilsonian concept analysis. *Nurse Education in Practice*, 14 (2014), 247–252.

Cialdini, R.B. (1984) *Influence: The Psychology of Persuasion*. Harper Business.

Clements, P. (2008) *The Diversity Training Handbook: A Practical Guide to Understanding and Changing Attitudes*. Kogan Page.

Cliff, M. & Noble, A.C. (1990) Time–intensity evaluation of sweetness and fruitiness and their interaction in a model solution. *Journal of Food Science*, 55, 450–454.

Columbia Accident Investigation Board, *Report Volume 1*, August 2003, p. 6.

Couttie, B. *The Case of the Unfamiliar Mariner*. http://maritimeaccident.org/2014/11/this-weeks-podcast-the-case-of-the-unfamiliar-mariner [accessed April 2017].

Covey, S. (2004) *The 7 Habits of Highly Effective People*. Simon & Schuster.

Cox, T. (1978) *Stress*. University Park Press.

Crabtree, S. (2013) *Worldwide, 13% of Employees Are Engaged at Work*. www.gallup.com/poll/165269/worldwide-employees-engaged-work.aspx [accessed April 2017].

Crichton, M. (2001) Training for decision-making during emergencies. *Horizons of Psychology*, 10 (4), 7–22.

Cruz, A. & Green, B.G. (2000) Thermal stimulation of taste. *Nature*, 403, 889–892.

Csíkszentmihályi, M. (1990) *Flow: The Psychology of Optimal Experience*. Harper & Row.

Damasio, A. (1994) *Descartes' Error, Emotion, Reason, and the Human Brain*. New York: Avon Books.

Darley, J.M. & Latané, B. (1968) Bystander intervention in emergencies: Diffusion of responsibility. *Journal of Personality and Social Psychology*, 8, 377–383.

de Crespigny, R. (2012) *QF32*. Macmillan Australia.

Deci, E. & Flaste, R. (1996) *Why we do what we do: Understanding self-motivation*. Penguin.

Dekker, S. (2005) *Ten questions about human error: a new view of human factors and system safety*. Lawrence Erlbaum Associates.

Dekker, S. (2006) *The field guide to understanding human error*. Ashgate.

Dekker, S. (2012) *Just Culture: Balancing Safety and Accountability*. Ashgate.

Department of Energy (1994) *Training Program Handbook: A Systematic Approach To Training*. DOE-HDBK-1078-94.

Descartes, R. (1637) *The Philosophical Works of Descartes*, rendered into English by Elizabeth S. Haldane and G.R.T. Ross, vol. I. New York: Cambridge University Press, 1970.

Dixon, N.F. (1976) *On the Psychology of Military Incompetence*. Futura Publications.

Dolan, P. (2014) *Happiness by Design: Finding Pleasure and Purpose in Everyday Life*. Penguin.

Drew, T., Võ, M.L-H. & Wolfe, J.M. (2013) The invisible gorilla strikes again: sustained inattentional blindness in expert observers. *Psychological Science*, 24 (9), 1848–1853. Sage.

Dreyfus, H.L. (1997) Intuitive, deliberative and calculative models of expert performance. In Zsambok, C.E. & Klein, G. (eds) *Naturalistic Decision-making*. Lawrence Erlbaum Associates.

Dreyfus, H.L. & Dreyfus, S.E. (1988) *Mind over Machine: The Power of Human Intuition and Expertise in the Era of the Computer*. Free Press.

Dreyfus, S.E. (2004) The Five-Stage Model of Adult Skill Acquisition. *Bulletin of Science Technology & Society*, 24, 177.

Driskell, J.E. & Johnston, J.H. (1998) Stress Exposure Training. In Cannon-Bowers, J.E. & Salas, E. (eds) *Decision-making Under Stress: Implications for Individual and Team Training*. American Psychological Association, p. 194.

Dubeck, D. (2014) *Healthcare Worker Fatigue: Current Strategies for Prevention*. Pennsylvania Patient Safety Advisory.

Dunbar, R.I.M. (1998) The social brain hypothesis. *Evolutionary Anthropology: Issues, News, and Reviews*, 6 (5), 562–572.

Economist Intelligence Unit (2009) *Global Diversity and Inclusion: Perceptions, Practices and Attitude*. Survey for Society for Human Resource Management.

Eisenberger, N.I. (2012) The pain of social disconnection: examining the shared neural underpinnings of physical and social pain. *Nature Reviews Neuroscience*, 13, 421–434.

Enter, D.H., Lee, R., Fann, J.I., Hicks, J.L. Jr., Verrier, E.D., Mark, R., Lou, X., & Mokadem, N.A. (2014) *"Top Gun" Competition: Motivation and Practice Narrows the Technical Skill Gap Among New Cardiothoracic Surgery Residents*. Presented at the Fiftieth Annual Meeting of The Society of Thoracic Surgeons, Orlando, FL, January 25–29, 2014.

Epley, N. (2014) *Mindwise: How we understand what others think, feel and want*. Penguin.

Ericsson, K.A., Charness, N., Feltovich, P.J. & Hoffman, R.R. (eds) (2006) *The Cambridge Handbook of Expertise and Expert Performance*. Cambridge University Press.

Ericsson, K.A. (2006) The influence of experience and deliberate practice on the development of superior expert performance. In Ericsson, K.A., Charness, N., Feltovich, P.J. & Hoffman, R.R. (eds) *The Cambridge Handbook of Expertise and Expert Performance*. Cambridge University Press.

Ericsson, K.A. & Pool, R. (2016) *Peak: Secrets from the New Science of Expertise*. Bodley Head.

Ericsson, K.A., Prietula, M.J. & Cokely, E.T. (2007) The making of an expert. *Harvard Business Review*, July–August 2007.

Erie Insurance (2013) *Erie Insurance releases police data on top 10 driving distractions involved in fatal car crashes*. http://investor.shareholder.com/erie/releasedetail. cfm?ReleaseID=754063 [accessed April 2017].

Etcoff, N.L. & Magee, J.J. (1992) Categorical perception of facial expressions. *Cognition*, 44, 227–240.

Eurocontrol (2012) *Some Perspectives on Fatigue Risk Management Systems*. March 2012.

Eurocontrol (2016) *Just culture*. www.eurocontrol.int/articles/just-culture [accessed April 2017].

European Agency for Safety and Health at Work (2013) *European Opinion Poll on Occupational Safety and Health*. Official Publications of the European Communities.

Festinger, L. (1957) *A Theory of Cognitive Dissonance*. Stanford, CA: Stanford University Press.

Fishbach, A. & Ferguson, M.J. (2007) The Goal Construct in Social Psychology. In Kruglanski, A. & Higgins, E. (eds) *Social psychology: Handbook of basic principles* (2nd ed.), Guilford Press, pp. 490–515.

Fisher, C.D. (1991) *Boredom at Work: A Neglected Concept, Discussion Paper No 19*. Bond University School of Business, p. 3.

Fisher, C.D. (2010) Happiness at work. *International Journal of Management Reviews*, 12 (4), 384–412.

Fixot, R.S. (1957) [no title] *American Journal of Ophthalmology*, August 1957.

Flight Safety Foundation (1993) Tire failure on takeoff sets stage for fatal inflight fire and crash. *Accident Prevention*, 50 (9).

Flight Safety Foundation (2000) Cabin crews must capture passengers' attention in pre-departure safety briefings. *Cabin Crew Safety*, July–August 2000.

Flin, R. & Maran, N. (2004) Crisis Avoidance Resource Management for Anaesthetists. *Quality and Safety in Health Care*, 13 (suppl. 1), i80–i84.

Flin, R., O'Connor P. & Crichton, M. (2008) *Safety at the Sharp End: A Guide to Non-Technical Skills*. Ashgate.

Forrester, J.W. (1975) *Collected papers of Jay W. Forrester*. Portland: Productivity Press.

Foster, C., Espig, S., Smoker, A. & Dillon, R. (2016) *The Future of Safety in ATM: NATS Safety Strategy for 2020*. NATS Ltd. Available at http://www.nats.aero/wp-content/uploads/2014/05/TheFutureOfSafetyInATM2014.pdf [accessed April 2017].

Foster, P. (2011) Chinese toddler run over twice after being left on street. *The Daily Telegraph*, 17 October 2011.

Frankl, V. (1959) *Man's Search for Meaning*. Beacon Press.

Fredrickson, B.L. (2001) The role of positive emotions in positive psychology: The broaden-and-build theory of positive emotions. *American Psychologist*, 56, 218–226.

Frey, B. (1997) *Not Just for the Money: An Economic Theory of Personal Motivation*. Edward Elgar.

Galton, F. (1889) *Natural Inheritance*. London: Macmillan.

Gibson, J.J. (1979) *The ecological approach to visual perception*. Boston, MA: Houghton Mifflin.

Gigerenzer, G. (2008) *Rationality for Mortals: How people cope with uncertainty*. Oxford University Press.

Gigerenzer, G., Todd, P. & ABC Research Group (1999) *Simple heuristics that make us smart*. Oxford University Press.

Gilbert, D. (2005) *Why we make bad decisions*. TED Talk. https://www.ted.com/talks/dan_gilbert_researches_happiness#t-963324 [accessed April 2017].

Gilbert, D. (2006) *Stumbling on Happiness*. Harper Perennial.

Ginnett, R.C. (2010) Crews as groups: Their formation and their leadership. In Kanki, B.G., Helmreich, R. & Anca, J. (eds) *Crew Resource Management* (2nd ed.).

Gollwitzer, P.M., Fujita, K., & Oettingen, G. (2004) Planning and the implementation of goals. In Baumeister, R.F. & Vohs, K.D. (eds) *Handbook of self-regulation: Research, theory, and applications*, pp. 211–228. New York: Guilford Press.

Green, G. (2003) *Inattentional blindness and conspicuity*. http://www.visualexpert.com/Resources/inattentionalblindness.html [accessed April 2017].

Gregory Harland Ltd (2006) *The collection and analysis of railway safety-critical communication error data (T365)*. Report for Rail Safety and Standards Board.

Gregory, D. & Shanahan, P. (2008) *Understanding Human Factors: a guide for the rail industry*. RSSB. Available by free download from the RSSB website at http://www.rssb.co.uk/Library/improving-industry-performance/2008-guide-understanding-human-factors-a-guide-for-the-railway-industry.pdf [accessed April 2017].

Gregory, D. & Shanahan, P. (2010) *The Human Element: a guide to human behaviour in the shipping industry*. TSO. Winner of the International Safety at Sea Award for Management & Operations (2011). Available by free download from the UK Maritime & Coastguard Agency website at https://www.gov.uk/government/uploads/system/uploads/attachment_data/file/283000/the_human_element_a_guide_to_human_behaviour_in_the_shipping_industry.pdf [accessed April 2017].

Gregory, R. & Cavanagh, P. *The Blind Spot*. http://www.scholarpedia.org/article/The_Blind_Spot [accessed April 2017].

Grossman, D. & Siddle, B.K. (2000) *Psychological effects of combat*. Academic Press.

Haidt, J. (2006) *The Happiness Hypothesis*. Arrow Books.

Hancock, G.D. (2009) *The efficacy of fragrance use for enhancing the slot machine gaming experience of casino patrons*. UNLV Theses/Dissertations/Professional Papers/Capstones, Paper 110.

Harari, Y.N. (2014) *Sapiens: a brief history of humankind*. Penguin Books: Vintage.

Harrison, Y. & Horne, J.A. (2000) The impact of sleep deprivation on decision-making: A review. *Journal of Experimental Psychology: Applied*, 2000, 6 (3), 236–249.

Hartley, L.P. (1953) *The Go-Between*. Hamish Hamilton.

Haynes, A. (1991) *The crash of United Flight 232*. Presentation to NASA Dryden Flight Research Facility staff.

Hedge, J.W. (2011) *Gaining Insight Into Decision-making Through a Virtual World Environment Application*. RTI International–Institute of Homeland Security Solutions.

Heffernan, M. (2015) *Beyond Measure: The Big Impact of Small Changes*. TED Books.

HeliOffshore (2016) *HeliOffshore Safety Strategy*. https://helioffshore.org/wp-content/uploads/2016/07/HeliOffshore-Safety-Strategy.pdf [accessed April 2017].

Helmreich, R.L. & Merritt, A.C. (2001) *Culture at work in aviation and medicine: National, organizational and professional influences*. Ashgate.

Herz, R. (2007) *The Scent of Desire: Discovering Our Enigmatic Sense of Smell*. Elsevier.

High Tech Edge (2016) *USS Trayer Disaster Simulator*. http://www.hightech-edge.com/navy-uss-trayer-disaster-simulator-battle-station-21/3265/ [accessed April 2017].

Hirsch, A.R. (1995) Effects of ambient odors on slot-machine usage in a Las Vegas casino. *Psychology & Marketing*, 12 (7), 585–595.

Hobbs, A., Avers, K.B. & Hiles, J.J. (2011) *Fatigue risk management in aviation maintenance: current best practices and potential future countermeasures*. Federal Aviation Administration. https://primis.phmsa.dot.gov/crm/docs/FRMS_in_MX_OAM_TR_HobbsAversHiles.pdf [accessed April 2017].

Hofstede, G. (1991) *Culture and Organisations: Software of the Mind*. McGraw Hill.

Hofstede, G. (2001) *Culture's Consequences* (2nd ed.). Sage Publications.

Hollnagel, E. (2006) Resilience – the challenge of the unstable. In Hollnagel, E., Woods, D. & Leveson, N. (eds) *Resilience Engineering: Concepts and Precepts*. Ashgate.

Hollnagel, E. (2009) *The ETTO Principle: Efficiency-Thoroughness Trade-Off: Why Things That Go Right Sometimes Go Wrong*. Ashgate.

Hollnagel, E. (2014) *Safety – I and Safety – II: The Past and Future of Safety Management*. Ashgate.

Hollnagel, E., Hounsgaard, J. & Colligan, L. (2014) *FRAM – the Functional Resonance Analysis Method – a handbook for the practical use of the method*. Centre for Quality in the Southern Region of Denmark. http://www.centerforkvalitet.dk/wp-content/uploads/2016/03/FRAM-Functional-Resonance-Analysis-Method-2013-uk.pdf [accessed April 2017].

Hopkinson, M. (2014) *Compassionate Leadership: How to create and maintain engaged, committed and high-performing teams*. Piatkus.

Horck, J. (2005) Getting the Best from Multicultural Manning. *Bimco Bulletin*, 100 (4), 28–36.

Hsee, C.K. & Weber, E.U. (1999) Cross-National Differences in Risk Preference and Lay Predictions. *Journal of Behavioral Decision Making*, 12, 165–179.

Hudson, P.T.W. (2004) Just culture model from Shell's Hearts and Minds Project. In *GAIN Working Group E: A Roadmap to a Just Culture: Enhancing the Safety Environment*, September 2004. Flight Ops/ATC Ops Safety Information Sharing.

Hunt, V., Layton, D. & Prince, S. (2015) *Why diversity matters*. McKinsey & Company.

IATA, IFALPA & ICAO (2011) *Fatigue Risk Management System (FRMS) Implementation Guide for Operators.*

IMO (2001) *International Maritime Organization, Guidance on Fatigue Mitigation and Management*. MSC/Circ 1014, 12 June 2001. The recent international study into fatigue at sea, Project Horizon, has proposed an update to this guidance.

International Association of Oil & Gas Producers (2013) *Shaping safety culture through safety leadership, Report No. 452*. Available online at http://www.iogp.org/bookstore/product/shaping-safety-culture-through-safety-leadership [accessed April 2017].

James, W. (1890) *The Principles of Psychology*, 2 vols. Dover Publications, 1950.

Janis, I.L. (1982) *Groupthink*. Houghton Mifflin.

Kabat-Zinn, J. (1994) *Wherever You Go, There You Are: Mindfulness Meditation in Everyday Life*. Hyperion Books.

Kahneman, D. (2011) *Thinking, Fast and Slow*. Allen Lane.

Kahveci, E., Lane, T. & Sampson, H. (2002) *Transnational Seafarer Communities*. SIRC: Cardiff University.

Kanki, B.G., Helmreich, R. & Anca, J. (eds) (2010) *Crew Resource Management*. Academic Press.

Kanizsa, G. (1955) Margini quasi-percettivi in campi con stimolazione omogenea. *Rivista di Psicologia*, 49 (1), 7–30.

Kanizsa, G. (1976) Subjective contours. *Scientific American*, April 1976.

Kanwisher, N., McDermott, J. & Chun, M.M. (1997) The fusiform face area: a module in human extrastriate cortex specialized for face perception. *Journal of Neuroscience*, 17 (11), 4302–4311.

Kelly, T. (2011) Black Friday: Target Shoppers Step Over Walter Vance As He Collapses, Dies. *Huffington Post*, 30 November 2011.

Kemeny, J.G. (1979) *Report of The President's Commission on the Accident at Three Mile Island: The Need for Change: The Legacy of TMI*. Washington, D.C.: The Commission.

Kirkpatrick, D.L. (1998) *Evaluation Training Programs*. Berrett-Koehler.

Klein, G. (1996) The effect of acute stressors on decision-making. In Driskell, J.E. & Salas, E. (eds) *Stress and Human Performance*, pp. 49–88. Lawrence Erlbaum.

Koh, T.S. & Rowlinson, S. (2014) *Project team social capital, safety behaviors, and performance: A conceptual framework*. Creative Construction Conference.

KVH Media/Pukka Films & gs partnership (2012) *The Human Element: a film about the role of human behaviour in safety at sea*. Training film, Runner-up in the 'Safety at Sea' category in the 2014 Seatrade Awards. http://traininglink.kvh.com/public/catalogue.28.192.php [accessed April 2017].

KVH Media (2015) *Complacency at Work? Managing Risk, Routine and Uncertainty*. Training film. http://traininglink.kvh.com/public/catalogue.28.204.php [accessed April 2017].

Latané, B. & Darley, J.M. (1968) Group Inhibition of Bystander Intervention in Emergencies. *Journal of Personality & Social Psychology*, 10 (3), 215–221.

Laughery, K.R. (undated) *Human Error: Current Perspectives and Implications for Assessing Blame*. Rice University, Houston, Texas.

Learmount, D. (2000) 'Poor repair' to DC-10 was cause of Concorde crash. *Flightglobal*. https://www.flightglobal.com/news/articles/39poor-repair39-to-dc-10-was-cause-of-concorde-crash-121739 [accessed April 2017].

Lehr, D. (2010) *The Fence: A Police Cover-Up Along Boston's Racial Divide*. Harper Paperbacks.

Lepori, G.M. (2010) *Positive Mood, Risk Attitudes, and Investment Decisions: Field Evidence from Comedy Movie Attendance in the U.S.* Available at https://ssrn.com/abstract=1690476 or http://dx.doi.org/10.2139/ssrn.1690476 [accessed April 2017].

Lerner, J.S., Li, Y., Valdesolo, P. & Kassam, K.S. (2015) Emotion and Decision-making. *Annual Review of Psychology*, 66, 799–823.

Levine, A.I., DeMaria Jr, S., Schwartz, A.D. & Sim, A.J. (eds) (2013) *The Comprehensive Textbook of Healthcare Simulation*. Springer.

Lewis, D. (2014) *Impulse: Why We Do What We Do Without Knowing Why We Do It*. Random House.

Liberman, V., Samuels, S. & Ross, L. (2004) The Name of the Game: Predictive Power of Reputations versus Situational Labels in Determining Prisoner's Dilemma Game Moves. *Personal & Social Psychology Bulletin*, September 2004, 30 (9), 1175–1185.

Lochbaum, D., Lyman, E., Stranahan, S.Q. & The Union of Concerned Scientists (2015) *Fukushima: The Story of a Nuclear Disaster*. The New Press.

Loftus, E. & Palmer, J.E. (1974) Reconstruction of automobile destruction: An example of the interaction between language and memory. *Journal of Verbal Learning and Verbal Behavior*, 13, 585–589.

Lovell, J. & Kluger, J. (1995) *Apollo 13*. Coronet.

Lund, I.O. & Rundmo, T. (2009) Cross-cultural comparisons of traffic safety, risk perception, attitudes and behaviour. *Safety Science*, 47 (2009), 547–553.

Machiavelli, N. (1532) *The Prince*. Penguin Classics, 2011.

MAIB (1997) *Safety Digest*, 02/1997. Marine Accident Investigation Branch.

MAIB (2004) *Report on the investigation of the grounding of the Italian registered chemical tanker* Attilio Ievoli *on Lymington Banks in the west Solent, South Coast of England 3 June 2004*. Marine Accident Investigation Branch, Report No. 2/2005.

MAIB (2008) *Report on the investigation of* Sichem Melbourne *making heavy contact with mooring structures at Coryton Oil Refinery Terminal on 25 February 2008*. Marine Accident Investigation Branch, Report No. 18/2008.

MAIB (2012) *Report on the investigation of the fatal accident of a crew member on the Woolwich ferry* Ernest Bevin *on the River Thames, London 3 August 2011*. Marine Accident Investigation Branch, Report No. 22/2012.

MAIB (2014) *Report on the investigation of the grounding of* Danio *off the Longstone, Farne Islands, England 16 March 2013*. Marine Accident Investigation Branch, Report No. 8/2014.

MAIB (2015) *Collision between MV* Orakai *and FV* Margriet *North Hinder Junction, North Sea 21 December 2014*. Marine Accident Investigation Branch, Report No. 16/2015.

MAIB (2016a) *Report on the investigation into the listing, flooding and grounding of* Hoegh Osaka *Bramble Bank, The Solent, UK on 3 January 2015*. Marine Accident Investigation Branch, Report No. 6/2016.

MAIB (2016b) *Report on the investigation of the grounding of the cruise ship* Hamburg *in the Sound of Mull, Scotland 11 May 2015*. Marine Accident Investigation Branch, Report No. 12/2016.

Malone, T.W. & Bernstein, M.S. (2015) *Handbook of Collective Intelligence*. MIT Press.

Marcellin, J.D. (2014) *The Pilot Factor: A fresh look into Crew Resource Management*. CreateSpace Independent Publishing Platform.

Marescaux, J., Clément, J.M., Tassetti, V., Koehl, C., Cotlin, S., Russier, Y., Mutter, D., Delingette, H. & Ayache, N. (1998) Virtual reality applied to hepatic surgery simulation: the next revolution. *Annals of surgery*, 228.5 (1998), 627.

Marine Administration Oaseirys Lhuingys (2001) *Casualty Investigation Report CA 68 EMILIA THERESA Cargo Tank Explosion 17/01/2001*.

Maritime Accident Casebook (2016) *Did jetlag fuel cableship burn?* 28 January 2016. http://maritimeaccident.org/categories/fatigue [accessed April 2017].

Maritime & Coastguard Agency (2014) *Human Element Guidance – Part 1 Fatigue and Fitness For Duty: Statutory Duties, Causes Of Fatigue And Guidance On Good Practice*, MGN 505 (M).

Maritime & Coastguard Agency (undated) *Leading for Safety: A practical guide for leaders in the Maritime Industry*. Available online at https://www.gov.uk/government/publications/leading-for-safety [accessed April 2017].

Masicampo, E.J. & Baumeister, R.F. (2012) Committed But Closed-Minded: When Making A Specific Plan For A Goal Hinders Success. *Social Cognition*, 30 (1), 37–55.

McGonigal, K. (2012) *Maximum Willpower: How to Master the New Science of Self-control*. Macmillan.

McGurk, H. & MacDonald, J. (1976) Hearing lips and seeing voices. *Nature,* 264 (5588), 746–748.

McKeever, G. (2014) *Procrastination doesn't pay.* https://www.workboat.com/blogs/maritime-matters/procrastination-doesnt-pay/ [accessed April 2017].

McKinney, E.H. & Davis, K.J. (2003) Effects of Deliberate Practice on Crisis Decision Performance. *Human Factors,* 45, 436–444.

McNamee, D. (2014) The hormone that allows us to love may also encourage us to lie. *Medical News Today,* 5 April 2014. http://www.medicalnewstoday.com/articles/275040.php [accessed April 2017].

McPherson, B. (2007) *Elephant in the Room: An Equality and Diversity Training Manual.* Russell House Publishing.

McSweeney, B. (2002) Hofstede's model of national cultural differences and their consequences: A triumph of faith – a failure of analysis. *Human Relations,* 55, 89.

Meadows, S.O., Miller, L.L. & Robson, S. (2015) *Airman and Family Resilience: Lessons from the Scientific Literature.* RAND Corporation, RR106, p. 10.

Mearns, K. & Yule, S. (2009) The role of national culture in determining safety performance: Challenges for the global oil and gas industry. *Safety Science,* 47, 777–785.

Merton, R. (1936) The unanticipated consequences of purposive social action. *American Sociological Review,* 1 (6), 804–904.

Michel, C., Velasco, C., Salgado-Montejo, A. & Spence, C. (2014) The Butcher's Tongue Illusion. *Perception,* 43, 818–824.

Miller, L. (2008) *METTLE: Mental Toughness Training for Law Enforcement.* Looseleaf Law Publications, p. vii.

Miyazaki, K. & Ogawa, Y. (2006) Learning absolute pitch by children: A cross-sectional study. *Music Perception,* 24 (1), 63–78.

Moreby, D.H. (1990) Communication problems inherent in a cross-cultural manning environment. *Maritime Policy and Management,* 17 (3).

Morieux, Y. (2013) *As work gets more complex, 6 rules to simplify.* TED Talk. https://www.ted.com/talks/yves_morieux_as_work_gets_more_complex_6_rules_to_simplify?language=en [accessed April 2017].

Morley, N. (1999) *Writing Ancient History.* London: Duckworth.

Murphy, P.J. (2002) *Fatigue management during Operations: a Commander's Guide.* Defence Science and Technology Organisation, Australian Dept. of Defence (Army).

Nagler, M.G. (2011) Does Social Capital Promote Safety on the Roads. *Economic Inquiry,* 51 (2), 1218–1231.

Nahapiet, J. & Ghoshal, S. (1998) Social Capital, Intellectual Capital and Organizational Advantage. *Academy of Management Review,* 23 (2), 242–266.

Nakamura, J. & Csíkszentmihályi, M. (2001) Flow Theory and Research. In Snyder, C.R., Wright, E. & Lopez, S.J. (eds) *Handbook of Positive Psychology.* Oxford University Press, pp. 195–206.

National Commission on the BP Deepwater Horizon Oil Spill and Offshore Drilling (2011) *Deep Water: The Gulf Oil Disaster and the Future of Offshore Drilling – Report to the President*. January 2011, p. ix.

National Transportation Safety Board (1973) *Aircraft Accident Report, Eastern Airlines, Inc. L-1011, N310EA, Miami, Florida, December 29, 1972*, Report No. AAR-73/14.

National Transportation Safety Board (1979) *Aircraft accident report, Japan Airlines Company, Ltd., McDonnell-Douglas DC-8-62F, JA 8054, Anchorage, Alaska, January 13, 1977*, Report No. AAR-78/07.

National Transportation Safety Board (1982) *Air Florida, Inc., Boeing 737-222, N62AF, Collision with 14th Street Bridge near Washington National Airport, Washington, D.C., January 13, 1982*, Report No. AAR-82/8.

National Transportation Safety Board (1991) *Avianca, The Airline Of Columbia Boeing 707 Fuel Exhaustion Cove Neck, New York*, Report No. AAR-91/04.

National Transportation Safety Board (1997) *Grounding of the Panamanian passenger ship Royal Majesty on Rose and Crown Shoal near Nantucket, Massachusetts, June 10, 1995*, Report No. MAR-97/01.

National Transportation Safety Board (2000) *Aircraft Accident Report: Controlled Flight Into Terrain Korean Air Flight 801 Boeing 747-300, Hl7468 Nimitz Hill, Guam*, Report No. AAR-00/01.

National Transportation Safety Board (2002) *Aircraft Accident Report: Loss of Control and Impact with Pacific Ocean Alaska Airlines Flight 261 McDonnell Douglas MD-83, N963AS About 2.7 Miles North of Anacapa Island, California January 31, 2000*, Report No. AAR-02/01

National Transportation Safety Board (2009) *Marine accident report, allision of Hong Kong-Registered Containership M/V Cosco Busan with the delta tower of the San Francisco-Oakland Bay Bridge, San Francisco, California, November 3, 2007*, Report No. MAR-09/01.

National Transportation Safety Board (2010) *Midair Collision Over Hudson River Piper PA-32R-300, N71MC and Eurocopter AS350BA, N401LH, Near Hoboken, New Jersey August 8, 2009*, Aircraft Accident Summary Report, Report No. AAR-10/05.

National Transportation Safety Board (2016) http://www.ntsb.gov/safety/mwl/Documents/MWL_2016_factsheet01.pdf [accessed April 2017].

Neisser, U. (1967) *Cognitive psychology*. Englewood Cliffs: Prentice-Hall.

Neisser, U. (1976) *Cognition and reality: Principles and implications of cognitive psychology*. New York: Freeman.

Network Rail (2014) *Everyone: Network Rail's Diversity and Inclusion Strategy 2014-2019*.

Newcott, B. (2009) Wisdom of the Elders. *AARP Magazine*, May–June 2009, 52.

Newport, C. (2016) *Deep Work: Rules for Focused Success in a Distracted World*. Piatkus.

Nursey, J. (2016) Leonardo Ulloa reveals the secret to Leicester City's success this season as Foxes eye Premier League title. *Mirror*, 9 February 2016.

Orasanu, J., Fischer, U. & Davison, J. (1997) Cross-Cultural Barriers to Effective Communication in Aviation. In Oskamp, S. and Granrose, C. (eds) *Cross-Cultural Work Groups: The Claremont Symposium on Applied Social Psychology*. Sage Publications.

Ordóñez, L.D., Schweitzer, M.E., Galinsky, A.D. & Bazerman, M.H. (2009) *Goals Gone Wild: The Systematic Side Effects of Over-Prescribing Goal Setting*, Harvard Business School Working Paper, 09-083.

Oswald, A.J., Proto, E. & Sgroi, D. (2015) Happiness & productivity. *Journal of Labor Economics*, 33 (4), 789–822.

Parrott, D.S. (2011) *Bridge Resource Management for Small Ships*. International Marine.

Patrick, J. (1992) *Training Research & Practice*. London: Academic Press Ltd.

Penn, R. (2012) *Bridge Resource Management*. The Rexford Penn Group.

Perrow, C. (1984) *Normal Accidents: Living With High Risk Technologies* (Revised edition, 1999). Princeton, NJ: Princeton University Press.

Peters, S. (2012) *The Chimp Paradox: The Mind Management Programme to Help You Achieve Success, Confidence and Happiness*. Vermilion.

Phillips, K.W. (2014) How diversity makes us smarter. *Scientific American*, 1 October 2014.

Pink, D. (2011) *Drive: The Surprising Truth About What Motivates Us*. Canongate Books.

Queensland Health (2009) *Fatigue risk management system resource pack*. http://enhancingresponsibility.com/wp-content/uploads/2014/01/Queensland-Health-Fatigue-Risk-Management-System-resource-pack-2009.pdf [accessed April 2017].

Read, P.P. (1993) *Ablaze: The Story of Chernobyl*. Secker & Warburg.

Real, L.A. (1991) Animal choice behavior and the evolution of cognitive architecture. *Science*, 253, 980–986.

Reason, J. (1990) *Human Error*. Cambridge: Cambridge University Press.

Reason, J. (2000) Safety paradoxes and safety culture. *Injury Control and Safety Promotion*, 7 (1), 3–14.

Reason, J., Hollnagel, E. & Paries, J. (2006) *Revisiting the 'Swiss Cheese' model of accidents*, EEC Note No. 13/06, Project Safbuild, Eurocontrol.

Registered Nurses' Association of Ontario. (2011). *Preventing and Mitigating Nurse Fatigue in Health Care: Healthy Work Environments Best Practice Guideline*. Toronto.

Rigoni, B. & Nelson, B. (2016) Engaged Workplaces Are Safer for Employees. *Business Journal*, 24 May 2016. http://www.gallup.com/businessjournal/191831/engaged-workplaces-safer-employees.aspx [accessed April 2017].

Riordan, C.M. & O'Brien, K. (2012) For great teamwork, start with a social contract. *Harvard Business Review*, April 2012.

Ripley, A. (2009) *The Unthinkable: Who Survives When Disaster Strikes and Why*. Arrow Books.

Rizzolatti, G. & Craighero, L. (2004) The mirror-neuron system. *Annual Review of Neuroscience,* 27 (1), 169–192.

Roberts, K.H. & Rousseau, D.M. (1989) Research in Nearly Failure-Free, High-Reliability Organizations: Having the Bubble. *IEEE Transactions on Engineering Management,* 36, 132–139.

Rogers Commission (1986) *Report of the Presidential Commission on the Space Shuttle Challenger Accident.*

Rose, D. (2001) Doomed: The Real Story of Flight 4590. *The Observer,* Sunday 13 May 2001.

Rosekind, M. (1996) *Cross-Cultural Barriers to Effective Communication in Aviation.* NTRS.

RoSPA (2011) *Driver fatigue and road accidents.* Road Safety Information, 11 June 2011. The Royal Society for the Prevention of Accidents.

RSSB (2012) *Managing Fatigue – A Good Practice Guide,* RS/504, Issue 1. Rail Safety & Standards Board.

RSSB (2016) *Supporting a fair culture – creating appropriate plans after incidents (T1068).* Rail Safety & Standards Board. http://www.rssb.co.uk/pages/research-catalogue/t1068.aspx [accessed April 2017].

RT.com (2016) *Pilots 'worked to death': Flydubai whistleblower says fatigue-related crash predicted.* 22 March 2016. https://www.rt.com/news/336514-flydubai-pilots-fatigue-crash/ [accessed April 2017].

Sacks, O. (1997) *The Island of the Colorblind.* AA Knopf.

Salas, E., Nicholls, D.R. & Driskell, J.E. (2007) Testing Three Team Training Strategies in Intact Teams: A Meta-Analysis. *Small Group Research,* 38 (4), August, 471–488.

Sams, M., Mottonen, R. & Sihvonen, T. (2005) Seeing and hearing others and oneself talk. *Cognitive Brain Research,* 23 (1), 429–435.

Schein, E.H. (1985) *Organizational Culture and Leadership.* University of Illinois at Urbana-Champaign's Academy for Entrepreneurial Leadership.

Schneier, B. (2008) *Schneier on Security.* Wiley Indianapolis.

Schwartz, B. (2015) *Why we work.* TED Books.

Schwartz, S.H. (1999) A theory of cultural values and some implications for work. *Applied Psychology: An International Review,* 48 (1), 23–47.

Seppala, E. & Cameron, K. (2015) Proof That Positive Work Cultures Are More Productive. *Harvard Business Review.*

Sergent, J. (1992) Functional neuroanatomy of face and object processing. A positron emission tomography study. *Brain,* 115 (1), 15–36.

Sharps, M.J. (2009) *Processing Under Pressure: Stress, Memory and Decision-making in Law Enforcement.* Looseleaf Law Publications.

Sheen (1987) *mv Herald of Free Enterprise,* Report of Court No. 8074, Formal Investigation. Department of Transport, HMSO.

Sherif, M. (1988) *The Robbers Cave Experiment: Intergroup Conflict and Cooperation.* Wesleyan University Press.

Shin, J. & Milkman, K.L. (2016) How backup plans can harm goal pursuit: The unexpected downside of being prepared for failure. *Organizational Behavior and Human Decision Processes,* 135, 1–9.

Skinner, S.K & Reilly, W.K. (1989) *The Exxon Valdez Oil Spill: A Report to the President.* National Response Team.

Smith, A. (1776) *An Inquiry into the Nature and Causes of the Wealth of Nations.* W. Strahan and T. Cadell.

Snowden, D. (2016) *Making sense of complexity in order to act.* http://cognitive-edge.com [accessed April 2017].

Soon, C.S., Brass, M., Heinze, H. & Haynes, J. (2008) Unconscious determinants of free decisions in the human brain. *Nature Neuroscience,* DOI: 10.1038/nn.2112.

Spangenbergen, S., Baarts, C., Dyreborg, J., Jensen, L., Kines, P. & Mikkelsen, K.L. (2003) Factors contributing to the differences in work related injury rates between Danish and Swedish construction workers. *Safety Science,* 41, 517–530.

Spicer, A. & Cederström, C. (2015) The Research We've Ignored About Happiness at Work. *Harvard Business Review.*

Stanford Business School (1999) Diversity and Work Group Performance. *Insights by Stanford Business,* 1 November 1999.

Starren, A., Luijters, K., Drupsteen, L., Vilkevicius, G. & Eeckelaert, L. (2013) *Diverse cultures at work: Ensuring safety and health through leadership and participation.* European Agency for Safety and Health at Work, 2013.

Stone, D., Patton, B. & Heen, S. (1999) *Difficult conversations: how to discuss what matters most.* New York: Penguin.

Størkersen, K.V., Antonsen, S. & Kongsvik, T. (2016) One size fits all? Safety management regulation of ship accidents and personal injuries. *Journal of Risk Research.*

Strauch, B. (2010) Can Cultural Differences Lead to Accidents? Team Cultural Differences and Sociotechnical System Operations. *Human Factors: The Journal of the Human Factors and Ergonomics Society,* 52 (2), 246–263.

Subsecretaría de Aviación Civil (1978) *KLM B-747 PH-BUF and Pan Am B-747 N736 collision at Tenerife Airport Spain on 27 Mar 1977.* Released in both Spanish and English.

Susetyo, D.A. (2010) *Multinational And Multicultural Seafarers And Met Students: A Socio-Cultural Study For Improving Maritime Safety And The Education Of Seafarers.* Masters Thesis, World Maritime University, Malmo, Sweden.

Swift, G. (2016) *Mothering Sunday.* Scribner.

Taras, V., Steel, P. & Kirkman, B.L. (2011) Three decades of research on national culture in the workplace: Do the differences still make a difference? *Organizational Dynamics,* 40, 189–198.

Teach, E. (2004) *Avoiding Decision Traps*. CFO (17 June 2004). http://ww2.cfo.com/human-capital-careers/2004/06/avoiding-decision-traps [accessed April 2017].

Teekay (2016) *External Navigation Review (ENR)*. Teekay Shipping, Glasgow.

The New York Times (2015) *Los Angeles and New York Differ in Their Responses to a Terrorism Threat*. http://www.nytimes.com/2015/12/16/us/los-angeles-schools-bomb-threat.html [accessed April 2017].

Thompson, H.L. (2010) *The Stress Effect: Why Smart Leaders Make Dumb Decisions – And What to Do About It*. Jossey-Bass.

Tichon, J., Wallis, G. & Mildred, T. (2006) *Virtual Training Environments to Improve Train Driver's Crisis Decision-making*. Proceedings of SimTecT, Melbourne, Australia, May 2006.

Trehan, K., Kemp, C.D. & Yang, S.C. (2014) Simulation in cardiothoracic surgical training: Where do we stand? *The Journal of Thoracic and Cardiovascular Surgery*, January 2014.

UK Health and Safety Executive (2016) *What is stress?* http://www.hse.gov.uk/stress/furtheradvice/whatisstress.htm [accessed April 2017].

US Coast Guard (1997) *Investigation into the circumstances surrounding the loss of propulsion on the bulk carrier* Bright Field *and allision with the Riverwalk Shopping Complex on December 14 1996 in New Orleans, Lousiana with multiple injuries and no loss of life.*

US Nuclear Regulatory Commission (2009) *Fatigue Management For Nuclear Power Plant Personnel*, Regulatory Guide 5.73.

Usborne, S. (2011) BA pilot hero – 'The day that changed my life for ever'. *The Independent*, Culture/Books/Features: Sunday 23 October 2011.

Van Wyk, E. & de Villiers, R. (2009) *Virtual reality training applications for the mining industry, Proceedings of the 6th international conference on computer graphics, virtual reality, visualisation and interaction in Africa*. ACM, 2009.

Varela, F.J., Maturana, H.R. & Uribe, R. (1974) Autopoiesis: the organization of living systems, its characterization and a model. *Biosystems*, 5, 187–196.

Vaughan, D. (1986) *The Challenger Launch Decision: Risky Technology, Culture, and Deviance at NASA*. University of Chicago Press.

Viscog Productions, Inc. (2003) *Surprising studies of visual awareness*, volume 1 (DVD). Champaign, IL: http://www.viscog.com [accessed April 2017].

Ward, P.A., Williams, M. & Hancock, P.A. (2006) Simulation for performance and training. In Ericsson, K.A., Charness, N., Feltovich, P.J. & Hoffman, R.R (eds) (2006). *The Cambridge Handbook of Expertise and Expert Performance*. Cambridge University Press.

Warsash Maritime Academy (2012) *Project HORIZON – a wake-up call: Research into the effects of sleepiness on the cognitive performance of maritime watchkeepers under different watch patterns, using ships' bridge, engine and liquid cargo handling simulators*. http://www.warsashacademy.co.uk/about/our-expertise/maritime-research-centre/horizon-project/about-horizon.aspx [accessed April 2017].

Watson, G.W., Scott, D., Bishop, J. & Turnbeaugh, T. (2005) Dimensions Of Interpersonal Relationships And Safety In The Steel Industry. *Journal of Business and Psychology*, 19 (3), 303–318.

Webb, C. (2016) *How to have a Good Day*. Macmillan.

Weick, K. & Sutcliffe, K. (2001) *Managing the unexpected: assuring high performance in an age of complexity*. Jossey-Bass Wiley.

Weisinger, H. & Pawliw-Fry, J.P. (2015) *How to perform under pressure: The science of doing best when it matters most*. John Murray Learning, p. 277.

Wheeler, M. (2016) *Asiana Airlines: "Sorry, Captain. You're wrong."* Airlines & Aviation, LinkedIn. https://www.linkedin.com/pulse/20140217220032-266437464-asiana-airlines-sorry-captain-you-re-wrong [accessed April 2017].

Wikipedia entry for *2011 M5 motorway crash*. https://en.wikipedia.org/wiki/2011_M5_motorway_crash [accessed April 2017].

Wikipedia entry for *British Airways Flight 38*. https://en.wikipedia.org/wiki/British_Airways_Flight_38 [accessed April 2017].

Wikipedia entry for MS *Herald of Free Enterprise*. https://en.wikipedia.org/wiki/MS_Herald_of_Free_Enterprise [accessed April 2017].

Williams, K.D & Nida, S.A. (2011) Ostracism: Consequences and Coping. *Current Directions in Psychological Science*, 20 (2), 71.

Wise, J. (2009) *Extreme Fear: The Science of Your Mind in Danger*. Macmillan.

Wollert, T.N., Driskell, J.E. & Quail, J. (2011) *Stress Exposure Training Guidelines: Instructor Guide to Reality-Based Training*. Federal Law Enforcement Training Center. Available at http://www.virtualtacticalacademy.com/files/stress_exposure_training_manual_9-26B.pdf [accessed April 2017].

Woods, D. (2006) Essential characteristics of resilience. In Hollnagel, E., Woods , D. & Leveson, N. (eds) *Resilience Engineering: Concepts and Precepts*. Ashgate.

Wright, D. & Wareham, G. (2005) Mixing sound and vision: the interaction of auditory and visual information for earwitnesses of a crime scene. *Legal and Criminological Psychology*, 10, 103–108.

Yerkes, R.M. & Dodson, J.D. (1908) The Relation of Strength of Stimulus to Rapidity of Habit-Formation. *Journal of Comparative Neurology and Psychology*, 18, 459–482.

Zaragoza, M.S., Belli, R. & Payment, K.E. (2007) Misinformation effects and the suggestibility of eyewitness memory. In Garry, M. & Hayne, (eds) *Do Justice and Let the Sky Fall: Elizabeth F. Loftus and Her Contributions to Science, Law, and Academic Freedom*, pp. 35–63. Mahwah, NJ: Lawrence Erlbaum Associates.

Index

Being Human in safety-critical organisations